CONTEXTUAL SUBJECTS

ROBERT LECKEY

Contextual Subjects

Family, State, and Relational Theory

UNIVERSITY OF TORONTO PRESS
Toronto Buffalo London

© University of Toronto Press Incorporated 2008
Toronto Buffalo London

www.utppublishing.com

Printed in Canada

ISBN 978-0-8020-9749-1

Printed on acid-free paper

Library and Archives Canada Cataloguing in Publication

Leckey, Robert
    Contextual subjects : family, state and relational theory / Robert Leckey.

    Includes index.
    ISBN 978-0-8020-9749-1

    1. Law – Canada – Philosophy. 2. Domestic relations – Canada.
    3. Administrative law – Canada. 4. Contextualism (Philosophy).
    I. Title.

    KE427.L42 2007   340′.10971   C2007-905056-5

University of Toronto Press acknowledges the financial assistance to its
publishing program of the Canada Council for the Arts and the Ontario Arts
Council.

University of Toronto Press acknowledges the financial support for its
publishing activities of the Government of Canada through the Book
Publishing Industry Development Program (BPIDP).

This book has been published with the help of a grant from the Canadian
Federation for the Humanities and Social Sciences, through the Aid to
Scholarly Publications Program, using funds provided by the Social Sciences
and Humanities Research Council of Canada.

For my parents,
and for José

Contents

Acknowledgments

This book is the fruit of my doctoral studies at the Faculty of Law, University of Toronto. I am indebted to my supervisors, David Dyzenhaus and Brenda Cossman, and to the members of my committee for their generosity and enthusiasm. David was the first to read the entire draft dissertation, doing so in two days over a summer long weekend. Brenda challenged me to take a critical distance from issues in family law to which I stood too close. The third reader, Audrey Macklin, suggested I rewrite the penultimate chapter late in the process when it would have been simpler to sign off. The fourth member, Jennifer Nedelsky, has continued the conversation following my defence. Despite having assumed less academic duties, Alison Harvison Young graciously served as external reviewer and commented perceptively. I have difficulty imagining a more supportive committee.

This book benefited greatly from the ideas and feedback of many people. Though conscious of the risk of omissions, I wish to acknowledge conversations with Eric Adams, Robin Ambrose, the Hon. Allan Blakeney, Daniel Borrillo, Jillian Boyd, Marie-France Bureau, Geneviève Cartier, John Coleman, the late Marie-Jeanne de Haller Coleman, Justice John Evans, Pascale Fournier, Evan Fox-Decent, Janet Halley, Nicholas Kasirer, Hoi Kong, Mary Liston, Roderick Macdonald, Desmond Manderson, José Medina, Denise Réaume, Sean Rehaag, Carol Rogerson, Jeffrey Simpson, Lorne Sossin, Pierre-Hugues Verdier, Eric Ward, Daniel Weinstock, and Robert Wintemute. Andrea Brighenti commented on chapters 1 and 8, and Jillian Boyd and John Haffner commented on chapter 4. Eric Adams provided helpful comments on the entire manuscript. I benefited from the feedback of audiences at my S.J.D. presentation at the University of Toronto, my job talk at the

Faculty of Law, McGill University, and a presentation at l'Université de Sherbrooke. Both anonymous readers for the University of Toronto Press gave me useful feedback on the manuscript, and I acknowledge the enthusiasm and encouragement of Len Husband and Richard Ratzlaff of the Press. At the outset, when I was applying to graduate schools and for funding, Justice Michel Bastarache pressed me, with his customary directness, to state my argument more simply.

I was fortunate to benefit from substantial financial and institutional support. I undertook my research as a Trudeau scholar, and I acknowledge the generous funding of the Pierre Elliott Trudeau Foundation, as well as the kindness of the Foundation's staff. I transformed my dissertation into a book during a wonderful year as a visiting scholar at the Centre de recherche en éthique de l'Université de Montréal (CREUM), and I am grateful for the warm hospitality of Martin Blanchard and others there. The Wainwright Fund of McGill University made possible the research assistance of Seth Earn during late revisions. Thomas Lipton patiently composed the index. I acknowledge the ongoing support of my dean, Nicholas Kasirer.

It is not, of course, only institutional and intellectual support that makes a book possible. During my research, I benefited especially from the encouragement and support of my parents, Robert and Catherine Leckey; my sister, Amelia Leckey; my grandmother, Jean Nesbitt; and my aunt and uncle, Judith and George Mills. Last, I thank my husband, José Navas, who has believed unwaveringly in this book, and who inspires me always.

CONTEXTUAL SUBJECTS

1 Introduction

Who is the legal subject? Who or what thinks about and produces law? To what subject does law speak? How do legislatures and judges understand the human beings whom they seek to regulate? And to the extent that one ascribes constitutive power to law, what subjects does law produce? What forms of being does law promote? What does law make visible, and conversely, what subjectivities does law occlude and efface? Which legal subjects are unspeakable, even unthinkable?

This book's short answer, shorn of nuance and definitions, denuded of examples, restrictions, and caveats, is that law has come to suppose and produce *contextual* subjects. Or at least it has done so in two legal fields in Canada, family law and administrative law. Contextual subjects, that is, subjects regarded as rooted in their relationships and social settings, have come to replace ones defined rather more abstractly by legal categorizations. But it is jarring to present the book's conclusion up front. Much more needs to be said to make this affirmation intelligible. Let me begin with the subject.

For decades now, post-structuralist theorists have criticized the liberal humanist construction of a universal, coherent, and self-constituting subject (e.g., Cadava, Connor, and Nancy 1991; Copjec 1994). As a legal scholar summarizes, 'with the postmodern rejection of all projects claiming to be universal, the unity of the subject is deconstructed and revealed as plural, fragmentary, and contingent' (Stychin 1995, 20). Among feminists, debate ensued as to the political consequences of deconstructing the notion of the subject. Some scholars, following Foucault, appeared to claim that the subject is so strongly constituted by discourse as to leave virtually no space for agency. Judith Butler, for example, argues that power 'assumes a psychic form that constitutes the subject's self-identity' (1997b, 3; see also 1999; cf. Magnus 2006). Some theorists argue that deconstructing the subject impedes any action whatever (Benhabib et al. 1995). Others claim that it is possible to acknowledge the constitutive role of discourse and context without conceding all possibilities of agency and political action (Vasterling 1999). Recent scholarship highlights the extent to which the later Foucault himself acknowledges the possibilities of agency. In the second and third volumes of his *History of Sexuality*, Foucault refers to practices of freedom (1990b; 1988). Indeed, Carlos Ball argues that the later Foucault had a conception of the self 'that allows for an understanding of its capacity for autonomy as constituting a universal good' (2003, 185). He holds that Foucault's later work reduces the schism between conceptions of liberal autonomy and postmodernist agency. In a similar vein, Dianna Taylor and Karen Vintges argue that for Foucault, 'an ethos characterized by critical, creative engagement with one's present constitutes the work of freedom, where commitment and responsibility materialize from the bottom up instead of from the top down' (2004b, 3). If one accepts such arguments, the dispute about agency is not one between followers of Foucault and those who, for strategic reasons, seek a theory of agency. Rather, the tension is one internal to Foucault. Perhaps, as David Weberman argues, 'it is sensible to think that subjectivity is a kind of hybrid resulting from both the productive effects of social power and self-determination (*rapport à soi*) as well as their interaction' (2000, 261).

Concerns with the constitution of the subject have special purchase in the legal setting. Foucault and Butler emphasize the constitutive or productive effects of legal rules and categories as instruments of regulation. Butler argues that the norm of sex has a power to produce, 'demarcate, circulate, differentiate' the bodies it controls (1993, 1). Kathryn Abrams writes that regulation, 'as a paradigmatic legal assertion of power – does not simply repress but rather inaugurates new forms of behavior and subjectivity in often unpredictable trajectories' (2005, 335). A French disciple of Foucault frames the point that repressive power is not exercised upon 'autonomous and preexisting' individuals. Rather, it collaborates in producing those individuals (Eribon 2004, 294). Juridical rules, prohibitions, and procedures are thus seen as playing a crucial role in constituting subjects.

A number of scholars, especially readers of Foucault, have remarked on this exclusionary and productive tendency of norms and categories. Butler has written about the constitution of subjects through 'the force of exclusion and abjection,' a process that produces an abjected outside (1993, 3). The objection arises that such a view tends monolithically to denounce all exclusions without critical differentiation. Nancy Fraser argues that exclusions are not all equally bad. It is therefore appropriate to attempt to distinguish legitimate from illegitimate exclusions (1995, 68). Butler subsequently admits that 'there are better and worse forms of differentiation, and that the worse kinds tend to abject and degrade those from whom the "I" is distinguished' (1995, 140). The concession here is that it is worth assessing different juridical exclusions and differentiating their productive effects.

It may be helpful to think of the notion of dynamic nominalism. Ian Hacking observes that people spontaneously come to fit their categories. A kind of person comes into being at the same time as the kind itself is being invented. The 'possibilities for personhood' change through a process he calls 'making up people' (1986, 229; cf. Butler 1997a, 28–38). These categories and legal labels have discursive and material effects on those subjects which they produce.

In the legal setting, what theorists mean by the 'subject' varies. Pierre Schlag defines the subject as the 'who or what' that thinks about and produces law (1990, 1629n6). Jack Balkin regards a legal subject as 'a person who attempts to understand the law, legal doctrine, and the legal system' (1993, 106n1). Abrams defines the subject as 'courts' paradigmatic accounts of who human beings are and how they are connected to the social world around them' (2001, 27). These definitions are suitable for their respective inquiries into legal production, legal hermeneutics, and judicial politics. My project here makes another definition appropriate, one slightly different from that offered by Abrams. Her reference to courts' paradigmatic accounts implies that the object of her inquiry is the explicit, official story by which courts operate and which their judgments perform and sustain. My concern is with the subjectivities produced through the 'multiplicity of discursive fields' (Cossman 1994, 16). To Abrams's attention to courts, I add legislatures and legal scholars. Moreover, the production of subjectivity that interests me does not rely exclusively on the explicit, official stories. It also traces aspects of the subject emerging from the interstices, delineating the productive effects of discursive performances of which the juridical actors themselves may be unconscious.

My focus is consistent with a number of accounts in the legal literature on the value of examining the legal subject. James Boyle argues that contemporary legal and political argument can 'best be understood as a debate over the essential characteristics of the subjects whose actions those arguments describe and prescribe' (1991, 524). Abrams contends that 'accounts of the legal subject can tell us crucial things about the legal world in which we live,' both descriptively and normatively (2001, 28). What I would add to these accounts is that a focus on the subject produced by a given juridical regime provides a fruitful way of bringing into view the negative impacts on those whom that regime marginalizes or excludes. Such a focus captures the manner in which the legal system structures identity and reconfigures the field of social possibilities in ways over which individuals do not exert full agency. A focus on the subject highlights the ambivalent impacts of juridical reforms, such as the way in which endorsement of certain kinds of same-sex relationships has simultaneously reinforced the production and vilification of 'bad' gay subjects (Cossman 2002b, 246–9; 2007). It is these negative dimensions that direct me to speak of the legal subject, with its simultaneous and conflicting suggestions of action and sufferance, rather than of the legal agent (cf. Macdonald and Sandomierski 2006). Furthermore, I shall argue throughout this book that attention to the subject brings into view the extent of a legal methodology of contextualism.

It is not that legal regimes produce a single, unified subject position. Instead, consistent with the deconstruction of the universal subject, the subject positions that these regimes produce are multiple and shifting (Diduck 1995; Collier 2006). Reference to the legal subject in the singular is a form of shorthand. Nor do I succumb to lawyerly hubris by claiming that law is the dominant subjectifying apparatus. Rather, law, with other competing apparatuses, merits deeper reflection for its constitutive effects (Jones 2006).

As a methodological matter, accounts of the subject must generally be drawn from 'the interstices of judicial argument' (Abrams 2001, 30). The legal subject produced is not a function merely of the set of juridical rules in force, but is, more broadly, a product of legal discourse generally. Balkin argues persuasively that a jurisprudence of the subject is preponderantly a '*cultural* jurisprudence, for it is culture that creates legal subjects as subjects' (1993, 108). Thus in this book I pay attention not just to the positive law of enacted and unenacted rules and how judges speak (MacDougall 2000, 12), but also to the scholarly literature to get a sense of legal culture. This approach does not depend on a presumption that legal scholarship or doctrine amounts to law. It presumes instead, more modestly, that legal scholarship contributes to legal culture.[1]

An inquiry into the legal subject could combine law with anthropology, sociology, psychoanalysis, the history of science, political theory, philosophy, and doubtless other disciplines. In this book I restrict the inquiry largely to political philosophy, particularly to a strand of feminist political theory. The strand of political theory is relational theory, a fruitful development that has been elaborated in the past twenty years and one that continues to attract scholarly attention. Specifically, this book argues for the emergence of a new conception of the legal subject using relational theory.

Relational theory is not an officially constituted school, and its boundaries are contestable. It can be seen as comprising several connected and overlapping areas of work. One proposes and elaborates an ethic of care. Such scholarship draws attention to the crucial relations of dependence and care on which each individual inevitably relies at some point. It emphasizes the ethical differences between men and women, the ethics of care relationships, and the extent to which caring work is overwhelmingly performed by women (Gilligan 1982; Noddings 1984; Kittay 1999; West 1997). Another area consists of literature analysing rights as relational. Its scholars dispute the reification of rights as non-negotiable givens. They cast rights instead as tools revisable in the service of desirable relationships (Brennan 2004; Minow 1990; Minow and Shanley 1996; Nedelsky 1993b). A connected scholarship seeks to reconfigure the liberal ideal of autonomy by envisioning what it calls relational autonomy (Nedelsky 1989; Mackenzie and Stoljar 2000a). This range of perspectives ensures that the account of relational theory I sketch for present purposes is partial, though I think it is a reasonable one. A jurisdictional caveat is in order. To the extent that scholarship within relational theory differs from my account, it falls outside the scope of this book.

Describing Subjects and Autonomy

Relational theory takes as its point of departure what I call its *descriptive premise*. Its conviction is that 'persons are socially embedded and that their identities form within the context of social relationships.' Intersecting social determinants such as race, class, gender, and ethnicity shape those identities (Mackenzie and Stoljar 2000b, 4). The diverse feminist perspectives on the relational self share the insight that 'mutual, reciprocal, communicative social interactions are necessary for the formation, sustenance, and repair of the self' (Allen 2004, 240). In Jennifer Nedelsky's formulation, 'We come into being in a social context that is literally constitutive of us. Some of our most essential characteristics, such as our capacity for language and the conceptual framework through which we see the world, are not made by us, but given to us ... through our interactions with others' (1989, 8). Another theorist writes that the self is intrinsically social, 'constructed in a relational matrix' that always includes aspects of the other (Chodorow 1986, 204). The 'self exists *fundamentally* in relation to others' (Donchin 2000, 239). The effect of these relations over time is crucial: the view of the self is also historical (ibid.); selves are 'formed in time and in relational space' (Williams 2000, 138). The 'historical self' may entail the idea of obligations implied by the 'sense of being historically rooted in a set of defining familial, institutional, and national relationships' (Fletcher 1993, 21). Some relational theorists emphasize the necessity for human selfhood of sharing one's narrative with others, an act that is inherently relational (Brison 1997, 21–2; Cavarero 2000, chs. 3, 5).

In its descriptive enterprise, relational theory opposes what it designates as the liberal conception of the subject. The presumption is that while relational theory concerns itself with relationships, liberalism does not. According to relational theory, the Western liberal subject is a 'self-possessing individual linked to others only by agreement' (Minow and Shanley 1996, 12). Liberalism is predicated on self-sufficient individuals independently pursuing their respective life plans. In juridical language, the liberal self is an autonomous, rational agent that chooses its relationships and obligations through the instruments of private property and contract. It is characteristic of relational theorists to contrast the liberal idea of obligation, which is voluntarily undertaken, with their notion of responsibility, which may be involuntary. They perceive interdependent relationships as generating, over time, obligations in excess of those devised by voluntary contractual undertakings (Regan 1993, 4; also Lloyd 2000). Relational theorists tend to object to strict reliance on contract on the basis that the normative content of relationships is not transparently predictable ex ante (Minow and Shanley 1996, 12). This criticism of liberalism for denying that the self is essentially social forms a constant refrain in relational theory. Individualism, as one theorist observes, is for many critics 'the evil demon of modern Western social and political life' (Friedman 2003, 16; see also Code

2000, 183; Dodds 2000, 216; Abrams 1999, 807; West 1988). These criticisms of liberalism may be viewed as forming part of what some think of as postliberalism (Reece 2003, 5).

The objection arises that relational theory ascribes too much unity to liberalism. Colin Bird has felicitously described liberalism as less 'a harmonious federation of moral ideals bound together under a constitution of individualism' than 'an unstable alliance of antagonistic principles and ideals' (1999, 3). The liberal tradition is perhaps best viewed not as 'a body of ideas' but as 'a collection of sources and interpretations of sources' (Appiah 2005, x).

A more significant objection is that relational theory overstates the charge that the liberal tradition presupposes and endorses an atomistic view of the individual. A number of liberal theorists have recently reminded communitarians and relational theorists that the liberal tradition takes the social character of individuals into account.[2] Liberals have pointed out that significant strands of liberalism accept fully that it is within society, institutions, and relationships that individuals flourish and make choices. Kwame Appiah argues that the self whose choices liberalism celebrates is not 'a presocial thing' or 'authentic inner essence independent of the human world,' but instead the product of social interaction from infancy (2005, 20). He writes that individuality presupposes sociality, not merely 'grudging respect for the individuality of others.' Furthermore, Appiah declares that properly valuing individuality entails acknowledging that each individual's good depends on relationships with others (ibid., 20, 21). Will Kymlicka argues that since liberals believe that people will form and sustain social relations without governmental action, while communitarians suppose that such governmental intervention is required, liberals actually believe in the social character of individuals more than do communitarians (1989, 904). More specifically, several scholars have rejected the contention that Kantian ethics postulate atomistic individuals (Schneewind 1998).[3] Others have emphasized the extent to which John Stuart Mill's conception of individuality is profoundly social. Wendy Donner argues that Millian individualism assumes social beings, 'not isolated individuals lacking deep social bonds' (1991, 146; see also Taylor 1997, 185). Other rejections of atomism underscore the social nature of language (Taylor 1985). If liberalism does not subscribe to an atomistic view of individuals, but rather accepts that individuals are formed within relationships and communities, relational theorists' disagreements with liberals should not be attributed to divergent descriptions of human nature.

Rather, the nub of such disagreements may be thoroughgoingly normative: namely, the appropriate political responses to the fact of humans' embedded existence.[4]

These objections aside, relational theory to this juncture fits rather neatly with so-called communitarian critiques of liberal atomism or the liberal unencumbered self (Sandel 1982; MacIntyre 1984). Soon, however, relational theory departs from the strongest implications of communitarian scholarship, as indeed do many communitarians. As Elizabeth Frazer and Nicola Lacey argue, the communitarian view of personhood renders women in a sexist and patriarchal culture 'peculiarly powerless' (1993, 151). It permits no means of attaining a critical consciousness (Nussbaum 1999, 71). It is on this basis that Marilyn Friedman characterizes communitarian philosophy as a 'perilous ally' for feminist theory generally (1989, 277). Relational theory distinguishes itself from communitarianism in its commitment to the capacity for individuals, especially women, to revise their life plans and choose ways of living other than those presented to them by the social contexts in which they are embedded and by which they are constituted. It is awareness of the oppression of unchosen attachments that prevents relational theory from rejecting core elements of liberalism, such as the priority of individuals. The focus on autonomy enters the picture here.

Relational theory holds that autonomy is necessary in order 'to consider which particular attachments we should reshape, which to reject, which to choose, and which to promote' (Barclay 2000, 68). For the relational theorist, autonomy is not a capacity that can be exercised in isolation. Rather – and this is presented as the crucial insight – autonomy depends 'not only on background facilities and welfare levels but also on our relations with others' (Frazer and Lacey 1993, 180; also Donchin 2000, 239; Anderson and Honneth 2005). Relational autonomy requires attention to the 'impact of social and political structures, especially sexism and other forms of oppression, on the lives and opportunities of individuals' (McLeod and Sherwin 2000, 260). Becoming autonomous – being able to find and live in accordance with one's own law – is necessarily social in two dimensions. First, the capacity to find one's own law 'can develop only in the context of relations with others' (Nedelsky 1989, 11). It is not separation but relationship that makes autonomy possible (Nedelsky 1996, 429; O'Donovan and Marshall 2006, 104). Second, the 'content' of one's own law 'is comprehensible only with reference to shared social norms, values, and concepts' (Nedelsky 1989, 11). Autonomy becomes possible in social interaction through relationships, such as those with parents, teachers, friends, and agents of the state (ibid., 10–12; Friedman 2005, 156–7; 2003, 15–17; Ball 2005, 357–9; Anderson and Honneth 2005, 131–2). Relatedness is seen as a precondition of autonomy, with interdependence one of its constant components. The autonomous self and the relational self are 'interdependent, even constitutive of one another' (Brison 1997, 29).

A couple of distinctions have arisen under the umbrella of relational autonomy. Relational theorists distinguish a view of agents as *intrinsically* relational, on the basis that their identities or self-conceptions are constituted by elements of the social context in which they are embedded, from a *causal* relational conception, which attends to the ways in which socialization and social relationships impede or enhance autonomy (Mackenzie and Stoljar 2000b, 22).

Theorists also differentiate *procedural* or content-neutral conceptions of autonomy from *substantive* conceptions. Procedural or content-neutral conceptions regard the initial 'content of a person's desires, values, beliefs, and emotional attitudes' as irrelevant to the inquiry whether the person is autonomous in respect of the motivations and actions flowing from them (Mackenzie and Stoljar 2000b, 13). Procedural conceptions fasten on the processes by which a person arrives at her desires and objectives and whether she has 'subjected her motivations and actions to the appropriate kind of critical reflection' (Mackenzie and Stoljar 2000b, 14; see also Christman 1991). The notion is that content-neutral procedural conditions are necessary and sufficient for autonomy.

In contrast, substantive theories of autonomy hold that procedural conditions for autonomy are necessary but insufficient. Substantive theories respond to objections to procedural accounts that derive from socialization, namely, the idea that oppressive socialization can undermine agents' normative competence (Mackenzie and Stoljar 2000b, 19–20). For proponents of substantive conceptions, some preferences and decisions are so harmful to the agent that they could not have been truly chosen autonomously. As Natalie Stoljar writes, 'preferences influenced by oppressive norms of femininity cannot be autonomous' (2000, 95). Proponents of substantive theories argue that norms oppressing women need to be criticized from a feminist point of view for their content. It is inadequate to criticize the reasoning processes undertaken by those whom the oppressive norms influence (ibid., 109).

Relational theory inscribes itself within feminist political philosophy or theory, but it does not content itself with abstract efforts to define its terms. Instead, it often turns to concrete legal issues. Thus relational theorists have analysed examples drawn from family law (Minow and Shanley 1996; Cossman 1990), constitutional law (Brison 2000; Nedelsky 1993b), administrative law (Nedelsky 1989; Cartier unpublished, ch. 5), antidiscrimination law (Koggel 1998), property law (Nedelsky 1993a; 1996), and tort law (Bender 1993).[5] These excursions onto legal terrain indicate an intention on the part of relational theorists that lawyers engage with their scholarship, an invitation I take up in this book. In addition to arguing for the emergence of contextual legal subjects, I shall argue that the presentation of relational theory's valuable insights, particularly for law, can be sharpened. For reasons I explain presently, this book adopts two substantive fields of law for its study: family law and administrative law.

Two Takes on a Relational Approach

Departing from what I have called the descriptive premise, relational theorists formulate what they call a relational approach or inquiry. It directs theorists, policy makers, legislatures, and lawyers to 'focus on *relationship*' (Nedelsky 1993a, 365), to pay 'attention to the claims that arise out of relationships of human interdependence' (Minow and Shanley 1996, 23). The idea is to see the 'human interactions to be governed' not primarily 'in terms of the clashing of rights and interests, but in terms of the way patterns of relationship can develop and sustain both an enriching collective life and the scope for genuine individual autonomy' (Nedelsky 1996, 429). The objective becomes to foster optimal relationships in a given setting. Consistent with the observation that relational theory is not a rigidly unified body of work, relational theorists articulate the relational inquiry in different ways. There are unacknowledged tensions, however, between two basic ideas about the relational approach, and this even within the work of the same scholars.

An ambiguity in the relational literature passes unnoticed in family law, but emerges in administrative law. The issue is whether relational theorists are interested in assessing and aiding relationships of any kind or whether they have in mind a quite specific idea of constructive relationships joined with the further objective of ultimately promoting relational autonomy. In the family setting, relational theorists call for sexual equality and diversity of family forms, for taking seriously the responsibilities generated by family relationships, and for recognizing the role of the larger society in sustaining families (Minow and Shanley 1996, 4).

Good family relationships will be marked by duration, mutuality, and interdependence.[6] What is unclear is whether those attributes were brought to the scene in the relational approach a priori or whether they emerged a posteriori after a relational investigation. The administrative law setting will highlight the ambiguity. It is not prima facie obvious that thick, interdependent relationships are appropriate in a bureaucratic setting.

I think two instantiations of a relational approach are identifiable in the literature. One is content-neutral, what I call the *weak* version. The other is fully normative, what I call the *strong* version. Before I sketch these two versions, I should specify that this contrast is different from the one mentioned above between procedural and substantive conceptions of relational autonomy. The point here is not the conception of relational autonomy, but the substance of the relational approach, one in which relational autonomy of either kind may operate to varying degrees.

The *weak* conception of the relational approach is methodological and largely content-neutral. This conception, exemplified in work by Nedelsky, holds that a relational approach is useful to people of varying political convictions. Its 'focus on relationship provides a useful framework for exploring ... issues and arguments more fully' (Nedelsky 1993a, 355). It helps 'to identify the issues at stake' (ibid., 344). The relational inquiry attempts to identify the constellation of relevant relationships around a given individual or the parties to a dispute. The claim is that issues can be better understood and debated 'if we focus on the kinds of relationships that are involved and the kinds of relationships we think a given legal regime is likely to foster' (ibid., 344). One of the relational approach's virtues is that 'it often exposes arguments that turn out to rest on superficial parallels of language' (ibid., 364). Nedelsky is explicit that her relational approach is not necessarily tied to specific substantive commitments. Her focus on rights as structuring relationships leaves open 'the question of which relationships we want' (Nedelsky 1993a, 345). The relational 'framework seeks to offer a better way of understanding the claims even of the positions to which it is clearly unsympathetic' (ibid., 346). Martha Minow and Mary Shanley argue that a relational approach can 'provide the analytic, intellectual, and rhetorical resources for approaching' the difficult questions in family law (1996, 25). For instance, progress in addressing complex family issues is likeliest 'to develop from a political and legal theory that focuses on the relationships that constitute family life and the precon-

ditions necessary to sustain such relationships' (1996, 25–6; see also
Regan 1999, 13–25).[7] Again referring to the family setting, another relational theorist argues that 'a discourse framed around individual rights
and interests is bound to neglect other significant features of family
bonds' (Donchin 2000, 248).

The crucial point to retain from the weak conception is that relational theorists suggest, implicitly and explicitly, that simply thinking
about relationships or focusing on them generates results. Reconfiguring theoretical and legal debates in terms of relationship facilitates the
resolution of controversial questions: 'a focus on *relationship* can shift
the terms of debate onto a more constructive path' (Nedelsky 1993a,
365). Similarly, 'shifting attention to the relational situation that frames
the conflict opens possible routes to further strategies for resolving tensions, reducing injustices, and reconfiguring self-understandings'
(Donchin 2000, 248). Given the feminist political orientation of relational theorists, I think there is an implication that merely undertaking
a relational inquiry is likelier than not to lead to policy outcomes congenial to feminist missions. This implication is discernible in the preceding passage's suggestion that 'attention to the relational situation'
may reduce injustice. When giving this sense, relational theory implies,
I think unhelpfully, that the basis for dispute between relational theorists and others will not be, as it sometimes is, normative disagreement
over the definition of *desirable* relationships, but simply the difference
between those who have turned their minds to relationships and those
who have not (Nedelsky 1993b, 14; Minow and Shanley 1996, 25–6).

By contrast, the *strong* conception of a relational approach is frankly
substantive and normative. It is not indifferent to the kinds of relationships that should be regarded as desirable in a particular setting. The
normative conception dives right into substantive debates. Nailing its
colours to the mast, it adopts relational autonomy as its highest or one
of its highest values.[8] It is committed to promoting optimal relationships, and it has a substantive criterion for identifying them. Optimal
and desirable relationships are ones that foster or promote relational
autonomy. Its concern is with 'structuring the relations between individuals and the sources of collective power so that autonomy is fostered
rather than undermined' (Nedelsky 1996, 430). While I shall return to
this question much later in the book, it appears that those who subscribe to the substantive version of the relational approach have a fairly
specific idea of the kinds of relationships that do foster relational autonomy. These are thick, interdependent relationships, such as those with

family members, friends, neighbours, and teachers. Indeed, Minow and Shanley refer to such relationships in their definition of what it means to focus on relational rights and responsibilities: it means drawing attention 'to the claims that arise out of relationships of human interdependence' (1996, 23). Nedelsky writes of the need to 'pay attention to the conditions that foster people's capacity to form caring, responsible and intimate relationships with each other – as family members, friends, members of a community, and citizens of a state' (Nedelsky 1993a, 355).

Though in the literature one can find depictions of both weak and strong forms of relational inquiry, the distinction is unstable. Neutral inquiries gradually transform into normative ones. Relational theorists are too committed to relational autonomy as a primary, if not the preeminent, value to approach a relational inquiry with a blank slate. In their ostensibly neutral investigative efforts to apply the weak relational approach, they seek to accomplish the same work under the guise of the descriptive premise that their *consœurs* achieve using the strong version. Efforts to work within the weak, neutral conception thus place too great a burden on accurate descriptions of embedded selves. The notion is that, instead of engaging in a normative enterprise, theorists applying the weak form of relational inquiry are clarifying the starting points and the values at stake, aided by their detailed and complete conception of the individual.

Minow and Shanley's essay on family law models the slippage from accurate description and weak, neutral relational analysis to strong, normative relational analysis. After identifying three main orientations within the literature – contractarian, communitarian, and rights-based – they criticize these positions for failing to address two 'paradoxical features.' One is that people are simultaneously individuals and deeply involved in interdependent relationships. The other is that families are simultaneously private associations and socially shaped entities. The authors argue that family disputes oppose one individual to another without attending adequately to the 'web of relationships that is not reducible to individual claims' (1996, 5–6). They assert that contractual ordering 'fails to deal with the fact that certain dependencies that develop in intimate relationships can not be adequately addressed by contract' (ibid., 12). The reference to 'fact' jars with the vocabulary of adequacy's testimony to a value-based evaluation.[9] They also argue that a focus on relational rights and responsibilities in a child custody dispute would give great weight to preserving continuity of relationships (ibid., 24). Without disputing that continuity likely is a *normatively* desirable element of constructive relationships, one can observe that it is not entailed by the mere exercise of 'focusing' on relationships. It is, rather, part of a substantive conception of *good* relationships. Indeed, the structure of their paper contrasts a relational approach with other patently substantive contractual and communitarian political theories. If one has such a vision, why not advocate for it explicitly instead of suggesting that it results, neutrally, from the mere exercise of thinking about relationships?

As I shall argue, relational theory does disservice to itself and its objectives when it locates controversial and debatable normative matters in the ostensibly factual space of its descriptive premise and in the content-neutral space of 'thinking about' or 'focusing on' relationships. Doing so implies, erroneously, that points of disagreement would dissolve if only everyone adopted the same accurate description and everyone took the time to think about relationships.

Similarly, in a paper on property issues raised by reproductive technologies, Nedelsky demonstrates how the weak relational inquiry leads easily into the normative form. Announcing her intention to 'spell out a bit more how a focus on relationship provides a useful framework for exploring these issues and arguments more fully' (1993a, 355), she identifies the relationships to be borne in mind when dealing with the problems posed by potential life. These are relationships of 'respect and appreciation for children'; 'relationships of respect for women and honouring of their reproductive capacities and labour'; and 'relations of equality, between people of all classes and backgrounds as well as between men and women' (Nedelsky 1993a, 355). She writes that, 'finally, at the broadest level, we also need to pay attention to the conditions that foster people's capacity to form caring, responsible and intimate relationships with each other – as family members, friends, members of a community, and citizens of a state' (ibid., 355). Identifying and promoting relationships of this kind is a deeply normative project. What becomes harder to pin down is how much work, independent of the normative attachment to the 'need to focus on the relationships that foster respect and equality for women and respect and appreciation for children' (ibid., 364), is being done by the neutral 'focus on relationship' itself. It is clear that Nedelsky is much more interested in promoting a particular kind of relationships, in attending to the 'conditions that foster people's capacity to form caring, responsible and intimate relationships with each other' (ibid., 355), than in enhancing whatever relationships happen to be around. The weak relational approach does not manage to do much analytic labour. It simply gives the normative project an entrée through a side door. My sense is that the space for the weak approach is narrow and tenuous. For example, I shall show later in the book that initiatives of relational theorists in administrative law do not restrict themselves to the weak conception of a relational approach but instead apply the strong normative conception.

Relational theorists tend to cast the descriptive premise and the relational inquiry as their flagship contributions to political theory (Minow and Shanley 1996; Nedelsky 1993b). Yet relational theory's contribution to political theory and practical analysis may not be its descriptive or ontological claim about sociality. Examples in this book will suggest that calls for simply thinking about relationships or focusing on them may prove less productive than relational theorists hope. Emphasizing the descriptive premise and the relational inquiry to this extent unhelpfully diverts attention from other, more promising elements. As I have shown, the weak, neutral version of a relational inquiry tends to slip into the strong, normative version. Furthermore, the strong version is so substantive that its heft is misrepresented by the shorthand 'focus on relationships.' It is much more than a focus or inquiry. It is a feminist political project.

Distinguishing Two Elements of the Relational Approach

Past the descriptive premise, relational theorists would do better to disaggregate their relational approach into two elements: a *contextual methodology* and their *normative commitments*.

There is already substantial support for identifying a *methodology of contextualism* in relational theory. Relational theorists consistently advocate close attention to the contexts in which individuals interact.[10] Catriona Mackenzie and Natalie Stoljar observe that feminist critiques underscore that 'an analysis of the characteristics and capacities of the self cannot be adequately undertaken without attention to the rich and complex social and historical contexts in which agents are embedded' (2000b, 21). Nedelsky adopts the feminist precept 'that any good theorizing will start with people in their social contexts' (1989, 9). She characterizes as 'crucial' the feminist insistence on context and particularity instead of abstract universality (2001, 135). Attention to context is seen as enabling 'attention to the assumptions and frameworks underlying any given expression and any given interpretation' (Minow and Spelman 1990, 1615). This insistence on context indicates that the relational inquiry's enjoinment to focus on relationships comports a methodological call to examine context. But what is the connection between relational analysis and contextual analysis? Are the two equivalent?

Where Christine Koggel writes that 'a relational approach begins with the individual in social practices and political contexts' (1998, 131), what she means by a relational approach is attention to context. If Nedelsky is correct that 'a focus on relationship automatically turns our attention to context' (1993b, 10; 1993a, 364), it is difficult to see why the inquiry should not begin there, or why the two are not interchangeable. At times relational theorists explicitly indicate the substitutability – the direct equivalence – of 'relational' and 'contextual': Nedelsky refers to a 'contextual or relational account of autonomy' and to 'the influence of personal relationships and social structures' (Nedelsky unpublished b, 21, 19). McLeod and Sherwin refer to 'relational (or contextual) autonomy' as involving 'explicit recognition of the fact that autonomy is both defined and pursued in a social context' (2000, 259). But other articulations indicate that the two are not identical. In a paper on family law, Roxanne Mykitiuk argues that determinations of filiation demand an analysis 'reflective of complex social and material relations and of the asymmetrical and diverse connections of multiple persons to a particular child' (2001, 791n68). By 'relations' she gestures towards a contextual methodology, one exceeding personal relationships. Likewise, when Minow and Shanley speak of intimate relationships as 'embedded in relationships of neighbors, religious and ethnic groups, and even relationships of strangers, all deeply affected but not entirely determined by the political system and economic circumstances' (1996, 24), their thrust is, likewise, less relationships tout court than it is context. Here is where the substantive distinction between relationships and context arises. The reference to the political system and economic circumstances hints that the context to which relational theorists refer includes the set of a subject's personal relationships existing at a given moment, but is greater than that set. It also includes political, socio-economic, and cultural conditions. As Martha Minow and Elizabeth Spelman observe, 'the demand to look at the context often means a demand to look at the structures of power, gender, race, or class relationships ... The emphasis on context often means identifying structures that extend far beyond the particular circumstance' (1990, 1651). Context is larger than the set of personal relationships.

It is worth distinguishing a subject's context from the set of her relationships because the former is likelier than the latter to leave open a wider range of political responses. The concern is not a conceptual one about the possibilities of the notions of context versus relationships *in abstracto*. It is simply that the account of relational autonomy has so coloured or signified the term 'relationship' that it has lost its edge as a descriptive and analytical tool and become instead, as a practical matter, a vehicle for relational theorists' normative vision of good relationships. By contrast, the idea of context is not yet firmly associated with particular normative views of appropriate relations. It is an examination of context, then, that is likely to prove more flexible and adaptable to different settings in which, for example, it may not really be 'caring, responsible and intimate relationships' (Nedelsky 1993a, 355) or 'relationships of human interdependence' (Minow and Shanley 1996, 23) that are desirable. The relational theoretic literature shows that when relational theorists speak of relationships, they tend to drag with them their normative commitments. This is a negative way of putting it. Positively, the point is that the contextual methodology towards which relational theorists gesture has value in a wider set of domains than does their normative commitments. A 'contextual' approach appears more open than a 'relational' one to different normative presuppositions and conclusions. A contextual approach can be appropriate for analysing structural and institutional relations; the normative commitment to promoting relational autonomy cannot be.

The second element to draw from the relational approach and to distinguish from the contextual methodology is the *normative commitment*. Most relational theorists have, I think, a substantive or normative commitment to the capacity for relational autonomy and to promoting constructive relationships conducive to it. It is this commitment that underwrites the theorizing of most who identify their analysis as relational. The abstract ideal of constructive relationships then demands particularization in different domains, such as the family, schools, and the bureaucracy. Indeed, as Amy Allen argues, 'even if we all agree that the self is social or relational, our work has just begun' (2004, 251).

Articulating and embracing relational theory's normative dimension is imperative. Failing to do so – leaning primarily on the ostensibly neutral relational inquiry – can leave relational theorists struggling to distinguish good from bad relationships. Nedelsky argues that a relational conception of the self (descriptive premise) emphasizes the difference between bonds that are constructive and those that are not, thereby supplying a standard by which to evaluate existing relationships (2001, 134). But the idea that the self is partially constituted by relationships does not per se dictate *which* relationships are constructive. Only substantive criteria can do so. Such evaluative means will derive from a developed normative account of good relationships, a specification of the qualities that promote the capacity for autonomy. Timidity in foregrounding the normative commitment impels Nedelsky elsewhere to acknowledge 'troubling historical examples' of judges adopting 'what one might call a relational approach' that have harmed women's interests (unpublished b, 21). She cites the judicial condonation of a murderous reaction on the part of a husband who stumbles upon his wife and her lover. The characterization of such an outcome, if only provisionally, as consistent with a relational approach shows a mistaken attachment to the view that the minimum requirement for a relational approach is some kind of attention to some kind of relationship. Calling such an outcome 'relational' shows faith that, at least most of the time, politically desirable results will come from the mere fact of examining relationships and inquiring how they can be fostered. It misleadingly suggests that relational theorists, contrary to their substantive commitments, are neutrally concerned with identifying and enhancing whatever relationships happen to exist. If relational theorists stow away their normative commitments, the consequence is that they can find themselves stranded with no tools to contest obviously bad situations.

Other rich examples are the homosexual panic cases. These concern self-identifying heterosexual men who react violently to real or perceived sexual advances from gay men and later plead a defence of provocation (Howe 2001). I do not think that relational theorists would wish to waste time exploring the way in which condoning the straight assailant's conduct is 'relational' in the sense of enhancing, say, his relationship with his female partner. But it is only by recourse to a normative vision that one can deny such condonation the dignity of being called a relational approach. Moreover, the normative vision cannot be as thin as a total rejection of violent means, since relational theorists explore ways in which a battered woman may legitimately deploy violence against her abuser (Nedelsky, unpublished b). Nor is the normative vision as simple as the fulfilment of relational responsibilities, whatever that means. Relational ties can threaten autonomy, 'for responding to others' needs and fulfilling one's responsibilities to them can become so consuming that the individual is deprived of any opportunity to pursue personal goals and projects' (Meyers 2004, 52). Put another way, some relationships enhance the autonomy of one individual at another's expense. So the criteria for identifying constructive relationships need to be fairly detailed.

The conundrum vanishes once relational theory shifts its emphasis to highlighting its normative commitment to a particular substantive kind of relationships, thick ones that enhance the relational autonomy of each individual involved. Normative resources are then available for criticizing the judge who excuses the homicidal cuckold. It is only from a normative standpoint that one can criticize such examples and undertake the evaluative work necessary for feminism's political project. This example (and there are many others where an objectionable legal norm must be conceded to serve one conception of relationships or another) shows that the relational inquiry, without revealing, explicating, and defending its normative underpinnings, does not move us forward through contentious thickets. The basis of criticism in these cases is not inattention to relationships. It is the normative definition of *appropriate* relationships. Only when relying on a normative foundation can one evaluate and distinguish good and bad actions and laws, good and bad relationships, and good and bad contexts. Such evaluation is critical because, after all, 'it is one thing to say that selves are formed in and through a social context, quite another to say that this is always a good thing' (Bird 1999, 207). As I shall argue, family law in the recent past was substantively objectionable to relational theorists, but the basis for the objections was not inattention to relationships. The problem was not that family law was non-relational. If anything, it permitted relationships to abridge individual autonomy too much. As I shall show, the objections to historical family law lay in its acontextual methodology and its particular criteria for identifying good relationships.

Separating the contextual methodology from the normative commitments is valuable as they should not always go together. In administrative law, the contextual methodology can be appropriately applied without the normative commitment to thick relationships. Furthermore, my discussion of family law will highlight occasional instances where a formal and abstract method – typically associated by relational theorists with liberalism – turns out to serve relational interests. Relational theory fails its own deepest convictions when it attempts to pass them off as necessarily embedded in the relational inquiry. The interesting questions on which relational theory has much to offer concern the normative conceptions of relationships that should be adopted and promoted in particular settings and the methods suitable in doing so.

Relational theorists have developed a sophisticated vocabulary and approach for tackling precisely such questions. Throughout the book I shall be hinting at the importance of normative commitments, and not simply because they animate a contextual approach. Norms are also important because of their role in partially defining contexts.

This book will distinguish three kinds of contributions that relational theorists may make in legal fields. One is methodological, namely, advocacy for contextualism. Another is normative, calling for attention to the relationships that enhance the capacity for autonomy. And the third is a hybrid, concerning the norms that structure and define what counts as the context. Human judgment always requires defining the context and structuring the way in which information is organized. As Kim Scheppele argues in a discussion of sexual assault, a story 'only makes sense against a background that limits the range of things that might be said. To describe the whole truth is impossible; to describe a coherent partial truth means having some background standards for deciding what is relevant and what is not' (1987, 1108). One signifies or sees some facts as salient and is blind to others (Medina 2003, 663; see also Koggel 1998, 34). The standards or norms that determine salience often remain implicit, though they are well understood and are relied on by a great many social actors. In applying a contextual method, a key issue is often the boundary determining what does and does not legitimately count. That boundary often depends on controversial normative decisions. Take rules in family law that characterize any person who is not a child's biological or adoptive parent as a legal stranger. In such a regime, the legal rule excludes as irrelevant the child's relations with a non-parent – a godfather, a family friend, the gay lover of one of the parents – from even entering the context. Relational theorists have much to say on such normative matters. In this book, by emphasizing context instead of relationships, I leave the questions more open to a variety of answers.

This Book's Path

I shall pursue three major claims, which will be of different interest to various readers. The first claim is that, in the contemporary period, both family law and administrative law have adopted a contextual view of legal subjects and law. By contrast, in the earlier periods, the legal subjects were *acontextual*. In family law, subjects were tightly ensnared in family relationships, yet their legal statuses were determinative and other contextual factors were irrelevant. In administrative law, subjects were thin, their interests sharply constrained by formal distinctions, and, similarly, their context was irrelevant. Though I focus on the Canadian setting, the way in which human rights norms are rendered concrete via a contextual methodology has resonance for other contexts, such as the United Kingdom with its Human Rights Act 1998, and European countries more generally, which are subject to the European Convention on Human Rights.

The second claim, which I have already begun to argue, is that relational theory sells itself short and obscures crucial debates by hiding, in an undifferentiated relational inquiry, its contextual method and its normative commitment to promoting relational autonomy via thick, interdependent, enduring relationships. This strand will be of greatest interest to political theorists as well as to those concerned with feminist interventions in political philosophy.

The third is that the contextual method has a utility broader than the appropriate purview of relational theory's normative commitments. Distinguishing contextualism from the normative commitments it serves within relational theory opens the possibility that it may be a suitable methodology to deploy even where no commitment to thick relations is appropriate. In other words, the contextualism sketched within relational theory can and should be applied in settings in which it is unsuitable to foster thick, interdependent relationships in the service of relational autonomy. Moreover, this detachment of contextualism from thick relationships is already happening. And where contextualism is adopted, the challenge arises of how to define it. This discussion will speak to lawyers and judges confronted with the challenge of practising contextualism. I believe it takes the discussion of context within Canadian law to a new level.

I have mentioned case studies of family law and administrative law. These are not the only legal fields that relational theorists have argued would benefit from a relational approach. But they will serve as a fitting canvas for this book's project. The conjunction of these two fields is unusual and controversial. In law's many mansions, family law and administrative law occupy decidedly different wings. The disciplinary division of public law and private law – family law is private, administrative law, public – should, in principle, ensure their perpetual segregation one from the other. Scholars do not typically regard the two as companionate or even as constructively contrastive. My argument is that despite their substantive, procedural, and institutional differences, the two are worth holding up to each other. In the past thirty or so years, both fields have adopted a methodology and discourse of contextualism. Both have come to produce contextual subjects. Both reveal that human rights norms can be applied through a contextual method: human rights norms expressed at an abstract level need to be made concrete in individual contexts. What makes the comparison of the two so fruitful is that, while both have turned to contextualism, the normative commitments of relational theory apply much more suitably in family law than in administrative law. The two fields together will substantiate my claim of the utility in disentangling relational theory from its unclear 'relational approach' into a contextual method and its normative commitments. Both fields will also show the complicated normative issues raised by the enterprise of defining the relevant context in given settings.

It is this challenge of defining the relevant context, and the disputes to which it gives rise, that makes administrative law a more productive public law field for study than constitutional law. Constitutional law, particularly the interpretation of the written constitution of the United States, is riven with debates about the appropriateness of recourse to context. Originalists seek to restrict the textual interpretation to what may have been intended at the time. Proponents of context 'seek to challenge the claim that the texts stand free of the situation in which they were produced' (Minow and Spelman 1990, 1602; see also White 1990, 137–8). It is a big binary debate: is context in or out of constitutional construal? As I shall show, the Canadian administrative law setting – less spectacularly, with considerably less domination of global public law discourse – is one in which the general acceptance of the appropriateness of contextualism leaves many contentious issues. Contextualism has won. What is revealing is not the question of context or not but instead the challenges raised by operationalizing contextualism. Moreover, the administrative law setting, in which courts develop the common law of procedural fairness and review decisions made under a broad delegated discretion, will show a wider application of contextualism than could be demonstrated by the constitutional setting, which in countries with written constitutions focuses on interpreting entrenched texts. The study of administrative law will show that what courts have now is not just a contextual approach to interpreting texts, but a contextual view of legal subjects.

Relational theory accords rather well with contemporary family law, by which I mean from 1975 to the present. Indeed, it is precisely because the fit is so snug that it is possible to discuss contemporary family law issues through the lens of relational theory without distinguishing the contextual methodology from the normative commitment to thick, constructive relationships. The mainstream of Canadian family law today seeks to foster the particular thick relationships in which individuals are embedded, and this mainstream position embraces a diversity of relational forms. A sustained examination of earlier family law, however, hints at the benefits of separating the relational approach into the two elements I have identified: contextual method and normative commitment. As chapter 2 recounts, family law between 1950 and 1975 laboured conscientiously to foster the sort of thick relationships it thought desirable. What distinguishes it from contemporary family law is its commitment to legitimate relationships, ones defined by a structure that rendered illegitimate those relations between unmarried couples and between individuals of the same sex. This commitment obtained in both the common law and the civil law of Quebec. In its emphasis on legitimacy, the body of positive law and scholarly writing was generally acontextual in a way at odds with relational theory's openness to social and institutional settings and informal as well as formal elements. Although any temporal division will be to some extent arbitrary, a divided appellate judgment warrants 1975 as a cutoff. *Murdoch v. Murdoch* (1975) serves as a pivot between the second and third chapters because the majority exemplified the formalist, acontextual method of the earlier period while the dissent presaged subsequent developments by modelling the contextual methodology of relational theory.

Chapter 3 discusses the rise of contextualism and the normative commitment of relational theory in developments in contemporary family law. A contrast emerges between the second chapter's abstract practices and more contextual methods in which judges attempted to take into account a number of contextual elements and make a decision influenced by all of them. I shall note settings in which the normative structuring of context proved particularly crucial. This chapter's presentation of the recognition of same-sex marriage as consistent with prior adoptions of contextualism constitutes an important intervention in debates on definitions of family and the impact of the Canadian Charter of Rights and Freedoms.

Chapter 4 uses the example of consensual ordering among adults to highlight the limits of taking a relational approach to resolving disputes. This chapter shows that, past a certain point, a contextual assessment of a situation demands a normative decision. Relational theory is no longer an outsider position, speaking relational truth to liberal power from the margins. Its intuitions and commitments have been largely absorbed by the judges of the Supreme Court of Canada in family law. Once the grander dichotomy of abstract liberalism versus relational contextualism is set aside, it becomes necessary to draw lines on thoroughly contextual, relational ground. Together, the three chapters will indicate that normative emphasis on thick relationships can be separated from a contextual methodology. The second site of inquiry, administrative law, further illustrates the separability of relational theory's elements.

Chapter 5 recounts that administrative law mid-century – from 1950 to 1975 – generally subscribed to none of relational theory's elements. It was not particularly concerned with the relationships of individual citizens, focusing more on the institutional alignment of courts and administrative tribunals. Administrative law's methodology was formalist, abstract, and acontextual. Its normative commitments included protection of property rights but did not concentrate on those thick relationships that are central to relational theory.

Chapter 6 narrates the emergence of a contextual methodology, as judges departed from formal classification exercises in favour of more contextual inquiries. Contextualism is detectable at different levels and in different kinds of relations, beginning in the *démarche* by which courts determine the content of the duty of procedural fairness that bears on administrative agencies. It is further discernible in the approach developed for determining the standard of review for agencies' substantive determinations. Last, it has emerged in the view that administrative decision makers are contextually embedded, as manifested in elaborations of the doctrine of bias and in the way that the impact of decisions on individuals are now taken into account.

Chapter 7 addresses relational norms in the administrative setting. Relational theory implicitly, and at times explicitly, presumes that similar ambitions are appropriate for the whole set of relations from the family to the administrative state. I will argue that in administrative law, the ideal of interdependence and intimacy is misplaced, but that the contextual method is appropriate. Even the weak version of a relational approach is problematic. Relational theory has a blind spot: its 'relational' orientation drives it to personalize its analysis, so that its work on administrative law, typically focusing on the optimal bureaucrat–citizen relationship, obscures broader structural elements of administrative

processes. My claim will be that relational theory's contextual methodology should be retained in administrative law but detached from that
theory's normative commitments.

It is worth anticipating an objection. The objection is that for a
project studying contextualism, this book concerns itself with lofty texts
that are somewhat removed from the lives of ordinary individuals
(Collier 2006, 244–5). It is true that the significant role assumed by contextualism warrants further study, including empirical work and
research on how contextual methodology operates in a variety of juridical forums, but the need for such work is not inconsistent with the
present project. A caveat is in order: this book is not a historical or sociological study, and while I speculate from time to time, I do not present
a causal explanation for the turn to contextualism. This book's drawing
together of the emergence of contextualism in family law and administrative law is itself a novel contribution, as is the sustained examination
of those fields through the lens of relational theory. (A further novelty
in the Canadian setting is the extended treatment together of family law
in the common law and civil law traditions.) By contrast, most of the
relational theoretic literature is short essays with few extended case
studies. Further research on what caused the rise of contextualism
remains to be done. Given the sense that contextualism is here to stay,
it is important to understand better how it functions and the norms that
animate it – matters I address in the book's substantive chapters. The
examples narrated here will serve to make the discussion of context less
abstract (see, similarly, Minow and Spelman 1990, 1639).

Let me conclude this introductory chapter by repeating my three
major claims. The first is that the domains of law I discuss now constitute contextual subjects. Judges and scholars have adopted contextualism not only in interpreting enacted texts, but in viewing and analysing
legal subjects more generally. This change in method has had discursive
and material effects. The second is that relational theory obscures
crucial debates by hiding its normative commitment behind the relational inquiry and the contextual method. Relational theory's intuitions
and commitments are normatively attractive and should be articulated
openly rather than masked. The legal developments I recount are
revealing because they show how normative engagements operate
through a judicial method of contextualism. Along the way, I shall
examine the interplay between changing normative commitments and
changing methodologies, identifying the challenge of defining what

counts as context. The third is that the contextual method that produces those legal subjects I have noted – arguably relational theory's
major contribution to theoretical debates – reaches more widely than
the appropriate application of relational theory's normative commitment. As these legal case studies will show, relational theory's value and
impact can be improved and intensified if it reconfigures its admirable
project.

PART ONE

Family Law

2 Thick Subjects in the Past

Family law in the mid-twentieth century poses a paradox for relational theorists. They know they do not like it. The law sanctioned women's adultery more harshly than men's. Illegitimate children suffered for their parents' immoral conduct. In Quebec, matters were worse. Under the long reign of the nineteenth-century civil code, married women did not even have civil rights. From today's perspective, family law fifty years ago is a shop of horrors, inconsistent with relational theory's vision of promoting relational autonomy, especially for women. But relational theory's 'relational inquiry' does not help target the problems.

Family law's subjects were thickly embedded in the bonds of social relationships and religion. Indeed, at junctures state family law incorporated by reference the regulatory norms of non-state orders such as religion and society, most obviously in Quebec. The resemblance with the thick subject associated with conservative stripes of communitarianism comes to mind (Whitehead 1992; Elshtain and Buell 1991; Sommers 1994). If anything, the subjects that law produced were too thick, with little space for departures from prevailing roles. There was much 'focus on relationship' and attention to the ways in which institutions and rules induced relational conduct coded as appropriate. A firm commitment prevailed to promoting those family relationships regarded as good, which were thick and interdependent. Relational theorists' basis for criticizing family law in the earlier period will not be the difference between their account of subjects as embedded and family law's story of subjects as abstracted and atomistic. Nor will it be that earlier family law failed to think about relationships and how constructive ones could be promoted and enhanced. The relational inquiry, as often framed, misses the mark.

I argue in this chapter that family law between 1950 and 1975 bears out the importance of disuniting relational theory's project. Dividing the relational approach into the methodology of contextualism and the normative commitment to thick, autonomy-enhancing relationships will provide the entry point for critical engagement with the law of this period. Family law presumed a thick description of subjects, but it followed, by and large, an acontextual, formal, and abstract methodology for treating family relationships. By formalism, I mean a practice of requiring judges to operate with categories and distinctions that determine results without judges' having to deploy the substantive arguments underpinning those categories and distinctions. Within such formalism, manipulation of categories replaces reflection on substantive concerns. Family law deployed a formal, acontextual methodology, one that relied on formal categorizations and that frequently permitted a single salient legal characterization to determine the outcome. It relied little on multifactored tests and open-ended criteria. For example, the roles of husband and wife were sharply differentiated and dragged a package of standard rights and duties. Consequently, in marital disputes, husbands and wives were regarded as instantiations of universal figures of Husband and Wife, rather than as individuals whose particular relationship had developed a unique normative content. What mattered for juridical purposes was correctly labelling someone as *what* she was, rather than piecing together a narrative of *who* she was (Cavarero 2000, 50).

Furthermore, family law's underlying normative commitment to *legitimate* family relationships appears highly objectionable by the contemporary standards of relational theory. The salient marker of desirable relationships was their religious and legal legitimacy. Marriage and legitimate filiation occupied the field of legitimate relationships exclusively. An explicit voluntary act of enlightened consent by two parties instated the thick status of marriage. Recognizable relationships did not emerge from informal or implicit ordering; functioning as a conjugal couple was insufficient. The norms of legitimacy that constituted some subjects as participants in valid relationships simultaneously excluded and devalued others. They explicitly prohibited conduct in ways that unquestionably 'abjected' the subjects in relationships figured as illegitimate (Butler 1993, 3). The prevailing juridical ethos thus emphasized explicit over implicit ordering. At times, the legal order acknowledged that Roman Catholicism or Protestant Christianity furnished the normative basis for defining 'legitimacy'; on other occasions, jurists cloaked similar substance more decorously as 'morality' or public order.

Within the Canadian state legal order, family law is conventionally regarded as a matter of private law (Leckey 2007b). Excepting the federal power over marriage and divorce, general legislative jurisdiction over family law falls to the provinces as a matter of property and civil rights. Significant substantive differences distinguish family law in the common law provinces from the regime in Quebec. In Quebec, the civil law provides the foundational law of property and civil rights. From 1866 until 1994, the Civil Code of Lower Canada, subject to piecemeal amendments, provided Quebec's general regime of the family. This code reflected the values of a rural, parochial, and Roman Catholic society; and well into the period, it corresponded with the prevailing conservatism.[1] During and after the Quiet Revolution of the 1960s, however, a sense emerged that the nineteenth-century code no longer reflected or served Quebec society. It should be noted that there are different ways of defining family law. The set of legal instruments, texts, and practices that constitute the family in law far exceeds those legal sources conventionally labelled as comprising family law. Taxation and immigration policies, for example, produce the family in law (Leckey 2002b, 226–33; also Diduck and O'Donovan 2006). For present purposes, however, I restrict the compass of family law to what has been traditionally regarded as the core: matters of status and property. It is time to turn to marriage.

Legitimate Unions

From a legal perspective, rhetoric about the 'family' as the bedrock of society is inaccurate. The family per se, devoid of legal personality and status, is typically invisible in the law's eyes. Indeed, there is no authoritative and accepted definition of 'family' (Millard 1995, paras. 26–7, 8). For lawyers in both traditions, the family is simply the hodgepodge of legal relations accruing among its individual members and between them and their property. The civil law classically recognizes two legal institutions as the means for establishing legitimate family bonds and as the source of status, rights, and obligations. *Marriage* is the means of founding the legitimate family, and *filiation* is the means of expanding that family (Marty and Raynaud 1956, para. 384). In the common law, family law is preoccupied with the legal effects of the relationships between husband and wife and between parent and child (Bromley 1957, 1).

Marriage's cultural and symbolic significance ensured its regulatory apparatus a signal role in the constitution of legal subjects. The institution of marriage, which then as now enjoyed an iconic status, provided the *normal* form for sexual relations, using that adjective in the robust, regulative sense. While some tolerance for diversity within the institution of marriage had characterized Britain's colonial and imperial days (Walters 2003, 95–100), matrimonial law had become by 1950 decidedly homogeneous. Within private international law, for example, different types of marriage incited considerable anxiety (Castel 1958).

Entry into a valid marriage required the voluntary consent of both parties, full compliance with the legal requirements of publication and solemnization, and an absence in the parties of incapacity respecting age, physical capability, and relationship by blood or marriage (*Moss* 1897, 268). Conversely, the common law grounds of nullity consisted of the opposite of these requirements: lack of consent, failure to comply with prescribed formalities, nonage, impotence, insanity at the time of solemnization, relationship within the prohibited degrees, and prior existing marriage (Hahlo 1972, 654). In Quebec, the civil code enunciated 'the qualities and conditions necessary for contracting marriage' (arts. 115ff. C.C.L.C.). Several features of the rules governing entry bear especially on the legal subject.

Marriage's consensual character attracted much attention. Although marriage's institutional aspect also attracted doctrinal concern (Carbonnier 1955, 288), scholarly writing in the period focuses on marriage as a contract. My account here unfolds against the backdrop of relational theory's tendency to regard reliance on contracting as a defining feature of thin, atomistic liberal conceptions of the subject. Chief among marriage's contractual elements were the choice of matrimonial regime and the conclusion of particular agreements by individual couples. Such agreements specified, among other things, generous gifts from the husband to the wife to ensure her economic future after his eventual death (Fontaine 1927). A high degree of detail frequently characterized these contracts, and the regime of matrimonial property, once chosen, remained immutable throughout the marriage. In Quebec the immutability of marriage contracts testified to the dominant paradigm of wealth in 1866, one in which immovable property predominated over volatile movables such as securities (Baudouin 1967, 224). Then, as now, class considerations restricted the set of unions for which contracts redistributing immovable property were relevant. In formal terms, the freedom to contract was virtually unlimited. In Quebec, marriage contracts, concluded under the watchful eye of a notary, were constrained only by law, good morals, and public order (arts. 1257, 1258 C.C.L.C.). The constraints of good morals in a profoundly religious, agrarian society should not, however, be underestimated.

Relational theory suggests two interpretations of these contractual practices. First, the relational theorist may protest that the practice of unalterable marriage contracts fails to take into account the ways in which married subjects become embedded in their relationship. Relational theorists tend to object to strict reliance on contract on the basis that the normative content of relationships is not transparently predictable ex ante (Minow and Shanley 1996, 12). They perceive interdependent relationships as generating, over time, obligations in excess of those devised by voluntary contractual undertakings (Regan 1993, 4). The strict enforcement of these contracts and the impediments to altering the matrimonial property regime appear to overlook the cognitive impairments that plague contracting. Such impairments are likely to be especially severe where, as during engagement, parties may tend towards what cheerless economists regard as irrational optimism. Enforcement of these agreements implies confidence that a single moment of contracting can achieve exhaustive and final provision for the future (Baudouin 1954–5).

The second, arguably superior reading acknowledges that the immutability of the parties' choice of property regime and of their marital contract contemplates that the spouses will change as they age and endure life's vicissitudes. The husband will die, and the wife will require maintenance in her declining years. Indeed, it is precisely because the thick, largely indissoluble relationship of marriage will alter the parties – in particular rendering the wife more vulnerable – that securing her economic future upfront is crucial. The marriage contract composed a framework or 'patrimonial constitution' (Brierley and Macdonald 1993, para. 313) within which the parties' interdependence (or, to avoid false hints at gender equality, the wife's economic dependence) intensified. Moreover, the contract would have been negotiated by the woman's father on her behalf, distinguishing it from the hastily signed prenuptial agreements that occasionally trouble the case law today. The function of these immutable contractual distributions of property should caution relational theorists against uniformly connecting formal reliance on contractual ordering with thin conceptions of legal subjects. Instead, these contracts operated to produce and protect thick, embedded, economically vulnerable female subjects.

By contrast, the strictness in policing the solemnization of marriage functioned less consistently in the protection of vulnerable subjects. Scholars disputed whether the law knew a 'common-law marriage.' They used the term to mean not mere prolonged cohabitation, but a marriage resulting from a consummated agreement to marry between persons legally capable of making a marriage contract, *per verba de præsenti*, followed by cohabitation. The extent to which a valid marriage might obtain despite imperfections in solemnization varied across the dominion. The civil law of Quebec knew no such informal marriage, although a marriage declared null continued to produce civil effects vis-à-vis the parties if they had contracted it in good faith (art. 163 C.C.L.C.). In Ontario, prevailing opinion held that common law marriages were invalid, although legislation provided that if the parties lived together as man and wife after an attempted solemnization of marriage, the marriage would be deemed valid despite an 'irregularity' respecting the licence, the banns, or the person solemnizing (Marriage Act 1950, s. 44). The state's interest in finding a marriage to be valid occasionally impelled courts to enlarge the statute's curative provision. In *Alspector v. Alspector* (1957), the court upheld the validity of a marriage celebrated by a cantor in accordance with Jewish rites, but for which no civil licence had been obtained. The difficulty was that total failure to procure a licence exceeded the category of statutorily condonable 'irregularities.' In Manitoba, the status of common law marriages was unclear (Cherniak and Fien 1974). In Nova Scotia, legislation explicitly nullified a marriage for non-compliance with the conditions of solemnization (Marriage Act 1954, s. 11). These varying positions exemplify a tension. Promoting legitimate marriages solemnized in compliance with state requirements affirmed the state's institutional prerogatives. But the interest in protecting vulnerable individuals militated towards recognizing marriages that, although imperfect, were substantively similar to perfected marriages.

In Quebec, the role of organized religion in solemnizing marriage constituted subjects as deeply embedded in religious traditions. No concept of civil marriage profaned Quebec law. The priests and ministers of recognized religions – operating on robust assumptions as to the things appropriately rendered unto God – monopolized the celebration of marriage. It was testimony to the Roman Catholic Church's sway in Canada East that the codifiers in 1866 took the Code Napoléon of 1804 as their model but did not replicate its exclusively civil marriage as a 'civil sacrament' (Carbonnier 2001, 310). To contemporary eyes, such a state of affairs is glaringly incompatible with a liberal state's neutrality. Yet religion permeated legal discourse to such a degree that for one prominent commentator, the civil law would satisfy its principles of neutrality if the state recognized as valid a marriage performed by the minister of one faith for the adherents of another (Baudouin 1951). By the 1960s, however, criticisms of this situation proliferated, stimulated by increasing secularization. The population's growing mobility and urbanization separated people from their natal villages, and it seemed less appropriate to maintain records parochially (Baudouin 1967, 225). Yet it was not until 1968 that the legislature introduced civil marriage (An Act Respecting Civil Marriage 1968). The construction of legal subjects in Quebec during this period is thus patently inseparable from religion.[2]

It is the way of the world that not all affections achieve their apotheosis in a solemnized marriage. When love did not culminate in marriage as promised, jurists mobilized contract in the service of relational interests. The culturally shared understanding of marriage as a contract underwrote treatment of the breach of a promise to marry. The common law notionally regarded a promise to marry as any other 'ordinary' contract, albeit one with special features. Its ostensible ordinariness ensured the possibility of an action for breach (Baxter 1963, 44). By this period, courts no longer ordered specific performance of the marriage promise; that is, they no longer ordered a defendant to marry a successful plaintiff. They did, however, award damages (Stranger-Jones 1951, 78). Today it may seem peculiar for courts to assess the fallout of a broken engagement in terms of compensation, but doing so showed contextual sensitivity to the circumstances of the jilted party. Damages were awarded to indemnify plaintiffs for their 'loss of positive advancement in the world,' which included loss of an establishment in life and of a share of the defendant's affluence. But awards were also made for 'sentimental damages' in respect of the 'injury to the feelings, affections, and wounded pride' (ibid., 78). To the extent that these are the compensable damages, the promise to marry seems rather unlike an ordinary contract. Damages for a broken engagement did not, of course, constitute a fully satisfactory solution. As Albert Mayrand observes, the law offers just and equitable means for resolving the problems born of a broken engagement, but only honour and a sense of decency – attributes exercisable in the non-juridical, social sphere – can inspire 'elegant' solutions (1963, 44). The evidentiary rules regulating a promise to marry provide a further sign that jurists labouring in this cranny of family law were marshalling the formal doctrines of contract law to vindicate a thickly embedded subject.

The alleged promise to marry required corroboration by material evidence, but such evidence did not need to be 'of a robust kind.' Corroboration could consist in the parties' conduct prior to the alleged making of the promise (Stranger-Jones 1951, 79). For example, were it impossible to prove a promise by letters or an explicit undertaking in the presence of a third party, the plaintiff might tender 'evidence of the conduct of the parties, and how they were regarded by their relations and friends,' showing that their intimate acquaintances treated them as an engaged couple (ibid., 79). Here again the courts were not modelling the ordinary approach to contracts. Indeed, it becomes apparent that actions for breach of promise to marry subtly transformed non-marital, dating relationships into legally recognized premarriage relationships (Dubler 2003, 1657). It is paradoxical that here the formal doctrines and mechanisms of contractual enforcement served to intervene in comparatively informal relational disputes. The socially embedded character of regulation of premarital relations emerges further from the possibility of an action against a third party for unlawful interference with the promise to marry (Baxter 1963, 47).

It is worth pointing out a distinction between the treatment of promises to marry in the common law and in the civil law. Civilian commentators objected that enforcing contracts to marry would impermissibly fetter the parties' freedom of consent at the celebration of their marriage. This concern led some doctrinal writers to characterize a broken engagement not as a breach of a promise to marry, but as a delict. This juridical characterization had consequences: the rules of evidence required a writing where damages sought for breach of contract exceeded fifty dollars, and while simple non-performance founded a claim in contract, one in delict demanded proof of fault (Pineau 1972, 27). A number of judges, prudently sidestepping this contentious doctrinal terrain, awarded damages without characterizing the claim they allowed (Mayrand 1963, 12–15, 52). The civil law thus shows an odd mixture of abstraction and contextualism. The concern that militated against framing claims in contract – the supposition that both parties routinely approached the celebration of marriage with untrammelled freedom of consent, at a time when women's leading option for a socially validated life outside matrimony was the veil – exemplifies the thinnest, most abstract conception of subjects as choosing agents. But the willingness to award damages, especially where the basis for doing so remained murky, bespeaks attention to the needs of subjects embedded in their social relations and context. It was, of course, more common for a promise to marry to lead to solemnization and the couple's embarkation on the blessed enterprise of married life, two spirits in one flesh.

Under the common law, husband and wife each had a right to the consortium of the other. In its primary sense, consortium meant living together. On a more sentimental level, it connoted as far as possible the sharing of a common domestic life. A leading English author writes that it was difficult to define the duties that the spouses owed each other more precisely: it was a 'matter of common knowledge rather than a subject for legal analysis' (Bromley 1957, 148). This 'common knowledge' suggests a role for custom and practice, and indeed the inaptitude of enacted rules, in regulating marriages. In contrast, the civil law was unencumbered by such timidity. The civil code enunciated the spousal obligations in its lapidary fashion: 'Husband and wife mutually owe each other fidelity, succour and assistance'; 'A husband owes protection to his wife; a wife obedience to her husband' (art. 173 C.C.L.C.). A wife was obligated to live with her husband, and he to supply her with the necessaries of life (former art. 175 C.C.L.C.). The legal or default regime in the civil law was community of property.[3] Crucially, it was the husband who administered that community. The law of marriage constituted legal subjects in complicated ways; one of the most revealing is married women's subjection to their husbands.

It is telling that within the common law's many, unsystematic mansions, relations between husbands and wives occupied a doctrinal room adjacent to the association between masters and servants. Legal rules and practices constituted wives as discursively and materially inferior to their husbands. For some, women constitute the unrepresentable, a 'linguistic absence' (Butler 1999, 14). Yet the difficulty with family law in this period is less women's unrepresentability or absence than the manner of their representation. Adriana Cavarero's account of gender within the philosophical tradition has analytical currency for family law: 'the woman is notoriously in the position of the object; ... she is thought, represented, defined from the point of view of the Man.' The woman consists in a 'series of images, which represent, from time to time and according to the context, *what* a woman must be in the economy of masculine desire: for the most part a mother or a wife' (2000, 50). After marriage, men remained men, and women became married women, a status entailing significant legal disabilities. Today's speech would call a woman raising children alone a single mother, which still implies that mother tout court is not single but in relationship with a man. The earlier period, however, used the term 'deserted wife.' This category appeared in legislation resulting from efforts to secure the economic interests and survival of indubitably vulnerable women. It was well intentioned, yet its discursive effect was to reinforce these women's passivity. The term ratified a masculine economy in which men, at their will, supported their women or abandoned them. Moreover, the law instated material incentives to keep women in their place. It was not enough for the property regimes to ensure that women lacked the resources to leave their marriages. The law, resting on a distasteful package of orthodox justifications (Roy 2002, 16–17n23), sanctioned women's infidelity more harshly than men's. In the common law provinces, a wife's adultery typically precluded her from claiming maintenance (Jacobson 1975, 560). In Quebec, the regime of separation from bed and board penalized the woman financially for her adultery (former arts. 208, 211 C.C.L.C.; Baudouin 1962). Under this regime, into the 1950s, a husband's adultery did not amount to a ground for separation unless he 'kept' his concubine in the matrimonial home.

Regulation of the married woman's civil capacity forms a rich site for inquiry. The common law, reflective of wives' general subjection to their husbands, strictly limited a married woman's capacity to initiate legal action and own and dispose of property. In the late nineteenth century, the Parliament of the United Kingdom displaced these rules by statute, so that married women were permitted to acquire and hold property free from any rights of control in their husbands (Married Women's Property Act, 1882). The Canadian common law provinces soon duplicated this development. Under these enactments, the husband and wife's unity in matters of property ceded to a strict policy of separatism. In the eyes of third parties, the married woman now equalled her husband as an abstract juridical subject. But the socio-economic forces that distributed property continued to subordinate women as wives in a masculine economy. The juridical equality in which this legislation enfolded married women veiled the material reality of how few women owned how little property. For the most part, this new equality was largely formal.

In Quebec, by contrast, the married woman's incapacity incapacitated her for another eight decades. Consistent with its philosophically and religiously grounded premise of resistance to change, Quebec preserved the married woman's civil inferiority largely intact into the 1960s. The civil law traditionally conferred on the husband the role of *chef de famille* (the Roman paterfamilias). One juridical instantiation of this role was the concept of paternal authority, which is the totality of the father's rights and duties regarding his non-emancipated minor children. The other was the married woman's civil incapacity. Above the nitty-gritty of the codal provisions, the idea of the married woman glittered as 'a sort of legal icon,' a symbol untouchable on pain of displacing foundational virtues (Brisson and Kasirer 1996, 411). Indeed, even when the married woman's emancipation finally arrived in 1964 (An Act Respecting the Legal Capacity of Married Women 1964), it came 'cloaked in this same conservative spirit' (Brisson and Kasirer 1996, 415).

Legislative reforms to both paternal authority and the capacity of married women were timid and fragmentary. The amended civil code declared paternal authority to vest in a child's father *and* mother; but, retracting with one legislative hand what it had given with the other, it reserved exercise of that authority during the marriage to the father (former art. 243 C.C.L.C.). The effect was a notional equality of spouses but a stark inequality of fathers and mothers (Pineau 1965–6, 214). The 1964 reforms granted the married woman contracting rights, management of her own property, and the capacity to appear in judicial proceedings, but the emancipation was incomplete. For example, community of property remained the legal regime and the husband retained the right to administer the community while a marriage endured. The husband also kept the right to choose the family residence. The wife was permitted to exercise certain functions only when the husband was unable to do so, and the amended code implicitly required the husband's consent for his wife's commercial activities (art. 182 C.C.L.C.). No corresponding obligation on the wife's part mirrored the husband's obligation to provide his wife with 'all the necessities of life according to his means and condition' (art. 176 C.C.L.C.). Indeed, it is arguable that, despite the amended regime's ostensible collegiality, enough of the husband's prerogatives survived to maintain him, at least implicitly, as the head of the family (Pineau 1965–6, 209–12). The laggardly emancipation of the married woman under Quebec law indicates the grip of governing ideas of the family on the legal imaginary and the difficulties they pose for law reform. Legislative preoccupation with impersonal roles such as Husband and Wife, applicable to all marriages, hinted at a preference for universals distant from the 'living singularity' of particular alliances (Cavarero 2000, 9). The description of subjects is thick, but the methodology is acontextual insofar as individuals' facts and circumstances are excluded. Yet despite the constellation of legal, social, and economic pressures operating to deter marriage breakdown, some alliances foundered and one spouse or both sought an escape.

Exit from marriage entwines matters of civil status and of property and maintenance. Despite the more pressing practical importance of property issues, legal discourse fixated on the question of status. Thus the Divorce Act (1968), when finally enacted, relegated maintenance and custody matters to status's shadow, regarding them as 'ancillary' or 'incidental.' The lawyerly preoccupation with status fortified the symbolism of the legitimate family, inscribing itself in the same discursive line that made an icon of the married woman. But to mention the Divorce Act is to anticipate.

Quebec law contemplated no voluntary termination of the status of marriage. In the civil code's unambiguous formulation: 'Marriage can only be dissolved by the natural death of one of the parties; while both live, it is indissoluble' (art. 185 C.C.L.C.). The availability of divorce varied across the country. Though divorce was not obtainable in courts in Quebec or Newfoundland, it could be procured by Senate resolution. Predictably, these constraints on the availability of divorce channelled the energies of unhappy spouses to the means of annulling marriages by virtue of defects in their solemnization. Desperate spouses scrutinized their history for one of the grounds of nullity. Where Quebeckers failed to make the case for annulment, they had to content themselves with separation from bed and board (*séparation de corps*). Separation from bed and board is a judicially pronounced attenuation of the marital bond. It relieves the spouses of the obligation of consortium but otherwise leaves the status of marriage intact. The preservation of the marital bond and its civil status at virtually all costs affirmed that marriage's role was not, as it became during the contemporary period, the public affirmation of a particular relationship (Coontz

2005). Rather, marriage's vocation was to assimilate individuals into the structure of legitimacy, an assimilation that tenaciously survived the wrenching disintegration of the particular pragmatic or affective relationship that had initiated it. Many couples never secured a legal separation and were 'forced' into extralegal relationships, undoubtedly, at the time, a 'degrading and demeaning' state of affairs (Foster 1968, 24). Reliance on informal marriage as an alternative to divorce and remarriage was particularly extensive in working-class communities (Chambers 2007, 143). Achievement of the Divorce Act in 1968, which made divorce uniformly accessible across the country, thus marked a profound change.

As for pecuniary matters, in Quebec, the husband's matrimonial obligation to maintain his wife subsisted during the marriage, including separation from bed and board. This obligation expired only on the marriage's dissolution, when the consorts became (somewhat implausibly) once again strangers to each other. Before the enactment of the Divorce Act, it was often perilous for a wife to proceed with a divorce unless she had already secured satisfactory financial arrangements, since the divorce would obviate any further maintenance claim against her husband (Walker 1965, 17). The corollary support provisions in the federal Divorce Act, by which an obligation of maintenance could arise on divorce, thus assumed crucial importance. Both separation from bed and board and divorce triggered separation of property, giving the wife the right to obtain restitution of her dowry and the property she had brought into the marriage and to claim the benefit of all the gifts and advantages conferred on her by the marriage contract. Legal separation and divorce initiated a species of secession from the marriage's patrimonial constitution. As with marriage contracts, the class effects were pronounced: for a large segment of the population, this patrimonial distribution on marriage's premature end would have been negligible.

In the common law provinces, claims for maintenance were framed under maintenance statutes. The civil emancipation of married women in the late nineteenth century had led to a regime of separate property under which marriage created few property rights apart from the inchoate right of dower (a life estate in one-third of the late husband's lands). In determining a husband's and wife's respective interests in property, Canadian courts strove – again, implausibly – to apply the same principles of property law as governed disputes between strangers (Cullity 1972, 183). (An exception is the effect, in the prairie provinces, of homestead legislation protecting the matrimonial home.) Equity added the presumption of resulting trust, which could find entitlement to a beneficial interest in land on proof either of a common intention to that effect or that the spouse who did not hold legal title – almost invariably the wife – had contributed directly to the purchase (ibid., 185). Evidence of a common intention respecting property for an eventual marriage breakup was usually scant, as few couples plan during their sunnier days for an eventual parting. Wives were mostly cornered into attempting to demonstrate ex post a direct financial contribution to the purchase. In assessing such claims, courts brushed aside indirect contributions to the purchase price or general contributions to household wealth as largely irrelevant. If courts were reluctant to accord weight to indirect financial contributions, they were still less inclined to recognize labour as a contribution capable of seeding a property entitlement. Although this strict approach was ostensibly intended to achieve the lawyerly desideratum of certainty, a measure of unpredictability seeped into the cases as a result of varying judicial classifications of wifely contributions (White 1969, 296–7).

The tensions generated by judicial application of property law to spouses are exemplified in a rich judicial text, the Supreme Court of Canada's divided judgment in *Murdoch v. Murdoch* (1973). During twenty-five years of marriage, Mr and Mrs Murdoch laboured for ranch owners and, later, bought and worked their own ranches. As was typical, Mr Murdoch held title to all the properties. Mrs Murdoch's father, on his death, had left life insurance proceeds to his wife, Mrs Nash. Some of these moneys were deposited in a bank account in Mrs Murdoch's name, and the funds later used by Mr Murdoch to buy land. In 1968, after a domestic altercation in which Mrs Murdoch sustained a broken jaw,[4] she left her husband and initiated two actions against him. One was a claim for judicial separation, custody of their son, alimony, maintenance for the child, and sole possession of the family home. The other action, consolidated with the first at trial, was a claim for an undivided one-half interest in two sections of land and in her husband's other assets. The basis for this claim was that the two of them had been equal partners and that Mr Murdoch was a trustee of her half.

Mrs Murdoch's litigation was not especially successful. Although the trial judge granted her a decree of judicial separation and monthly maintenance of $200, he gave custody of the son to Mr Murdoch. He dismissed entirely the second action for the property interests. At trial there was a dispute over the use of the insurance moneys to purchase some of the land. Mrs Murdoch and her mother testified that the funds were Mrs Murdoch's and thus constituted a direct contribution to the purchases. Mr Murdoch, whom the trial judge believed, testified that the funds belonged to his mother-in-law and were a loan to him (*Murdoch* 1971).

The Appellate Division dismissed Mrs Murdoch's appeal in a few lines. The majority regarded the trial judgment, in its award of maintenance and rejection of the property claims, as indivisible. For them, Mrs Murdoch's acceptance of maintenance since the trial judge's order debarred her from subsequently appealing that order (*Murdoch* 1972). A dissenting judge thought it possible to construe the appeal as touching only the claim for an interest in property, not the alimony that Mrs Murdoch had putatively endorsed by taking the money.

At the Supreme Court of Canada, the majority judges held it unnecessary to pronounce on the severability of the trial judge's order and the effect of taking the maintenance. In their view, Mrs Murdoch's claim, even if permissible, would have foundered on the merits. They rejected her claim of a resulting trust on the basis that the evidence failed to establish a financial contribution to the purchase price of any of the properties. Her sole contributions were, in Martland J.'s memorable phrase, the work done 'by any ranch wife' (*Murdoch* 1973, 436). Laskin J. alone dissented. The case swiftly achieved public notoriety and galvanized legislative reform, reactions which indicate that the majority decision had misjudged and misrepresented social attitudes towards married women. Much has been said about the decision's defects and its distributive effects in ratifying a transfer of labour from wife to husband. Its relevance here is the relationship between the majority judges' normative commitments and the methodology employed to operationalize them.

One reading suggests that the majority judges were constrained by a thin conception of the legal subject and a formal methodology. Martland J. modelled judicial formalism, cleaving closely to precedents. A line of English cases had interpreted a statutory power to resolve spousal property disputes as authorization to deviate from property and trust law's rules of title.[5] Commentators had derided this discretionary approach (in a turn of phrase pregnant with ethnocentrism) as palm-tree justice (White 1969), and the Supreme Court of Canada had repudiated it more than a decade prior to *Murdoch* (*Thompson* 1961). In good formal fashion, Martland J. adhered to this rejection, affirming that no legislation granted the courts discretionary jurisdiction to disregard property rights (*Murdoch* 1973, 432). Accordingly, in conformity with orthodox property law, he assessed Mrs Murdoch's claim for a resulting trust strictly, as if the transactions had occurred between strangers. His account of the facts reflected his reliance on conventional property law: he focused on the dates and amounts of transactions (ibid., 427–8). To this point, the reading of Martland J. is consistent with a formal judicial method and reveals little about his underlying normative position.

Yet the suggestion that a thin, atomistic conception of the subject drove the majority's reasons raises complications. Martland J. treated two of the characters abstractly, Mr Murdoch and Mrs Nash. He regarded them as parties at arm's length, the idea being that Mrs Nash transacted business with her son-in-law like a broker on a trading floor. Martland J. made no effort to situate these two within the contours of a field of interdependent subjects connected by family relationships. As a commentator observed cogently, Mrs Nash would not likely have lent Mr Murdoch the money were he not married to her daughter, nor would she have intended to assist him in executing a transaction that excluded her daughter from its benefits (Jacobson 1974, 313). The hypothesis of abstract subjects becomes less plausible still when applied to the characterization of Mrs Murdoch. Martland J.'s view that her labours were the work of 'any ranch wife' hinted at a thick conception of status, one distant from the free contracting agents that were Mr Murdoch and Mrs Nash. An inconsistency appeared in the way that Martland J. constituted the set of subjects. The effect was that the majority judgment operated as if the emancipation of married women had never occurred. Mrs Murdoch had spent a quarter-century toiling for her husband and owned almost nothing. But she held a bank account, into which were deposited the life insurance moneys. Prior to the Married Women's Property Act, that bank account in her own name would have been impossible. The trial judge found that the moneys, despite having been deposited in Mrs Murdoch's bank account, belonged to her mother and were then lent to Mr Murdoch. Distinguishing the two women is critical. Even at common law, it would have been possible for Mrs Nash, as a widow, to hold and manage assets. It was only Mrs Murdoch who, as a married woman, depended for her legal capacity on the statutory displacement of the common law's legal unity of spouses. Finding that the moneys were a loan from Mrs Nash to her son-in-law rendered nugatory Mrs Murdoch's civil emancipation and the fact that, during an intermediate stage, she controlled the moneys in her bank account.[6] Indeed, the deposit of the moneys in that account altered nothing. How is one to make sense of the distinction between Mrs Murdoch and her mother?

At least a provisional answer is to be found in the fact that only Mrs Murdoch was regarded as a wife. Martland J. did not attempt to reconstruct the terms of the Murdochs' marriage. Mrs Murdoch was seen as enmeshed in wifely obligations; those obligations, however, were not particular to her. Martland J. expended little effort attempting to reconstruct the terms of their common life or to distinguish Mrs Murdoch's role from that of universal Wife (*Murdoch* 1973, 427–9). Though regarding a man and a widow as abstract, choosing agents and a wife as deeply embedded in a universal status seems inconsistent, it resonates with the ethos of family law depicted so far. Recall that the slow emancipation of married women in Quebec conjoined a conception of men as contracting agents with an iconic ideal of wives. Perhaps Martland J. was straitjacketed by his preconception of the wifely role to an extent that he was closed to anything accidental or exceptional. His understanding of Wife perhaps functioned as an epistemic obstacle (Bachelard 1983), preventing him from apprehending the Murdochs' narrative otherwise. According to this reading, once he recognized the familiar status of 'wife' and applied it to Mrs Murdoch, there was no possibility of imagining the relationship and its property effects otherwise. Mrs Murdoch was never a 'who,' a particular wife in unique circumstances, but only a 'what,' a universal Wife, suffering the effects of her role's 'abstract valence' (Cavarero 2000, 50). According to this hypothesis, what propelled Martland J.'s judgment was a brew of formalism mixed with conceptions of most subjects as atomistic contracting agents but wives as bearers of a universal status.

This hypothesis implies that a turn to relational theory might have altered Martland J.'s judgment. But on closer examination, the example shows the value of my proposal for separating the relational inquiry's normative commitment from its descriptive premise and contextual method. The descriptive premise that subjects are thickly embedded in social, relational contexts might have obviated the view of Mrs Nash and her son-in-law as transacting at arm's length. A contextual methodology would have revealed labours on the farm to be the sole way in which one could ever expect a typical ranch wife to contribute to her husband's real estate purchases. While there is much that is worth taking from this reading and the supposed effects of an encounter with relational theory, a focus on descriptive and methodological matters is incomplete. Such a reading of Martland J.'s reasons overlooks an important element: their *normative* vision of family relations. The charge of formalism and acontextualism presupposes that Martland J. might have wished to reach another outcome had he only had the tools to do so, or that he neglected to reflect on his normative position. But he did not fail to 'focus on relationship.' In the majority reasons, I sense neither reluctance nor thoughtlessness along these lines. Instead, the majority judges successfully advanced their normative vision of appropriate family relationships. Although the judges did not address the matter explicitly, conservative social standards would have characterized Mrs Murdoch as a bad wife. She had shown wifely disloyalty by seeking hospitalization after a physical clash that Martland J. subsumed, indifferent to gender, under the rubric 'marital difficulties' (1973, 429). She walked out on her husband and sued him. That she left her husband may, one can conjecture, have influenced the prior award of custody of the child to the husband.[7] Perhaps Martland J. wished to pre-empt the moral hazard that would arise should wives perceive themselves as having financial incentives for leaving their husbands. Perhaps the judgment's thrust, on some level, was to keep women in their place.[8] Martland J. may have been using a discourse of formalism and a method of acontextualism to justify a normative decision made all too contextually. The majority judges may have made a substantive and contextually rooted decision as to Mrs Murdoch's unworthiness, numbering as relevant contextual factors that relational theorists, on account of their normative commitments, would have eliminated as irrelevant (that she had initiated the separation, that a trial judge had already preferred the husband for custody). This alternative account of the judgment suggests the importance of the implicit and explicit normative rules that define different contexts and the interaction between normative commitments and contextual methodologies. For all her woes, however, the thickly embedded subject representing Irene Murdoch advanced her claims from the privileged terrain of legitimate marriage.

Couplings outside Marriage

When marriage was the sole legitimate locus for sexual relations, the law figured the couplings of men and women not married to each

other as illegitimate. It would be inaccurate to speak of unmarried
'close personal adult relationships' (Law Commission of Canada
2001), because it would imply that relationships outside marriage gar-
nered the social approbation or indifference they do now. Doing so
would confer a false validation on the past's significations of sexual
relations (Halperin 2002, 84–9). Not surprisingly, couples outside the
marriage norm were 'in some sense being defined still in relation to
it' (Butler 2004, 42). Heterosexual couplings outside marriage functioned in a couple of ways. Their juridical and social treatment attests
to the law's fixation with categories of legitimacy. They provided a constitutive outside against which marriage was defined and constantly
reinforced, and they served as instruments for the production of bastards (Cretney 2003, 516–17). The law marginalized the entire set of
heterosexual couplings outside marriage; at the same time, it established a spectrum of shame running from unmarried cohabitation,
the least objectionable, through adultery to incest. The common law
essentially ignored unmarried unions. In Quebec, the civil law on the
whole did not regulate the de facto family explicitly; unmarried
couples (*unions libres*) were almost but not quite outside the explicit
posited law. One small, negative acknowledgment regarded gifts: the
law would enforce inter vivos gifts to a concubine classifiable as maintenance, but nothing more generous (art. 768 C.C.L.C.). Though the
civil code constituted the central articulation of family law, in the
twentieth century the legislature introduced social programs affecting
family relations through ordinary legislation. For some purposes, such
social legislation included de facto spouses (Popovici and Parizeau-
Popovici 1971, 53–5; Baudouin 1966, 161–2). Yet the civil code's iconic
importance in Quebec legal culture is such that relegation of rules
treating de facto unions to ordinary legislation indicates an understanding that such unions did not constitute true families. It is chiefly
in extralegal literature by psychologists, sociologists, and social
workers – primarily published in French within Quebec – that a sense
emerges of the family as a functional unit providing economic and
affective security irrespective of its inscription in relation to the axis of
legitimacy. The social and legal disapproval of these illegitimate couplings manifested itself materially in the laws respecting illegitimate
children.

    The measures regulating children's illegitimacy epitomize the viru-
lence with which family law enforced its ideal of legitimacy. Legal rules
and discourse, in a vector of labelling imposed from above (Hacking

1986, 234), constituted children born out of wedlock as bastards, illegitimate children, the children of unmarried parents, and natural children. A lexical observation: the disjunction legitimate–natural tacitly acknowledges that legitimate children and legitimate families are 'unnatural,' the product of law's operation within a contingently constructed social and juridical context.[9] The substantive concern animating those legal rules was a determination to provide no incentives for illegitimate families (Baudouin 1966, 173–6). The consequences of a child's illegitimacy, unlike those entailed by dissolution of marriage, do not divide easily into those pertaining to status and those to property. A child's status vis-à-vis his biological mother or father often emerged implicitly from the latter's legal obligations.

At common law, the traditional criterion for legitimacy was the parents' lawful marriage at the time of the child's birth. The common law distinguished between the biological parents. Only the mother, to the exclusion of the father, had the same rights regarding her illegitimate child as both would have had vis-à-vis legitimate children. At common law, neither parent was liable to maintain an illegitimate child. By the historical period, legislation had displaced this rule (Bromley 1957, 344, 348–9). In Ontario, for example, the statutory scheme provided for financial contributions by both parents of a child born out of wedlock. It stipulated further that a maintenance agreement or filiation order bound the father's estate (Children of Unmarried Parents Act 1950, ss. 13, 14, 23). Despite these measures, the law reinforced the normative and material priority of legitimate over illegitimate children. This priority is evident in the stipulation, still preserved at the time of writing, that the maintenance obligation binding the father's estate must not interfere with maintenance of his widow and legitimate children, and that the widow and legitimate children were to be provided for before illegitimate children (Children of Unmarried Parents Act 1950, s. 23(2)). Moreover, the procedures for an unwed mother to claim child support were degrading and invasive (Chambers 2007, ch. 2). At common law, an illegitimate child could not participate in the intestacy of either parent – another harsh rule somewhat palliated by legislation (Bromley 1957, 453).

In Quebec the situation was similar. The conservatism that hampered the married woman's emancipation had fully paralysed the legislature concerning illegitimacy. The civil code in its first century underwent no change whatever in this matter (Baudouin 1966, 161). Unlike the common law, the civil law treated both parents of an illegitimate child equally. Natural children had a claim against their parents for food, but no other rights.[10] The juridical link created by the natural child's alimentary claim and the parents' correlative obligation was purely personal. This parental support obligation established an attenuated family bond between parent and natural child, but it did not ensconce the child in a larger family unit. Thus the natural child remained a legal stranger towards her natural grandparents. The justification for confining the support obligation so narrowly was that permitting a child to claim support from her natural grandparents would have linked her and her ascendants, threatening the legitimate family by erecting an illegitimate parallel structure (Baudouin 1966, 168). The implication is that the personal support obligation between parent and child did not generate a family. Natural children had no claim under the rules regulating intestate successions (arts. 606, 636 C.C.L.C.). They enjoyed, however, the right to receive testamentary gifts from their natural parents. Here the concern to penalize illegitimacy submitted to the codifiers' general principle, one with complex historical antecedents, of unlimited testamentary freedom (Brierley and Macdonald 1993, para. 336). Lesser scope for generosity on the part of a natural parent was enforceable when it came to inter vivos gifts. The civil code calibrated permissible measures using the spectrum of shame, prescribing that the class of 'other illegitimate children' could receive by inter vivos gift like anyone else, but that adulterine and incestuous children, like concubines, could receive only gifts classifiable as maintenance (art. 768 C.C.L.C.).

The legal treatment of illegitimate children did not escape criticism. Some commentators recognized that it was perverse, in the interests of deterring adultery, to penalize the innocent third parties it engendered. Jean Goulet remarks critically that adultery's principal sanctions 'se retrouvaient massées sur la tête de l'enfant naturel dont il en est le fruit' (1965–6, 265). A few criticisms justified themselves by reference to common decency and social mores. Arguments for reduced discrimination against natural children referred occasionally to international law, notably to the UN's Declaration of the Rights of the Child (ibid., 285). Nonetheless, the organizing matrix of legitimacy was so firmly established that even those critics who advocated incremental reforms to palliate the detriments inflicted on illegitimate children did not seek to topple the fundamental concept. Instead of proposing an alternative substantive basis for filiation, they continued to presuppose a legitimacy–illegitimacy dichotomy, one firmly rooted in the legitimate family's moral superiority. A prominent Quebec commentator rebuffs an American sociologist's assessment that the chief problem was value judgments about the goodness of legitimate parenthood (Baudouin 1967, 230). Another calls, similarly, for a 'more human' understanding, without tumbling into the 'excesses,' committed elsewhere, of legitimating adulterine children (Bergeron 1961, 31). The common law provinces narrowed the class of illegitimate persons by permitting legitimation if the parents married one another after the child's birth. Yet such incremental reduction of the class of bastards still ratified the premise that a class of bastards should subsist (Green and Winter 1965, 182). Even technological innovations failed to disturb the law's configuration around legitimacy. Jurists regarded the problem of classifying a child born as the result of artificial insemination of a woman with sperm not her husband's as a puzzle to be solved within the existing framework, not as an opportunity to rethink the whole approach. Scholars reached different conclusions as to how to affix such cases in the matrix of legitimacy (Baudouin 1967, 231; Tallin 1956, 11–27). They did not, however, doubt the appropriateness of such taxonomic acrobatics. A conception of filiation not inscribed in terms of legitimacy and illegitimacy seemed unthinkable.

My discussion so far operates as if the categories of legitimacy and illegitimacy exhausted the field of family relations. Neither category, however, included homosexual couplings.[11] One could argue, borrowing from Judith Butler, that homosexual couplings occupied 'a field outside the disjunction of illegitimate and legitimate' (2004, 105). Homosexual transactions were not regarded as giving rise to thinkable relationships, let alone ones that might be characterized by the lexicon of legitimacy and illegitimacy applicable to relations between a man and a woman. The criminal law's prohibition against homosexual conduct persisted into the late 1960s, targeting discrete acts regarded as morally repugnant. Neither the prohibition nor other legal features evinced a conception of homosexual relations as potentially mature, enduring, and enriching. The homosexual represented the 'negation of familial ties' (Girard 1987, 1). One judge pronounced homosexuality 'an antithesis of marriage and … an obvious repudiation of the marital state' (*Guy v. Guy* 1982, 589). The marriage of two homosexuals or even their forming an illegitimate family unit was patently unthinkable. In the words of the same judge: 'marriage is a heterosexual, legal relationship' (ibid.). To the extent that this period debated a gay marriage question, it was whether homosexuality on the part of one party constituted an impediment to marriage to someone of the opposite sex. Several experts affirmed that it was, on the basis that a homosexual could not be a satisfactory spouse, sexually or emotionally, to a 'normal person' (Bordeleau 1968, 245–6). The asymmetrical but symbolically significant opposition *normal/homosexual* was not unintended.

Law's prohibitions and penalties produced homosexual subjects in many ways (Davidson 2001; Halperin 2002). In the federal statute book, the structure of the 1968 Divorce Act is telling. Previous cases had refused to regard homosexual conduct as adultery, so the legislative drafters faced the choice whether to accept their terms or overrule them. Parliament opted for the former. Thus it did not inscribe engagement 'in a homosexual act' as a species of adultery, which it made the first statutory ground for divorce. Adultery could only be committed with persons of the opposite sex. Instead, Parliament located commission of a homosexual act as one of the 'unnatural offences,' akin to guilt of sodomy, bestiality, and rape (Divorce Act 1968, s. 3(b)). That the statute did not classify homosexual acts by a spouse as adultery is evidence that homosexual relations were not illegitimate, but rather unthinkable and 'unnatural.' The drafting was admittedly infelicitous. A judge observed that Parliament had neglected to define 'homosexual act' but that practices of statutory interpretation mandated that such an act should be taken as distinct from sodomy, which was mentioned in the same subsection. Parliament's reticence in defining 'homosexual acts' shifted the unenviable task of doing so to the courts (*M. v. M.* 1972, 115, 124). One judicial stab at a definition posited 'homosexual act' as including 'any act of physical conduct between two persons of the same sex having as an object gratification of the sexual impulses or drives of either or both participants, the sexual quality of the act being the determining ingredient' (*T. v. T.* 1975, 61). One judge admitted that although in other cases he would have inferred (opposite-sex) adultery, the 'unnatural' and 'abnormal' quality of same-sex sexual conduct led him to prescribe 'cautious scrutiny' of the circumstances disclosed by the evidence (ibid., 62–3). To think of homosexual conduct as a species of adultery would have been to prefigure the possibility of relationships that were not pathological, but like concubinage, only illegitimate. Thus the period's regulation of couplings produced largely a heterosexual subject. Legal regulation of families included no resources that could help a homosexual subject acquire respectability and make life more livable.

Yet illegitimate subjects were not immutably fixed on the wrong side of the line. Some subjects managed to cross the privileged border. And to complement our understanding of law's productive power, it will be revealing to examine in some detail the modalities of these forms of border crossings, beginning with children.

Border Crossings

Legitimate filiation never depended solely on brute biological facts. Even filiation by blood, to use the contemporary civil law term, is a social construct, one mediated by juridical norms. The regime of legitimacy included presumptions that placed a child provisionally within the category of legitimate children. Where a married woman gave birth, her husband was presumed to be the father. A presumption applied if the child was born after the death of the mother's husband (Stranger-Jones 1951, 317–18; Bromley 1957, 258–61; Pineau 1972, 90–7; Ouellette 1980, 198–9). It must be understood that in a number of cases, the presumptions constructed a relation of legitimate filiation between an adulterine child and the mother's cuckolded husband. The gesture of presuming legitimacy where possible constituted the set of legitimate children as a default class, home to those who had not yet fallen out of it.[12] One might remark, influenced by Foucault, on the disjuncture within the apparatus of filiation between biological truth and what the law makes function as the juridical truth of legitimacy (Rabinow and Rose 2003, 316). Failing the 'true' filiation, we seek 'relative truths' (Cornu 1998, 32). Across this contingent border between legitimacy and illegitimacy, the law enabled limited migration. Here are instances of 'shifting' family subject positions (Cossman 1994, 16).

In Ontario and Quebec, for example, the law permitted ex post legitimation by subsequent intermarriage of the child's natural parents (The Legitimacy Act, 1961–62; art. 237 C.C.L.C.). In such instances it was the formal union of the biological parents that triggered legitimation, not the coalescence of a de facto family unit that recognized and nurtured the child (Baudouin 1966, 163). This avenue of legitimation was evidently foreclosed to adulterine and incestuous children, whose parents could never marry each other. The effect was to constitute adulterine and incestuous children as society's 'true pariahs' (Baudouin 1967, 229). It was not only upward movement into the category of legitimacy that was possible. Illegitimacy, too, could arise some time after a child's birth. If a putative marriage was declared null, the status of any children of that union depended on the good faith of the parents. If the parents had attempted to marry in good faith, the children remained legitimate. If the parents had attempted marriage in bad faith, the children were retroactively bastardized (arts. 163, 164 C.C.L.C.). These movements across the border separating and constituting legitimacy and illegitimacy altered the legal status of a child vis-à-vis his or her presumed biological parents. Another avenue for an illegitimate child to acquire a legitimate filiation was through adoption by strangers.

Adoption did not exist historically at common law or in the civil law. Although historically, many illegitimate children have been raised by adults who were not their biological parents, the law until the twentieth century constructed no filial bond between a child and such adults. The possibility of adoption arrived by statute (Adoption Act 1921; An Act Respecting Adoption 1923–24). It was not just anyone who could adopt. Although Ontario's adoption legislation made no mention of religion, most children's aid societies rejected declaredly atheist or agnostic couples as adoptive parents (Chaikoff 1964). Religious considerations also restricted the set of potential adoptive parents for a particular child. The notion of 'interfaith' adoption provoked anxieties. In those days, an example of an 'interfaith' adoption was a Protestant couple attempting to adopt a baptized Roman Catholic child (Dehler 1962; cf. Markle 1964). Unsurprisingly, religion played a larger part in Quebec. That province's legislation enshrined religious imperatives, demanding that one of the adopting parents profess the same religious faith as the adopted child (Adoption Act 1969, s. 5, para. 1). It is a sign of the thick conception of legal subjects that the legislature regarded juridical rules as capable of overriding legal identity but not religious affiliations. The adoption regime's imbrication with religion ensured that the regime intensified the legal subject as a product of religion.

Adoption is paradoxical, simultaneously subversive and conservative. It departs from the foundational social and legal practice of locating a child in relation to her presumed biological parents and characterizing that relationship by reference to the juridical bond between those parents. In this period, it assimilated illegitimate children into legitimate family structures, 'washing away,' one author writes with a biblical flourish, 'the original stain' (Bergeron 1960, 14). It is subversive because conferral of legal filiation on what would otherwise be a de facto relationship hints that the categories for creating legitimate family bonds are not closed. It is conservative because it is a filiation 'by imitation,' seeking to duplicate legitimate filiation (Carbonnier 1955, 557) or to graft itself onto it (Cornu 1998, 131). By providing a means for illegitimate children to achieve legitimacy, adoption ratified and reinforced legitimacy's dominance and underscored the pains of illegitimacy for children who were luckless enough to remain unadopted. In its simultaneous subversiveness and conservativeness, adoption presaged the contradictory approbation and disruption of marriage that characterize the contemporary quest for same-sex marriage (Cossman 2002b, 239). Perhaps legislatures and courts recognized the potential transgression in this breach in filiation's foundation. In any case, adoption confronted sustained difficulties in achieving substantive equivalence with legitimate filiation. Two points of resistance, the adoption process and its legal effects, illustrate these difficulties.

Legislation typically provided for a child to be placed for adoption if the natural parent gave consent to adoption or abandoned the child. The child would be placed with prospective adoptive parents for two years before a final adoption order could be made. The Ontario and Quebec acts stipulated that a court could, exceptionally, dispense with parental consent, but were silent respecting the retraction of consent already given. Three Supreme Court of Canada cases from the 1950s dealing with conflicts over consents to adoption are revealing: *Re Baby Duffell* (1950), *Hepton v. Maat* (1957), and *Re Agar* (1957). This trilogy held that, any time prior to the making of the adoption order, the natural parent could withdraw her consent. Indeed, the Supreme Court developed a sturdy presumption that in such cases the interests of the child mandated the return of that child to his or her biological parent(s). In response, the legislatures of Ontario and other common law provinces amended their statutes to specify that consent could be withdrawn only if doing so was, with regard to all the circumstances, in the child's best interests (Child Welfare Act 1958, s. 3). Courts in most jurisdictions subsequently read such statutory provisions as overruling the practice in *Baby Duffell* (*Re Goldstein and Brownstone* 1970; *Ex parte Worlds* 1967, 258; *Re Wells* 1962, 247). Ontario courts and the Supreme Court of Canada then rejected the contention that this statutory amendment superseded the trilogy. Instead, held those judges, the trilogy's privileging of biological bonds aided in interpreting the new restriction on withdrawal of consent (*Re Mugford* 1969, 609). In the case in which they made this determination, a two-year-old child who had spent most of his life with his adoptive parents was returned to his biological mother. A public outcry ensued, and within weeks the legislature ·passed a further amendment (The Child Welfare Amendment Act 1969). Under this second amendment, a Crown wardship could no longer be terminated once the child had been placed in the home of a person who had given notice of intent to adopt. This pattern of decisions from appellate courts disconnected from public opinion replicates the experience in *Murdoch.*

The courts in these cases made interesting methodological moves. The selection of authorities was notable, and the judges appeared somewhat deaf to the statutory commands of legislatures, resisting the statutory adoption regime's displacement of the common law. In *Hepton*, for example, Cartwright J. wrote that a child's natural parents had a right to its custody, which, 'apart from statute,' they could lose only by abandoning the child or by gross misconduct (1957, 615). He neither characterized a consent to adoption as abandonment nor recognized the adoption statute as falling within his caveat respecting statutes. In the same case, Rand J. referred to the centuries-old legal rule regarding custody. In doing so, he accorded minimal weight to the much more recent legislative alteration of the common law rule (ibid., 608). The judges' fidelity to the common law despite contrary legislative signals resembled the stance frequently adopted in administrative law.[13] It is also notable that the judges relied on English authorities that no longer represented the state of English law, applying them far from their original context. Cartwright J. likened a parental consent to adoption to an unenforceable contract signed by a parent to place her child temporarily in one of Dr Barnardo's homes (*Re Baby Duffell* 1950, 744). The judges did more than simply refer to old common law rules and cases; they virtually replaced the open-ended inquiry mandated by the statute with a formal rule favouring a child's natural parents. The judges committed themselves to a robust presumption that the natural parent should be allowed to revoke her consent to adoption. This hollowing out of consents appeared succinctly in *Hepton*: in the Supreme Court's estimation, the trial judge had erred by failing to give 'due weight' to the fact that the respondents were the children's natural parents and by attaching 'undue importance' to the consent to adoption (1957, 616).[14] Observe the analytical burden placed on those slight adjectives. By the final case of the trilogy, the presumption had ossified to the extent that Locke J. regarded himself as compelled to grant custody to the biological mother despite his conviction that the child would fare better if left with the adoptive parents – a state of affairs he explicitly regretted (*Re Agar* 1957, 55–6).

In turning from direct legislative sources, the judges referred to non-legal normativity. Rand J. declared that a child is not free from 'natural parental bonds entailing moral responsibility' (*Hepton* 1957, 607). Perhaps, by implication, deliberately receiving a child into one's home engendered no moral responsibility. The 'natural' parental bonds entailing 'moral responsibility' marked a shift to non-legal normative terrain. This shift occurred more clearly still in the Ontario Court of Appeal's reasons in *Re Mugford*. The court affirmed its deep commitment to natural filiation over adoption: 'One cannot over-estimate the importance to a child of living, moving, and having its being in an environment shared by its own blood kin where it will enjoy the warmth and affection of the mother who gave it birth.' The court anchored its commitment to the bedrock of religious values by using scriptural language ('For in him we live, and move, and have our being ...' [Acts 17:28]). The considerations moving the court were 'but a part of the intangible values which flow from a custom deeply rooted in our way of life' (*Re Mugford* 1969, 609). 'Intangible values' and custom functioned here to impede the implementation of a scheme of positive law in the interest of the orthodox economy of the biological family. Indeed, contrary to the court's qualification, these values proved strikingly tangible, successfully thwarting what appeared to be the statutory intention.

The judges placed little weight on the prior parental consent to adoption. The natural parents in these cases had signed a consent form, and there was no evidence of factors vitiating consent. The majority judges nevertheless declined to view the parents' consent combined with placement of the children with foster parents as extinguishing old relationships and generating new ones. It was argued in *Re Baby Duffell* that, from the perspective of the child welfare agencies, the two-year probation period between placement of a child and the final adoption order served to permit the agency better to assess the adoptive parents. From this perspective, it was critical to provide incentives for prospective adoptive parents to undertake adoption; such incentives would be undermined if the probation period simply prolonged the time during which the natural parents could revoke their consent and assert their blood rights. Yet the courts in these cases permitted revocation of consent by the biological parents at any point during the probation period.

The construction of the facts and assessment of the child's interests in these judgments is revealing. The judges appeared to adopt a one-sided contextualism shot through with norms favouring the biological parents. They dwelled on the attractive features of the biological relatives and constructed elaborate ex post justifications for the natural mothers' initial decisions to hand over their children (*Re Baby Duffell* 1950, 741; *Hepton* 1957, 608–9; *Re Mugford* 1969, 604). The corollary of this favourable construction of the blood relatives was an occlusion of the existing relationship between foster parents and child. In *Re Baby Duffell*, the foster parents raised the child for two years before the Supreme Court hearing. Cartwright J. conceded their 'admirable' care for the infant and devotion to him, but invested these observations with little normative heft (1950, 740). The courts conceived of foster parents' potential contributions as material, not affective. Cartwright J. wrote that the court should not deprive a mother of her illegitimate child simply because 'a nice balancing of material and social advantages' made it plain that others wishing to do so could provide 'more advantageously' (ibid., 746). His discourse of 'material advantages' was a revealingly reductive way of characterizing the connection between a child and those who had nurtured him in their home throughout his first two years. The appellate court in *Re Mugford* modelled a similar stance, referring dourly to the 'superior material advantages which a child may enjoy in the home of strangers in blood' (1969, 609). It seems that the judges regarded affective contributions as a prerogative of caregivers related by blood, and commitment to this view influenced their delineation of the context. What is to be made of these judicial manoeuvres?

One possibility is that the judges were suspicious of the consent given by the biological mothers. Perhaps the judges were moved by a contextual assessment of the circumstances in which the biological parent consented to adoption and gave up her child. Lori Chambers argues that in formulating the adoption solution, social workers failed to consider the impact of relinquishment on women. Although the hard evidence required to vitiate the consent in an individual case may have been lacking, the social pressures and shame bearing on unwed mothers may have impelled them to consent too hastily to adoption. Unmarried mothers may have 'chosen' adoption in a context of powerlessness (Chambers 2007, 95–105).

An alternative reading, which also warrants considerable weight, is that the judges resisted accepting the fundamental legitimacy of the adoption regime. While their primary loyalty was to legitimate biological filiation, their secondary loyalty went not to adoption but to illegitimate biological bonds. On this reading, it was the judges' normative commitment to blood relationships that led them to ignore legislative commands in favour of old common law rules, and to construct the cast of characters so that return of the child to the biological parents was seen as satisfying that child's best interests. The two readings are not mutually exclusive.

The crucial observation to be taken from these cases is the importance of the normative commitments brought to decision making. The different methodological tendencies noticed here – formulation of a rule favouring the biological parent, construction of the context that emphasizes biological parents' affective gifts and adoptive parents' material resources – operate not neutrally but in the service of specific normative commitments. To reach different outcomes – say, the attribution of greater significance to the relationship unfolding between foster or adoptive parent and child – being more contextual is not enough. Nor is thinking about relationships or focusing on them. What matters is the norms structuring such contextualism. Though it is unnecessary to choose between the two readings just presented, support for the second one – judicial resistance to adoption – emerged from the institution's evolving effects. I mean here the extent to which adoption placed a child on footing equal to that of legitimate, presumedly biological children.

At different junctures, legislatures and judges toiling in this area of adoption law demonstrated intense commitment to the biological family. In the first half of the period, legislatures resisted making adopted children fully equivalent to children born in wedlock. In Ontario, for example, an adoption order maintained links to the child's natural parents by conserving property rights to which he would have been entitled but for the adoption order. Furthermore, initially the adoptive filiation between a child and her adoptive parents applied only between them: the adopted child was not deemed to be the child of those parents in the eyes of third parties (The Adoption Act 1950, ss. 12(3), 12(7)). If this were an attempt to preserve the prohibited degrees of marriage between the child and members of his biological family, it could have been achieved more narrowly. In Quebec, until 1969, the adopted child was not fully integrated into the adoptive family and acquired no inheritance rights except from the adoptive parents (Coderre 1965, 38–40). It is a conservative commitment to biological family bonds that best explains the judicial resolution of disputes regarding the status of adopted children in the conflict of laws and interpretation of wills. Uncertainty reigned in both civil law and common law regarding choice of law for recognizing a foreign adoption. At the root of a number of testamentary conundrums lay the presumption that in a writing, 'child' means 'legitimate child.' The solution, one called for repeatedly before legislatures acted, was to legislate that a child validly adopted anywhere is presumed to come within the meaning of child tout court (Baxter 1961, 337, 339). But as testamentary disputes show, resolute judges could impede even legislation explicitly equating the statuses of adopted and legitimate children 'for all purposes' (An Act to Amend the Child Welfare Act, 1954, 1958, s. 3). An exemplary case concerned a will written prior to the legislative amendment to the status of adopted children (*In re Gage* 1962). While acknowledging the amendment, the majority of the Supreme Court of Canada held that the will could not have intended to include persons other than legitimate children of the body. The majority deployed property discourse, holding that to read the legislation as retroactive would amount to a confiscation by the state of the property of one class (the biological legitimate children) and its distribution to another. In this case, where the concern was the testamentary intent of a deceased testator, there was much less justification for distorting the governing legislation than there might have been in cases where the judges sensed that a mother had been pressured into relinquishing her child. Confirmation that the majority in this case misread the legislature's intention is found in the subsequent amendment. The amendment supplemented 'all purposes' with the specific injunction that testamentary references to 'children' should be read as including adopted children (The Child Welfare Act, 1965, s. 82(3)).

Family law in this period shared with relational theory a thick description of subjects as embedded in social relations and context. Yet substantively its rules and ethos were objectionable in light of contemporary standards, in particular those of feminist political theorists, including relational theorists. The objections come into view not through the lens of a 'relational approach' per se, but rather through a differentiated examination of the period's acontextual methodology and its normative assessment of the marker – legitimacy – for identifying desirable relationships. Legal rules materialized this thick conception of subjects in various ways, including the definition of married women in relation to their husbands and the construction of children as legitimate or illegitimate in virtue of their parents' civil status. Legal recognition of religion – in religious solemnization of marriage, say, and in the constraints on interfaith adoptions – was a further sign of this embeddedness. The general indissolubility of marriage prior to the enactment of the Divorce Act in 1968 represented a sense that subjects were so embedded that their subsequent interactions were unable to touch their civil status. Internal tensions are worth noting: I remarked on the dissonance between the thickly differentiated statuses of Husband and Wife and the principle of freedom of contract regarding marriage contracts and the management of married women's property.

One critical point of difference from relational theory concerns statuses and time. While the legitimate status roles contemplated that dependencies would deepen within a family, a static quality derived from the treatment of illegitimate subjects. No interaction, interdependence, or reliance developed across time could alter the status of an illegitimate relationship. When subjects crossed the border between legitimacy and illegitimacy, they did so instantly; there was no halfway house at which to stop between the two zones. Nor, similarly, did property rights arise on the basis of temporally sustained interactions. It would have made no difference to the majority in *Murdoch* had the pair been married just two years rather than twenty-five. What precluded the wife's claim was plain failure to satisfy the formal conditions.

For the most part, the period's methodology was acontextual and formal. With some exceptions, the criteria determining legitimacy and other matters were formal, technical ones: such determinations did not need to refer to less formal factors or to the context in which a particular relationship played out. Judges, legislatures, and commentators privileged explicit and formal means of changing rights and obligations rather than implicit, inferential, or informal methods. In *Murdoch*, for example, the majority judges focused on formal and technical elements to the exclusion of evidence that would have given a sense of the couple's particular marriage and the wife's specific contributions. Similarly, where a biological parent sought to revoke consent for the adoption of her child, the rule favouring that parent effectively excluded consideration of the affective bond developed between foster parents and the child. It is this acontextual method that leads to my conclusion that family law in this period produced thick subjects but not contextual subjects. Those relationships that anchored subjects were identifiable, in the paradigm cases, by formal criteria.

Relational theorists associate strict enforcement of contracting with liberal legalism and an atomistic legal subject. The cases of marriage contracts and breaches of promise to marry were revealing because enforcement of contracts in those instances served the interest of vulnerable parties and indicated sensitivity to subjects' contextual embeddedness. Yet even where hints of contextual reasoning were detectable, they were discreetly masked behind formal doctrines. Thus breach of a promise to marry was characterized as breach of an ordinary contract. And the return of a child to his biological mother was done on the basis of old precedents and formal presumptions, rather than contextual acknowledgment that the initial consent to adopt may have been procured under conditions of intense social pressure. At times there appeared to be, as an *arrière-pensée* in the service of the thick subject, a sort of second-order contextualism, a sensitivity to context underlying the outcome that could not be articulated. Contextualism dared not speak its name. Given the way that contract doctrines can function to defend vulnerable relational interests, it seems that relational theorists should be cautious in presuming the effects of contracting and the subjects presupposed and produced by those effects.

The acontextual and formal methodology of the period served and entwined with family law's normative commitments. These commitments resembled those of today's conservative communitarian theorists of the family. Those relationships worth promoting were those inscribed as legitimate, and those that were illegitimate called for sanctions. Family law constituted the legal subject in relation to axes of legitimacy and illegitimacy, thus fixing subjects on one side or the other of a bright line. Most commentators who criticized the impact of illegitimacy on children did so on the basis, not that it was wrong to organize the family around legitimacy, but that in penalizing children the disincentives to immoral conduct were inaccurately imposed. Even advocacy for reform during the period implicitly ratified the legitimate family's 'rightful first rank' in the hierarchy (Bergeron 1961, 31). In the obscurity beyond the domain of legitimate and illegitimate heterosexual couples, homosexual relationships occupied a space in which they could barely be discussed. Such relationships were not yet thinkable even as an object of illegitimacy, nor were they acknowledged as potentially constituting couples.

The earlier period of family law produced thickly embedded subjects, but ones situated with regard to formal legal categories, not less formal contextual factors. The regime's objectionable features come into view best when attention turns from relationships generally to the legal method adopted and the normative commitments about precisely which sorts of relationships warranted support. Subtleties come into view once the relational approach is disentangled in this way. It is time to turn from the earlier period's thick family subjects to the succeeding period's contextual subjects.

3 Contextual Subjects in the Present

This chapter turns to developments in family law over the past thirty years. My argument is that contemporary family law substantially reflects relational theory's elements. Family law appears to accept relational theory's descriptive premise of the socially constituted self. It manifests normative commitments to thick, interdependent, autonomy-enhancing relationships, irrespective of their inscription as legitimate or illegitimate. Most notably, legislatures, judges, and scholars have adopted a method of contextualism. The view taken of subjects is much more particular and fact-specific than previously. The effect is to constitute legal subjects as embedded in social and institutional contexts that have become legally relevant – that is, as contextual subjects.

A handful of stories in family law scholarship will set the stage. For the most part, scholars have not spun grand narratives for the gamut of changes in Canadian family law. Instead, several fragmentary accounts and discourses organize contemporary scholarship. Three interrelated lines of feminist scholarship are discernible. One, particularly active in the 1980s, applies feminist analysis to reveal the extent to which traditional family law is gendered and the distributive effects of that gendering. Such a project inscribes itself within the larger enterprise of unmasking and critiquing the 'patriarchy behind purportedly ungendered law' (West 1988, 60–1). Its targets – typically identified with a view to reform of the positive law – include marriage as a patriarchal institution, the distribution of matrimonial property and allocation of spousal support, and the attribution of child custody. A signal concern of this scholarship is the material injustice of relations between men and women. One of its achievements has been to publicize the detrimental economic impact of divorce on women. The contention is that family law regimes instantiate liberal values of equality and independence, values rendered inappropriate by the material conditions of women's oppression (e.g., Mossman 1992; 1994; Mossman and MacLean 1986; Boyd 1989; Weitzman 1985; see also Boyd and Young 2004, 546–8). A second line of scholarship approvingly detects and promotes a shift from formal to functional conceptions of 'family' (Freeman 1994; Harvison Young 1998; see also Bala 1994). The third scrutinizes the distribution of support responsibilities between the state and the family. This scholarship argues that dual expansions in the quantum of private support obligations and the set of potential support debtors legitimate the neoliberal retrenchment of the welfare state. The effect is a privatization of the state's support burden and a downloading of social reproductive costs (Boyd 1994; 1996; Fudge 1989; Cossman 2002a). Another rough narrative, generally implicit in the literature, is less pessimistic. It sees judicial and legislative developments of the law touching family property and spousal support as evolving appropriately since the 1970s towards an equitable sharing of the economic consequences of conjugal relationships (Rogerson 1985, 481; Kasirer 1994, 572). Finally, a distinct subset of scholarship emphasizes the transformative role of the Canadian Charter of Rights and Freedoms. The argument here is that the Charter has altered family law substantially, directly in the form of equality challenges and indirectly through its influential values and methodology (Harvison Young 2001; Bala 2001; L'Heureux-Dubé 2001; see also Boyd 2000; but see Leckey 2007b). My argument about contextualism complements these narratives, especially the discourses of privatization and of the impact of the Charter.

It is through separations that we make sense of marriage, begins a recent history (Hartog 2000, 1). This is a faintly morbid and distinctly lawyerly approach, akin perhaps to a medical claim that the autopsy makes sense of life. Nonetheless, the view is ingrained in the legal literature, and my argument touches down on the messy intervention of law at the end of love. I return to a dispute introduced in the previous chapter, deepening the analysis.

Patrimonial Matters on Marriage's End

Martland J.'s majority judgment in *Murdoch v. Murdoch* denied the wife's property claim, demonstrating formalism as well as reliance on abstract, universal roles for husband and wife. Contrary to the majority, Laskin J.

sided with Mrs Murdoch in a solitary dissent. He would have declared Mr Murdoch to be a constructive trustee of a beneficial interest on the part of Mrs Murdoch.[1] In disagreeing with his judicial brethren, Laskin J. viewed Mrs Murdoch's contributions not as those of an ordinary ranch wife, but as 'extraordinary' (*Murdoch* 1973, 439). I argue that, in hindsight, the elements of relational theory are detectable in Laskin J.'s dissent. The reasons for caution here are obvious. Some commentators regard the dissent as somewhat conservative. They point to the dissent's framing of the issues in narrow technical and doctrinal terms, not bolder ones of equality or fairness (Harvison Young 2001, 755), and to its concern with the appropriate roles of the legislative and judicial branches of government (Rogerson 1985, 499–505). Moreover, Laskin J.'s contributions to family law, viewed collectively, do not cast him as a standard bearer for progressive law reform. My claim, then, is not the rash one that Laskin J. was fully aware of the radical potential detectable in his text – his biographer calls him an 'unlikely harbinger of female emancipation' (Girard 2005, 399) – nor that his dissent caused the subsequent legislative reforms. My more modest contention is that the dissent contains the analytical resources marshalled in subsequent reforms and that it models the contextual methodology characteristic of contemporary family law.

It will be fruitful to compare the majority reasons with the Laskin dissent. One hypothesis is that Martland and Laskin JJ. both operated within the same methodology. The two camps concurred as to what evidence was relevant. Both agreed on the meaning of the crucial terms: marriage, wife, and so on. Within this hypothesis, both camps agreed that a wife who makes an ordinary contribution to her husband's farming enterprise will not thereby have made a legally significant contribution to that enterprise, at least nothing germane to winding up the marital venture. In this version, Martland and Laskin JJ. parted ways when, after scrutinizing Mrs Murdoch's contributions, Martland J. concluded that they were normal and Laskin J. concluded that they were not. It is an evaluative difference, not a methodological one. This reading of the case is conservative and ultimately affirms the status quo. By grounding Mrs Murdoch's entitlement on the basis that she made extraordinary contributions, Laskin J. implicitly ratified the majority's view that a normal wifely contribution generates no property entitlement.

Yet this hypothesis is unsatisfactory. It fails to correspond to how the judges approached their task. Martland J. did not, in fact, scrutinize Mrs

Murdoch's contributions in any serious way to compare them with the standard of the normal ranch wife. Nor did he indicate any particularly firm idea of what that standard might be.[2] Instead, he emphasized the dates and amounts of transactions, data conventionally signified as legally relevant, but expended little effort attempting to reconstruct the terms of the Murdochs' common life. Martland J.'s standards privileged the rules of property law, the details of formal property transactions, and the conventionally differentiated roles of husband and wife. Laskin J.'s standards included much more. His dissent produced a subject not defined by ideal roles, but anchored in particularity. In his account of the facts, he noted a 'physical clash' that resulted in Mrs Murdoch's hospitalization; by contrast, Martland J. spoke much more discreetly and abstractly of 'marital difficulties' (*Murdoch* 1973, 443, 429).[3] The fight informed Laskin J.'s general context. Evidence of the physical labour performed by Mrs Murdoch was 'central' to his assessment, and he catalogued her ranch work by quoting her evidence in chief: 'haying, raking, swathing, moving, driving trucks and tractors and teams, quietening horses, taking cattle back and forth to the reserve, dehorning, vaccinating, branding, anything that was to be done' (ibid., 441, 443). These details of Mrs Murdoch's activities during the couple's life assumed normative importance when Laskin J. characterized them as indirect contributions towards the purchase of the properties. A comparison of Martland J.'s listing of the dates of the property purchases with Laskin J.'s fuller account of married life calls to mind Gérard Cornu's observation that in the daily life of families, 'il n'y a pas que des dates; il y a la durée.' He remarks that 'la vie est jalonée d'événements majeurs entre lesquels s'étale le cours ordinaire de l'existence' (Cornu 1998, 152). The two judges were undertaking substantially different methodological inquiries: Martland J.'s was acontextual, Laskin J.'s, contextual. But to leave the characterization at this level overlooks the importance of norms in structuring contexts, in coding some factors as salient while excluding others.

It is inadequate to assess Martland J.'s examination of the formal evidence without attention to the norms that structured his enterprise. Despite his words, his examination did not turn entirely on an empirical assessment of the relative normality of a wife's contributions. He was less open to the possibility of wives being normal or abnormal than he was transfixed by the abstract ideal of Wife. It was Mrs Murdoch's being a wife that, for Martland J., barred her contributions from legal significance.[4] For Martland J., at least as he revealed himself in this judgment, every wife will be normal.

By contrast, the normative framework within which Laskin J. operated was one in which it was necessary for a wife to demonstrate, in a fact-specific way, extraordinary contributions. But it was one in which it was possible for her to do so. Laskin J.'s contextual approach presumed both a flexibility on the part of the actions that different characters can perform and a close attention to detail. Indeed, he was anxious to specify that he was not instating a formal signification of 'wife' – the opposite of Martland J.'s – according to which simply being a wife entailed a share of property. To this end, he clarified that the court was not being asked to declare an interest in Mrs Murdoch 'merely because she is a wife and mother' (*Murdoch* 1973, 451).[5] In Laskin J.'s way of seeing, legal subjects were much less abstract and formal than in his colleague's. The need to demonstrate the basis for the claim in each case partly explained his attention to the facts. Laskin J. provided a determination based on the narrative of what Mrs Murdoch did (specific labours), not what she was (wife) (Cavarero 2000, ch. 1).

Contemporary feminism and queer theory indicate that Laskin J.'s text exceeded his relatively modest intentions. He could not, he wrote, 'share the trial judge's appreciation of normalcy' (*Murdoch* 1973, 439). His analysis, which intended simply to show that one wife crossed the threshold of ordinary labour, destabilized family roles, showing them to be contingent and shifting. Fifteen years later, Judith Butler would argue that gender is performative, constituting the identity it is purported to be, and constituted by those very expressions said to be its results (1999, 41–4). In other words, there is no identity that pre-exists its ongoing enactment. In *Murdoch*, Laskin J. demonstrated that the family roles 'husband' and 'wife' are performative and that the set of subjects capable of performing each is not fixed. Mrs Murdoch, in the text, is more than an extraordinary wife. She becomes oddly, or rather, queerly, a man and a husband. In her own account, she 'worked outside with him [Mr Murdoch], just as a man would.' A bit prior in the text, she becomes her husband: 'Undeniably, however, the wife again did *a* husband's work'; 'the wife did *her* husband's work' (*Murdoch* 1973, 443, 442 [emphasis added]). Mrs Murdoch becomes fabulously androgynous, liberated within the text from the gender role that constitutes and constrains her. In her material deprivation, Irene Florence Murdoch the person remains all too clearly gendered. But as a legal construction in the text she transcends her gender role.[6] Indeed, it is only once a judge sees her as performing maleness that he is willing to share material privilege with her. These passages are unsettling. If Mrs Murdoch is performing her husband's work, on what basis does the husband retain title to his privilege? It is not that Laskin J. was conscious of this sense of family roles as performative, nor of the potential disjuncture between performance and legal category. Yet precisely such a sense would infuse many family law developments over the following decades. It is, for example, a similar sense of family roles as performative that makes thinkable the recognition of unmarried couples as substantially equivalent to married couples, or of de facto parents as assuming rights and obligations proper to biological and adoptive parents.

The Supreme Court's decision in *Murdoch* arrived at a time when shifting social attitudes had ripened the moment for reform. The judgment precipitated widespread outrage, and every provincial legislature eventually introduced reforms. These reforms far exceeded Laskin J.'s reasons. The new legislation ensured that 'merely' being a wife did entail property rights: the new regimes established presumptions of sharing flowing from the fact of marriage. Theorists of metaphor contend that substantive consequences flow from the different metaphorical ways in which marriage is conceptualized (Lakoff and Johnson 2003, 243–4). If they are correct, it is significant that the preamble to Ontario's Family Law Act (1990) declares it necessary to 'recognize' both the equal position of spouses as individuals within marriage and marriage as a form of partnership. The legislature uses the verb 'recognize' in the robust, normative way; the equality to which it refers did not pre-exist the legislative utterance. Spouses retain separate property during the marriage, but once the marriage disintegrates, its profits are divided equally between the two spouses (subject to exceptions where equal division would be unconscionable). The equalization measure explicitly recognizes child care, household management, and financial provision as joint responsibilities of the spouses, declaring, optimistically, that equal contribution in these matters inheres in the marital relationship (s. 5(7)). This and similar regimes in other common law provinces permit domestic contracts to override the equalization of property.

In Quebec, the civil code designates for all married couples a specified mass of property as their 'family patrimony.' This mass includes the family residences, their furnishings, motor vehicles used by the family, and certain pension moneys. In the event of separation from bed and board or dissolution of the marriage, the value of this mass of property is divided between the spouses, irrespective of who holds title. The code also provides for the possibility of a compensatory allowance payable by one spouse to the other in respect of unjust enrichment. Furthermore, the reforms have established partnership of acquests as the default property regime (arts. 414, 416, 427, 432 C.C.Q.).

Comparing the criticisms levied against these regimes by scholars in the respective legal traditions is revealing. Typical common law criticisms attack the distributive outcomes. In contrast, civilian scholars have expended considerable energy criticizing the compensatory allowance and the family patrimony for their ostensible incompatibility with the logic of the civil law's traditional regulation of matrimonial property (Caparros 1994). The leading criticism relevant for present purposes, however, is that the marital property regimes reproduce the abstracted, stripped-down rational agent attributed by relational theory to classical liberalism. This criticism arises in work inscribing itself within the gendered distribution line of feminist scholarship noted earlier. Critics detect this supposedly liberal abstractness in the preamble to Ontario's act and the equal division of matrimonial property, which is executed for the most part irrespective of the spouses' contributions or needs (Klein 1985). The charge is that, in the typical fashion of liberalism, equal division presumes a level playing field, thereby obscuring systemic structures of patriarchy and oppression (Fineman 1983). Admittedly, the terms need to be complicated somewhat, since scholars in both Quebec and the common law provinces have characterized these regimes as communitarian (Kasirer 1995, 821; Mossman 1989, 209–10). I argue that it is inaccurate to regard equal division of property as presupposing and constituting atomistic legal subjects.

To elaborate my argument, it will be helpful to rely on the distinction I have proposed between relational theory's elements. Commentators who criticize the equal division of matrimonial property for its ostensible atomism are advancing, under the guise of the description of subjects, what is better acknowledged as a normative evaluation. It is arguable, normatively, that equal division is not an optimal distributive outcome. Such arguments could lean on the considerable disadvantage experienced by women who take time from their careers to raise children. But the charge that equal division presumes and reproduces abstract contracting agents, at a descriptive level, is unpersuasive. A presumption of equal sharing thickens the status dimension of marriage in recognition of the relational entanglements that develop during conjugal life. Equal division presumes that fact-specific interaction will occur in the context of each union. It seeks to respond to the dynamism and unpredictability of married life. Indeed, it represents a rough measure by the legislature, drawn in a state of imperfect information since 'love and trust discourage all but the most cynical spouses from keeping accounts' (Kasirer 1995, 802). The rule of equal division may also reflect the context-specific legislative judgment that in an accounting contest, women from a household that divided labour 'traditionally' would fare poorly relative to men. Forensic evidence of women's traditional contributions may be lacking, and in any case, the market undervalues those contributions (Knetsch 1984, 275–81). By contrast, men are likelier to marshal clear proof of their pecuniary contributions to the marital enterprise. A rule of equal division amounts to a normative and pragmatic determination that the give and take of sustained relationship make impossible a precise accounting of contributions to a marriage (Kasirer 1994, 599). Only on the surface is equal division abstract.

Moreover, the gender-neutral presumptions of equality depart from the previous reliance on preconceived, distinctly unequal roles of Husband and Wife. The main effect of matrimonial property statutes is to confer property rights on those with the status of wife, 'a status that barely one hundred years ago deprived its holder of any property interest whatsoever' (Mossman 1985, 649). The rule of equal division seeks to take into account the informal exchange relations that were invisible to the majority in *Murdoch*. The contrast with unjust enrichment substantiates the point. This equitable doctrine is less abstract, based as it is on clear proof of contributions made by one spouse to the other's property.[7] Yet many commentators regard it as procedurally cumbersome and substantively less satisfactory than a formal rule. In any event, the property regimes, which regulate only part of the reconception of the family's functioning as an economic unit, entwine with statutory support obligations.

The Divorce Act authorizes a court to order spousal support after considering the condition, means, needs, and other circumstances of each spouse (1985, s. 15.2; see also Family Law Act 1990, s. 33; art. 587 C.C.Q.). These considerations include length of cohabitation, the functions performed by each spouse during cohabitation, and agreements relating to the support of either spouse. In a legislative effort to define what the context excludes, the Divorce Act declares spousal misconduct irrelevant (1985, s. 15.2(5)).[8] Parliament articulated four objectives of spousal support: recognition of economic advantages or disadvantages arising from the marriage or its breakdown; apportionment of financial consequences arising from child care; relief of economic hardship arising from the marriage breakdown; and promotion of economic self-sufficiency 'in so far as practicable' (s. 15.2(6)). While formal rules of property division presume relational interaction, these factors and objectives call for case-by-case application in the context of each relationship.[9] The spousal support factors neither reflect abstract ideal roles nor do they deem contributions to the marital enterprise to be equal. They demonstrate the contextual method of the *Murdoch* dissent according to which what matters is the narrative of the parties' patterns of conduct. For the most part, recent judicial practice applying those provisions produces a variable, thoroughly contextual subject.

Relational theory regards contract as the primary form of ordering for abstract liberal subjects. The relationship between the statutory scheme and private contracts thus constitutes a revealing site for investigation. In *Pelech v. Pelech* (1987), the Supreme Court of Canada ratified the enforcement of consensual agreements (collectively with *Richardson v. Richardson* (1987) and *Caron v. Caron* (1987), the 'trilogy'). The Court held that a contract in which a spouse waives her right to support should be enforced unless the contract is unconscionable or the parties' circumstances have undergone a radical change that is causally connected to the marriage. This judgment has provoked extensive criticism consistent with the first line of feminist scholarship's attention to distributive effects. Other criticism refers to the legal subject produced by the judgment. Brenda Cossman argues that Wilson J.'s 'causal connection' inappropriately abstracts the particular parties from a broader context of women's economic dependence and inequality, ignoring the constitutive effects of social institutions and relationships (1990, 327–9). Martha Bailey writes critically of the trilogy's 'atomistic view of the family' as consistent with 'dominant liberal discourse,' a discourse that 'represents the oppressive relationship between husband and wife as a freely chosen contract between rational, unencumbered, autonomous individuals' (1989–90, 616; see also Rogerson 2003, 303). It is not my ambition to defend the judgment's distributive outcome, and the charges of the contracting liberal subject's thinness have some merit. Yet in two overlooked respects, the reasons in *Pelech* connect with elements of relational theory.

The first concerns the subject's constructedness. Alison Harvison Young has remarked on the trilogy's progressive style of reasoning in the sense that principles and policies implicit in the statute explicitly drive the majority's reasons (2001, 765). Wilson J.'s acknowledgment of the competing judicial stances towards contracts – from automatic enforcement to paternalist rewriting – foregrounds the sense in which the subject in family law, as Cossman puts it, 'does not exist prior to language or discourse, but rather, is constituted in and through multiple and conflicting discourses' (1994, 14). Contrary to the view that the trilogy's notion of subjectivity 'ignores any social construction of self' (Bailey 1989–90, 616), Wilson J.'s recognition of judicial policy choices in formulating a stance towards contracts hints at subjects' contingency. As a normative matter, *Pelech* inaugurates a policy that many feminist scholars would not have chosen. The core of the disagreement is not, however, that the majority presumes the subject's prior and independent naturalness while relational theory recognizes its embeddedness. *Pelech*'s subject is contingently constructed, the product of social interactions, including government regulation.

The second feature is attention to the institutional structures that allow autonomy to flourish. Wilson J. writes that, failing a radical change in the parties' circumstances causally connected to the marriage, the obligation to support the former spouse should be, 'as in the case of any other citizen, the communal responsibility of the state' (*Pelech* 1987, 852). Mrs Pelech was receiving welfare at the time of her petition, so the majority judges were not trading in counterfactuals. Today this presumption of a communal obligation to support needy individuals is commonly conscripted as a foil to recent judicial references, in widening support obligations, to the imperative of alleviating claims on the public purse. My point here, however, is that in enforcing the waiver of support, Wilson J. referred to an institutional context partly constituted by the provision of public assistance. It is much less abstract to enforce separation agreements on the basis that adequate public support will compensate for the waived entitlement than on the sole basis that it is the state's role to uphold all contracts resulting from parties' bargaining and their exchange of consent. The adequacy of public support at that juncture is contestable as an empirical matter. But Wilson J.'s determination of the enforceability of private ordering remained embedded in a presumed institutional context. The judgment demonstrated a normative definition of the relevant context that regards a pair of contracting spouses not as self-contained, but as socially situated.

The Supreme Court revisited *Pelech* in *Miglin v. Miglin* (2003). A majority of the judges attenuated the presumption in favour of enforcement to agreements, crafting a test that agreements must, to be binding, reflect the original intentions of the parties and comply substantially with the objectives of the Divorce Act. The definition of the relevant context alters again in a couple of support judgments where there was no agreement.

Moge v. Moge (1992) concerned a pair of Polish immigrants. Despite the rigours of a grade seven education in her native Poland, Mrs Moge remained economically dependent sixteen years after separation from her husband. Leaning on the statutory objective of promoting self-sufficiency 'so far as is practicable,' the trial judge had found that Mrs Moge had had time to become financially independent and that her husband had supported her as long as he could be required to do. The Court of Appeal set aside the judgment and ordered indefinite spousal support. The Supreme Court of Canada affirmed, emphasizing the Divorce Act's compensatory elements. *Moge* marks an important progression in the contextualization of subjects in family law. In the majority reasons, L'Heureux-Dubé J. rejected what she called the 'mythological stereotypes' ingrained in a dichotomy between 'traditional' and 'modern' marriages (ibid., 847; see Sheppard 1995, 314–22; Diduck and Orton 1994, 700). In so-called modern marriages, the wife's work outside the home ostensibly secured her self-sufficiency, obviating recourse to alimony. Instead, L'Heureux-Dubé J. privileged the particular over universal roles. In its attention to the detail of the lived relationship and the concomitant rejection of iconic ideals of Wife, *Moge* is reminiscent of the dissent in *Murdoch*. It exceeds that dissent, however, in delineating the context. In *Murdoch*, Laskin J.'s gaze remained fixed on the household, implicitly reinforcing the classic liberal divide between the private sphere of the household and public matters. *Pelech* blurred this line in referring to the institutional conditions of public income support. In *Moge*, the norms structuring the context adjusted once more. L'Heureux-Dubé J. scrutinized the Moges' household, not only for its internal economy of exchange, but also for its institutional relationship with external conditions. It is important when reading the act, enjoined L'Heureux-Dubé J., 'that judges be aware of the social reality in which support decisions are experienced' (*Moge* 1992, 874). *Moge* stands, then, as a redefinition of the context that includes societal treatment of women; marriage and child rearing's mediation between the spouses and the market; and the market's valuation of reproductive and domestic labour.

L'Heureux-Dubé J. immediately secured the viability of the redefined context by a skilful tactical move: she declared the detrimental impact of divorce on women to be amenable to judicial notice. In other words, not only is the broader social context admissible and relevant, but the claimant is spared the burden of submitting evidence to reconstruct it.[10] *Moge* thus exemplifies, methodologically, the turn to contextualism, and normatively, the critical importance of specifying those norms which structure the apprehension of contexts. This normative delineation is controversial. It is arguable that even this enlarged site of examination remains too limited. It may fail to address the 'larger societal context' of Zofia Moge's economic insecurity, the failure to train immigrants, and the persistence of sex discrimination in labour markets (Sheppard 1995, 286).

It is appropriate here to anticipate the objection that I exaggerate the novelty of this contextualism. Certainly it is possible ex post to reconstruct the institutional and social realities in which prior regimes were embedded. Prior abstract approaches were themselves 'rooted in particular contexts and operate[d] within contexts with real and particular effects that often benefit[ed] some people more than others' (Minow and Spelman 1990, 1628). The immutability of matrimonial property regimes under the Civil Code of Lower Canada, for example, reflected an economy based on immovable wealth of predictably stable value. But the degree to which explicit reference was made to social conditions was much less. Spousal support under the 1968 Divorce Act turned on the 'condition, means and other circumstances' of the parties, but these factors were construed as mandating a narrow inquiry, one to be conducted within the four walls of the (unhappy) matrimonial home. By contrast, *Moge*'s explicit injunction requires judges to regard the external social context as relevant and important.

The analytical utility of separating the 'relational approach' into methodological and normative elements is revealed further by a spousal support case in which a contextual method arguably disserved relational theory's normative commitments. *Bracklow v. Bracklow* (1999) concerned the claim of a wife who developed severe physical and psychological health problems unrelated to the marriage. In an effort to reconcile the previous cases with its inclination to allow Mrs Bracklow's claim, the Court distinguished three models for spousal support: contract, compensation, and a non-compensatory or mutual obligation model. On the basis of the third model, the Court found for Mrs Bracklow an entitlement to spousal support with an unspecified term. The mutual obligation model enriches – or at least complicates – the Court's theory of the sources of obligations bubbling up between legal subjects in intimate relationships. McLachlin J., writing for all the judges, deployed relational theory's descriptive premise and contextualism in two moves that generated tension with relational theory's normative commitments to autonomy.

The first move concerned the relationship between a divorcing couple and the broader social institutional context. The Court followed *Pelech* to the extent of regarding a couple as embedded in a setting that included government income support programs. The crucial difference made by the dozen years since *Pelech* was that the Court drew a normative conclusion from this contextual examination opposite to that in the earlier case. Recall that Wilson J. regarded the community as obligated to support a divorced spouse who had validly waived her right to alimony. In *Bracklow*, the normative concern animating the judges was the injustice of downloading a family support obligation onto the state. Without reference to *Pelech*, McLachlin J. spoke indignantly of the 'potential injustice of foisting a helpless former partner onto the public assistance rolls' and of the desirability of placing the primary burden of support for a person who cannot achieve post-marital self-sufficiency not on the state, but on her former partner (*Bracklow* 1999, para. 31). This position stood in opposition to the political engagements of many relational theorists, who tend to favour robust state income programs to compensate for the ways in which family income distribution fails vulnerable individuals.

The other move engaged the temporal definition of context and its impact on relational autonomy. The Court wrote that marriage creates interdependencies that cannot be easily unravelled, which in turn create legally recognizable and enforceable expectations and obligations. During family cohabitation, wrote McLachlin J., people's affairs may become 'intermingled and impossible to disentangle neatly' (*Bracklow* 1999, para. 31). Here is the language of relational theory. The judicial account of relationships and their ensuing responsibilities resonates with an argument, explicitly situated within relational theory, that it is impossible to delineate the responsibilities that arise from deep relationships (Lloyd 2000). The Court at this point was far from any abstract liberal subject voluntarily selecting its obligations. McLachlin J.'s view of family relationships was complex, distant from the stance modelled by the majority in *Murdoch*. The objection for some critics was that *Bracklow*, in striking the balance between social relations and independence, came down too heavily on the side of relational embeddedness. Although the parties had previously cohabited for four years, the marriage in *Bracklow* lasted just three years. Even if one combined the de facto and de jure periods, the relationship was not especially long. It was thus on the basis of a relatively short relationship that the Court recognized enduring obligations. The support obligation in *Bracklow* was arguably incompatible with a regime that, in other respects, increasingly recognizes the reality of divorce and second families (Cossman 2000, 449). The notion of relational autonomy draws attention to the possibilities for exiting relationships and initiating new ones. The contention that recognition of a potentially lifelong support obligation towards a former spouse is inappropriate foregrounds the need in such areas to make normative decisions. Context can be relied on in ways that can be evaluated as good or bad. Limits are appropriately imposed on the presumptions of relational responsibility.

The subject constituted by judicial discourse in *Bracklow* nevertheless retained traces of liberal contractualism. Perhaps disconcerted by the disjuncture between the view of obligations growing over time and marriage's voluntarist past, the Court alternated between stressing the factual messiness of shared life and the formal consent secured by marriage. The judges attempted to cast ascribed obligations as the fruit of consent. Recognition of deep support obligations entails no loss of autonomy, McLachlin J. asserted somewhat unconvincingly, because autonomy is voluntarily ceded in the formalization of marriage. One hurdle for this explanation is that legislation in the common law provinces imposes virtually identical support obligations on unmarried cohabiting couples. Thus, in at least the circumstances of unmarried couples, it must be the tacit commitments of shared life that justify the statutory support obligation, not the formal exchange of consent in marriage (Leckey 2002c, 40–4). Thus, reference to the voluntary cession of autonomy was a rhetorical attempt to justify obligations only tenuously voluntary. Implicitly, McLachlin J. was presuming a 'social commitment to the view that relationships of interdependence can give rise to responsibility in ways that a purely voluntary conception of obligation can't fully capture' (Regan 1993, 4). By the time legislatures have entrenched spousal support obligations for unmarried spouses – and obligations can long survive a relationship – the best conclusion may be that the legal subject is more relationally embedded and much less the rational contracting agent of liberalism than McLachlin J. was able comfortably to admit. Family law is producing contextual subjects, though the normative commitments may raise some cautions for relational theorists. These are concerns internal to a 'focus on relationship,' ones best explored more thoroughly within explicit articulation of the kinds of relationships that promote relational autonomy. Another area into which contextualism has spread and in which normative questions arise is the regulation of parent–child relationships.

Filiation

In the late 1970s and 1980s, most Canadian jurisdictions abolished the distinction between legitimate and illegitimate filiation. Typically these abolitions declared a person's status as the child of his or her parents to arise independently of whether the child was born within or outside marriage. Caveats followed so as to avoid nullifying adoptions. While legitimacy dropped away, paternity retained its significant material and symbolic consequences. For the purposes of determining paternity, the law of filiation preserved the presumptions and means of proof developed during legitimacy's hegemony. Prior reforms – diminution of the class of illegitimate children and incremental palliation of its economic and social consequences – had left the foundational dichotomy of legitimacy and illegitimacy intact. By eliminating this distinction, abolition was breaking radically with those earlier reforms. Filiation irrespective of the parents' marital status repudiated the idea that filiation draws its value from marriage; children's equal status affirmed filiation's intrinsic value (Cornu 1998, 378).

Fiats declaring the equality of the status of children do not represent a reduction in formalism. The biological and social criteria that determine paternity remain relatively formal. For example, no requirement calls for demonstration of a functional bond of care or any emotional commitment on the part of the biological parent (Jacobs 2004). Nonetheless, legislative abolition marked a shift in the vocation of filiation from the service of legitimacy to the service of children's identity and material support. The reforms eliminated fault from the law of filiation and of successions, so that at least in this regard, children no longer paid for their parents' sins. Abolition eliminated much of the prior law's explicit disapproval of family units not founded on marriage. In Quebec, where the law once recognized only the legitimate family founded by matrimonial union, the code now implicitly recognizes family groups united by blood alone (Pratte 1982, 174). It is here that the potential for less formalism and greater contextualism emerges: it becomes increasingly thinkable to recognize relationships not juridically constituted by the state-sanctioned exchange of consent to marriage.

The justification for these amendments is noteworthy, as is their reception by society. The abolition of illegitimacy derived from explicit concern for justice and equality, which seem to be values implicit in the foundational family law of the various jurisdictions (Leckey 2007b). Most of the enacted amendments were not the fruit of court challenges by parties claiming under entrenched bills of rights. These reforms were warmly received, popularly regarded as necessary and normal. Understandably, in light of the broad reforms of which they were part, the changes to filiation in Quebec were thoroughly glossed and critiqued. In the common law provinces, however, the abolition of illegitimacy proceeded so smoothly that within several years, texts in post-abolition jurisdictions either significantly understated the transformation of family law's ambitions or no longer addressed illegitimacy, even as a matter of historical interest.

The increasing acceptance of adoption as a legitimate mode reveals a less formal, more performative view of filiation. Recall that in Quebec, adoption was initially introduced by ordinary statute as opposed to amendment of the civil code. This choice signalled adoption's relative inferiority as a derogation from the filial regime. The new book of family law, grafted by the legislature onto the civil code in the early 1980s, shepherded adoption into the code, ameliorating its status.[11] Furthermore, judges demonstrated themselves more reluctant to allow biological parents to revoke their consent to adoption. The previous chapter's account of adoption cases from the 1950s demonstrated how judges, eager to reclaim children from the arms of their adoptive parents, had privileged claims of blood over those rooted in affective bonds. By contrast, judges in the 1980s explicitly detached the legislative command to privilege the best interests of the child from their earlier, almost irrefutable presumption that the claim of the biological parent would best serve those interests. In *King v. Low*, McIntyre J. held that the adopted parents had 'come to look on the child as their own, as a member of their family to whom they have become attached as to their own children' (1985, 102). The result was a greater willingness to recognize ties that arose, factually, between a child and caregivers unrelated by blood. Here was acknowledgment that biology (signified as legitimate or illegitimate) did not exhaust the field of culturally and legally intelligible parental relationships. The legal subject thus emerged, at least in the adoption cases, as the product of particular facts and experiences rather than the more abstract product of universal categories regarded as 'natural.' Yet adoption remains always self-evidently artificial. It includes a formal element, in the adoption order, but that formal element occurs in the expectation that the adoptive parents will subsequently warrant that order by performing as parents (Bordo 2005, 235).

Adoption introduces a performative dimension to family law: it is understood that adoptive parents will perform as parents. The increasing acceptance of adoption's legitimacy represents a degree of openness to the way in which different types of relationships may figure as familial. At the same time, it is important to recognize that adoption, until recently, has largely reproduced the orthodox model of the heterosexual nuclear family. The standard aim of adoption was the erasure of all ties with the biological parents. To this end, adoption records were sealed and contact between biological parents and their adopted child prohibited or stringently regulated. These measures aimed to enclose the adopted child within the 'circle of his new family' (Fraser and Kirk 1984, 116; also Lavallée 2005). The heterosexual nuclear family's ability to absorb and normalize adoption perhaps exemplifies the 'rather remarkable adaptive character' of privileged identities (O'Connor 2005). So long as the closed adoption model prevails and adoption is regarded as the replacement of one family with a new nuclear family, adoption's subversive dimension appears substantially tamed. The settings in which it becomes thinkable and recognizable for the performance of parenthood to warrant the status of parenthood remain tightly circumscribed.

The open-ended 'best interests' rule is an obvious invitation to contextual assessment. It has distributed its effects so unevenly, though, that it cautions against uncritical calls for more contextualism. Most notably, scholars have documented the differential impact of child welfare laws on First Nations communities. This problem reveals the critical importance of the normative rules that structure contextual approaches. For members of the white majority, the standard of the child's best interests appears sufficiently open-ended to embrace all that could be relevant within its contextual purview. Marlee Kline argues, however, that the notion of an individual child's best interests abstracts him from his cultural context, instating basic tenets of liberal ideology such as universality and impartiality (1992). She delivers an incisive critique of *Racine v. Woods* (1983), in which the Supreme Court of Canada applied the best interests test to affirm the de facto adoption of a First Nations child. The Court refused to take the girl from her 'psychological parents' to return her to her biological mother. As Kline argues persuasively, the expert witness relied on by the judges effaced the cultural context. The witness opined that the passage of time demanded the supersession of the ethnic and cultural background by the new mother–child relationship (*Racine* 1983, 188). Kline observes that the best interests rule typically looks only to the competing parents at issue, the biological parents versus the prospective adoptive parents. The analysis eclipses the value of a First Nations community as a place in which child rearing is valued and practised as a collective endeavour. The effect, she argues, is to privatize child rearing (Kline 1993). What is revealing is that the outcome for which Kline argues – including an independent First Nations child welfare regime – is not a return to the prior approach, in which biological bonds and ostensibly universal roles trumped. Rather, what she argues for, grounding her claims on the cultural community, is a differently structured and defined contextualism.

Provincial statute books hint that the law of filiation has stabilized around natural and adoptive parents. Established notions of filiation confront a reminder of their artificiality and contingency, however, in the form of assisted reproductive technologies. While the law tolerates a distinction between the legal 'father' and the biological father, it typically presumes an unproblematic unity of legal 'mother' and biological mother. This juridical naturalization of maternity has precluded legal thinking about maternal attributes as distributable in a way similar to paternal attributes (Mykitiuk 2001; Meyer 2006). But assisted reproductive technology introduces the possibility of two or three women with a claim to legal 'motherhood.' Providing the egg, carrying the child, and commissioning this process are separable acts that different women may perform (Jackson 2006). In what some may regard as an attack on 'monomaternity' (Cornu 1998, 123), new reproductive technologies demonstrate that what is regarded as 'natural' is itself the product of social and legal creation (Dewar 1998, 483). Canadian legislatures have for the most part shrunk from tackling these complex issues (Campbell 2007).[12] What is significant for this chapter, besides the evident performativity of parental roles, is that resolution of these issues requires normative definitions as to the relevant context. Some scholars argue that the way to advance policy discussion is to analyse relationships, to reflect on 'asymmetrical and diverse connections of multiple persons to a particular child' (Mykitiuk 2001, 791n68; also Minow and Shanley 1996, 23–4). But analysing relationships is impossible until there is some sense as to which relationships may be counted and scrutinized. Some will be in, others out. Thus a 'focus on relationship,' or a contextual scrutiny of relationships tout court, both advocated repeatedly by relational theorists, begs one of the central and thorniest questions. Controversial normative rules are required to structure the contextual inquiry and assessment.

One further regime, this time in federal legislation, constitutes subjects through filial bonds. Federal law recognizes a child support obligation on the part of step-parents. Specifically, the Divorce Act contemplates corollary support in respect of every 'child of the marriage,' including any child of whom one spouse is parent and for whom the other 'stands in the place of a parent' (1985, ss. 2(2)(a), 15.1(1)). Similar definitions appear in family maintenance acts in nearly all common law provinces. By contrast, in Quebec the law of filiation circumscribes the reciprocal obligation of support. In divorce proceedings in that province, the Divorce Act does not preserve an existing family obligation, but creates a new one. *Chartier v. Chartier* (1998), the leading case, models the contextualism emergent in family law. The dispute concerned a woman's claim for child support from her estranged husband, who was the natural father of the younger but not the elder of her two children. The question was whether, as the father contended, a person standing in the place of a parent could unilaterally terminate that relationship. Authorities on the point conflicted. The Supreme Court of Canada precluded unilateral repudiation of the quasi-parental bond, holding unanimously that Mr Chartier stood 'in the place of a parent' within the statutory terms at the relevant time. Having established a parent–child relationship, the stepfather could not unilaterally end that relationship, even though the marital relationship with the child's mother was expiring. If, as the classic formula holds, 'si l'on peut divorcer du conjoint on ne peut divorcer de ses enfants' (Philippe 2003, 131), the question who are one's children becomes paramount.

The Court set out a fact-specific, highly contextual approach for determining the 'nature' of an adult–child relationship. This approach contrasts with the formal rules of filiation, which would otherwise characterize the relationship between an adult and a child. The inquiry in *Chartier* includes the child's perspective and the step-parent's representations. It seeks express and tacit signals of intention. Contextual factors in defining the parental relationship include whether the child participates in the extended family as would a biological (and, presumably, adopted) child; whether the person provides financially for the child; whether the person disciplines the child as a parent; whether the person represents to the child, the family, and the world, explicitly or implicitly, that he or she is parentally responsible to the child; and the child's relationship with the absent biological parent. The best interpretation requires that children be able to rely on the continuity of parentlike relationships (*Chartier* 1998, para. 32). In this reasoning, the judge gathers evidence of the context and organizes it according to a normative – specifically, performative – view of parental relationships. The approach is consistent with an ethic that 'takes the relationship as a given and seeks ways to nurture and sustain it' (Regan 1999, 29).

The effect of the Divorce Act is that a step-parent legally becomes a parent in limited respects. The Court addressed the objection that obligations to support all 'children of the marriage' under the federal legislation render adoption (a provincial matter) otiose. Adoption retains legal importance, noted the Court, in the law of successions. Almost in passing, Bastarache J. remarked that the step-parent not only incurs obligations, but also acquires the right to apply under the Divorce Act for custody or access (*Chartier* 1998, paras. 43, 39). The judgment thus serves as reminder that relationships with children are not to be undertaken lightly (Cossman 2000, 440). Given the Court's comment about the corollary right to claim custody and access, the message is also that one should not lightly frame and substantiate a claim for child support on the basis that, during rosier times, one's estranged spouse stood in the place of a parent. Being a child of the marriage is not, strictly speaking, a modality of filiation, but it functions strikingly like one. In at least practical terms, the Court's claim that the Divorce Act leaves intact the provincial regulation of filiation is unpersuasive. It is worth distinguishing adoption. Adoptive filiation depends on formal legal acts. The adoption order, preceded by the biological parent's giving of consent, formally demarcates a normative site in which a legally cognizable bond of parenthood can accrue. By contrast, the sort of quasi-filiation that arises when a person stands in the place of a parent requires only the formal act of the marriage of the two adults where the Divorce Act applies. Where provincial legislation applies in the common law provinces, the family unit's informal cohabitation suffices.

Subsequent cases hint at controversy over the norms structuring the contextualism that *Chartier* demands. In its reasons, the Supreme Court denied the possibility of an intermediate position between stranger and parent. Once a person stands in the place of a parent, that person is to be treated the same as any parent (*Chartier* 1998, para. 42).[13] The effect is that the consequential analysis occurs at the threshold inquiry whether a step-parent stands in the place of a parent. If so, the quantum of support becomes the mostly mechanical matter of reading the guideline table. The result is an all-or-nothing venture that channels the step-parent to contest, not the quantum of his obligation, but the prior formation of a parental relationship. In Carol Rogerson's analysis, this status question (parent/not parent) eliminates the possibility of dealing with issues contextually, which might 'generate differentiated notions of parenthood in different contexts.' Rogerson further objects that trial courts assimilate step-parents to parents too quickly, after a period as short as two years. She points to sociological research that demonstrates that it takes a long time for step-parents to assume a role equivalent to parents. The upshot, she argues, is to force step-parents to assume parental obligations before a truly parental relationship has developed. Rogerson advocates 'a more nuanced, less rigid approach,' in which quantum and duration may vary more in response to factors such as the length and nature of the relationship and the impact of the relationship on the child, including its effect on other sources of support (2001, 153–4, 102, 156). Instead, current practice seems to consecrate one or two factors as determinative, the effect being that marriage and the fact of living together as a family pull vigorously towards a conclusion that a step-parent 'stands in the place of a parent.' Despite the aspiration of contextual sensitivity, cohabitation with a child's mother for two or three years may stiffen into a criterion for ascription of parental status nearly as formal and automatic as biological paternity.

Another issue is that a number of judges structure their inquiry around the assumption that children need a father. In *Chartier*, Bastarache J. identified as one of the factors the 'nature or existence of the child's relationship with the absent biological parent' (1998, para. 39). The biological father in that case was fully absent, so the Court understandably did not model the way that a judge should incorporate this factor. Rogerson argues that judges perceive an imperative to provide 'replacement social fathers' for children whose biological fathers have abandoned them. She detects 'pervasive cultural assumptions' that a 'normal' family consists of children with one mother and one father, noting that where the biological father is absent, courts lower the bar for recognizing the stepfather (Rogerson 2001, 95–6). In such cases, the court often states that the stepfather was the only father the child had known. The turn to contextualism exemplified in *Chartier* has been significant in loosening the category of parent. Yet readings of the judgment as simultaneously affirming the possibility of more than two parents and as empowering judges to construct traditional nuclear families hint that the norms guiding contextualism matter tremendously. Thinking about relationships, and about the relationships that rights and entitlements structure, as urged by relational theorists, is insufficient. What is needed is refinement of relatively precise guiding norms, norms that should be the product of articulated debate.

It is peculiar that the Court speaks of the 'nature' of the adult–child relationship, as opposed to its character or quality. As Martha Nussbaum observes, people use that word in 'multiple and slippery ways' (1999, 255). After all, it is precisely not the relationship's nature, in a biological sense, that the step-parent disputes engage. The crux of the inquiry is the relationship's artificiality, its constructedness as a symbolic, communicative, and material project sustained through time, its performance. Then again, the Court's diction is perhaps fitting, as a radical – surely unintended – observation that by the end of the twentieth century, the 'nature' of a parental relationship can arise from conduct, not only from mediated biological facts and judicial orders. The inference seems to be that parenthood thus has no essence but arises in several ways and in varying degrees.[14] The number of family subject positions that an individual can occupy have multiplied. A child may have more than two fathers (Harvison Young 2000), and a person's parental obligations may extend beyond the class of his biological and adopted children. Definitional disputes may persist, but family law is nonetheless producing contextual subjects. Contextualism and norms interweave further in the realm of non-marital adult relationships.

Outside Marriage

Diminished emphasis on the legitimacy of adult relationships secured through marriage has further reconstituted family law's subjects. Four stages of change are discernable on the 'muddled terrain' outside marriage (Dubler 2003, 1656). Two have been primarily legislative and the other two primarily judicial. The first is the legislative repeal of rules penalizing unmarried relationships, such as invalidations of inter vivos gifts and prohibitions on testamentary gifts. The second is the ascription to unmarried opposite-sex couples of support obligations akin to those applicable to married couples. Beginning in the 1970s, legislatures in all the common law provinces enacted such statutory support obligations (e.g., Family Law Act 1990, ss. 29 'spouse,' 30). The justification for the new measures supplied by Ontario's attorney general at the time is revealing. The government proposed that 'persons living in a relationship of some permanence' bear responsibility for their mutual support. The driving concern was the exploitation of women in these relationships: 'many people ... have been induced to enter into the relationship and to stay home and raise the children,' entailing a position of total dependency on account of their absence from the labour market (Ontario, Legislative Assembly, *Debates* (18 November 1976), 4793 (Mr McMurtry)). Legal subjects 'induced' to enter relationships and thus disadvantaged in the market were no longer the subjects presumed to negotiate their marriage contract and formally to assume a package of reciprocal obligations. The legislature departed from an emphasis on bargaining and volition, and the minister's remarks showed a conception of feminine subjects distinctly different from the formally equal subject produced by the Married Women's Property Acts. By contrast, Quebec has not legislated any support obligation between de facto spouses. The civil law regards de facto spouses for the most part as linked in no way whatsoever, no matter the duration of their shared life. The corpus of social legislation, however, which delineates entitlements under government programs and other collective schemes, treats de jure and de facto spouses together (Tétrault 2005, 549–51).

In the judicial theatre, a line of cases resolving property disputes between unmarried cohabitants have used constructive trusts to remedy the unjust enrichment of the partner holding title. In the contextual style of the dissent in *Murdoch*, these judgments focus on the particularity of each unmarried relationship, conferring visibility and legal relevance on patterns of indirect contributions to the purchase and improvement of property. The temporal dimension is crucial. In *Sorochan v. Sorochan*, for example, the Court wrote that the longevity of an unmarried relationship militates in favour of proprietary relief (1986, 53). It was argued in another case that the Ontario legislature's expansion of 'spouse' in delineating support obligations but not family property implicitly prohibited courts from applying general equitable principles to property disputes between cohabitants. Dickson J. rejected this contention, finding no basis for distinguishing in the equitable division of assets between marital and less formal relationships. He reasoned that the parties 'lived as man and wife for almost twenty years. Their lives and their economic well-being were fully integrated' (*Pettkus v. Becker* 1980, 850). In treating married and unmarried couples together, there is a sense of spousal roles as performative – *living as* substitutes for *being*. Dickson J. made the negative statement that the absence of a statutory scheme requiring division of assets does not bar the availability of an equitable remedy. What he left implicit was the affirmation that the legislative recognition of a support obligation between unmarried partners shows that such couples already perform a legally cognizable spousal relationship. The legislation not only preserves the possibility of an equitable remedy in a property dispute, but fortifies it.

These stages' implications for the legal subject are substantial. The earlier period produced a static, formalistic subject. An intimate relationship engendered obligations only once inscribed as a legitimate marriage, sanctified by 'l'établissement, la solennité inaugurale' (Cornu 1998, 154). Significant changes in the entitlements and duties of that subject arose from formalized, consensual acts, the effects of which were for the most part permanent. Think of the indissoluble status of marriage and the immutability of marriage contracts. Where a privileged status proved impermanent – say, the declaration of the nullity of a putative marriage void ab initio – the better way to regard the situation is that the permanent status of legitimacy never attached and the law merely rectifies an error ex post. Such shifts from presumed legitimacy to illegitimacy occur in strict on/off fashion, with no intermediate phase. Marriage does not serve as a proxy for the diachronic emergence of obligations. It stands as a punctual commitment to future obligations. By contrast, the developments surveyed here constitute subjects in more dynamic, informal terms. Legislative recognition of a support obligation within couples having cohabited three years represents an extraordinary shift. The three-year threshold functions as a proxy for a gradual emergence of economic reliance and vulnerability. Such enactments show legislatures alert to the 'possibility of new, legally enforceable obligations calcifying in the interstices of lived interaction' (Leckey 2002c, 18). Similarly, judicial determinations that shared conjugal life and informal and indirect contributions to property are equivalent to formalized contributions of purchase money constitute a subject whose daily life has joined its juridical acts as legally relevant. Daily life now arguably not only complements, but also rivals formal law (Cornu 1998, 154). Though the conjugal household remains an economy of exchange, the set of recognizable exchanges has expanded, reflective of the *Murdoch* dissent, to include informal ones. Here, as in the case of the step-parent obligation interpreted in *Chartier*, the legislatures understand kinship as 'not a form of being but a form of doing' (Butler 2000, 58 [endnote omitted]).

The potential abuses of such recognition underscore the need to scrutinize the norms underlying this contextualism. In the mid-1990s, for example, the Ontario government revived the so-called 'spouse in the house' rule to curtail its social assistance obligations. Its definition of 'spouse,' though facially gender neutral, had the effect of presuming that a man living in a woman's household supported her. The definition deemed spousal, for example, the relationship between a person with a disability and his cohabiting friend. In *Falkiner* (2002), the definition was successfully challenged as discriminatory contrary to Section 15 of the Charter. The contextual approach I have sketched in this section takes tacit ordering into account; the objections raised by the regime in *Falkiner* serve as a reminder that the basis for presuming such ordering is open to scrutiny. The difficulty in *Falkiner* was the disjunction between any implicit support undertakings by the deemed 'spouses' in the houses and the immediate clawback of welfare entitlements. As the courts observed, the definition wrongly assumed equivalency between a cohabitation relationship with support obligations and one without (*Falkiner* 2002, para. 58; Cossman 2002a, 208–9). In a sense, rather than constructing the relation from the context of individuals' lives, the government's scheme inferred a context of undertakings of mutual support in virtue of the simple fact of a shared roof.

The final stage of recognition of unmarried opposite-sex couples has been litigation under the Charter and the legislative amendments in its wake. In *Miron v. Trudel* (1995), the Supreme Court recognized marital status as analogous to those prohibited grounds of discrimination in Section 15 of the Charter. A majority of the Court read an insurance regime's definition of 'spouse' as including unmarried couples. The determination that excluding unmarried cohabitants violated their constitutional right to equality triggered a number of legislative reforms. This judgment serves as reminder of the bluntness of constitutional litigation as an instrument for fashioning social policy. The Supreme Court has subsequently declared that inclusion among the analogous grounds is permanent (*Corbiere* 1999). The judges' intention was presumably to spare vulnerable equality claimants the burden of proving each time that a basis for exclusion is justifiably regarded as an analogous ground. A worrisome potential effect, however, is the propensity for reifying markers and categories of oppression. Where distinctions between married and unmarried couples are signified as discriminatory and offensive to the human dignity of unmarried couples, it is difficult to resignify unmarried cohabitation as an alternative family form valuable, in part, for its difference from marriage. Thus while the general disadvantage and stigma associated with unmarried cohabitation have diminished further in the decade since *Miron*, marital status remains entrenched as an analogous ground. Has the judicial gaze, in an instance of the Medusa syndrome, turned the group of cohabitants to stone? (Appiah 2005, 110). The binary discourse of inclusion/exclusion deployed in equality cases appears to rule out remedial regimes subtler than total assimilation and total exclusion (Barlow and James 2004). Furthermore, since parenthood and childlessness are not salient characteristics under Section 15, the Charter's logic is unlikely to encourage efforts to distinguish cohabitants raising children from those who are not. Yet this is arguably a crucial proxy for commitment and economic dependence (Conway and Girard 2005, 729–31). Indeed, whereas the contextualism associated with relational theory, in its alertness to the deepening of relational obligations and interdependencies across time, would aspire to recognize a spectrum of different autonomy-promoting relationships, *Miron*'s effect appears somewhat cruder. There are now, one surmises, two classes of unmarried couples, those whom the legislature regards as akin to marriage on the basis of the duration of their cohabitation, and those who, having lived together for a day or more less than the statutory threshold period, are entirely invisible (*Brebric v. Niksic* 2002).

Miron is arresting in the equality field for finding discrimination where ostensibly the claimants could have avoided that discrimination by choosing to marry. McLachlin J. distinguished the theoretical proposition that one is free to marry from the practical reality of legal, financial, social, and religious constraints on that choice. 'Marital status,' she wrote, 'often lies beyond the individual's effective control' (1995, para. 153). The recognition that a couple should be regarded as married on the basis of shared life departs from the liberal emphasis on consensus and choice in the law of marriage. Yet in broader family law terms, McLachlin J.'s acknowledgment of individuals who lack effective control over their marital status parallels the account of vulnerable cohabitants induced by their partners to stay home and raise children sketched by Ontario's attorney general two decades prior. One further site of change remains.

Beginning in the 1990s, Canadian courts and legislatures departed from the strictly heterosexual legal subject produced by family law in the earlier period. Same-sex unions achieved gradual entry into the field of legible relationships.[15] Admittedly, Trudeau had achieved the decriminalization of homosexual sex in the late 1960s. But the justification for that decriminalization was privacy and a Millian harm principle, not the claim that homosexual couples should be thinkable as families (compare Herman 1990; Cossman 1994). The early family cases in which homosexuality emerged – in which, say, a gay or lesbian parent sought custody or access – struggled to conceive of homosexuality as compatible with family (Gavigan 2000). Even the remarkable inclusion of sexual orientation as a prohibited ground in Quebec's Charter of Human Rights and Freedoms in 1975 did not translate directly into revised conceptions of family. In the early 1990s, prior to any of the major Charter litigation, the Ontario Law Reform Commission contemplated including same-sex couples in provincial legislation in recognition 'that the social practice of family life has substantially expanded beyond the confines of traditional marriage' (McCamus 1993, 466). By that juncture, a few courts had already allowed claims in unjust enrichment from one same-sex partner to another of the sort made by members of unmarried heterosexual couples (*Anderson* 1986; *Forrest* 1992).

The challenged laws concerned public entitlements in some cases and private obligations in others. The applicant in one unsuccessful effort sought bereavement leave to attend the funeral of the father of his same-sex partner. Brian Mossop argued that exclusion of a same-sex relationship from employment legislation counted as discrimination on the basis of 'family status' in the sense of federal human rights legislation (*Canada (A.G.) v. Mossop* 1993). The claim was framed as a statutory interpretation matter respecting the enabling statute, not a Charter claim attacking it. Although Mossop lost, his case is notable for the dissenting reasons of L'Heureux-Dubé J., who articulated a richly contextual and functional vision of family. Indeed, a number of the unsuccessful demands around this time led to split decisions in which forceful dissents testified that homosexual unions were becoming legible as family. In another such case, *Layland* (1993), two male applicants sought judicial review of a municipal refusal to issue them a marriage licence. The applicants lost, but their case made a rich contribution in the dissenting reasons of Greer J., who wrote presciently – in language redolent of relational theory – that it is in the state's interest 'to foster all family relationships' and that it is discriminatory to urge the state to preserve only traditional heterosexual families (677).

It is a mistake to regard these Charter challenges regarding gays and lesbians as detached from the prior legislative developments regarding unmarried heterosexual cohabitants. By introducing an explicitly performative sense of marriage, those legislative amendments paved the way for the Charter claims by gay and lesbian couples. This point that legislation tilled the soil for the Charter claims is demonstrated nicely in *Knodel* (1991). The case concerned a claim that a definition of 'spouse' in medical regulations that excluded a same-sex couple was discriminatory on the ground of sexual orientation contrary to Section 15 of the Charter. The court allowed the claim and, as a remedy, read 'spouse' as including a member of a same-sex couple. The regulation had already extended 'spouse' beyond married individuals to cover 'a man or woman who, not being married to each other, live together as husband and wife' [*sic*]. Rowles J. read the phrase 'live together as husband and wife' as intended to exclude relationships not marked by emotional and sexual commitment, but noted that the phrase did not require a couple to be husband and wife. Here the drafter's inclusion of 'as' emerged as crucial. The judge then saw Knodel and his partner as having performed as husband and wife: 'They were deeply committed to each other emotionally and sexually, exchanged vows and rings in a private ceremony, established a home together, pooled their finances, and shared bank accounts and credit cards' (*Knodel* 1991, paras. 81, 82, 83). In this and other cases, application of the Charter introduced same-sex spouses into a category of spouse already loosened by legislation.

Egan v. Canada (1995), another Charter case, underscored the relationship between context and norms. The appellants, James Egan and John Nesbit, were a gay couple who had lived together for nearly forty years. They challenged the definition of 'spouse' that restricted a federal pension benefit to married persons and, as in *Knodel*, cohabiting opposite-sex couples. La Forest J., for himself and three others, accepted that sexual orientation is an analogous ground under Section 15. But he concluded that the definition of 'spouse' did not infringe the equality guarantee. Cory and Iacobucci JJ. (L'Heureux-Dubé and McLachlin JJ. concurring) held that the definition discriminated and, moreover, that it was not a justifiable limitation under section 1. Sopinka J. broke the tie in brief reasons. He agreed that the definition discriminated, but he upheld it under Section 1 in deference to the legislature's choices on account of limited resources and the 'novelty' of recognizing same-sex relationships. In contrast, Cory J. adopted the view of kinship as a form of doing, so that he moved between *being* and *performing*: the appellants 'are a homosexual couple,' he wrote; 'they refer to themselves as partners.' Clearly, being a couple is the cumulation of multiple sustained performances: 'They have lived together since 1948 in what is obviously an intimate, caring, mutually supportive relationship. They have shared and continue to share bank accounts, credit cards and property ownership. By their wills they have appointed each other their respective executors and beneficiaries' (*Egan* 1995, 577). In the same way that Mrs Murdoch performed a husband's work, Egan and Nesbit performed as a couple.

What is revealing for present purposes is the contrast between La Forest J.'s and the dissenting judges' framing of the relevant contexts. L'Heureux-Dubé J. regarded the context as including broader socioeconomic conditions. She remarked that the appellants, as elderly and poor homosexuals, stood 'at the margins of an already marginalized group within society' (ibid., 567). La Forest J., for his part, defined a social context that excluded gay couples. Indeed, he arguably figured gay couples as not-family and as less than human (Butler 2004, 30). Since Parliament had already added unmarried heterosexual couples to married couples in the scheme, he had his work cut out for him. He justified the pension benefit for married couples on the basis that marriage had been grounded in 'our legal tradition' from 'time immemorial.' But for the inclusion of unmarried opposite-sex couples, he necessarily sought a justification less formal and more functional.[16] He distinguished them from (necessarily unmarried) homosexual couples on the basis that many of the former cohabit indefinitely, produce children, and 'care for them in response to familial instincts rooted in the human psyche' (*Egan* 1995, 536–7). Nurturing within gay households, by implication, did not draw from these same familial and human instincts. Even when La Forest J. acknowledged that gay couples perform as family, it was part of a brutal exclusionary move that simultaneously erased them. He wrote that homosexual couples 'undoubtedly provide mutual support for one another, and that, no doubt, is of some benefit to society. They may, it is true, occasionally adopt or bring up children, but this is exceptional and in no way affects the general picture' (ibid., 538; see Beaman 1999). Observe the curious contrast between La Forest J.'s certitude as to the social benefit derived from same-sex couples' mutual support ('undoubtedly,' 'no doubt') and that support's normative irrelevance. Since telling stories and seeing context requires viewing some factors as salient and being blind to others (Scheppele 1987; Minow and Spelman 1990), it is especially apt that the metaphor La Forest J. used to erase same-sex couples was a visual one (Brighenti 2007). He invoked a conception of society in which the 'general picture' was altered 'in no way' by the realities of same-sex couples raising children. It is one thing to argue that particular occurrences do not justify changes to social policy, and another entirely to state categorically that those occurrences are appropriately rendered invisible. The judge's deployment of the language of certainty – undoubtedly, no doubt, truth, in no way – sought to 'establish a set of norms that are beyond power or force' (Butler 1995a, 39), and to secure for his pronouncements an incontestable status as foundational, prepolitical, and prejuridical. It is plain that the disagreement between La Forest J. and his colleagues was not methodological but normative. To explain the addition of heterosexual cohabitants in the scheme, he accepted the performativity of family relationships and the relevance of the contexts in which they raise children. The differences between the judges may have deep normative roots, but if so, it is through contrasting definitions of the context that their foundational commitments operate.

The next major case returned from public to private entitlements. In *M. v. H.* (1999), the Supreme Court held that it was discriminatory to restrict a spousal support obligation to unmarried cohabitants of the opposite sex. This judgment, while groundbreaking in its recognition of the legitimacy of gay and lesbian relationships, was doctrinally cautious. It cleaved to the technical elements of Charter jurisprudence, steering clear of any broader discussion of family social policy, changing family demographics, and family diversity (Cossman 2002b, 236). In this way *M. v. H.* retreated from the broader approach modelled by L'Heureux-Dubé J. in *Moge.* Legislatures responded in various ways (Murphy 2001). Parliament 'modernized' benefits and obligations in nearly seventy statutes so as to include same-sex couples (Modernization of Benefits and Obligations Act 2000). Nova Scotia defined 'common-law partners' irrespective of sex and provided for consensual declaration of same- and opposite-sex domestic partnerships (Law Reform (2000) Act 2000). Ontario, rather grudgingly, created a new category, 'same-sex partner'

(Amendments Because of the Supreme Court of Canada Decision in M. v. H. 1999). Alberta legislated more broadly in respect of interdependent adult relationships (Adult Interdependent Relationships Act 2002), perhaps hoping to 'dilute' the equivalency of same-sex and opposite-sex conjugal relationships by submerging the former in a deep pool of functionally equivalent non-marital relationships (Cossman 2002c, 504n14). The legal subject is thus constituted somewhat differently in this respect from province to province.

The final stage (so far) is that superior and appellate courts have struck down as discriminatory both common law and enacted definitions of marriage as between one man and one woman. In *Halpern v. Canada (A.G.)* (2003), the Court of Appeal for Ontario addressed the claim that marriage is heterosexual because it 'just is.' The judges dismissed this argument out of hand as circular. In the court's words, denying same-sex couples the right to marry perpetuated the view 'that same-sex couples are not capable of forming loving and lasting relationships, and thus same-sex relationships are not worthy of the same respect and recognition as opposite-sex relationships' (ibid., paras. 71, 94). The court in this way made a normative assessment of the value of same-sex relationships as similar in salient respects to heterosexual marriages. In the midst of these court decisions, Quebec instated a new institution, the civil union, which is available to opposite-sex and same-sex couples and substantially reproduces the legal regime of marriage (An Act Instituting Civil Unions and Establishing New Rules of Filiation 2002).[17] Most recently, the Parliament of Canada has changed the definition of marriage (Civil Marriage Act 2005). Same-sex relationships have moved from the terrain of the unthinkable to the thinkable; what was once 'behind closed doors' has been rendered public in a powerful and unsettling way (Collier 2001, 176). This movement has been accomplished, incrementally, through a method of contextualism. Private law values of family law and the constitutional right to equality have descended from abstraction and been rendered concrete in the particular facts of domestic life (Leckey 2007d).

Family law in the contemporary period can be regarded as reflecting the major elements adumbrated by relational theorists. Relational theory departs from a description of selves or subjects as constituted by their social context and embedded in relationships. It contrasts this understanding with a view of subjects as atomistic choosing agents who voluntarily select their relational obligations and structure them contractually. As in the earlier period, family law in the contemporary era follows a thick conception of subjects, although the role of religion has been considerably reduced – at least in the explicit state regimes (compare Shachar 2005). A rejection of the priority of contractual choosing is apparent in the repeal of direct legal prohibitions and penalties affecting so-called illegitimate adult relationships. The reforms acknowledge that adults do not always choose their deepest attachments consciously and with full freedom. The contemporary period recognizes that, absent formal legal acts, the obligations and recognizable relations between subjects alter across time as a result of sustained interactions. Contemporary family law uses time in a constructive manner: time allows the establishment of bonds (Philippe 2003, 132). A sort of customary law is recognized as arising between family members. The constituting factors of subjects are no longer simply the civil status inscribed in a government registry.

The separation of a relational approach into constituent elements for which I argue in this book helps us hold the contemporary period up against the past. The major distinction from the previous era, and the most important way in which family law has moved closer to elements of relational theory, is found in this period's methodology and normative commitments. The substance of the differences is better specified in these terms than addressed in a general way by the question of whether or not the law attended to relationships. As in the previous era, these elements intertwine. Some authors describe the shift as one from a formal vision of the family to a functional one. Such accounts can be problematic in that they attempt to compare incomparable features. The methodological change is one from formal inattention to context to an informal contextualism. The normative change is one from commitment to legitimacy to commitment to families, which, in their functioning irrespective of formal legal markers, provide affective and economic support to their members. Once the prior era's deep commitment to legitimacy is acknowledged, the norms it applied and the means of doing so appear functional in the sense that they served the foundational ends. Indeed, what the formalism-to-functionalism account elides is that family law has changed not only in method, but also in its normative commitments.

The contemporary era subscribes to a performative understanding of family that depends much less than the previous era on juridical legitimacy. Children obtain status independent of their parents' civil status. Adults can have recognizable relationships outside marriage. Step-parents may be required to support children towards whom they have performed as parents. The law acknowledges existing relationships and ascribes obligations on the basis of those relationships. Put another way, where there have been sustained patterns of interaction, the absence of consensual undertakings does not preclude the recognition of enforceable obligations. A further change is that the norms are no longer exclusively heterosexual, nor is the subject of family law necessarily heterosexual. The sense of the performativity of parenthood helps secure the cultural and legal intelligibility of parenting by gay men and lesbians. Such parenting is itself always 'an active process of achievement, performance and enactment' (Haywood and Mac an Ghaill 2003, 59). The method has shifted to one in which explicit reference to context has become frequent and indeed imperative in adjudicating family matters. Subjects are constituted not only by a single salient status – such as being a wife – but also by an aggregation of contextual factors. They are contextual subjects.

Yet it is important not to exaggerate the move towards the informal and the tacit. In Quebec, in particular, a heavy emphasis on consensual statuses persists, one derived from the civil law's classical veneration for freedom of the will. This emphasis is seen in the legislative refusal to recognize support obligations between de facto spouses and to impose child support obligations on step-parents. That emphasis led the Quebec legislature to respond to the same-sex issue by enacting a new consensual civil status, the civil union. A hardy strain of formalism subsists, though in the case of civil unions, the willingness to revisit the class of family couples that merit access to a consensual civil status demonstrates contextualism and a sense of family's performativity. This case suggests a fruitful collaboration between contextualism and more formal reliance on consent. The legislature, the gatekeeper to the set of consensual regimes, is open to altering the entry rules in response to contextual observations.

What is the relationship between normative and methodological elements? In the move from the prior period's family law, normative and methodological steps alternated. At bottom, however, my sense is that the normative change was most crucial. Relational theorists call consistently for a contextual approach, urging 'attention to the rich and complex social and historical contexts in which agents are embedded' (Mackenzie and Stoljar 2000b, 21). They address less often and less directly the way that norms determine what will be regarded as a relevant element of the context. The characterization of context as 'rich' hints that contextualism entails evaluations, but the matter is rarely tackled. Recall that in *Egan* (1995), the La Forest camp upheld the pension legislation's restriction of a benefit to married and unmarried heterosexual couples and the Cory–Iacobucci camp would have included homosexual couples. Had the legislation included only married couples, it is possible that the contest would have been one between formal (reliance on juridical status) and informal (attention to tacit and interactional elements) methodologies. But Parliament's prior inclusion of unmarried opposite-sex couples precluded such an opposition. Instead, the contrast was between two camps of contextualists, one of which regarded homosexual couples as irrelevant for present purposes: same-sex couples were invisible to La Forest J.'s 'general picture.' It is the norms that constrain the possible set of contextual readings. Similarly, the normative definition of the context proves crucial in applying the step-parent support provision in the Divorce Act: it is significant whether or not a judge operates on the assumption that a child should, where at all possible, have a 'father.' Recall, too, that criticisms of the effects of the 'best interests' rule for First Nations posited the need for a context that would encompass child rearing as a collective enterprise, casting its net wider than the dyad of biological parents. Relational theorists have treated with comparative neglect debates over the norms that inform contextualism.

The ways in which norms constrain context lead me to hypothesize that the shifts in family law of the past three decades have been the result of normative changes rather than the result of methodological shifts. During the earlier period, when legitimacy and formalism reigned, criticisms were made on the basis of decency, fairness, and equality. Over time, society came to regard these underlying values of family law as translating into different juridical norms than those obtaining. Once the norms shifted, it became clear to some judges and scholars that a contextual methodology would better serve those substantive commitments. The public's expectations and demands of family law altered, and family law responded. It is perhaps relatively recently, especially on the same-sex questions, that judicial developments have preceded social change on the normative matters. This idea of a mutually reinforcing shift in method and normative commitment over the past thirty years leads to two comments on the family law scholarship sketched at the outset.

One literature is critical of the enlargement of spousal support and of redefinitions of 'family' that expand the set of potential debtors. The basis for its criticism is the understandable fear that such developments permit the state to reduce its social spending (Boyd 1996; Cossman 2002a). Scholars detecting the state's privatization of social costs would benefit in argumentative force by articulating their normative commitments more fully. They do not denounce the enactment of adoption, the abolition of illegitimacy, and the equalization of matrimonial property as foot soldiers of the welfare state's retreat. These critics of privatization notably do not sympathize with the majority in *Murdoch*. Yet the effect of these reforms has been to increase private obligations and reallocate private resources so as to reduce claims against the state. Even those alarmed by a phenomenon of privatization regard these earlier reforms as appropriate legal responses to the contextual legal subject, accepted as suitable background conditions for the flourishing of relational autonomy. It is not, then, that the critics of privatization oppose on principle all redefinition and enlargement of 'family.' Their objection is not to expansions of family that reduce the state's obligations per se, but more narrowly to expansions they characterize as inappropriate. Once this is recognized, it emerges that what is missing from their accounts is a clearer delineation of the basis for marking some expansions but not others as problematic.[18]

As for the accounts that emphasize the Charter's impact, they underestimate the continuity in normative commitments and contextual elements across the contemporary period. Robust claims for the Charter's efficacy and influence in family law understate the degree to which its triumphs hinge on the contextual subject already produced by developments squarely within the private law of the family.[19] The changes noted by these scholars depended on the particularistic, as opposed to universal, approach and the relational sense of family roles as performative modelled by the *Murdoch* dissent and instantiated in legislative reforms. Recognition of same-sex relationships is not the upshot of abstract application of a rule of universal equality to individuals (Leckey 2007d). It is implicit in the judicial performance in the major judgments that the courts are assessing relationships, not vindicating the equality claims of individuals. Consider the extent to which those judges sympathetic to the claimants in *Egan* lingered on the particular facts of Egan and Nesbit's performance of conjugality (see also *M. v. H.* 1999). Such detailed evaluation of same-sex couples would have been unnecessary were it just a matter of applying the proposition that once government provides a benefit, it must do so equally (*Eldridge* 1997). Claimants on other grounds need not prove their worthiness. The law's recognition of same-sex relationships is not a mechanical application of a universal rule of equality to individuals, but instead a validation of same-sex alliances closely resembling heterosexual marriages.[20] The pedigree of the judicial reasoning that led to same-sex marriage has implications for the charges raised by critics of so-called judicial activism. Here again, as in the case of critics of privatization, there can be an unhelpful failure to specify the objections. Would the critics of the Charter and judicial activism denounce the dissent in *Murdoch* and the subsequent judgment in *Rathwell v. Rathwell* (1978), where the wife won, as activist usurpations of family policy? If not, it would be helpful for them to draw a line between those judgments and the Charter cases of the 1990s. Attention to continuities in the constitution of contextual subjects over thirty years are unlikely to pacify the fiercest critics of these reforms, but they potentially blunt the charges of novelty and abrupt transformation.

Some theorists attentive to law's productive capacity posit that every act of inclusion necessarily excludes others. Queer critics argue, for example, that the attainment of same-sex marriage worsens the discursive and material conditions affecting alternative sexual arrangements, exacerbating the shame attached to queer relationships that do not imitate marriage (Warner 1999, ch. 3). It is certainly arguable that marriage's regulatory force exceeds its formal borders and that it preserves its 'legal and ideological supremacy' as the norm for all intimate relations (Dubler 2003, 1712). While the legal subject is no longer produced in a strictly heterosexual matrix of legitimacy, conjugal relations remain paradigmatic, and alternative family forms are regarded as 'modalités imparfaites et minoritaires' (Cornu 1998, 43). Though scholars have criticized the enduring emphasis on conjugality (Fineman 1995, 228–30; Cossman and Ryder 2001; Bottomley and Wong 2006), they have interrogated rather less the continuing presumption that natural filiation provides the norm to which alternatives should be assimilated, or that children should have two parents. Some argue that there should be greater recognition of families in which more than two adults function as parents (*A.A. v. B.B.* 2007; Jackson 2006), or in which there is just one (Noreau 2002). Law, even with all the contextualism, functionalism, and openness in the world, continues to govern using categories. It seems that the project of governance by law ultimately requires such categories, and one is forced to attempt to evaluate the exclusionary effects that arise by implication from these instruments. It is unhelpful, in subscribing to the idea that all regulation is exclusionary, to regard as equally exclusionary and equally damaging criminal prohibitions against homosexual conduct with the fact that, say, Ontario's family regime does not acknowledge unmarried couples cohabiting less than three years. The exclusions need to be evaluated on several levels, including their degree of permanence (a cohabiting couple will, eventually, cross the legislative three-year threshold) and the measure of material and symbolic harm inflicted. These are deeply normative matters, well within the compass of relational theory's normative commitment. As the case studies in the next chapter will show, judges can agree on descriptive, methodological, and many normative elements adumbrated within relational theory and still disagree on where to draw lines.

4 Contracting and Disputes within Relational Theory

'The best sort of love between persons,' remarks Martha Nussbaum, 'is highly vulnerable to happenings in the world' (1986, 359). So, it turns out, are the agreements that people once in love conclude with each other. This chapter engages with instances of formal ordering that seek to curtail the extent of relational obligation and interdependence. My starting point is three judgments from the Supreme Court of Canada that increased the weight accorded to private ordering in adult intimate relationships. The judgments treat a separation agreement, a prenuptial agreement, and a cohabiting couple's failure to marry. The majority enforced the two contracts and refused to include unmarried couples within the matrimonial property regime. In their reasons, the majority judges spoke repeatedly about autonomy and choice. By contrast, the dissenting judges would have set the agreements aside, and one dissenter would have assimilated unmarried couples into the matrimonial regime on the basis that failure to marry cannot be taken as an affirmative rejection of that regime.

A couple of stories can be told about these judgments. One recounts that in each case, the majority held people to their choices. By contrast, the minority determined that, all things considered, the individuals were not making choices to which they should be held. This story evokes an important theme in relational theory, that is, the rejection of an atomistic liberal view of subjects as choosing agents in favour of recognition that selves are embedded in their context and relationships and do not necessarily choose freely.

Another story, arguably more persuasive, can also be told. This story too draws on relational theory, but in another way. In this version, the majority and minority positions are much closer than the first story depicts. The second story recounts that the majority and minority reasons testify to common acceptance of relational theory's descriptive premise, contextual methodology, and a number of its normative commitments. All the judges acknowledged that people's contexts and relationships strongly influence their choices. Despite recognition of such influence, all judges agreed that it is necessary to chalk out some scope for individual choice. Disagreements arose at the point where the facts were subjected to more or less shared principles.

My ambition in this chapter is to adjudicate between these two stories, reflecting on the implications for family law and relational theory. I contend that the disagreement in the cases is best seen as a dispute internal to a group of contextualist judges. This suggests the limits of relational theory in analysing specific examples. Once one identifies the context of interdependent relationships, one must eventually decide in each case where to draw the line between recognition of the influence of social context and deference to human agency.

Relational theory traditionally understands its mission as countering abstract liberal approaches to political and legal analysis that fail to focus on relationships. But the traditional way of framing relational theory's 'relational inquiry' or 'relational approach' ill serves it where all sides to a dispute do attend to relationships and adopt a contextual methodology. Relational theorists ought to focus on their normative commitments and try to work them out more precisely, balancing competing interests of protection and autonomy. This chapter's demonstration of methodological convergence, contrasted with some normative divergence, serves as a reminder of the limits of the descriptive and methodological elements of relational theory, hinting that it should wear its normative commitments more boldly. Indeed, it appears that the imperative for relational theorists to articulate their normative commitments is strongest where a contextual methodology is already present.

Two Contracts, a Nonfeasance, and an Uproar

Miglin v. Miglin (2003) concerns a separation agreement. Eric and Linda Miglin were married for some fifteen years. On separation, they negotiated a lengthy separation agreement that, among other things, divided their assets, secured child support to Ms Miglin, and waived each party's statutory right to spousal support under the Divorce Act (1985). Five years after the divorce, Ms Miglin nonetheless applied for spousal support. At that time, her assets totalled some three-quarters of a million dollars. The Divorce Act requires a court making an order for spousal support to 'take into consideration' any 'agreement or arrangement relating to support of either spouse' (s. 15.2(4)(c)). It was a point of controversy exactly what it means for a court to take such agreements into consideration. The Supreme Court's rusty leading authority, *Pelech v. Pelech* (1987), enjoined judges to enforce waivers of support strictly. Since its release, however, commentators had savaged the case and judges had not followed it consistently. In this climate of juridical uncertainty, Ms Miglin's challenge of her waiver of spousal support succeeded at trial and withstood appeal. The Supreme Court reversed. Bastarache and Arbour JJ., writing for a majority of seven, identified certainty, finality, and autonomy among the Divorce Act's general objectives. They declared that, when an agreement was unimpeachably negotiated and complied substantially with those objectives, it was presumptively dispositive. In the majority's view, such an approach left the parties room 'to apply their own values and pursue their own objectives in reaching a settlement.' It ensured spouses the 'autonomy to organize their lives as they see fit and to pursue their own sense of what is mutually acceptable in their individual circumstances' (*Miglin* 2003, para. 55). In their dissent, LeBel and Deschamps JJ. emphasized the high emotions and vulnerability of parties negotiating separation agreements and the need to ensure that agreements are objectively fair when evaluated by the legislative standards for judicial orders of support.

Hartshorne v. Hartshorne (2004) tested the mettle of a prenuptial agreement. A pair of lawyers, Robert and Kathleen Hartshorne, cohabited for four years, had a child together, and finally married. It was a second marriage for both. On the demise of his first marriage, Mr Hartshorne had surrendered considerable assets by virtue of British Columbia's statutory presumption that matrimonial property be shared equally. On the threshold of the second marriage, he held assets valued at $1.6 million and she, having entered the legal profession a decade behind him, dragged substantial debts. Before they married, Mr Hartshorne expressed an aversion to risking a second division of property. He drafted an agreement that departed from the default regime, stipulating that he and his wife would be separate as to property. This proposed agreement granted Ms Hartshorne a 3 per cent interest in the family home for each year the parties were married, up to a maximum of 49 per cent. Ms Hartshorne received independent legal advice that the proposed agreement was unenforceable; her lawyer assessed it as 'unfair' in the sense of applicable provincial legislation (Family Relations Act 1996, s. 65(1)). On their wedding day, both of them signed the agreement. Throughout their marriage, Mr Hartshorne worked in his law firm and Ms Hartshorne was a full-time homemaker and mother. When the marriage ended nearly a decade later, Ms Hartshorne argued that the marriage agreement was unfair and should be overridden. She prevailed at trial and on appeal, but the Supreme Court allowed Mr Hartshorne's appeal. The agreement failed to strike the majority as 'unfair' in the statutory sense. In any case, wrote Bastarache J., having received legal advice that the contract was unfair, Ms Hartshorne should not have signed it did she wish not to be bound. Deschamps J., writing a dissent with which two colleagues concurred, articulated her understanding of a legislative intention 'that only fair agreements be upheld.' In her view, 'fairness' should be taken as an internal reference to the legislation's default regime, rather than a more flexible, external reference to the parties' sense of fairness. For the dissenting judges, the consequences flowing from the decision to marry included all the pecuniary responsibilities of the default regime (*Hartshorne* 2004, paras. 69, 91).

Nova Scotia (A.G.) v. Walsh (2002) assessed the constitutionality of the legal consequences of unmarried cohabitation. Susan Walsh and Wayne Bona lived together for a decade. When they parted ways, Ms Walsh challenged Nova Scotia's matrimonial property legislation under the equality guarantee in Section 15 of the Canadian Charter of Rights and Freedoms. Her complaint targeted the restriction of the presumption of equal division of property to married couples. She contended that this restriction discriminated against her, as someone who had cohabited but not married, on the basis of marital status. The high card in her hand was the Supreme Court of Canada's decision in *Miron v. Trudel* (1995). That judgment had invalidated as discriminatory distinctions between married and unmarried couples in insurance legislation. Ms Walsh lost at trial but won on appeal. The provincial appellate court applied *Miron* to hold that denying unmarried cohabiting couples the presumption of equal property division violated their essential human dignity. In the Court of Appeal's view, the regime's restricted application indicated that the legislature regarded unmarried relationships as inferior to marriages. Eight judges of the Supreme Court of Canada reversed. Bastarache J.'s reasons for the majority revealed choice to be trumps. Where legislation drastically altered the legal obligations of partners inter se, 'choice must be paramount.' In his view, many people in circumstances similar to those of Ms Walsh and Mr Bona had chosen to avoid marriage and its legal consequences. Furthermore, despite functional similarities between married and unmarried couples, significant heterogeneity characterized the latter group (*Walsh* 2002, paras. 43, 39). In her dissent, L'Heureux-Dubé J. emphasized the historical disadvantage of unmarried couples, their functional similarity to married couples, and their absence of effective choice.

Scholarly responses to these judgments typically expressed shock. *Miglin* came to one prominent commentator as a deep 'surprise' (Rogerson 2003). *Walsh* was characterized as a 'stunning reversal' (Mitchell 2003, 123), a development 'starkly at odds with decades of legislative initiatives and Supreme Court of Canada rulings anchored in a functional approach to family relationships' (Rogerson 2003, 274; Lessard 2006). The judgments were criticized for departing from prior jurisprudence (Mitchell 2003, 125; Rogerson 2003, 274; *Miglin* 2003, paras. 204, 207, LeBel J., dissenting)[1] and for economically disadvantaging women who were already vulnerable (*Hartshorne* 2004, para. 91, Deschamps J., dissenting; Shaffer 2004a, 433–5). Attention to the women's disadvantage typically comported a procedural branch (contracting processes disadvantage women particularly) and a substantive branch (contracts inappropriately 'privatize' family law by supplanting public norms) (*Hartshorne* 2004, paras. 78–82, Deschamps J., dissenting; Shaffer 2004b, 289; see also Bryan 1999; Singer 1992). One other form of argument is present in the literature, framed in the familiar terms of relational theory and its opposition to abstract liberal subjects.

Atomistic Liberals Confront Relational Theorists?

Relational theory opposes itself to what it designates as the liberal conception of the subject. According to relational theory, liberals conceive of the subject as an autonomous, rational agent that selects its relationships and obligations through the instruments of private property and contract. Liberals, according to this view, regard choosing as the 'pre-eminent human deed' (Brown and Halley 2002, 17), fostering a vision of the person as a 'choosing machine' (Douglas and Ney 1998, 184). In contrast, relational theorists understand that subjects are socially constituted, embedded in their contexts, their selfhood and agency formed by thick relationships with others.

The other form of criticism of the majority judgments combines political theory and sociology. It is akin to relational theory's descriptive premise and contextual methodology. On the descriptive, theoretical side, it holds that these three judgments rested on crude, simplistic, or abstracted conceptions of autonomy and choice (Rogerson 2003, 299–300, 323; Shaffer 2004a, 431; 2004b, 284–7).[2] The judgments marked the return to family law of the 'liberal individual unfettered by gender or familial ideology' (Boyd and Young 2004, 567). On the sociological side, the charge is levied that the majority judges pursued ideological or normative concerns at the expense of sociological accuracy. It protests the enforcement of explicit formal agreements on the basis that they inaccurately reflect the 'true' normativity of cohabitation relationships (Rogerson 2003, 298–300; Shaffer 2004b, 287). Together these strands can be regarded as the liberal abstraction thesis, which convokes what I shall call the enforcement and antienforcement camps. These terms are preferable to intervention versus non-intervention, which would fail to recognize that the enforcement of contracts depends on state institutional structures. It would be premature to identify the enforcement camp with liberalism and the antienforcement camp with relational theory. The immediate inquiry is whether it is appropriate to view the antienforcement position as congenial to relational theory.

The views of the enforcement and antienforcement camps are extreme. It should be admitted, nevertheless, that a glance at the judgments suggests that these positions have analytic purchase. The presence of divisions in the three cases and the consistency of the judges' membership in one or the other of two groups – five resolute judges stood in the majority in all three cases – hint further at the existence of starkly divided camps within the Court. Unmodified references to choice and autonomy pepper the majority judgments, and those judges did not refer to the resources within the liberal tradition that might have thickened their core notion of autonomy. It seems fair to hypothesize that the majority reasons constitute a thin, atomistic subject disengaged from its relationships. The majority's references to autonomy do not appear to take into account theoretical work on relational autonomy as a capability that can be exercised only when enabled by relationships. It is possible to conjecture, for the sake of argument, that the references to autonomy in *Miglin* and to choice in *Walsh* derive from a liberal universe of negotiated transactions in which, even in matters of the heart, individuals pursue their own self-interest without regard for those with whom they bargain. Indeed, this reading owes less to liberalism than to libertarianism. Its exemplar par excellence is perhaps the majority's enjoinment in *Miglin*: 'Parties must take responsibility for the contract they execute as well as for their own lives' (2003, para. 91).

As for the dissenting judges, they appeared acutely sensitive to the embedded nature of individual subjects, alert to the deep influence exercised on women by their more potent male partners. They were concerned with achieving substantively fair responses to states of inequality irrespective of the legal matrix in which they arise. A reluctance to enforce explicit contractual ordering in family matters was grounded on concerns with the bargaining process and the substantive outcomes. As for process, the individuals whom the dissenting judges in *Miglin* and *Hartshorne* would have released from their written agreements had the benefit of independent legal advice. The one whose contracting process was hastier was herself a lawyer. The other's negotiation process stretched over fifteen months and featured a costly cast of professionals. Antienforcement dissatisfaction with these circumstances hints that satisfactory bargaining conditions between a breadwinner and a homemaker will rarely obtain.[3]

As for substance, under the agreements the two women had not insignificant assets. The hesitation to enforce may focus less on each claimant's particular circumstances than on the general impropriety of contracting out of the default regime. It is the dissent in *Hartshorne* that comes closest to a judicial denial of the normative acceptability of private ordering in departure from public norms. In the view of the dissenting judges, the legislation does not entitle one party to stipulate that he or she will receive more than a fair share of the total family wealth. Rather, it permits the parties to determine which assets (cottage versus ski chalet?) each will take in executing the default division (2004, para. 79). Though the legislative invocation of 'fairness' appears to refer to something external to the act, for the dissent the referent of 'fairness' was simply the substance of the default regime. This interpretation largely guts the statute's enablement of private ordering.

In family matters today, few are likely to adopt a hard libertarian approach along the lines of full enforcement of all contracts. Too much is known about contracting failures and exploitation (Trebilcock and Keshvani 1991, 550). It is thus possible to bracket rather than engage with the libertarian reading of the majority texts. As for the extreme reading of the antienforcement texts as virtually vacating a role for contract, the gestures in this direction warrant further comment. The strong antienforcement arguments potentially undermine political efforts within feminism.

The antienforcement camp relies on a handful of dichotomies: strong/weak; explicit/implicit; independent/dependent; voluntary/involuntary; market/family; reason/emotion. Such dichotomies are not only a way of thinking, but also the medium through which people experience their lives (Olsen 1983, 1561). The dissenting judicial performances map gender onto these dichotomies, rendering explicit what was implicit, linking feminine subjects with the weaker element of each pair. While the intention is to highlight empirical disadvantage, the unintended effect is to cement in legal discourse the structural arrangement in which female subjects are inferior to male subjects (Halley 2006). Specifically, the strongest judicial and scholarly articulations from the antienforcement camp problematically intertwine exaggerated discursive constitutions of women as emotional and as economically dependent on their male partners.

The antienforcement camp constructs the women as emotional. In his dissent in *Miglin*, LeBel J. quoted Ms Miglin's own account of the negotiation period as 'a very confusing and emotional time' and cautioned about the effects of the 'emotional upheaval and the pressures.' In his view, even where, as in the Miglins' case, the parties negotiate over a lengthy period, advised by independent counsel, the parties' emotional vulnerabilities affect the separation agreement in subtle ways quantifiable only with difficulty (2003, para. 244; see also Shaffer 2004a, 433; 2004b, 265). It is not that the conditions in which spouses negotiate domestic contracts are a purely private concern (Herring 2005). But there are potential insidious effects of producing legal subjects whose degree of emotion undermines their capacity to consent.

A rapidly expanding literature, ranging from philosophy to neurology and including law, aims to deconstruct the dichotomy between (masculine) reason and (feminine) emotion. It seeks to underscore the cognitive value of emotions, elucidating emotion's role as a component of reason (e.g., Meyers 1997a; Nussbaum 1999, 72–7; Nussbaum 2001; Damasio 1994; Evans and Cruse 2004; Ball 2005). Kathryn Abrams argues that 'earlier dichotomous characterizations of reason and emotion' as the provinces, respectively, of men and of women now seem 'reductive and outdated' (2005, 334). Claims that a woman should be released from her undertakings on the basis that she was 'emotional' *and therefore irrational* undercut such investigative scholarship and its progressive potential. Indeed, the claim that women should be released from their agreements on this basis tacitly ratifies the contestable patriarchal construction of men as rational and women as emotional. It

implies that the only conduct that can be taken seriously in the juridical sphere, and to which autonomy can be ascribed, is unemotional.
Such an implication stands in direct opposition to relational theorists'
efforts to reconceive autonomy in embodied, relational terms (Mackenzie and Stoljar 2000a; Nedelsky 1989). Asserting the unenforceability of
contracts concluded by emotional women reinforces the ideal that
women, to contract effectively, should strive to be unemotional and
more like men. On the contrary, the strategic objective must surely be
to foster a state of affairs in which there is space for all subjects, irrespective of their gender, to be simultaneously emotional and reasonable, emotional and autonomous. The presence of emotion should not
lightly be coded as indicative of the absence of agency and thus of
consent.[4]

Is it possible that the majority judges sensed that too ready a judicial
recognition of women's emotion as vitiating their capacity to make decisions might have unintended consequences? Once family law leans far
towards regarding the decision making of emotional women as unreli-
able, it is unclear that only the woman herself would be able to raise the
point, and at strictly her strategic convenience. Perhaps the majority
judges shrank from the prospect of counsel for non-custodial fathers
citing *Miglin* and *Hartshorne*, had the dissenters' approach prevailed,
when contesting decisions regarding their children's medical treatment
or education on the basis that the custodial mothers who made those
decisions were 'emotional.' A view of law's power as 'more limited and
more contingent' can make instrumental revisions of legal rules to
advance 'an emotionally infused perspective' appear a 'less decisive or
compelling normative move' (Abrams 2005, 335).

The antienforcement camp's other problematic tendency is the exag-
geration of women's economic dependence and the domination it
implies. It is true that Ms Miglin and Ms Hartshorne would have been
better off materially had they won, and concerns for the judgments' distributive effects are not without legitimacy. The economic disadvantage
should, however, be interrogated rather than assumed, and the parties'
privation should not be exaggerated. Ms Miglin's assets approximated
$750,000; Ms Hartshorne had her share of the matrimonial home and,
by the time of the legal proceedings, had found work as a lawyer.
Indeed, the exceptional extent of the assets in *Miglin* and *Hartshorne* –
perhaps unstartling, given the costs of litigating to the Supreme Court
– makes it perilous to predict the impact on women nearer the poverty
line. It is pertinent that the majority signal their view that *Miglin*'s thrust

is not necessarily the enforcement of waivers of support where a party is significantly more vulnerable than was Ms Miglin. Noting that during the early years of the marriage she earned a university degree, the majority judges specified in a telling caveat that they need not determine whether the Miglins' separation agreement would have survived a challenge on facts closer to those in *Moge v. Moge* (1992; *Miglin* 2003, para. 98). In that case, the wife, still dependent on the husband years after the marriage, had merely a grade seven education from Poland. Given the Miglins' and Hartshornes' relative wealth, it is not clear, as some observers fear, that the judgments effectively repudiate the 'new notion of substantive justice within marriage' (Leckey 2002c, 38) previously identifiable.

The construction of Kathleen Hartshorne as hapless victim is particularly troubling. At the time of the wedding, the Hartshornes had a toddler and Mr Hartshorne had been supporting Ms Hartshorne for close to two years. Without explaining why, the dissenting judges expressed concern that Ms Hartshorne had been out of the workforce and dependent on Mr Hartshorne for that time, and that during the eight years since her call to the Bar, she had worked as a lawyer only in Mr Hartshorne's firm. 'The agreement,' Deschamps J. wrote, 'was concluded under pressure with the wedding fast approaching' (2004, para. 90; see also Boyd and Young 2004, 566). 'These facts made Mrs. Hartshorne emotionally and economically dependent upon Mr. Hartshorne' (Shaffer 2004b, 284). The intense concern about the timing of the wedding and the fact of the child intimate, in doubtless unintended ways, that Ms Hartshorne was a fallen woman whose redemption depended on securing marriage to the father of her child. Critics accept that the threat of calling off the wedding was a card in Mr Hartshorne's hand alone. Yet this presumption that a cancelled wedding would have harmed Ms Hartshorne more grievously than Mr Hartshorne resonates more of *Pride and Prejudice* than of contemporary feminism. In addition, for the dissenting judges, Ms Hartshorne's remaining at home for the rest of the marriage caring for the couple's children 'further illustrates the power dynamics' (2004, para. 90). The assumption that Ms Hartshorne cannot really have consented to staying at home, combined with the view of full-time homemaking as self-evidently a badge of exploitation, is worrisome (compare Yuracko 2003, 88–9). The decision to raise children does not per se indicate exploitation and is not conclusive evidence as to the power dynamics within the couple.[5] Also problematic is the suggestion that Ms Hartshorne had ceased operating as an informed economic agent. One commentator queries whether Ms Hartshorne, herself a lawyer, 'actually turned her mind' to the economic consequences of waiving her property entitlement (McLeod 2004, 15). Observe the inconsistency between some of the criticisms: most commentators agree that Ms Hartshorne's degree of emotion was high, yet surely the basis for that elevated emotion is precisely that she had turned her mind to the draft contract's economic upshot. In decidedly unattractive ways, these criticisms constitute women as permanent victims with impaired agency.

Fixing women on the losing side of these dichotomies has a couple of effects. As a methodological matter, the adoption of a fixed, gendered distribution of power departs – ironically, for interventions motivated by feminist concerns – from relational theory's contextual and particularistic approach. What vanishes is what Foucault has called the 'strictly relational character of power relationships' and the consciousness of power not as something acquired and held but as dynamic and changeable (1990a, 94–5). Recall that in *Murdoch v. Murdoch* (1973) it was a particularistic, contextual aesthetic that opened Laskin J.'s eyes to the possibility of the wife's performing her husband's role. When the dissenting judges read the fact of full-time homemaking as evidence of domination, they are not drawing a highly context-specific inference about Ms Hartshorne, but reinforcing stereotypes. It is striking how rapidly an ostensibly contextual approach manifests the imprint of presumptions and prior models.[6]

More substantively, the antienforcement position pays insufficient attention to the detrimental effects of constituting women as subjects who cannot make agreements they are expected to uphold. The law traditionally recognizes that children are not to be held to disadvantageous contracts. But it marks a significant regression for feminism to undermine married women's emancipation by arguing that educated women, even on receipt of independent legal advice, are not presumptively bound by their agreements. Indeed, to make the point tendentiously, was the objection to the married woman's civil incapacity that the woman herself lacked power to make her own legally binding decisions or, rather, that power over the woman was entrusted to her husband rather than to the benevolent legislature?

Neither the libertarian enforcement position nor the strong antienforcement position can be comfortably adopted. In any event, the antienforcement position drawn from the dissents and some of the commentary is too crude to be regarded as compatible with relational theory. It is this characteristic that necessitated the interrogation point in this part's heading. It is not self-evident that the enforcement and antienforcement camps map, respectively, onto groups of atomistic liberals and relational theorists.

What is relational theory's stance towards contractual ordering in the family setting? Relational theory's opposition to the liberal legal emphasis on contract leads to caution against enforcement of contract in matters of thick relationship. The idea is that the obligations of relational ties exceed the set of strictly voluntary undertakings assumed by contract. Yet despite the shared vocabulary of context and deep relationship, relational theory's stance vis-à-vis the antienforcement camp is best regarded as ambivalent. Relational theorists emphasize the necessary role of relationships in making autonomy possible. They also oppose, however, the idea – implied too strenuously by the antienforcement camp – that women are simply stuck within relationships and social contexts. Relational theorists reject the idea that women are unable to take a critical distance and choose different lives and relationships for themselves. Motivated by the political necessity of revising oppressive identities and roles, relational feminists distance themselves from strands of communitarianism (Goodin 1996). It is on this basis that they defend their commitment to at least a revised version of autonomy. The central concern is 'freeing women to shape our own lives, to define who we (each) are, rather than accepting the definition given to us by others (men and male-dominated society, in particular)' (Nedelsky 1989, 8–9; also Friedman 2005, 151).

Relational theory's position regarding contract must be more complicated than that of the antienforcement camp. Its normative commitments to relational autonomy and to diversity of family forms are sometimes served by the flexibility in structuring families that contract can facilitate. For those for whom 'traditional' family models are unsatisfactory, the development of alternatives may depend on robust recognition of the exercise of agency through private ordering (see Reece 2003, 103–5). Surrogate motherhood contracts come to mind, as do agreements delineating the relationship between a prospective mother, her lesbian partner, and a sperm donor. It is contract that may liberate parties from the constraints of a default regime structured around the biological parenthood of 'natural' mothers and fathers (for example, Quebec's rules relating to a 'parental project': arts. 538ff. C.C.Q.; see also Gavigan 2000). In reference to the concerns raised by emotion, such agreements are predicated on the legitimacy of formal explicit ordering on acutely emotional turf. In parenting matters, parties contract specifically because emotions will be high and they might not subsequently reach the same agreement. Contracts seek to project present intentions forward into time, allowing the parties scope to plan their lives. Admittedly, the extent to which strict enforcement of such contracts is appropriate may vary. Commentators who might permit a birth mother to renege on a surrogacy contract or prior consent to adoption as the upshot of a relational analysis (Minow and Shanley 1996, 12) might reasonably favour more stringent enforcement of a sperm donor's waiver of paternal rights where the autonomy of two lesbians to raise their child free from male intervention is at stake (Arnup and Boyd 1995, 81–93). Relational theory objects that the formal character of contractual ordering seems at odds with the contextual methodology of relational theory and its description of subjects embedded in relations that exceed their choosing; but at times relational autonomy's focus on the choice to form and sustain constructive relationships depends on contract.

A further complication, and a further reason that the extreme antienforcement position sketched above should not be viewed as the one of relational theory, is that resisting enforcement of contracts ratifies, at least by implication, the existing default regime's distribution. Condemnation of a contractual derogation slides, by implication, into an endorsement of the standard regime. In doing so it forfeits relational theory's customary critical distance and attention to the social background conditions necessary for autonomy. When the future projection of present intentions produces severe material disadvantages for one of the contracting parties, it is appropriate to ask questions. But normative commitments within relational theory – to diverse forms of relationship, to critical examination of background conditions, and indeed to autonomy – entail a rejection of the extreme antienforcement position as incompatible with the rich mix of relational theory's resources.

Before I reread the cases with relational theory in hand, it is helpful to review recent scholarly interventions concerning structure and agency. The questions confronting the Supreme Court in the three cases evoke ancient philosophical debates over determinism and will. More contemporary language would refer to structure and agency. Unresolved tensions in recent interventions in this debate will inform the more moderate account of the judgments that follows.

Debating Structure and Agency

Theorists have proposed various dialectics to resolve the supposed tension between structure and agency. Some take the former as enabling the latter and regard structure as itself constituted by social practices (Frazer and Lacey 1993, 174–8; also Hirschmann 2003, 99; Reece 2003, ch. 2). Recent readings of Foucault seek to combine the two. The starting point is the quandary of the relation between Foucault's earlier and later work. A number of scholars read Foucault's earlier archaeological and genealogical works as implying that the subject is 'nothing more than the effect of discourse and power' (Allen 2000, 115). They allege that Foucault's supposed eradication of the subject commits him to denying the possibility of moral or political agency. It follows, for these critics, that subjects have no capacity for reflection on or resistance to the forces operating on them. Such forces wholly determine the subject.

In a recent essay, Amy Allen seeks to combine agency and structure. She contends that Foucault's major project was not the eradication of the subject's agency. Rather, it was an account of the historically contingent way that subjects come to be constituted and to exercise a degree of agency. For Foucault, the subject is an effect of discourse and power, but not *merely* such an effect. Allen argues that her reading of Foucault has the potential to open up new ways of approaching the structure/agency problem: 'Far from coming down on the structure side of this divide, Foucault's work actually provides some of the theoretical and conceptual resources necessary for working out the interrelationship between structure and agency' (ibid., 120–2, 128). As David Weberman, another sympathetic reader of Foucault, puts it, 'subjectivity is a kind of hybrid resulting from both the productive effects of social power *and* self-determination ... as well as their interaction.' The subject is 'embedded in and always partly constituted by social power' (2000, 261, 263). It is Foucault's observation of the omnipresence of power that leads his critics to think that he implies total determinism. But Allen and Weberman argue that his position does not entail total determinism: the subject is constituted but not determined. Moreover, the subject's constitution in this way is the 'very precondition of its agency' (Butler 1995a, 46). It is, however, the case that there is no authentic subject untainted by relations of power; 'there is no power-free self or subject to which we might return' (Weberman 2000, 264).

Tackling the agency/structure debate, Kwame Appiah observes that when debates suppose an opposition between agency and structure, they are competing 'for the same causal space.' Insisting on agency within the discourse of structure – that is, seeing the two as sharing the same space – is changing the subject. Appiah proposes giving up viewing structure and agency as competing in this way. The logic of structure (which yields causes for action) and the logic of agency (which yields reasons for action) belong, he argues, to two distinct standpoints. Which standpoint people adopt in particular circumstances depends on their interests and purposes. Whether one pays attention to causes or reasons depends on the relevant practical purposes. In particular situations, the answer given will depend on the constitutive interests underlying the story being told: 'If we're interested in the conditions that make people act a certain way ... we tell one narrative ... If we're interested in retribution and blame, we tell another.' Where one seeks to understand people as intentional systems, one projects rationality onto them, despite awareness that people are never fully rational. It is what he calls an as-if exercise, operation by hypothesis. One conclusion Appiah draws from assigning agency and structure to distinct conceptual spaces is that positing that an agent had partial autonomy incoherently combines the two. Talk of partial autonomy is 'an ill-fated attempt to split the difference between two standpoints: one in which I have autonomy and one in which I do not' (2005, 56, 59, 60). Similarly incoherent, to Appiah, is the implication of the discourse of partial autonomy that 'full' autonomy is even conceptually possible (ibid., 52).

What can be taken for present purposes from Appiah's two standpoints and the readings of Foucault? One element of Appiah's account is that, when it comes time to attribute responsibility, agents should be regarded as if they are rational and autonomous. An analysis of the environmental factors that cause an agent to act in a certain way is conceptually distinct from an analysis of that agent's responsibility for his action. Such an implication would seem to militate for enforcement of domestic contracts: although socio-economic and relational factors might cause an agent to conclude a non-optimal or detrimental contract, a judge would operate as if the parties were rational and autonomous. As a legal matter, however, legislative fiat debars such a blunt application of Appiah's analysis. The Divorce Act at issue in *Miglin* does not dictate that agreements supplant the legislative support obligation; they are only a consideration. The Family Relations Act in

Hartshorne permits judges to deviate from agreements that are 'unfair.' The philosophical accounts obviously differ considerably, but one point may be productively regarded as common to both: agency is never perfect. Indeed, perfection and imperfection are wrong ways of thinking about it. The effect is that one does not wait for evidence of full rational agency before attributing responsibility. As for Foucault, the upshot is that there is no power-free subject to which to return. As the poet Joel Lane puts it, 'there's no place / called freedom' (1994). In *Miglin* and *Hartshorne*, all the contracting parties are partly constituted by power relations, discourse, and their social relations. Given the legislative injunctions against blind enforcement of contracts, the question is not whether the parties were free of influence, but whether the influence in the particular cases surpasses a threshold at which less than full enforcement is warranted. As for *Walsh*, the implication is that fully free choice is something of a chimera. The notion that no subject exercises choice fully free from power relations will illuminate my reading below of the majority and dissenting reasons. It is time now to take up the task of delineating a more moderate reading of the judgments, one more consistent with the richness of relational theory.

Contextual Subjects on Relationships' End

Deploying elements of relational theory, the majority reasons in all three cases show awareness of the contextual embeddedness of their subjects. I shall refer both to the reasons and to interpretations of them in subsequent cases.[7]

The challenged agreements in *Miglin* and *Hartshorne* differ in two structural respects. The first is the kind of agreement, itself a function of when it was concluded. Contract's usual function is to structure a relationship and channel parties' expectations forward in time. The Miglins' contract was a separation agreement, concluded near the dissolution of their marriage. A separation agreement alters rights and obligations that would otherwise obtain. The future into which it attempted to project Eric and Linda Miglin's intentions was their postmarital life, during which they would continue to share in the raising of their children. Under the test developed in *Miglin*, the question is how well life since separation has lined up with the expectations on concluding that agreement. In contrast, the Hartshornes' agreement was a prenuptial or marriage contract. The future into which a prenuptial agreement attempts to vault the parties' intentions is their married life.

The issue is how well the parties predicted what would happen during their marriage. Ex ante contracting attempts to nip support or property obligations in the bud by pre-empting sharing or dependence.

The second crucial difference is the kind of entitlement waived in the two agreements. When spouses divorce, settlement of their affairs is viewed globally, taking into account spousal support obligations and division of property. Yet division of property and spousal support rest on different bases. Equal division of matrimonial property is typically a presumption from which the trial judge may depart on the basis of enumerated exceptional factors. The entitlement to property division arises from the fact of marriage rather than from more specific facts. By contrast, entitlement to spousal support must be established in each case. Pertinent factors include the parties' needs and means and their respective contributions during the relationship, specifically whether one spouse is owed compensation for economic hardship wrought by the marriage or its termination. Application of these factors to particular parties is a highly fact-specific exercise, 'a contest between stories' (Leckey 2002c, 2). In both *Miglin* and *Hartshorne*, the primary controversy concerned just one kind of entitlement. Thus while the Miglins' comprehensive separation agreement divided their assets, the most controversial point was Ms Miglin's waiver of claims to spousal support. Taken at face value, her waiver essentially declared that she was not in need and was not economically disadvantaged by the years of marriage. Conversely, the Hartshornes' agreement left intact a possible entitlement to spousal support. Their agreement's controversial feature was the deviation from the presumption of equal property division. This deviation inscribed an intention that Ms Hartshorne would not, during the marriage, contribute to the increase of her husband's assets. It is time to turn now to explicit contracting ex post.

In *Miglin*, the majority and minority reasons converged on the descriptive claim of subjects as embedded, the methodology of contextualism, and normatively, the need to recognize the autonomy to craft intimate relationships on one's own model.

The *Pelech* trilogy forms the jurisprudential background to judicial assessment of contracting after marriage. Two decades ago, that trilogy imposed a change-based test with a high threshold for judicial overrides of separation agreements. The threshold set was a radical and unforeseen change that is causally connected to the marriage. The trilogy privileged the optimistic (if not deluded) idea that divorcing parties should seek a 'clean break.' In *Miglin*, the majority judges held that the trilogy's test was too rigid. *Pelech*'s singular emphasis on a clean break and self-sufficiency was inconsistent with models of spousal support developed in subsequent case law and with the variety of competing objectives in the legislation (*Miglin* 2003, para. 40). One might regard the change from *Pelech* to *Miglin* as shifting the pointer between structure and agency or autonomy. Yet what is apparent in *Miglin* and the subsequent cases is not only a bit more structure and a little less autonomy, but also a richer sense of autonomy, one consistent with the teachings of relational theory.

When a spouse applies for spousal support in a way inconsistent with a prior agreement, the approach in *Miglin* requires contextual assessment of all the circumstances. The majority and minority judges agreed on the appropriateness of such a methodology of contextualism, using interchangeable and indistinguishable wording (*Miglin* 2003, para. 46, Bastarache and Arbour JJ.; cf. para. 162, LeBel J.). Such agreement did not, of course, prevent the dissenting judges from arguing that the majority had failed its standard of contextualism, but neither should that agreement be overlooked. The majority structured a two-step investigation. Step one looks at the time of the separation agreement's formation. Step two turns to the time of the application for support.

At the first stage, the court should examine the circumstances in which the agreement was negotiated and executed to determine whether there is any reason to discount it. The majority did not subscribe to the liberal, atomistic view sketched earlier. Those judges were acutely conscious of the context of marital negotiations, 'a time of intense personal and emotional turmoil.' 'Unlike emotionally neutral economic actors negotiating in the commercial context,' wrote Bastarache and Arbour JJ., 'divorcing couples inevitably bring to the table a host of emotions and concerns that do not obviously accord with the making of rational economic decisions' (*Miglin* 2003, para. 74).[8] LeBel J.'s discussion of the circumstances of negotiation explicitly noticed factors that might disadvantage women vis-à-vis their male partners (ibid., paras. 214, 215), but was otherwise similar to that of the majority. The disagreement hinted less at a clash between rival camps than at a matter of emphasis. The majority did not ascribe an irrebuttable autonomy to the spouses by virtue of their rational personhood. They were, however, unwilling to place the burden of proof on the party who wished to enforce an agreement. Though cognizant of the contextual constraints on contracting spouses, they warned against presuming an imbalance of power. Bastarache and Arbour JJ. noted that recognition of the emotional stress of separation or divorce does not entail a presumption that parties are incapable of assenting to a binding agreement. They stated further that where a party is vulnerable, the presence of counsel or other professionals may effectively compensate for that condition.

On the facts of *Miglin*, the majority judges found nothing to indicate that the circumstances surrounding the negotiation and execution of the Miglins' agreement were 'fraught with vulnerabilities' (ibid., para. 22). The majority referred to the length of negotiations and the professional legal and financial advice received by Ms Miglin. By contrast, the minority sensed that there might be something in Ms Miglin's reports of her emotional upheaval (ibid., para. 244). Critics of the majority judgment who view Ms Miglin as having been highly vulnerable during the negotiations may worry that the failure to find her negotiation process problematic has shut the door to findings of vulnerability in other situations. The judgment appears not to have had exclusively such an effect.[9] Judges have not consistently read *Miglin* as dictating that the presence of legal counsel per se precludes a finding of vulnerability (*Kelly* 2004, para. 27).

Under the majority's approach, a judge examines the substance of an agreement as it was at the time of formation. The appropriate inquiry is whether the agreement takes into account the factors and objectives listed in the Divorce Act, thus reflecting 'an equitable sharing of the economic consequences of marriage and its breakdown' (*Miglin* 2003, para. 84). The majority identified the legislation's objectives as including finality, certainty, and autonomy. Their threshold for less than full enforcement was an agreement's failure to comply substantially with the legislative objectives. It is the references to autonomy that most fuel the atomistic liberal reading of the judgment. What exactly did the majority justices mean by autonomy? They stated that the parties had a large amount of discretion in establishing their own priorities and goals (ibid., para. 84). The autonomy to which the majority judges referred was the capacity of the couple to resolve their differences in accordance with their own values and understanding of their relationship. It was, consistent with the word's literal meaning, the idea of being 'governed by one's own law' (Nedelsky 1989, 10). Bastarache and Arbour JJ. demonstrated this sense of autonomy when speaking of the 'parties' right to decide for themselves what constitutes for them, in the circumstances of their marriage, mutually acceptable equitable sharing' (*Miglin* 2003, para. 73; also paras. 55, 66). As Piché J. has put it since,

'Ce qui est "juste" ne dépend donc pas seulement de la situation objective des parties, mais également de leurs idées, de leur mariage et de sa
dissolution de même que de leurs attentes et aspirations pour l'avenir'
(*R.L. v. D.L.* 2004, para. 12). As the majority judges conceived it, this
autonomy opposed not the individual spouses towards each other, but
rather the couple towards the community's norms. The majority judges
regarded their conception of autonomy for the couple as consistent
with their prior interpretation of the Divorce Act as recognizing the
'diverse dynamics of the many unique marital relationships' (*Bracklow*
1999, para. 35, quoted in *Miglin* 2003, para. 55). The idea that the
meaning of justice is to be worked out in a particular context is consistent with relational theory's contextual methodology.

In testimony to the narrowness of the gap separating the two groups
of judges, the dissenting judges concurred with their colleagues on the
necessity of space for the parties to structure their own relationship.
While the dissent would have tested the fairness of agreements by an
objective measure, it nonetheless contemplated a 'generous ambit'
within which reasonable disagreement would be possible. LeBel J. has-
tened to insist that his approach 'does not deny individuals the autonomy to organize their lives as they see fit,' nor did it prevent them from
bringing to negotiations their own concerns, desires, and objectives. His
approach 'accords parties a considerable degree of flexibility in negotiating arrangements that reflect their particular priorities' (*Miglin* 2003,
para. 235; also para. 241). The parties' 'own attempts to achieve the
objectives codified ... in the context of their unique situation should not
lightly be disregarded' (ibid., para. 232). Where, as here, both majority
and minority agreed on consent and the possibility of and need for the
parties to exercise autonomy, the points of disagreement were relatively
small.

A further point about the majority's conception of autonomy merits
mention. One of relational theory's insights is that autonomy is a capacity that can be measured, not something to be stipulated or universally
ascribed to agents. The ability to exercise autonomous choice is a function of the extent to which one has a 'wide enough range of available
significant options to yield an adequate capability set' (Brison 2000,
285). The attention to vulnerability during negotiation and the benefit
of professional assistance may help the majority understand autonomy
in this way as a capacity that must have been exercised for an agreement
to be upheld.[10] Even the explicit legislative objective of self-sufficiency
has been interpreted, following the general orientation in *Miglin*, as a

capacity rather than a responsibility. In the past, this objective had been seen as a justification for limiting the husband's obligation to the wife on the basis that it was her responsibility to become self-sufficient. In a post-*Miglin* case, however, an agreement was held to fail the standard of substantial compliance with the statutory objectives because it neglected to provide the wife with adequate resources to achieve self-sufficiency (*J.E.D. v. E.P.D.* 2003, para. 30). Moreover, judges in subsequent cases have not always regarded the legislative objectives of autonomy and finality in *Miglin* as inflexible trumps. As Slatter J. wrote in a later case, 'There is an ability to moderate the values of autonomy and finality to the extent necessary to accommodate changed circumstances, while still encouraging settlement' (*Hearn v. Hearn* 2004, para. 41). In the same spirit, it may be an error for a judge to accord the objective of autonomy 'decisive importance' (*M.C. v. P.B.* 2003, para. 42).

On the facts, the majority in *Miglin* found the agreement to have complied substantially with the Divorce Act at its formation. During the marriage, the spouses had jointly owned two roughly equal assets, the matrimonial home and the family business. The separation agreement required each to exchange half of one asset in exchange for the other's half of the other, leaving Ms Miglin sole owner of the house and Mr Miglin sole proprietor of the business. The majority presumed this swap to reflect the parties' (and their professional advisors') assessment of their respective needs, abilities, and interests. It seems reasonable to think that the arrangement was congenial to the parties, since Ms Miglin retained custody of the children and it was Mr Miglin who had always managed the business. The agreement secured Ms Miglin some $60,000 annually in child support. It also included a consulting agreement between her and the business, which would pay her $15,000 annually for five years. On the separation, Ms Miglin stopped receiving her regular salary from the family business, but as the majority observed, she also stopped working full-time for it. The majority found it not unreasonable that the agreement left Ms Miglin $75,000 annual income for her and the children, particularly since her expenses excluded any rent or mortgage payments (*Miglin* 2003, para. 97). LeBel J., for his part, viewed the agreement as unsatisfactory at formation. To him, the exchange of half the business, valued at $250,000, for half the house, valued at $250,000, was unfair on the basis that the business produced income while the house did not. It did not strike him as salient that sustaining the business's income would continue to demand Mr Miglin's full-time energies, whereas Ms Miglin's capital asset imposed no equivalent demands. LeBel J. also objected to the failure to secure Ms Miglin a greater stream of income (ibid., para. 245).

The second step of the majority's test in *Miglin* turned on the time of the application. The majority wrote that 'the vicissitudes of life' meant that the spouses might find themselves in circumstances not contemplated (ibid., para. 87). The court's inquiry was the extent to which enforcement of the agreement still reflected the parties' original intentions and still complied substantially with the legislative objectives. The issue was what had happened to the parties between the end of their marriage and the present, and how accurately they had projected postmarital life. Unlike the life changes necessary to amendment of an agreement under *Pelech*, changes here need not be radically unforeseen, nor must the applicant prove a causal connection to the marriage. Instead, the applicant must establish that 'in light of the new circumstances, the terms of the agreement no longer reflect the parties' intentions at the time of execution and the objectives of the Act' (ibid., para. 88). This element of the test is consistent with Brenda Cossman's recommendation for a broadly construed notion of causation in appreciation of 'the multiplicity of causal relationships in economic dependency' and 'an understanding of the interdependence of factors leading to dependency' (1990, 372). Ms Miglin's trouble in proving that her circumstances no longer reflected her initial intentions was that her circumstances were, in fact, largely those that she and Mr Miglin had contemplated. During negotiations, her financial advisor had drawn her attention to the consulting agreement's limited term. Financial projections had assumed that she would not seek paid work during the first five years, so her failure to secure employment hardly carried her outside her expectations.

Undoubtedly the multitude of factors make examination of an agreement a complex enterprise. Carol Rogerson criticizes the *Miglin* test for its complexity and uncertainty (2003, 320). But this rich complexity is precisely in line with relational theory's contextual approach. Cossman notes that a feminist critique of contract multiplies the set of relevant factors and thus renders evaluation of claims and resolution of disputes more difficult and more complex. She suggests that approaching a fair resolution may require complicating the resolution of these matters (1990, 362).

I have argued that the majority and the minority in *Miglin* concurred on the need to look to context and on the particular embeddedness of persons making contracts with their spouses. Both sides agreed on the need for attention to vulnerability in negotiation and on the need to ensure parties some autonomy to translate their own objectives into agreements. They agreed, to slightly varying degrees, on the need for arrangements to comply with the applicable legislation. For these reasons, it is inaccurate to suggest that the majority reasons produced abstract, disembodied subjects. Slightly more pronounced normative disagreements will become apparent – albeit snugly within relational theory – when we examine *Hartshorne* regarding the question of explicit contracting ex ante.

Contracting before marriage poses a couple of significant issues. The first derives from the processes of contracting and the difficulty in predicting how a relationship will evolve during marriage. The second questions the normative acceptability of contracting out of the state's default regime for marriage. The two concerns tug in different directions, and this is why in *Hartshorne* the majority refused to articulate a firm rule regarding the deference due to marriage agreements versus separation agreements (2004, para. 39). First, a serious challenge to prenuptial contracting is how difficult it is for the parties to predict how their economic relationship will evolve during their marriage. While it is difficult to assess accurately the past economic impact of a marriage in negotiating a separation agreement, it is harder still to predict that impact before the marriage. Moreover, prior to their marriage the parties may be less lucid than usual. The point of marriage is a time 'of hopes and dreams and good intentions' (Shaffer 2004a, 420), and many contract with an unrealistic sense of what their married future holds. Parties are likely to be 'unduly optimistic about the fate of their marriage,' overestimating the future propensity of the other to 'avoid opportunistic behavior or unfair manipulation' (Eisenberg 1995, 254, 251). Judges may draw practical points from these remarks. Acknowledgment of the difficulty of predicting may call for special, highly contextual sensitivity to differences between the terms of the agreement and the way that the parties' relationship developed. Furthermore, the elevated emotional state of parties about to marry may warrant particularly stringent review of their negotiating conditions. What attention to these points is visible in the judicial performance in *Hartshorne*?

Shaffer argues that the majority decision is disappointing for its lack of contextualism. She suggests that *Hartshorne*, like *Miglin* and *Walsh*, presumes a vision of choosing and bargaining that treats the spouses as formal equals but overlooks the myriad ways in which spouses do not act as commercial players at arm's length. They are, rather, 'enmeshed in a context of complex emotional dynamics and vulnerabilities' (2004a, 416–17, 431). Yet the majority judgment was more contextual than Shaffer acknowledges (Bailey 2004, 257). The majority was aware of the complex emotional dynamics but drew a different conclusion than did the dissenting judges and some critics. The majority weighted heavily the fact of Ms Hartshorne's being herself a lawyer. They were reluctant to accept that a lawyer would not understand the implications of a contract she signed. Those judges probably detected a whiff of bad faith on Ms Hartshorne's part that made them reluctant to minimize factors – such as her receipt of independent legal advice – that ought to have palliated any potential vulnerability. This sense of bad faith may be discerned in Bastarache J.'s discussion of the fact that the legal opinion obtained by Ms Hartshorne underscored the agreement's prejudice to her. 'It is trite,' he wrote, 'that a party could never be allowed to avoid his or her contractual obligations on the basis that he or she believed, from the moment of its formation, that the contract was void or unenforceable' (*Hartshorne* 2004, para. 61). Although this judgment dwelled on the facts less than did *Miglin*, what marked the majority judgment regarding the conditions of contract formation was arguably less an acontextual methodology than the emphasis it placed on a couple of salient facts, notably Ms Hartshorne's receipt of legal advice and her legal training.[11] The dispute among the judges evinced not a contrast between contextualism and abstraction, but rather a disagreement over the way that the context was framed and that some facts acquired salience. Bastarache J. leaned on legal training, Deschamps J. on child rearing and homemaking. But it would be an error to read *Hartshorne* as dictating that all persons be held unflinchingly to their ex ante marriage agreements. To the extent that the majority judgment underdeveloped the contextual considerations regarding prenuptial negotiations, it was because Bastarache J. believed the crux of the case to lie in other, more normative concerns.

Critics of *Hartshorne* assume that the difficulties in prediction led to a normatively relevant gap between the terms of parties' ex ante agreements and the normativity of their shared life. The concern is not the substance of contractual terms or interactional norms per se, but the imagined distance between them. In this way, critics suppose that even where parties contractually exclude the sharing of property, during the marriage they will nonetheless intermingle assets. Such suppositions are consistent with relational theory, which is open to the notion that relational interactions between individuals engender responsibilities exceeding contractual undertakings. Milton Regan Jr argues that inter-dependent relationships can 'give rise to responsibility in ways that a purely voluntary conception of obligation can't fully capture' (1993, 4 [endnote omitted]; see also Lloyd 2000). As Rollie Thompson puts it, in a slightly different context, 'as couples live together and merge their economic lives,' positive intention to share and support each other can be inferred from each partner's 'manifold and reciprocal daily adjust-ments and acquiescences' (2003, 90). The assumption is that tacit undertakings or relational conduct lead to greater intermingling of financial affairs and deeper obligations than contemplated within the formal, explicit modes of ordering such as the marriage contract in *Hartshorne*. There is a sense, drawing on the description of the contex-tual, embedded self, that where a conflict arises between explicitly artic-ulated ex ante norms and the 'tacit arrangements' that 'flourish' within families (Cornu 1998, 153), the latter have a persuasive claim for nor-mative priority. But the actual conduct in *Hartshorne* troubles this cheer-ful reading of domestic conduct as implicit ordering that should over-ride prior explicit ordering.

The problem in *Hartshorne* is not the gap between the contract and the Hartshornes' conjugal life. Their married life carried out precisely the terms of their agreement. Bastarache J. noted that 'both the finan-cial and domestic arrangements' between the two parties 'were unfold-ing just as the parties had expected' (*Hartshorne* 2004, para. 45). There was no commingling of funds, there were no significant joint bank accounts, and the husband retained his assets in his name. It is chiefly on this basis that the majority upheld the agreement, although they also argued for its substantive fairness, remarking that during the marriage Mr Hartshorne's net worth decreased while Ms Hartshorne's increased. Shaffer argues that these facts are best interpreted as 'Mr. Hartshorne living out *his* intention to maintain control of his income and his assets' (2004b, 285). Yet irrespective of whose will shaped the parties' lived reality, it is difficult to oppose to the contract any significantly different normative regime derived from conduct or custom. Contrary to the crit-icism, the Court's decision to maintain the Hartshornes' agreement was not promoting formal choice over the 'reality of the parties' circum-stances … during marital cohabitation' (McLeod 2004, 11). The reality of the parties' circumstances tidily bore out the terms concluded by contract. The question to explore further is whether the critics of *Hartshorne* really advocate a preference for implicit over explicit norms, as a methodological or procedural matter, or whether they seek to enforce a robust substantive vision of distributive justice based on the default regime. A spousal support case provides a good site for this query.

In *Bracklow v. Bracklow* (1999) the Supreme Court found entitlement to indefinite support on a non-compensatory basis. The spouses had no explicit contract; indeed, the judgment is typically viewed as silent on the issue of private ordering, ex ante or ex post. My reading of the judgment, however, reveals a not insignificant treatment of private ordering. McLachlin J. stated that when parties marry, there is a presumption of an obligation of mutual support, one that the parties may 'of course' alter 'through explicit contracting (usually before the union is made with a prenuptial agreement), or through the unequivocal structuring of their daily affairs, to show disavowal of financial interweaving' (ibid., para. 20). This statement signalled the Court's commitment to enforcing the outcome of explicit and implicit private ordering. What is notable in *Bracklow* is the disjuncture between this theoretical commitment to private ordering and the Court's practice in assessing the evidence. The trial judge had found that the parties had 'a modern marriage of two independent people' (ibid., para. 58). The Supreme Court declined, however, to find that the independent parties' conduct amounted to a disavowal of financial interweaving by the structuring of their daily affairs. For the Supreme Court, the imperative of responding to Mrs Bracklow's need trumped the parties' implicit private ordering (Leckey 2002c, 37).

In this example, the obligations detectable from implicit ordering were less than those imposed by the explicit default regime. The *Bracklow* case helps flush out the thrust of the criticisms of *Hartshorne*. The chief objection to enforcing the Hartshornes' agreement is not the methodological one that doing so privileges explicit norms over implicit understandings, but is instead the normative, distributive charge that the contract deprived a woman of access to the most favourable financial terms. If this is correct, it is time to take up the normative argument about default regimes.

The second issue raised by ex ante contracts is fully normative. To what extent should parties be permitted, even under optimal negotiating conditions, to derogate from the default matrimonial regime? The difference here between separation agreements and prenuptial contracts is substantial. Separation agreements generally accept the default regime in the Divorce Act. One defends a separation agreement by arguing that it instantiates the general legislative objectives. Adopting the statute's lexicon, Mr Miglin argued that their marriage did not dis-advantage his wife economically, with the consequence that no com-pensatory spousal support was warranted. He did not argue that their agreement rendered the statute's compensatory norm inapplicable. By contrast, a defender of a prenuptial agreement argues precisely that it displaced the default norms. Thus in defending the prenuptial agree-ment, Mr Hartshorne was not contending that it instantiated the norm of equal sharing in the context of their marriage. He was arguing that they had exempted their marriage from that norm. Mr Hartshorne's aim in concluding the prenuptial agreement was the one identified by the majority as most typical: 'a desire to protect pre-acquired assets ... for children of a previous marriage' (*Hartshorne* 2004, para. 39). How vigorously may a person pursue such an objective to the detriment of his future spouse?

Legislatures have haggled their way to different answers, though none garners universal approval. In Quebec the legislature has conse-crated equal division of the family patrimony as an obligatory matter of public order (art. 391 C.C.Q.). Ontario's statute, rather austerely, con-templates the setting aside of domestic contracts for a party's non-dis-closure, for a party's not understanding the agreement's nature or con-sequences, or otherwise in accordance with the law of contract (Family Law Act 1990, s. 56(4)). British Columbia's legislature has decided to permit all consensual regimes except 'unfair' ones, which of course bequeaths to the courts the question of statutory interpretation in *Hartshorne*. Deschamps J.'s reading of 'fairness' cleaved to the default regime. As evident from the judgment's opening sentence, Bastarache J.'s understanding differed: 'Domestic contracts are explicitly permitted by the matrimonial property regime in British Columbia' (*Hartshorne* 2004, para. 1). Both majority and minority judges felt themselves con-strained by the legislation. Shaffer draws out what she perceives as the majority's conception of fairness, nicely presenting the disputed point: 'Fairness ... is less about ensuring that agreements are substantively fair according to public norms of fairness, but more about ensuring that people are entitled to enter into and rely upon contracts that reflect their personal vision of fairness in the context of their intimate rela-tionships' (2004a, 426).

What might relational theory say on this question? The majority's recognition of the potential for contract to make space for diversity within the state's matrimonial regime resonates with a recent account of relational contract. Alain Roy argues that in an increasingly diverse society, it is inappropriate for the state unilaterally to impose a single conception of marriage. Individuals and couples vary, goes the argument, and it is appropriate to allow couples to vary their rights and obligations. According to this view, social, political, and economic justifications make contract appropriate when the role of the state may be viewed increasingly as one of coordinating regulation rather than of imposing substantive norms (2002, 310, 337). What is perhaps most suitable is a 'context-sensitive pluralistic legal regime' (Cohen 2002, 198). The point about diversity may push critics of the majority outcome to clarify their positions. Deschamps J. appeared to subscribe to the view that the statute in *Hartshorne* only permits the parties to determine the particular way that they will follow the statutory norm of equal division. Yet this reading probably overstates the extent to which she would regard couples as rigidly bound by the default regime. If a prenuptial agreement contemplated a distribution for the homemaker wife on separation superior to the statutory half, would Deschamps J. allow the breadwinner husband's subsequent challenge to the agreement in virtue of its unfairness to him? I suspect she would not. A trickier, borderline case might concern a middle-aged woman in a second marriage, determined to shelter the few assets she has laboriously accumulated for her children's education and her own retirement. Would the antienforcement camp override her negotiated derogation from the statutory redistribution? The position to be clarified is thus not fidelity to the statutory scheme so much as it is redistribution in the service of vulnerable subjects, particularly women. If such is the objective, it should be fleshed out more fully. Such an objective seems to require identifying within each relationship the strong and weak parties, an act that may respond with difficulty to shifting currents of power.

Crucial normative issues along these lines await serious debate, and I need not attempt to resolve them here. For present purposes, it is notable that they appear to be issues falling within the set of normative commitments I have identified with relational theory. Relational theory's normative commitment to promoting interdependent relationships can be regarded as militating against the possibility of a marriage in which the partners retain economic self-sufficiency. At the same time, the theory's commitment to the aspiration of autonomy and the idea that women, in particular, need to be able to criticize and revise the roles socially assigned to them incline against automatically enforcing the state's regime in order to invalidate relationship-specific arrangements. While an extended normative debate can occur within the terms of relational theory, the point to retain from this analysis is how little work is performed by relational theory's descriptive premise and contextual methodology. Adopting that method may reframe conflicts, but at least in these instances, it does not indicate how to resolve them. The points requiring further debate are identified more clearly once the relational inquiry's normative elements are separated from the others. Further normative questions, again distinct from the methodological ones, emerge from my rereading of the challenge to the matrimonial regime for excluding unmarried couples.

Unlike the previous cases, *Walsh* was not a case testing the application of family legislation to a particular dispute. It was a Charter challenge to the boundaries of a province's matrimonial regime. In most provinces, the fact-specific statutory support regime includes unmarried cohabiting couples. In contrast, the marital property regime, which consists of rules of division and protections for the matrimonial home, excludes them. An unmarried partner, though not benefiting from a presumption of equal sharing of property, may claim restitution for the other partner's unjust enrichment. Such claims are not easily proven, the litigation can be costly, and even successful claims are likely to fall short of equal sharing. For unmarried couples, then, unjust enrichment is not an alternative path to the result statutorily assigned to married couples.

Walsh serves as the basis for examining, from the perspective of relational theory, the appropriateness of preserving distinctions between married and unmarried couples. I argue that Bastarache J.'s reasons for the majority and L'Heureux-Dubé J.'s dissenting reasons exemplify a contextual methodology as well as tensions within relational theory's normative commitments.

The majority and dissenting reasons employ a methodology of contextualism. The majority judges observe that all married couples chose to marry and in so doing undertook the obligations of marriage. On the other side of the coin stands the presumption that unmarried couples did not choose to marry and have not undertaken those obligations. The heterogeneity of unmarried cohabitants raises a contextual concern for the majority judges. They are conscious that the Court is adjudicating not a single family dispute but a constitutional challenge to a broadly applicable regime. Bastarache J. responded to Ms Walsh's claim that the class of unmarried cohabitants reveals 'functional similarities.' To him, contextual analysis reveals that the argument based on such similarities fails adequately to address the 'full range of traits, history, and circumstances of the comparator group' (*Walsh* 2002, para.

39). L'Heureux-Dubé J. countered with an empirical claim. She referred to social science literature that suggests that couples do not plan their relationship with a clear idea of their legal rights and obligations or of the consequences of various relational forms. As she remarked tersely, 'most people are not lawyers' (ibid., para. 143). This is her reliance on context. How does one assess the relative merits of each position?

On a macro level, a study cited throughout the judgment reports that more than half of cohabiting couples eventually marry each other, typically within three to five years (noted in Rogerson 2003, 278n15). This is surely a clue that, as an empirical matter, unmarried couples do consciously distinguish the lesser commitment in cohabiting from what they understand as the deeper commitment signalled by marriage. On a micro level, the facts in *Walsh* show that Ms Walsh and Mr Bona held the conjugal home as joint tenants. They were not, it seems, totally oblivious to the legal consequences of their shared life or wholly haphazard in their planning. The passages I have noted in the two sets of reasons indicate that both refer to contextual factors, albeit to different ones. As in *Miglin* and *Hartshorne*, there are differences in emphasis and interpretation within the judges' contextualism. Here, however, I am not interested in mining these differences or undertaking an extended adjudication of the empirical dispute over the reality of couples. I want instead to highlight the tensions internal to the dissent, ones that engage relational theory's concern with autonomy.

Think of L'Heureux-Dubé J.'s argument that cohabiting couples do not consciously plan their relationship as the *inadvertence thesis*. She also argues that the ability to marry is inhibited whenever one partner wishes to marry and the other does not. Call this the *domination thesis*: the stronger partner determines the depth and form of the couple's commitment. The lowest, least committal common denominator prevails. The set of unmarried cohabiting couples is a large one, and it is possible that the inadvertence thesis accurately accounts for some of its members and the domination thesis for others. But it is unnerving that L'Heureux-Dubé J. should suppose so serenely that the two theses gesture towards the same outcome. Assimilation into the matrimonial regime would be an appropriate remedy for couples covered by the inadvertence thesis were there reason to think they would have married had they gotten around to it. The understanding is that unmarried couples, although they have not formally assumed obligations, have, through a succession of interactions, informally and implicitly assumed obligations of mutual care and sharing. Though L'Heureux-Dubé J.

presumably supposed such cases to be rare, her emphasis on thought-lessness implies *a contrario* that those couples who actually did think about it and decided they wished to retain separate property should be entitled to do so. By contrast, in the case of couples covered by the domination thesis, the trouble is not that they failed to contemplate the matter. These couples did think about it, and likely argued bitterly over it, but each person pressed a different desire. In such couples, one wants to get married and the other wishes to remain unmarried. Assimilating such couples into the matrimonial regime is not a matter of executing their mutual but unexamined, unarticulated wish, nor is it a matter of splitting the difference. In such cases, the dissent's remedy would reverse things entirely so that the domination shifts to the other side. In L'Heureux-Dubé J.'s performance, subscribing to the domination thesis generates a substantive argument that the default regime for marriage should uniformly apply, even – indeed, especially – where one party desires it and the other does not. If you wanted to split the difference, you could do worse than the state of affairs existing in most common law provinces, where cohabitation gives rise to need-based spousal support obligations but not division of property. At the very least, it is worth noticing the tension in a single set of reasons between the two accounts of why cohabitants do not marry.

With the domination thesis in mind, it is interesting to assess one proposal for resolving *Walsh*. Some suggest that it would have been preferable to shift the burden of proof, presuming inclusion within the matrimonial regime but with the possibility of explicit opting out (*Walsh* 2002, para. 77, L'Heureux-Dubé J., dissenting; Thompson 2003, 90). This idea of an opt-out is incompatible with the domination thesis and the kind of reasoning that animates the dissents in *Miglin* and *Hartshorne*. The process of opting out is vulnerable to the same potential for opportunism, cognitive limitations of ex ante decision making, and elevated degree of emotion characteristic of other family negotiations. If one would not trust the ex ante partial opting out in *Hartshorne*, there is little basis to rely on the informed consent of a cohabitant opting out of the full matrimonial property regime. In any case, the opt-out would be likeliest to arise in precisely the circumstances where the parties differed in their resources and relative strength. If one accepts the domination thesis enough to favour a presumption of inclusion, it is inconsistent to rely on a consensual waiver. Taking domination seriously does not permit taking it halfway.[12]

Perhaps the biggest theoretical questions are engaged by the relationship between unmarried cohabitation and marriage. It is here that *Walsh* connects with the questions of structure and agency. What animates the majority is clearly an attempt to vindicate concerns of autonomy, ones consistent, I argue, with relational theorists' normative commitments. For the majority, there are two interrelated lines of autonomy-related concern. One is the distinction between a formal undertaking, such as the exchange of consent in the marriage vows, and the implicit undertakings of tacit interaction (form). The second is the possibility for a diversity of regimes, that is, to structure the patrimonial dimension of intimate relationship otherwise than dictated by the state's default regime for marriage (substance). The majority detected in the Court of Appeal's decision in *Walsh* the erasure of both distinctions. And both distinctions are consistent with relational theory's interest in promoting autonomy and family diversity.

As for the form of relational ordering, is marriage qualitatively different from de facto relationships, or is it merely a matter of timing? Should living together be taken as a proxy for consent to the deep patrimonial undertakings of marriage? Does recognition of the embeddedness of subjects leave any space for the notion of a consciously chosen undertaking that has consequences significantly different from unconscious, tacit undertakings? Is there still space for an idea of deliberate consent? It should be remembered that in the area of sexual assault, women have battled to secure a privileged status for explicit expressions of will over inferences from their conduct. Relational theorists thus cannot avoid grappling with the need for a conception of consent, at least in some intimate relations between men and women.

The dispute between the majority and the dissent in *Walsh* turns on the question of choice. This emphasis on choice is consistent with equality law more generally (Leckey 2007b). In the presence of a legal status entailing substantial benefits and obligations, such as citizenship or marriage, discrimination should not be found too readily. It is appropriate in such cases to hold individuals to choices they make on a cost/benefit analysis without characterizing those costs as the unsavoury fruit of discrimination (Leckey 2002a, 455–9). Preserving some scope for choice is appropriate within family law because the alternative is to vacate the undertaking in formal commitments such as marriage (but see Lessard 2006).

The tentative conclusion I drew from the debate over structure and agency above was that, to some measure, choices are always shaped. At the same time, legal and social order requires that some notion of consent remain possible. In *Walsh* both Bastarache and L'Heureux-Dubé JJ. fetishized choice, making it talismanic. The majority judges upheld the distinction by attributing choice to cohabitants. The dissent would have struck down the distinction, effectively denying all choice to cohabitants, on the basis that some unmarried people have no authentic choice to marry. Once it is acknowledged that choices are never unconstrained, however, the focus must shift so that a policy decision can be made. The repeated references to choice in *Walsh* – in majority and dissenting reasons – miss the mark of the text's deepest concerns.

In both sets of reasons, it is more helpful to think of consent. When Bastarache J. wrote that married couples chose to marry and to accept the obligations and rights of marriage (*Walsh* 2002, para. 43), the key concept was not choice among a range of options, but consent to one of those options, marriage. It is not so important whether an individual could choose to marry or stay unmarried; there are always constraints on the capacity of unmarried individuals to persuade their partners to marry them, and the choice to marry may itself be ambivalent. What is most important is that consent to the codified matrimonial rights and obligations can reasonably be imputed only to those having affirmatively decided to marry.

L'Heureux-Dubé J.'s dissent replicates the majority's reference to choice, and here again the issue should really be consent. She wrote that whenever one of the two cohabiting partners wishes to marry and the other does not, 'it can hardly be said that the person who wishes to marry but must cohabit in order to obey the wishes of his or her partner chooses to cohabit.' In such circumstances, she wrote, it is 'patently absurd' to state that both chose to avoid the legal consequences of marriage (ibid., para. 152). Watch how the meaning shifts constructively when one substitutes 'consent' for 'choice.' Here is the flaw in the argument: That I prefer *M* but will meanwhile do or keep doing *C* in no way entails that I do not consent to *C*, nor even that I do not choose it. *C* is simply not my first choice. L'Heureux-Dubé J. overlooked the possibility of moral or political difficulties in imputing consent to the party who has affirmatively refused it. Where one partner would consent to the marital regime and the other would not, the clash calls for resolution on a principled basis. Moreover, her formulation undermines the agency of the person who would prefer marriage: it introduces the language of command and obedience, holding that the person must 'obey the wishes' of the other partner. L'Heureux-Dubé J. was concerned about the domination of the partner who must 'obey' the command to remain unmarried. Yet she invoked another, presumably preferable state of affairs in which the mere desire of one partner would conscript the other to marry, or at least to assume marriage's legal consequences. Surely both must consent to those potentially weighty consequences.

Equally surely, relational theorists who want to preserve a role for autonomy cannot jettison the idea of consent. Shaffer comments on the decision to marry in reference to the complexity of premarital negotiations. She argues that the desire to marry is such that it is too simple to say that Kathleen Hartshorne, had she objected to the contract drafted by her fiancé, should simply have walked from the negotiating able. The decision to marry is not reducible to 'an economic calculus,' being instead a 'profoundly personal decision' knitted with 'religious beliefs, social practices, family norms, and personal attitudes towards commitment and stability' (Shaffer 2004a, 432; on the decision to divorce, see Reece 2003). Even Shaffer, who regards subjects as deeply embedded within and constrained by a variety of forces including influence by the stronger partner, speaks of the profound importance of the decision to marry. This importance militates against equating patterns of implicit interaction with the formally expressed decision to wed. It is worth preserving space for the importance of the undertaking to marry. Relational theory's enterprise seeks to identify the complex factors that influence and shape preferences and choices. It is not to deny the possibility of their ever arising.

The other, substantive line of concern is the diversity question. Regarding cohabitation as triggering the panoply of matrimonial obligations further promotes the matrimonial regime as the single model of intimate relationship. The effect would be equivalency between the commitment signalled by a formal legal act and the fact of cohabiting for a legislatively prescribed period. As some have observed, the choice between various types of 'relationship status,' all attracting the same attributes, does not obviously advance autonomy (Conway and Girard 2005, 736). From the perspective of the judges in *Walsh*, matrimonial property was the last bastion of right and obligation that was exclusively marital. For judges concerned with affirming the consensual, chosen character of marriage, something must distinguish it from unmarried, de facto cohabitation. For their purposes, the logic of inscribing the line between spousal support and division of property is perhaps less important than the imperative of drawing a line somewhere.[13] Given how few rights and obligations had not been already extended to unmarried couples, matrimonial property became the judges' line of last defence. I think this accounts to some degree for the shrillness of the majority's references to choice. Those judges were less defending the choices of unmarried couples than they were championing the distinctiveness of the regime for those who consent to marry (compare Réaume 2006).

What one is left with, on distinctly normative terrain, is the need for attempting to negotiate the balance between recognizing the constraints on people's choices and preserving the scope for autonomy and difference. The Court in *Walsh* might better have acknowledged the complex choices facing it. It might have been preferable for the judges to admit that they were pinioned between deference to formal modes of ordering (including abstinence from an available formal mode, marriage) and deference to informal modes. The Court could then have admitted that, after recognizing informal ordering in prior judgments, it was in *Walsh* asserting the continuing importance of formal ordering. The judges were drawing the line at property division, although the line might have been drawn elsewhere, and there is something irksome about any bright line between support and division of property. The complicated interests and forces at play in the area perhaps impeded consistency from being the primary criterion.

As for relational theory, again it appears that judges can agree on the necessity of a thick description and a method of contextualism while still differing on how to cash out the common commitment to relational autonomy. It is not the case that the majority judges regarded family subjects as unattached atoms while the dissenting judges saw them as embedded.[14] If at times the majority reasons in *Walsh* lean towards producing a somewhat abstract choosing subject, they do so in the interests of avoiding the converse construction, a set of subjects so deeply embedded in relationships that the decision to marry makes little difference and choice and consent vanish. The dispute here seems to turn on normative workings out of relational autonomy in domestic settings. Indeed, it is arguably the majority's concern for preserving marriage as a special sort of deeper attachment that motivated its performance. It certainly cannot be said that the difficulty is that the majority judges failed to follow relational theory's enjoinment to 'focus on relationships.'

These three judgments are better understood, not as the product of rival camps of liberals against contextual feminists, but as proof of significant convergence on the part of the judges. This chapter detects significant commitment on the part of all judges to relational theory's elements. The concrete differences emerged, at least in *Miglin*, when it came to applying the method and principles to the facts. I admitted that the differences of principle are greater in *Hartshorne* and *Walsh*, where the majority was particularly concerned by the autonomy interest.

This second story of significant convergence around elements of relational theory attests to the theory's persuasiveness. Its contextual methodology and commitment to promoting interdependent relationships while preserving some space for agency and individual choices are compelling. Indeed, there is a sense in which the judges of the Supreme Court found themselves standing shoulder to shoulder on what could be called a contextual plateau. They agreed that what is necessary is a contextual assessment of instances of private ordering and of a multiplicity of factors in family life. A victory of sorts for relational theory is thus apparent. At the same time, this convergence on contextual method and the partial constitution of subjects by their relationships and social settings, moderated by the need for agency, did not lead to agreement when it came to adjudicating specific cases. Now, it is true that relational theorists do not claim that their theory can be mechanically applied to grind out answers. But they do, nonetheless, suggest that it can help clarify the factors to consider and untangle difficult problems in family law. The discussion in this chapter shows the extent to which judges can adopt relational theory and still find themselves at loggerheads, a sign of the internal tensions within that theory. It is not a criticism per se that there are tensions within the theory; it would be a thin theory indeed that had none. Yet to the extent that those tensions undercut the theory's analytical purchase when it comes to the sort of cases that pose difficulties in family law today, it bears notice.[15] Though a turn to relational theory does not per se resolve or clarify the tough issues, as some theorists suggest, relational theory has successfully articulated the tensions and formulated the vocabulary for continuing the difficult conversations. These are conversations that call for the taking of normative positions, for clearer articulation of how to instantiate relational theory's normative commitments. Adjudicating disputes between contextual subjects is a tough task. Tensions internal to relational theory have not been resolved, but it is time to turn the lens of relational theory on an area of public law.

PART TWO

Administrative Law

5 Thin Subjects in the Past

Legal historians and administrative lawyers tell at least two different stories about the administrative state in the twentieth century. What might be called the classic account relates that the minimalist government of the previous century gave way to the administrative state. Legislatures transferred the authority to determine classes of claims, such as tort actions by injured workers, from the common law courts to specialized boards (Risk 1983). The objectives for doing so included achieving a higher volume of processing at a lesser cost and confiding the decision-making power to tribunal members who would be less sympathetic than ordinary judges to the owners of hazardous industrial enterprises. Governments involved themselves in complex redistributive schemes, implemented through administrative agencies. In various combinations these agencies were delegated administrative, quasi-judicial, and legislative functions. The exigencies of the First and Second World Wars stimulated greater economic intervention by means of organs more responsive than legislatures to rapid change, as in the case of price controls. In turn, this delegation of power to administrative agencies provoked fears of loss of liberty (Hewart 1929), prompting judicial review of those agencies' functions. Administrative law, a nascent branch of public law, began to emerge. Some scholars regard this growth of the administrative state as the 'most important legal phenomenon' of the twentieth century (Dyzenhaus 1996, 133).

A revisionist story is somewhat different. On a substantive level, it emphasizes the historical continuity of state intervention in the marketplace and distribution of wealth, noting that nineteenth-century governments never restricted themselves to the night watchman minimalist model and themselves effected significant redistributions

(Horwitz 1992). On an institutional level, it underscores the historical pluralism of the institutions of governance, situating the twentieth-century administrative diversity of departments, tribunals, adjudicators, and ombudsmen in a historical continuity. Its claim is that it is erroneous to view the ordinary or superior courts of the nineteenth century as having monopolized adjudication, or at least as having done so for very long. Harry Arthurs argues in his influential book 'Without the Law' that 'legal centralism was essentially a Victorian artifact' and 'that we are not very far removed if at all from the days when English law was demonstrably pluralistic' (1985, 188). It follows that the administrative pluralism of the twentieth-century administrative state, in which government agencies interpret and apply law, is consistent with previous experience, not a radical break from it. There have always, on this view, been a diversity of court-like adjudicative agencies and a diversity of normative orders (Arthurs 1980; 1985). Some scholars would also point out that the traditional account's emphasis on the administrative state's growth in the first decades of the twentieth century is a parochial, distinctly Anglo-American narrative; in France, for example, the *droit public* developed much earlier (Lindseth 2005).

Administrative law, the subject of this and the following two chapters, is a branch of public law. In Canada it is rooted, as a matter of constitutional law, in the English common law. In principle it is uniform across the Confederation (but see Leckey 2004, 331–8; 2007c; Lemieux 2006). In the mid-twentieth century, administrative law as such in the Commonwealth countries remained a relatively new subject. The term did not yet appear consistently in the indexes to general legal texts. As a disciplinary construction, the subject was still developing in reaction to the proliferation of administrative tribunals or boards. Indeed, as late as the 1970s, it was possible to deny, though only polemically, the existence of any 'such thing as administrative law' (Estey 1971, 307). At the beginning of this chapter's period, Canadian administrative lawyers had not yet produced their first indigenous monograph, making do, in atavistic colonial fashion, with British texts. Yet despite ostensible similarities, institutional and substantive features distinguished Canadian administrative law from that of the mother country. The typical English administrative law scenario involved a decision by a civil servant ensconced within a ministerial or departmental hierarchy; the typical Canadian situation involved a decision by an independent board (Willis 1974, 230). This Canadian reliance on independent regulatory boards exercising economic control, a practice 'almost unknown' in England, was a borrowing from the United States (Willis 1959, 47). In Canada, the major substantive areas of executive action monitored by administrative law were land use zoning and building permits, labour relations, tax assessment, licensing, and professional disciplinary proceedings.[1] Land use was prominent in English administrative law as well, but there the labour relations, marketing scheme, tax, and immigration matters so crucial in Canada played relatively minor roles (Abel 1961, 135). All of these areas distinguish the administrative state from the ideal – however much or little it ever actually obtained – of the minimalist state restricted to core functions of public security and dispute resolution.

Definitions of 'administrative law' are controversial and contingent. D.J. Galligan distinguishes two senses. One refers to a body of legal principles created by the courts and having common application to all areas of government activity (the traditional sense of administrative law). The other refers to the law and practice relating to the various specific subjects regulated by the state, such as welfare, planning, and immigration (Galligan 1982, 258). There is yet another sense, one presented by critics of the first, traditional acceptation. Notice that the first sense refers to principles and rules created and applied by courts. Reference to courts in the administrative law setting means the decisions of courts when ruling on applications for judicial review. The third sense of administrative law, while it does not deny some supervisory role for courts, focuses primarily on the fostering of 'successful public administration' within government agencies and organizations. It attends more to the 'structures and processes of everyday governance' than to the 'episodic, *ex post facto* correction of "errors"' (Macdonald 2004, 159–60; Borgeat 1994). In these chapters I mean chiefly the first, general sense: judicial decisions on judicial review and administrative law scholarship.[2] This is the classic sense and it is revealing of the legal subject produced.

It is a definitional consequence of the focus on administrative law as the rules and principles created by the courts that its character is primarily common law. The norms are largely unwritten ones discovered or announced by courts, as opposed to ones enacted by legislatures or bodies to whom legislative power has been delegated. To supply what they discern delicately as the legislature's omission, judges invoke what they call the 'justice of the common law' (*Cooper* 1863).

A further consequence flows from administrative law's character as law announced and developed by judges in their judicial review of administrative action. It is helpful to regard administrative law as operating on two distinct planes. On one is the interaction of individuals with the bureaucrats working within administrative agencies or government departments. Judicial review proceedings call on courts to assess the legality of that interaction. On another, more structural plane is the interaction of courts with administrative agencies. Each judicial intervention in the relationship between individuals and the administration may be regarded as simultaneously an instance of readjustment of the relationship between the courts themselves and the administration. Thus judicial review of administrative action must take into account not only the appropriate relationship between the administration and individuals, but also that between the courts and the administration. Judicial intervention in administrative processes can be seen as an instantiation of broad, systemic views on the appropriate relationship between the state's apparatus and the structures of political economy. Issues of administrative law can, as has been observed, 'serve as proxies for a two-hundred-year-old political controversy: should the invisible hand of the market or the visible hand of the state determine the course of our lives?' (Arthurs 1985, 196 [endnote omitted]; see also Lindseth 2005; Leyland and Woods 1997).

John Willis, a prominent administrative lawyer, identifies two major characteristics in the development of Canadian administrative law between 1933 and 1973. The first he calls physical, a shifting of the line between private and public as government intruded into domains previously conceived of as private (Willis 1974, 233). The animating notion was that private interests could be sacrificed for the public good. Debates about where to halt the reach of government regulation and redistribution persist today, though the contemporary retrenchment, reorganization, and privatization of government have reconfigured them. Whereas earlier scholars fretted about excessive governmental incursions into private domains, today scholars may contend that public law should not retreat from overseeing the exercise of power in privatized governmental functions (Arthurs 2005, 813–14; Aronson 1997; Craig 1997; Freeman 2003). The referents of 'private' and 'public' are shifting and contingent.

Willis's second characteristic was psychological. It was the eventual acceptance of boards' legitimacy (Willis 1974, 233). For decades, Canadian administrative law scholarship devoted energy to wearying debates over boards' permanence as a feature of the legal landscape. Actors in the field were characterized as for or against the rise of the administrative state. Judges and practising lawyers tended to stress the dangers that administrative tribunals posed to liberty. Such opponents of boards regarded them as threats to fundamental principles of public law. As executive organs to which judicial functions had been consigned, they were seen as a threat to the separation of legislative, executive, and judicial functions (Rambourg 1969, 20). Furthermore, opponents regarded the substantial measures of discretion confided to boards as inconsistent with the rule of law, which they saw, after A.V. Dicey (1959), as requiring the subjugation of the administration to the law. The notion was that fairness and objectivity demanded that administrative action unfold within a framework of rules, rather than arbitrarily. Yet it is arguable that no state has ever conformed in all respects to Dicey's definition in the full sense of officialdom answering in the ordinary courts according to precisely the same law that binds citizens (Corry 1960, 545).

By contrast, teachers and scholars were more inclined to emphasize the importance of the state's new functions and the need for speedier, specialized procedures. Willis distinguishes what he calls lawyers' values from civil servants' values. In his assessment, the lawyer typically values a model of justice developed in the courts, emphasizing the formal rules of natural justice, while the bureaucrat values procedural efficiency and efficacy in implementing the objectives of a particular governmental scheme (1968). As subsequent scholars have noted, the distinction should not be overstated. It may be that the 'central problem of contemporary governance is less a "conflict of values" between public servants and the legal profession than a disagreement about how best to pursue public policy according to law' (Macdonald 2005, 452; see also Sossin 2005a, 446). Eventually, in any event, opponents were forced to concede boards' permanence (Reid 1971, xi). Considerable rivalry persisted nevertheless, at this institutional level, between courts and boards.

The tensions between those 'for' and 'against' the administrative state can be recast slightly by identifying two contrasting political orientations. One, influenced by Dicey, regarded the role of the courts as 'overwhelmingly negative,' that of protecting individual freedoms from governmental interference (Leyland and Woods 1997, 381–2). Subscribers to this view framed their concerns in abstract, distinctly liberal terms. What concerned them were notions such as the administration of justice, prevention of arbitrary or abusive governmental action, the appropriate relationship between state and private interests, and the 'general value of procedural fairness' (Beetz 1965, 250; Rambourg 1969, 11–12; Dussault 1969, 513; Hogg 1974, 173). The chief means for vindicating these concerns was judicial review. The other orientation was functionalist. Functionalism is used in a number of different ways, but what I mean here is the sociologically grounded view of society as a system with interdependent and mutually supportive parts, each with a function in the survival of the whole. Functionalism also includes a distinct pragmatism concerned with law's consequences and the pursuit of governmental programs to improve social welfare (Leyland and Woods 1997, 393; cf. Loughlin 2005). Functionalism in Canada was inspired by the American school of realist jurisprudence and the New Deal architects of social design during the 1930s (Gordon 2005, 417–21). Its Canadian incarnation par excellence is the work of John Willis (1935; see also Loughlin 2005, 398). For the most part, the functionalists pay little attention to the legal subject that underwrites their positivist projects of reform. Periodically I shall point to functionalist positions in this respect, arguing that their inattention to individuals undermined the force and attractiveness of their enterprise.[3]

My attention in this chapter focuses largely on the liberal vision represented by judges and commentators. Although important work could be done to assess administrative and parliamentary means of controlling administrative tribunals, my focus is judicial protections and controls. I argue that administrative law in this period subscribes for the most part to the thin, atomistic subject that relational theory attributes (however bluntly) to classical liberalism. This notion of the subject was produced, explicitly, by the era's discourse of citizenship, but also, more implicitly and interstitially, by the method and substance of judicially inferred procedural guarantees. Turning to the concerns of relational theory, the methodology of judicial review at this time is formal and acontextual. Its normative commitments concerned the negative idea of protection against government interference. As I will show, the legal subjects produced were decidedly thin and acontextual.

Institutional Rivalry

Disputes about the desirability of boards' existence per se sublimated into a sustained institutional rivalry between these boards and the courts. Judges regarded the creation of specialized tribunals as having reduced their own prestige. Courts evidently took umbrage to different degrees, some reacting more strenuously than others. Bora Laskin observes that the decisions of Saskatchewan courts quashing labour board decisions conveyed the impression that those courts were engaged in a 'bitter battle on social and economic policy in which they were determined to have the last word' (1952, 993–4; see also Fudge and Tucker 2001, 307). As one critique puts it, 'judges, given their pre-occupation with private law rights, lack the necessary knowledge and expertise, or are unwilling to take account of the social or economic purpose lying behind the law' (Leyland and Woods 1997, 397). Yet these realist analyses should not be taken as inconsistent with the notion that the opponents of the administrative state were sincere, and not only for self-interested reasons. It is reasonable to suppose that at least some of the critics were genuinely moved by disapproval of executive interferences in what had once been – or had been perceived as – the common law's sphere of free commercial action.

Supporters of the administrative state sought to end this rivalry by developing fully independent institutions. For believers in the institutional superiority of administrative tribunals over courts for dealing with the high volume of files generated by the state's regulatory and distributive initiatives, this was simply the upshot of their reasoning. If administrative tribunals are superior to courts at resolving certain disputes at first instance, they reasoned, an appellate administrative tribunal would also be preferable to an appellate court at adjudicating administrative appeals. Moreover, in the view of some commentators, judges' training, culture, and institutional self-interest rendered them incapable of exercising appropriate restraint and demonstrating due deference when reviewing tribunal decisions. Accordingly, a number of commentators advocated the creation of general administrative appeal tribunals (Willis 1935, 80–1). The separate administrative structure of France, including its Conseil d'État, stimulated particular scholarly interest (Leyland and Woods 1997, 389; see also Arthurs 1985, 211). In the ensuing decades, however, such an institutional development has occurred only in Quebec, and there only partially (Pépin 1997).

One fault line for the rivalry was the general issue of statutory interpretation. A statute serves as the authorization for all administrative activity. In administrative law, statutory interpretation thus assumes a crucial, and politically salient, importance. In private law contexts, the classic notion is that legislatures enact legislation in derogation from the foundational fabric of common law rules. The Statute of Frauds thus specifies a writing requirement for certain classes of contracts, departing from the unenacted rules that would otherwise apply. In the private law setting, courts apply these rules to trench disputes among private parties, construing narrowly the legislated derogations from the common law. The administrative law setting is radically different. In the typical administrative case, a legislature has created an agency and delegated authority to it by virtue of an enabling, constitutive, or organic statute. The enabling statute sets out the agency's mission in broad, open-ended terms. The normative language of regulatory statutes is 'often vague and uninformative: ... "may in its discretion approve," "public convenience and necessity."' Consequently, there is 'ample opportunity – often, indeed, a compelling necessity – for the administration itself to give meaningful specificity to such statutes' (Arthurs 1985, 204–5; see also Mashaw 2005, 510). To perform its assigned task, the agency was required to interpret its legislative mandate and operationalize it (Macdonald 1987). Since the sole basis for administrative action was statutory authorization, any action not authorized by the statute – extending beyond the statutory mandate – was illegal. The question of how those enabling statutes were to be interpreted was thus of prime importance. In a famous essay, John Willis identifies the 'social and political views of the men who happen to be sitting' as a major, entirely negative influence on statutory construction (1938, 13). Judges were scions of the propertied classes and resented redistributive programs and the curtailment of their courts' purview. They were thus, in Willis's view, inclined to quash the decisions of administrative tribunals as falling outside their statutorily assigned jurisdiction.

A subset of statutory interpretation so contentious it merits extended treatment was judicial interpretation of privative clauses and the construal of the boundaries of boards' jurisdiction. A privative, preclusive, or ouster clause is a statutory provision stating, in any of various ways, that courts shall not disturb a tribunal's actions. It is an assertion of legislative intention that the delegated administrative agency, not the courts, should make a particular kind of decision. There were three common forms: (1) 'no-*certiorari*' clauses, which provide that no action may be brought to disturb a tribunal decision; (2) 'finality' clauses, which provide that the tribunal's decisions shall be 'final'; and (3) 'exclusive jurisdiction' clauses, which confer on a tribunal exclusive jurisdiction over specified matters or everything before it (Reid 1971, 179–80).

The privative clause crystallized perhaps better than any other issue the divisions between commentators and judges over the appropriate degree of judicial intervention in tribunal decisions. One issue dividing commentators and judges was the legal possibility and propriety of judicial review in the face of a full privative clause. Such clauses intertwine with the concept of jurisdiction because even those who accept that such clauses validly shield a board's determinations within its jurisdiction would likely entertain arguments that legislative intent requires courts to nullify tribunal actions *exceeding* that jurisdiction (Willis 1935, 78). Thus the classification of a question as pertaining to jurisdiction provides a hook for courts to review the tribunal's determination on that point. In other words, the degree to which a privative clause serves to insulate decisions from review hangs on the court's restraint in classifying questions as jurisdictional. A court keen to intervene could characterize many issues as concerning jurisdiction. Some scholars were suspicious, contemptuous even, of the concept of jurisdiction as a means of distinguishing questions within a board's exclusive province from those reviewable by a court. Peter Hogg, for example, writes that 'the concepts of "jurisdiction" and "law" are sufficiently vague – some would say meaningless – to offer a means of review of any erroneous finding of fact or law' (1973, 204–5). One would expect, then, that eagerness to characterize questions as jurisdictional corresponded with antipathy towards the administrative state, whereas reluctance so to characterize matters corresponded with favour for it.

What predominated in Canadian courts was a narrow reading of privative clauses, with ready classification of questions as jurisdictional. Indeed, the tendency of Canadian judges to accord a restrictive interpretation to 'apparently unambiguous privative clauses,' effectively rendering such provisions nugatory, even attracted the attention of de Smith writing in the metropolis (1968, 347). Laskin writes almost despairingly of courts' refusal to adopt the broad view of privative clauses in the enabling legislation of labour arbitrators. He observes drily that with few exceptions, the courts exerted the same supervision over administrative agencies as they would absent any preclusive clause. Laskin blasts the courts for their 'evasion of privative clauses through specious interpretation and unsupported assumptions [a]s a trespass on the policy functions of another agency' (1952, 988, 991). His diction is revealing: 'another agency' is shunting aside the view of courts as trading in law (superior) and of boards as trading in policy (inferior). Instead, it constructs both courts and boards as agencies that perform, on the same plane, policy functions. The sense would have been very different had he referred simply to courts' trespass on 'the policy functions of *an* agency.' His defence of tribunal jurisdiction rests on political faith in the merits of administrative tribunals' capacity effectively to develop policy in their field.

There is perhaps one exception to prove the rule that political attitudes towards the administrative state determined one's approach to jurisdiction. D.M. Gordon, a practitioner in Victoria, expounded a 'pure' theory of jurisdiction. According to this theory, jurisdiction is an external constraint on power that precludes courts from considering the manner in which administrative bodies make their decisions and the quality of those decisions. For Gordon, this theory was grounded in a doctrinal coherence flowing from a Diceyan understanding of the rule of law. Jurisdiction was to him a categorical and bounded concept, and courts had no tools to enter a board's jurisdiction for the purpose of policing a decision's reasonableness or substantive merit. In other words, the scope of a tribunal's statutorily granted authority stood independently from the merits of the decisions it made in exercising that authority (Roach 1989). Gordon's formal methodology is typical of the reasoning during the period. While Gordon exemplifies formalism, he is atypical in virtue of his professed detachment from politics. He defended his theory, which if adopted would have shielded tribunal decisions, without conscious sympathy towards the administrative state. The concept of jurisdiction, as he understood it, left no room for qualitative judgments or the pursuit of social purposes (Gordon 1966, 520). Gordon concedes freedom to administrative bodies, not because he approves of the functional specialization of the labour of governance, but because he believes that boards' tasks do not involve the recognition of legal rights. Since no rights were implicated, no principled and consistent grounds justified judicial intervention (Roach 1989, 33). In his monograph, de Smith rejects Gordon's pure theory on the basis that, impractically, it reduced jurisdictional control almost to nothing. In contrast to Gordon's denial of the idea of judicial policy, de Smith admits that defining jurisdiction is a matter 'of public policy rather than one of logic' (1968, 98). The significance of Gordon's theory for present purposes stems from the contrast it presents with other, more political approaches to jurisdiction, though these other approaches also operated within a formal methodology and justified their outcomes by reference to the statutory text. His doctrinal purity is anomalous because debates about the interpretation of privative clauses generally engaged political questions about the appropriateness of the administrative state and institutional self-interest. Conflicting views of privative clauses – from Laskin's to Gordon's – give a sense of the institutional rivalry between courts and administrative tribunals and testify that attention focused on institutional jockeying more than on individual subjects. In the background of the relations of the individual to the bureaucracy lie always these larger, interinstitutional considerations.

Threshold Matters, Thresholds Matter

In private law cases the unsuccessful party appeals to a higher court. He appeals, as of right or by leave of the higher court, according to the rules set out in a Courts of Justice Act or a code of civil procedure. On appeal, the reviewing judge or panel of judges seeks to correct errors made by the deciding judge below. In administrative matters, where the decision maker is an administrative tribunal of some kind, wielding delegated authority, the matter is different. The individual dissatisfied with an administrative decision who wishes to challenge it must establish the basis on which a reviewing court may review the decision. And in a judicial review of administrative action, what is typically at issue is not the merits of the decision made, but whether the administrative decision maker complied with its enabling legislation. In the past, courts constrained the autonomy of administrative tribunals by reviewing their decisions for legal error, excess of jurisdiction, and breach of the safeguards of natural justice. Decisions regarded as outside jurisdiction or made in a process incompatible with the imperatives of natural justice were regarded as illegal: the statutory authorization did not extend to them.

Public law remedies historically took the form of the 'prerogative' writs, which were initially available only to the Crown and not to subjects. By exercising the prerogative remedies, the Crown 'could ensure that public authorities carried out their duties, and that inferior tribunals kept within their proper jurisdiction' (Wade and Forsyth 2004, 591). The remedies were intended to ensure efficiency and maintain order in the hierarchy of courts, commissions, and authorities. By the close of the sixteenth century, these remedies had become available to ordinary litigants, and applicants could initiate proceedings in the Crown's name without seeking permission to do so. The prerogative writ of habeas corpus would test the legality of a prisoner's detention. Certiorari and prohibition were designed for preventing the usurpation or abuse of power by inferior bodies, be they judicial or administrative (ibid., 615–30; de Smith 1968, 20–33). These ancient remedies were still the form for judicial review in the mid-twentieth century. At least in theory, courts reviewing administrative action do not assess the substance of the decision. They assess its legality, including its compliance with the enabling legislation and with the requirements of natural justice.

Access to the courts was restricted by considerations tied to the interest of the individual applicant (standing) and to the kind of administrative action impugned (crudely, reviewable or non-reviewable). These thresh-old issues exemplify administrative law's formal, abstract methodology.

Locus standi or standing means legal capacity to challenge an act or decision (de Smith 1968, 426). De Smith articulates the rationale for the doctrine of locus standi as a means of mediating conflicts between two aspects of the public interest: the desirability of encouraging indi-vidual citizens to participate actively in the enforcement of the law and the undesirability of encouraging the professional litigant to invoke judicial jurisdiction in matters not concerning him (ibid., 422). The period's judicial review proceedings demonstrated little sense of a coherent theory of standing. Reid's discussion of standing appears frag-mented throughout his book, the points appearing under different types of proceeding, such as certiorari and prohibition, declarations of right, and mandamus (1971, 349–50, 403–4, 392). Where the plaintiff or applicant was unable to satisfy the preliminary requirements, notably the necessary degree of personal interest, judicial relief could be unob-tainable. Different personal interests sufficed to support applications for mandamus, certiorari, and a quashing of compulsory purchase orders, and all differed from the interest required of plaintiffs in actions for injunctions (de Smith 1968, 22). While overall the threshold for standing was relatively high, standing turned rather technically on the nexus between the particular interest threatened and the prerogative writ or other remedy sought.[4] To the extent that one can generalize, courts took the view that to be legally aggrieved, a person must be not merely dissatisfied with or even prejudiced by an act or decision. Also, he must have been subjected to a legal burden or refused or deprived of something to which he was legally entitled (de Smith 1968, 424). The absence of any general approach to standing hints that the conception of the legal subject was a thin one.

One of the most concrete understandings of the subject appears interstitially in a criticism of excessive judicial review. This criticism anchors itself firmly in what Willis would call bureaucratic values. Albert Abel objects that an individual who can challenge an administrative decision affecting the interests of many persons, whole communities, or larger aggregates is permitted to postpone that decision's operation 'to the prejudice meanwhile of the indefinite many whose competing claims were recognized by the administrative award.' Abel's comments so far do not depart from the usual abstract sense of competing claims or interests. But he continues: 'Then, when the matter comes on for hearing at the appeal, *he* is represented but *they* are bodiless wraiths'

(1962, 75 [emphasis in original]). Implicit in this complaint is a sense that representation in the administrative and appeal processes renders someone corporeal so that his or her interests can be taken into account. One becomes physically embodied only once one has standing and one's interests are explicitly represented and noticed. Conversely, granting standing to an aggrieved individual has the effect, by implication, of rendering less material the interests of those unrepresented.[5]

Even where standing was established, courts' scope for review depended on the classification of the challenged administrative act as 'quasi-judicial' or 'administrative.' The leading Canadian text declares the outcome of this classification to be crucial for three reasons. First, the ancillary remedies such as certiorari lay only to judicial or quasi-judicial but not administrative functions; second, the rules of natural justice governed the procedure involved in exercising a quasi-judicial but not an administrative function; third, courts tended to see the exercise of a quasi-judicial discretion as subject to their supervision and an administrative discretion as not (Reid 1971, 111). Together the first and third reasons composed administrative law's 'primary question': Will the courts accept jurisdiction? (Canadian Bar Association 1948, 1350). Willis does not mince words in identifying the stakes in such inquiries, observing that whether or not certiorari lies in respect of any given decision is not a 'mere question of procedure,' but 'a question of power' (1935, 62). The process of locating administrative acts vis-à-vis the quasi-judicial/administrative dichotomy reveals the period's formalism and acontextualism.

Both the definition of 'quasi-judicial' and, correspondingly, its application were clumsy. The justifications for the classification and the method of performing it frequently blended. Reid notes four principal approaches to the classification problem, admitting candidly that the result obtained was a function of the approach selected (1971, 121–30). One approach focused on the nature of the administrative decision maker's process. Sir William Wade suggests that a quasi-judicial decision may be viewed as a judicial process from which one or more elements are missing, or preferably, in his view, as an administrative process to which one or more judicial elements are added (1949, 227).

A second approach targeted the nature of the result or the interests at stake. This approach held that acts affecting rights should be regarded as quasi-judicial, while acts affecting mere interests or privileges might rightly be categorized as administrative.[6] A minister choosing whether to confer a permit was a classic example of a discretion appropriately viewed as administrative on the basis that it did not affect rights (Brun 1974, 427–8). This approach was methodological, since correctly identifying the interest at stake as a right or a mere privilege dictated whether the rules of natural justice bound a process. Yet the approach was simultaneously justificatory in presuming and promulgating a normative message that interests and privileges warranted lesser protections than did rights.

A third approach concentrated on the nature of the power, or put another way, the normative sources on which the administrative decision relied. This approach, regarded as the most popular by Abel, dubbed as 'administrative' those decisions made according to policy or expediency and as 'judicial' those based on law and authority. In Abel's view, the problem with this distinction was that familiarity with courts' and agencies' operations brought the realization that it depended on ideal types, elevating differences of degree into differences in kind (1972, 62). Another problem, of course, is that this distinction presumed the mutual exclusivity of policy or expediency and law.

The fourth, most rigid view concerned the duty to act judicially. It held, in contradiction to the second, that characterization of an act as quasi-judicial was not entailed by an administrative body's simply having legal authority to determine questions affecting subjects' rights. Instead, even where a right was affected, there must have been 'super-added' the further attribute that the body have the duty to act judicially. This approach found its archetypal articulation in *Nakkuda Ali v. Jayaratne* (1951, 78; see also *Calgary Power Ltd. v. Copithorne* 1959). This ascription of a duty to act judicially was not linked to the body's general status, but turned in particular circumstances on the nature of the process by which a decision maker was empowered to reach a decision (*Nakkuda Ali* 1951, 75). The search for explicit legislative imposition of a duty to act judicially derives its justification from deference to parliamentary will and the assumption that exercises of discretion do not change the law, but only affect the legal rights and duties of a particular individual (Dyzenhaus 2002b, 541–2). It contemplates no duties or rights flowing from natural justice, procedural fairness, or any unenacted source. Like the first approach, the hunt for explicit authorization authorized by *Nakkuda Ali* serves simultaneously as method and justification. Turning from these abstruse debates to the mundane forum of public opinion, one might observe that the general public – rightly or wrongly, prevaricates an author – assimilated certain 'administrative' functions to the set of judicial functions, making it appropriate that those administrative functions comply with 'minimum norms' (Beetz 1965, 255).[7]

In light of these justificatory and methodological differences, it is unsurprising that making the characterization was difficult and that the quasi-judicial/administrative dichotomy generated much debate and criticism. One packet of criticisms charge that the classification exercise was unworkable. Reid characterizes the line between administrative and quasi-judicial powers as 'sometimes dim' (1971, 113), underscoring the enterprise's dimensions of 'illogic, arbitrariness and mystery' (ibid., 129). The result, he writes, is that judicial supervision of administrative action 'looks suspiciously like mumbo-jumbo, learned gobbledy-gook assumed as a facade for an exercise in arbitrariness' (ibid., 129–30). Frank Scott remarks on the lack of a clear definition and the classification's effect of enlarging judicial discretion (1948, 274–5). Willis derides the characterization exercise as 'inextricably confused' (1959, 54). Abel rails against the 'spurious dichotomy, two undefined terms in place of one' (1972, 62). These comments give a strong sense that the classification operated inefficaciously. Nevertheless, they do not rule out the possibility that a workable classification exercise would be acceptable. This critical view was not unanimous; Gordon held what Roach characterizes as a 'confident and categorical understanding of the distinction between administrative and judicial functions' (1989, 11).

Other criticisms strike more deeply to the distinction's normative basis. These criticisms protest that the classification exercise diverted attention from the impact of decisions on the individuals affected. Jean Beetz suggests that certain plainly administrative procedures could benefit from the procedures imposed on judicial and quasi-judicial decision making (1965, 255). For him, the characterization of an act as 'administrative' does not determine definitively the set of appropriate procedures. The McRuer Royal Commission suggests that a decision's impact might be more relevant to the determination of appropriate procedure than the institutional location in which the dispute was decided: 'The individual who suffers from an unjust decision made by a statutory tribunal suffers just as acutely as from an unjust decision made in the ordinary courts' (Ontario 1968, 4). The suffering and injustice contemplated here are not functions of classification of an interest as a right or privilege or a process as quasi-judicial or administrative. Willis, for his part, proposes jettisoning the quasi-judicial/administrative distinction in determining appropriate procedures. It would be preferable, in his view, to seek a 'reasonable balance' between the rights and feelings of citizens with whose possessions the administration interferes and the public interest, which dictates that administrative authorities not be frustrated in executing their duties (Willis 1959, 49). These criticisms indicate a loss of faith in the formal classification process as adequately representative of the underlying substantive concerns ostensibly justifying it.

It bears clarification that the two sets of criticisms – the classification's inefficacy and its normative dubiousness – blend together. Eric Tucker argues that the classification exercise need not have been as difficult as it seemed, and that the incoherence of the case law resulted to some degree from normative doubts as to the distinction's merits (1987, 583–4). Nevertheless, throughout the period the judges and commentators appeared, for the most part, to regard themselves as necessarily confined within the distinction. The classification exercise concerned itself with institutional prerogatives, not the appropriateness of processes in light of the impact of the decision on the individual. And the literature gives a sense of judges and some scholars engaged in an enterprise, not of deploying rights to structure relationships, but rather of manipulating rules for their own sake. To the extent that the right/interest distinction was an attempt to consider the impact on individuals, it did so crudely, a point to which I return. The thinness of the conception of the legal subject in the period flows significantly from the prominence of this quasi-judicial/administrative distinction at the expense of an approach concerned with the people affected. Once an applicant passed the threshold, it became possible to argue that the decision maker had lost jurisdiction by neglecting its duty to follow the procedural requirements of natural justice.

Procedural Safeguards

Procedural safeguards comprised a variety of statutorily and judicially imposed rights on the part of the individual affected by administrative action (de Smith 1968, 135ff.; Reid 1971, ch. 1, 2, 6). Judges inferred procedural safeguards as an exercise of statutory interpretation, supposedly serving legislative intent by filling in what the legislature would have wished had it considered the matter. Aside from the judicial fiction of fidelity to legislative intent, several other, more instrumental rationales for procedural safeguards circulated. Gilles Pépin enunciates a twofold need for subjecting administrative tribunals to appropriate procedural rules. The first imperative was to ensure the ordered functioning of tribunals and to facilitate their members in making the best deci-

sions possible. The second was to accord a minimum of protection to
the rights and interests of those subject to the administration, the
administrés (1969, 603). In R.M.W. Chitty's view, it was 'the Court's duty
jealously to protect the individual from the delusions of grandeur from
which all forms of bureaucracy so evidently suffer' (1964, 128). He fails
thus to contemplate the possibility that courts are themselves another
form of bureaucracy similarly susceptible (Macdonald 2005, 452; see
also Belley 2001, 349–53). Willis articulates a third, also instrumental
understanding of procedural fairness. He sees procedural fairness as
exercising a social control or legitimation function in the sense that the
average man will more readily accept decisions that he neither likes nor
understands where the procedure looks fair to him. In Willis's view, adequate procedures compensate for what he disparages as the 'unfamiliar
and unrealistic lawyer's reasoning' on which proceedings are based
(1959, 48). The courts are transparent in these understandings of procedural fairness: all attention is on keeping the bureaucracy in line and
on the bureaucracy's mode of interaction with citizens. The relationship
between the courts and the bureaucracy is invisible and immune to
assessment or criticism.

The two principles of natural justice in English law are *audi alteram*
partem, adequate notice and an opportunity to be heard, and *nemo judex*
in causa sua, that an adjudicator be disinterested and unbiased (de
Smith 1968, 135). For present purposes, bias can be addressed briefly.
Administrative law regarded the judging subject abstractly as a bundle
of interests. The decision maker's qualifications for his functions were
negative, notably the absence of any pecuniary interest in the case that
would impeach his neutrality and objectivity. Such a view of decision
makers makes their property interests determinative.

Audi alteram partem is the entitlement to a hearing and, where entitlement is found, the quality and characteristics of that hearing. The question of entitlement will reveal the period's method and notions of the
subject. A right to be heard might obtain in four situations: the statute
expressly or by implication required a hearing; the statute appeared to
dispense with a hearing but one was inferred; the statute conferred a
discretion to hold or dispense with a hearing; and the statute was silent
(Reid 1971, 15–38). In all but the first case, the common law might
interpret a governmental body's enabling statute as intending a hearing
where that body's action affected certain interests. In making such interpretations, judges regarded themselves as invoking the 'justice of the
common law' to supply the legislature's omission (*Cooper* 1863; de Smith

1968, 141). In Britain, the legal principle had coalesced that no person might be tried for his liberty or his property without being heard (de Smith 1968, 141). By contrast, Canadian judges were more restrained, abstaining from enunciating a general right to be heard before the making of an administrative decision. It is unlikely that the absence of this right was widely known; a commentator speculates that it would have startled many Canadians (Cormie 1961, 10). Absent any general right, the right to a hearing developed sporadically across different areas. The result was that where a statute did not provide for an oral hearing, the common law was 'wholly uncertain' (Willis 1959, 51), appearing 'subjective, *ad hoc*, contradictory and disarrayed' (Reid 1971, 2). Judges' determinations in this area reflected a tension between two competing values. As Reid notes, 'justice' pulled one way, expediency the other (ibid., 1). The connection between a hearing and justice is perhaps self-evident. As for expediency, it was noted that the urgency and complexity of the decisions assigned to administrative tribunals precluded the consultation of citizens and rendered detailed accountability by state agents impracticable (Rambourg 1969, 24). The contested question of entitlement to a hearing exemplified Willis's contrast between lawyerly and bureaucratic values (1968).

While the cases did not appear to instantiate a consistent principle, certain tendencies are identifiable. A hearing would be required for the exercise of quasi-judicial functions (Reid 1971, 14). The oral hearing was conceived of, for the most part, as arising in relation to property, the 'innumerable occasions on which civil servants or boards are entitled to interfere with the property or livelihood of the citizen – shutting down his business premises as insanitary, or cancelling his taxi-driver's licence' (Willis 1959, 51). A union was entitled to a hearing before undergoing decertification (*L'Alliance des professeurs* 1953). Likewise, a landowner was entitled to a hearing before his premises were condemned as unfit for human habitation (*Board of Health for Saltfleet Township* 1954). By contrast, a securities salesman was not entitled to be heard before the revocation of his licence (*Ontario Securities Commission* 1957). Confronted by this mosaic of case law (Reid 1971, 4ff.), one may attempt valiantly to make sense of it by hypothesizing that interference with rights attracted a hearing, while interference with privileges, such as the securities licence, did not. But such a distinction fails to reconcile all the cases. Interference with privileges occasionally moved judges to require a hearing.

Brief mention is warranted of the Canadian Bill of Rights (1960). It guarantees a right to a 'fair hearing in accordance with the principles of fundamental justice' for the determination of a person's rights and obligations (s. 2(e)). But this provision had little effect on the question of the necessity of a hearing, since jurisprudence already required a hearing when 'rights' were at stake (Reid 1971, 38).

In this era, administrative decision makers, like judges, were not required to give reasons for their decisions (de Smith 1968, 133). A failure to provide reasons would not usually be considered an error (Reid 1971, 253–4). Defenders of this status quo relied on several arguments. One was that the writing of reasons would burden the administrative process and substantially diminish its efficiency. This instrumental concern with efficiency reflects bureaucratic values and emanated from those favourable to the administrative state's flourishing. Another argument concerned the appropriate site of accountability. Wade writes that an obligation to provide reasons would conflict with the rule that Parliament was the 'primary place for the declaration and defence of political decisions' and the forum in which to obtain answers in particular cases (1949, 230). The volume of files passing through the British administrative state, even as he wrote, saps the credibility of the view of Parliament as an effective forum for accountability. A third argument is revealing not only of the debate over reasons, but more broadly of the understanding of administrative decision making. The claim is that there would be nothing to say: administrative decisions are essentially factual, and specifying reasons in each case would result in mere reiterations of the general policy. Wade suggests that many cases were 'little else than a fact-finding inquiry followed by a political decision' (ibid., 231). Repeating the policy in individual cases would, in his assessment, provide 'doubtful' satisfaction (ibid., 230). There is little sense, in this view, of the way in which a rule or policy might be inflected differently according to various facts. Facts and policies are not seen as engaged in a process of mutual constitution. Rather, the ontological assumption is that facts are unchanging inputs, the raw material on which policy operates.

In contrast, some commentators were troubled by the absence of a legal duty on administrative decision makers to provide reasons. One speculates that the failure to require reasons was the aspect of Anglo-Canadian administrative law that would strike an outside observer as most unfavourable (Cormie 1961, 10). Suggestions for a reasons requirement emerged, one applicable to agents exercising judicial and quasi-judicial functions (Dussault 1969, 538; see also Reid 1971, 254n25). Reasons were perceived as aiding individuals in better protecting their established rights. Specifically, arguments in favour of reasons seized instrumentally on the way in which reasons aided the individual in having a decision overturned on judicial review or on appeal. Willis notes that the absence of written reasons made it difficult for citizens to know whether they had grounds for resorting to the courts. Moreover, a lack of written reasons eliminated the possibility of an important ground for challenging a decision: error of law on the face of the record (Willis 1959, 53; see also Cormie 1961, 10). Where the citizen's recourse was not judicial review, but a statutory appeal, concern for the provision of reasons was particularly sharp. The view was that a board's remaining silent as to its reasons for decision inappropriately thwarted the individual's statutory appeal (*Re Ross* 1953, 568; Rogers 1953, 812–13).

Observe that opponents and proponents of administrative reasons shared joint occupancy of a narrow conceptual space. The point is perhaps best revealed by the silences in the debate. There is little sense that a requirement to give reasons – to motivate a decision, as it is said in French – might improve decision making. I mean the idea that a reasons requirement constrains the range of choices the decision maker may make by eliminating those choices not publicly articulable (Dyzenhaus and Fox-Decent 2001).[8] This is an instrumental argument, but it differs from Willis's point that the provision of reasons simply makes it easier to identify bad decision making. In theory, writing reasons sharpens a tribunal's reasoning process, thus reducing the likelihood that appeal would be desirable. But the period's debates over reasons seemed to presume that the quantity of objectionable decisions is a constant not reducible by a reasons requirement.

Moreover, neither side seems alert to the function of reasons as a means of justification in the sense of attempting to persuade the individual of the merits of an adverse decision. Receipt of reasons leads the individual either to fight the decision or to conclude that fighting it would be futile. Willis's comment that the appearance of fair procedures makes an adverse decision that an individual does not understand more palatable to him is, similarly, not a concern with justification. By contrast, the idea of reasons as justification aspires to present reasoning that the individual will understand and accept.[9] Yet in these debates there is little sense that the process of justifying a decision to the affected individual bridges, in an important way, the distance between agency and individual. There is no sense, as would follow much later in relational theorists' work on administrative law, of a relationship to be sustained and enhanced between bureaucrats and individuals.

Finally, both camps presuppose an atomistic conception of subjects and administration according to which administrative decision makers are engaged in a series of bilateral transactions with discrete individuals, not a multilateral, diachronic project of governance. Reasoned decisions are not understood as assisting those particular individuals and their peers to adjust their future conduct in light of how an administrative policy applied in particular cases. This vision of a string of distinct, unrelated cases reflects the view, noted in connection with the quasi-judicial/administrative dichotomy, that officials are not trading in law, a view reflected in the absence of any doctrine of precedent before administrative tribunals. Their enterprise – call it policy, call it expediency – does not engender rules of social conduct. It is time to turn from these discrete sets of rules and reflect on the ways in which administrative law produced identities, generating different senses of subjectivity and citizenship.

Contingent Citizens

Then, as now, citizenship was a complex, multifaceted production. In the period's judgments and scholarship, the concepts of different dimensions of citizenship and of the consequences flowing from citizenship functioned in different, mutually reinforcing ways to constitute legal subjects (Bosniak 2000; Dummett and Nicol 1990). Citizenship was intricately linked with economic rights (Marshall 1950). It was of the greatest importance, writes one scholar, to ensure the protection of the rights of citizens in the face of a growing administration (Dussault 1969, 513). But such statements problematically presume the naturalness and self-evidence of conceptions of citizenship and of rights.[10] Citizenship and rights appeared in administrative law in three ways, starting with the legal sense in which individuals were juridically subject to the law's privileges and protections by virtue of a national identity status.

International and domestic law defined citizens in relation to non-citizens or aliens, their constitutive outside. Traditional international law in no way restricted the right of any state to exclude or expel aliens and to devise whatever machinery it deemed necessary for exercising this prerogative. The view that follows is of immigration as a privilege to be bestowed or withheld at the pleasure of the host state. As John Hucker observes, in most countries procedural safeguards for immigrants had been slow to emerge (1975, 655–6; see also Corbett 1960, 489). Consistent with this general orientation, administrative law during this period discriminated on the basis of citizenship and domicile in bestowing its protections (Hucker 1975). Parliament granted immigration officials broad discretionary authority. Judges had classified as administrative, as opposed to quasi-judicial, a number of common acts of immigration authorities, such as a board of inquiry's issuance of a deportation order, the immigration minister's confirmation of a deportation order or consideration of an appeal, and an immigration officer's conduct of a hearing (Reid 1971, 131). Visa hearings were highly informal. Moreover, Parliament enacted into legislation its wish to pre-empt the courts from interfering with the immigration administration, simultaneously materializing the notion that immigration to Canada is a privilege, not a right.[11] The Immigration Act contained a strong privative clause that plucked from the courts jurisdiction to interfere with any decision within jurisdiction concerning any person not enjoying Canadian citizenship or domicile (1952, s. 24; Kronby 1959, 8–9). Immigration officials' decisions within their jurisdiction were largely unconstrained.

As today, immigration was the corner of administrative law in which personal relationships were perhaps threatened most acutely. In the historical period, the importance of relationships between family members or the impact on family members of another member's deportation drew little attention. A Supreme Court of Canada immigration case widely regarded as progressive for the time is revealing. In *R. v. Leong Ba Chai* (1954), the issue was the entry into Canada from China of a child whose father was already in Canada. The child's entry into Canada was contingent on his legitimacy, and that legitimacy was questionable. The primary issue for administrative law was not the child's legitimacy on the merits, but rather the immigration officer's refusal to consider the application. Taschereau J. held that mandamus lay directing the immigration officer to carry out his statutory duty to determine whether the child otherwise complied with the provisions of the Immigration Act. For the judge, the child's legitimacy was a simple conflict-of-laws issue: the personal status of the child as to his legitimacy was governed by the domicile of the father. Therefore, once it was established as a question of fact that the child had been legitimated in China, while his father had his domicile there, the law of Canada would recognize the legitimacy of that child (Castel 1958, 2–3). The child's legitimacy and thus his capacity to join his father was merely a somewhat technical matter of private international law. The impact on the child of an adverse decision was fully irrelevant to the administrative official and the judge. The file was to be dealt with not on the basis of any reference to the social context or any impact on the parties, but by reference to the local British Columbian expert in the Chinese law of legitimacy. There was no sense that the law, purposively, was structuring relationships (Nedelsky 1993b).

As in other areas of administrative law, a minority line of critical scholarly commentary transcended the formalism of the citizen/alien dichotomy. D.C. Corbett points to the oddity that Canada, which prides itself on the rule of law, should authorize such informal, unreviewable proceedings in immigration cases. Where a vital matter affects a Canadian citizen in Canada, he or she normally has access to the courts and enjoys the safeguards of court procedure. By contrast, a person applying as an immigrant does not get the same chance (Corbett 1960, 489). Such a comparison presumes some measure of human worth running across the citizenship/alien distinction. Similarly, John Hucker prefers to set aside formal classifications and instead consider animating values of natural justice and the administrative scheme's impact. The distinction between administrative and quasi-judicial acts, runs his argument, should not deter Canadian courts from relying on the precepts underlying natural justice to require good faith and fairness for immigration procedures (Hucker 1975, 662). Hucker compares the impact of deportation proceedings on the individual with the impact of criminal proceedings, noting that the latter attract substantial procedural protections. Deportation, particularly of individuals already resident in Canada, who usually have established family, personal, and economic ties, frequently entails a disruption of life at least as great as that inflicted by a prison sentence (ibid., 690n229). To Hucker, the view of immigration as a privilege was 'unduly formalistic' and wrongly ignored the 'gradual accretion of rights to the individual as he forges ties with this country through lawful residence here' (ibid., 682). This statement is a rare instance of spatial and temporal contextualism in the period. It shows a sense of the subject as socially embedded and developing over time, in that the lived experience of a person and his reliance on a given state of affairs serves, in some measure, to counter the formal classification of immigration as a privilege. These comments that transcend administrative law's formal, category-based approach constitute minority critiques of the existing regime. The main point to be drawn from an examination of state citizenship in the historical period is that the legal subject mattered to administrative law on the basis of its status as citizen of a sovereign state. While the citizen's mobility rights were clearly the product of the state, the category of property rights produced a different conception of the citizen, one regarded as based on rights pre-existing state action.

'Much of the history of judicial review of administrative action,' writes David Mullan, 'is wrapped up with the courts' vindication of traditional property rights in land, personalty, or money already possessed' (1980, 77; see also Dyzenhaus 2002b, 531–2). Many of the common law administrative principles developed in settings where courts intervened to constrain agencies' interference with proprietary rights. An early case, *Cooper* (1863), stands for the proposition that the grant of confiscatory power is subject to a qualification that no man is to be deprived of his property without his having an opportunity to be heard. The connection between procedural protections and protection of property, and the sense of property rights as crucial to individuals, is historically well established. Within Canada the protection of property rights was less stringent than in England. Canadian courts did not follow their English counterparts in unearthing in the common law the entitlement to a hearing prior to expropriation; they seem to have been less stringent in their defence of laissez-faire liberalism from state encroachment (Tucker 1987, 576).

At junctures, admittedly, it is unclear whether the Canadian judges are hashing out a coherent understanding of property rights more consistent than the English solution with local economic and geographical imperatives (cf. Watson 1993, ch. 4), such as the need for governmental construction of railways and other infrastructure, or whether they are fumbling in the dark. A case from the late 1950s is arguably more an instance of one formal dichotomy colliding with another than of coherent development of a theory of the relationship between the administration and property rights. In *Calgary Power Ltd. v. Copithorne* (1959), a public utility company failed in negotiating a right of way directly with the plaintiff. The utility subsequently obtained ministerial authorization for the expropriation of a right of way across the plaintiff's land. The minister's order was duly filed in the land titles office, although the landowner received no notice of any of these proceedings, nor was he given any opportunity to be heard by the minister. Two live issues before the Supreme Court were whether the minister's act was quasi-judicial, thus entailing notice and a hearing, and whether a right of way was an 'interest in land' and thus within the scope of things statutorily susceptible to expropriation. Martland J. for the Court reproduced passages from the strictest authorities on the classification of quasi-judicial acts, but spent little time applying them to the facts of the case. He concluded swiftly that the minister's decision was a policy decision for which he was answerable only to the legislature. As for the second issue,

Martland J. examined several real property statutes and concluded that the interest at stake was an interest in land. What is revealed here is a 'serious tension' in the libertarian position (Dyzenhaus and Fox-Decent 2001, 206n24). The libertarian opposes redistribution and wishes to protect private property, but he also opposes the welfare state, disdaining to dignify it as legal and thus amenable to rational supervision. Though the justifications are unclear, in *Copithorne* the latter wish trumped, leaving undisturbed a confiscation of property.

Nonetheless, while the letter of the *Cooper* law did not obtain in Canada, its spirit managed to sustain a considerable focus on proprietary rights. *Cooper* was present in the Canadian administrative law of the period less as a matter of positive law than of legal culture. When commentators are concerned about whether the absence of formality in administrative procedure risks harming 'les droits des citoyens' (Beetz 1965, 253) or that every agency must, in the course of its procedures, respect 'des droits et libertés des administrés' (Dussault 1969, 538; see also Prémont 1962, 56), those rights referred to are typically proprietary rights. Likewise, the concern with the 'existing rights' (Wade 1949, 233) or 'established rights' (*Board of Health for Saltfleet* 1954, 374) or 'droit possédé' (*L'Alliance des Professeurs Catholiques* 1953, 154) of private citizens is generally proprietary. One would not refer to human rights as existing rights but rather as inherent, intrinsic, or fundamental rights.

However they were called, property rights stood always in contrast with 'mere' interests or privileges. Interference with privileges did not attract due process in the same way as interference with rights. While judges often, though not always, held that interference with rights required a prior hearing, withdrawal of a privilege was much less likely to do so (Reid 1971, 34–5). Like the quasi-judicial/administrative distinction, the right/privilege distinction is slippery. The classification often turned on semantics. A view prevailed in some quarters that conferral of a new licence was a mere privilege, for the purposes of determining applicable procedural guarantees, but that interference with an existing licence constituted interference with an acquired right. This distinction was too nice for some (Brun 1974, 431). That it was governmental regulation which had created the need to obtain a licence further complicated the picture. Thus a regulatory regime that made licences necessary (privileges) had taken away the prior right to transact business free from regulation. In this respect, the withdrawal of a licence could be framed as a deprivation of the 'common-law right to engage in a business' (Rogers 1953, 814). In a similar vein, one commentator regarded as 'frightening' the official view of permits or licences as privileges permitting citizens to do what has been 'a free man's right for centuries' (Cormie 1961, 7–8). Not all commentators, however, believed the distinction to be tenuous. Gordon believed that the words of the statute conclusively governed the inquiry as to whether regulatory activities involve vested rights (1932). Beyond its uncertainty, the distinction warrants criticism in the light of today's standards because it failed to track a substantive distinction between important and unimportant impacts on the individual. Interests classified as 'privileges' were not necessarily trivial, nor did their withdrawal generate only minimal impacts on those affected. The licence associated with an occupation was typically regarded as a privilege, the cancellation of which was regarded as mere executive action. Parole was discounted as a mere privilege, and its inferior status as such furnished justification for the denial of due process in parole application procedures (Jobson 1972, 284).

In England but not in Canada, courts required a hearing before the confiscation of land. Willis regards it 'an amusing commentary on the wholly relative character of what is or is not fair in administrative procedure' that while the Englishman enjoyed this inalienable right to be heard before the confiscation of his land for public purposes, the Canadian had to make do with arguing in court over the amount of compensation owed him (1959, 47). But the distinction to which Willis draws attention does not underline only the relative and contingent character of fair administrative procedure. It also illuminates the meaning of the property right itself, since the meaning of the right is the way it functions within society. The way that commentators conceive of property rights vis-à-vis other interests is revealing. Speaking of the evolution of administrative law, Rambourg observes that the right of property lost its absolute character when the notion of the collective interest expanded (1969, 36). Angus argues for judicial restraint when property is in issue, suggesting that civil libertarian values warrant more rigorous protection than proprietary values. He notes that extensive judicial intervention to protect proprietary interests will thwart the effective achievement of statutory objectives through administrative action (Angus 1974, 192–3). Both commentators show themselves sympathetic to the bureaucratic objectives of the administrative state. Willis, a staunch functionalist and a self-proclaimed 'government man' (1974, 225), favours the collective interest. He agrees that judicial intervention in the service of property interests inappropriately impedes executive action. But he disagrees with Angus in the suggestion that courts intervene less in the interest of property and more in the interest of civil libertarian values. Indeed, Willis shows himself insouciant about both property interests and other individual interests. He disparages 'a number of currently fashionable cults and the damage they may do to effective government if they are allowed to infiltrate too deeply into the procedural part of administrative law.' As his first example, he provided, using eloquently dismissive inverted commas, the 'cult of "the individual" and claims by prisoners in penitentiaries, complaining of their treatment there or applying for parole, to a formal "right to be heard"' (ibid., 229).

Innovative ways of regarding property complicated further the already unstable distinction between rights and privileges. An influential article by Charles Reich (1964) provided an argument that privileges can be recharacterized as entitlements, 'a new property to be fairly and impartially dispensed according to law' (Jobson 1972, 287). While Reich's argument was not explicitly adopted in the administrative law of the period, glimmers appear of an expanding sense of property rights. David Mullan provides an instructive reading of Rand J.'s reasons in *Roncarelli v. Duplessis* (1959). *Roncarelli* involved a claim by a Jehovah's Witness restaurateur for civil damages against the premier of Quebec for requesting the cancellation of the restaurateur's liquor licence. Duplessis had wished to shut down Roncarelli's restaurant in retaliation for his having posted bail for many of his fellow Jehovah's Witnesses. Mullan observes that Rand J. emphasized the significance of occupational interests as a backdrop to his decision on the illegality of the premier's actions. By emphasizing the occupational interests, Rand J. showed a willingness to peer behind what Mullan calls the 'charade' that would legally classify such licences and interests as mere privileges. Rand J. wrote: 'As its [the licence's] exercise continues, the economic life of the holder becomes progressively more deeply implicated with the privilege while at the same time his vocation becomes correspondingly dependent on it.' He noted, too, that 'the field of licensed occupations and businesses of this nature is steadily becoming of greater concern to citizens generally' (*Roncarelli* 1959, 140). Mullan writes that from one perspective, all that Rand J. did was to equate occupational licensing with traditional property interests in land, goods, and money, on the basis that prior to state intervention, individuals were free to undertake the regulated action. This equation does not approach the recognition of sharply different kinds of property interest suggested by Reich's essay. Yet given the time and legal context, Mullan continues, Rand J.'s was a significant statement, 'cutting through as it did the unfortunate legal ramifications of the term "privilege" and foreshadowing the judicial development of recognition of both substantive and procedural rights in all sorts of employment situations in the sixties and seventies' (1980, 77–8 [footnotes omitted]). It is also significant that Rand J. awarded damages for future losses beyond the date of the licence's expiry, though Roncarelli had no right to a renewal (ibid., 74). Yet there is a further dimension that Mullan does not address.

Rand J. connected the potential of holding a licence, a mere privilege, with a legal concept grounded in rights, citizenship. Regarding the premier's definitive disqualification of Roncarelli from ever again obtaining a liquor licence, Rand J. wrote: 'This purports to divest his citizenship status of its incident of membership in the class of those of the public to whom such a privilege could be extended' (*Roncarelli* 1959, 141). This rhetorical gesture was astute because, strictly speaking, the law of the time recognized no right to belong to a class eligible to receive privileges. Indeed, even Rand J.'s notion of citizenship remained much thinner than, say, the conception of citizenship as including basic social rights such as health care and education (Marshall 1950). Moreover, there is no suggestion that Rand J.'s approach was typical of his colleagues on the bench or of commentators during the period. Indeed, *Roncarelli* merits its place in the pantheon of Canadian administrative law judgments in large measure by virtue of its having departed so markedly from contemporary judgments.

It is worth reflecting on the presumptions underlying the right/privilege dichotomy and its application. The present account shows a majority of participants in administrative law accepting the coherence of that distinction, and a minority questioning it. For those in the majority, their reliance on property and the importance of policing the boundary separating private property – acquired rights – from administrative action take property and the boundary as natural and unproblematic. They do not acknowledge that the right of property requires not only collective enforcement but also collective definition (Tucker 1987, 568; Nedelsky 1989, 18). The right of property is regarded as a thing to be protected, not one of several important values to be collectively determined (Nedelsky 1990, 165). Moreover, as it occurs in the period's literature and judgments, the idea that interference with property rights requires strict procedural protections is framed not as a qualitative assessment that this kind of government action is more serious than others, but rather as the assumption that until government starts to take something from a landowner, government has not already been acting. The reliance on property in administrative law presumes the coherence of a natural state of affairs in which a minimalist government does nothing and property holders simply enjoy their rights. In its neglect or refusal to acknowledge the contextual and social dimensions of property, this majority vision is thoroughly formal and acontextual. It is not apolitical, far from it (Dyzenhaus 2002b, 553); but it depends on a refusal to consider the context in which property rights are constituted and enforced. By contrast, subscribers to the minority view demonstrate a contextual recognition of the contingency of property rights.

One is left, then, with a sense of the legal subject as a bearer of property rights. It is interference with property rights that most impelled the intervention of judges to read procedural requirements into silent or ambiguous statutes. Moreover, the focus on property rights is constituted in relation to a lesser focus on interests or privileges. This distinction is drawn formally, not on any sound basis or assurance that deprivation of property rights caused greater harm to individuals than withdrawal of so-called privileges. The sense emerges for the most part, then, of an administrative law apparatus concerned with policing somewhat arid distinctions, consequently maintaining a view of individuals as property owners. The holding of property rights appears to have been the chief characteristic of individuals as they merited the judiciary's intervention on their behalf. I do not wish to suggest that administrative law judges engineered this focus on property. Material constraints doubtless played a role: it may often have been in the property cases that individuals had the private resources to bear the financial costs of the judicial proceedings (Angus 1974, 188–9). The overall effect, though, was to emphasize subjects as proprietors.

I noted earlier the notion that civil libertarian values deserved protection more rigorous than did proprietary interests. Angus's suggestion indicated a rudimentary view of the legal subject as a bearer of civil and political rights in a sense relevant for administrative law, as did a couple of judgments by Rand J. of the Supreme Court of Canada. The first case for this discussion is *Roncarelli*. What is relevant for present purposes is Mullan's reading of the case, specifically of Rand J.'s statement about the limits of statutory discretion. Mullan sees the judgment as indicating a vision of the Canadian constitutional system founded on shared values as to the freedom of religious beliefs and the right of individuals to exercise clear legal rights such as the posting of bail for people charged with criminal offences (1980, 76–7).

A second noteworthy case is *Smith and Rhuland Ltd. v. The Queen* (1953). This appeal concerned an order made by the Nova Scotia Labour Relations Board, rejecting an application for certification of a union as bargaining agent for certain employees in a collective unit. The board had found the unit suitable for bargaining purposes and determined that the other conditions for certification had been satisfied. Nevertheless, on the basis that the union's secretary-treasurer, who had organized the local body and signed the application, was a communist and the dominating influence, the board refused the certification. The Nova Scotia Court of Appeal had quashed the board's decision, and a majority of the Supreme Court of Canada dismissed the appeal. Rand J. observed that no law prohibited holding communist views or being a member of a group or party supporting them. In his view, treating the secretary-treasurer's political views as a ground for refusing certification evinced a want of faith in the intelligence and loyalty of the union's membership. He concluded that the board had not been empowered to act on the view that official association with an individual holding political views considered dangerous by the board is incompatible with formation of a labour organization. The values underlying Rand J.'s (and the Court of Appeal's) decision appear to be respect for civil liberty and political choice. Rand J.'s extrajudicial writings magnify the hints at civil libertarian values in this and other of his judgments (1960, 152–6; 1954; 1951). Admittedly, Rand J. is not articulating commitments generally shared by the majority of his colleagues or of his critical audience. Gordon blasts the judgment, largely on the basis that 'an administrative tribunal has always been considered to have a complete and unfettered discretion, one to be governed by considerations of policy and expediency, which are what the tribunal chooses to make them' (1954, 86).[12] Nonetheless, these judgments, even if exceptional in their time, attest that administrative law did not constrain only administrative tribunals' interference with property rights. The political rights of the citizen attracted at least some attention.

It is perhaps unsurprising that, in an era of rapid institutional development and change, scholarly attention focused more on institutional relationships than on the individuals in whose ultimate service the administrative state operated. As elaborated in the context of the quasi-judicial/administrative dichotomy and the right to a hearing, administrative law attended more to institutional arrangements and formal classifications than to the individual affected, the impact of administrative action on him or her, and the appropriate relationship between that individual and the administrative agency. The subject of administrative action was, for the most part, absent and disembodied. Indeed, the legal subject occupied an intermediate position of disadvantage between two possible positions.

On one hand, the legal subject of administrative action was regarded abstractly enough that particular facts of his or her experience over time were only rarely regarded as legally relevant. Where the individual was conceived of as embodied, it was negatively, as an isolated and vulnerable body. Manifesting the concerns relating to the growth of administrative tribunals, some commentators feared that the administrative might of the state threatened to crush isolated and vulnerable individuals (Prémont 1962, 64). Rand J. speaks of the 'isolated individual' tossed like a cork on the ocean of economic, social, and political organizations (1961, 189). Recall, too, Abel's objection to recognition of standing on the part of persons objecting to administrative decisions: such standing transformed the other members of the community who could benefit from the regime into 'bodiless wraiths' (1962, 75). It was exceptional for the facts of daily life to loosen the grip of legal dichotomies such as right/privilege, in the manner of Rand J.'s anomalous acknowledgment in *Roncarelli* of the dependence on a liquor licence increasing with time.

On the other hand, the legal subject was rooted enough that it was national law that governed, not universal human rights or notions of human dignity. The immigration setting made this point most sharply. It is chiefly in French-language scholarship that one can trace early expressions of concerns with the legal subject as a bearer of human dignity and with the sort of values that are viewed by some contemporary scholars as crucial to administrative law. For Rivero, participation in the administrative process would privilege a certain conception of the person and of human dignity. He writes that it is a 'conception de l'homme qui est au cœur du débat. Les procédés de concert, d'explication, d'adhésion, ne font que traduire une certaine idée de la dignité de la personne, qui "exige que chacun agisse suivant une détermination consciente et libre"' (1965, 832 [footnote omitted], cited in Pépin 1969, 605).

A final point related to dignity arises regarding democratic values. Some sense obtained that rights of participation in administrative decision making instantiated democratic values. Gilles Pépin states that procedure's value is not only defensive and conservative; it is by means of procedure that one assures the participation of *les administrés* in the process of elaborating, adopting, and applying the decisions that interest them. Procedure 'permet d'étendre le règne de la démocratie à l'action administrative qui, très souvent, fait large part à des éléments plus ou moins discrétionnaires' (Pépin 1969, 604). He sees procedural safeguards as transcending their instrumental, property-based concerns, concluding that 'la procédure peut largement contribuer à faire de l'administré, face à la décision administrative, non plus un sujet mais un citoyen' (ibid., 605). Another contrast draws out the significance of the difference between *administré* and *citoyen*. The notion of citizenship is 'imbued with the idea of participating in public life within the framework of the state, being one among equals in a republic.' As such it contrasts with *ressortissant*, which invokes, rather more narrowly, 'the person linked by nationality to a particular state' (Dummett and Nicol 1990, 9). Within the administrative law context in which Pépin was writing, the idea of administrative law's safeguards as democratizing the relationship between administration and citizen was relatively novel. If the function, in part, of procedural safeguards is promoting democracy, rather than defending or conserving property, the set of circumstances in which those safeguards become appropriate opens up. The basis for restricting procedural safeguards to the property settings to which they had been largely confined, or to decision making in which the tribunal's powers and procedures are judicial or quasi-judicial, disintegrates (Pépin, 608). Such a broad vision also emerges from Rand J.'s reasons in *Roncarelli*, for example his reference to 'the rule of law as a fundamental postulate of our constitutional structure' (1959, 141). In Rivero's view, participation in the administrative process terminates the status of the person concerned as a stranger to the act concerning him: 'entre l'autorité et lui, un dialogue se noue' (1965, 822; compare Cartier 2002). Charles Taylor might view the phenomenon Rivero contemplates as shared agency, with two actors acting simultaneously. They are not merely coordinating their actions, but actually acting together (1997, 171–2). By contrast, a much thinner conception of democracy sees the democratic state as protecting the rights and freedoms of citizens from encroachment by the administration, without concern for the citizens' involvement in the process (Dussault 1969, 528).

The rules, practices, and scholarship of administrative law in the period 1950 to 1975 produced a thin legal subject. Part of this was a function of the scant attention paid to the individual. As shown by the institutional rivalry of which privative clauses formed the lightning rod, much of the energy expended by those active in administrative law went to negotiating and contesting institutional boundaries. The emphasis on the relationship between institutions – boards and courts – left scarce attention for the description of the subject or explicit consideration as to which relationships were appropriately promoted. The conception of the legal subject was also thin in the sense of comprising narrow legal categories but little of lived experience, relationships, and commitments. From the liberal orientation towards judicial review, the availability of procedural safeguards to individuals interacting with administrative decision makers frequently hinged on a classification exercise, with protections attaching to one side of a dichotomy and not the other. I am thinking of dichotomies and their classification exercises concerning the process legally required (quasi-judicial or administrative), the endangered interest (right or privilege), and the claimant's status (citizen or alien). For example, certiorari was possible only where judges construed a statute as demanding a 'quasi-judicial' process of the decision maker. In contrast, 'administrative' or 'executive' decisions were virtually unreviewable. Reliance upon on/off status or classifications, such as citizen or privilege, eliminated possible inquiries as to the impact of decisions on individuals, in particular, impacts that intensify with time. References to situations changing over time – I noted exceptional ones regarding a licence holder and a non-citizen making a life in Canada – were rare. Nor was there much attention to the context in which a particular administrative act occurred, or to the institutional context of the tribunal itself. The debates over the appropriate interpretation of privative clauses, though engaging political stakes, were largely channelled within a formal, acontextual method. One can thus observe the thin subject and formal, acontextual method criticized by relational theory. From the functionalist perspective, the individual subject was virtually invisible; what mattered, instead, was expedience in executing the administration's program. Neither orientation I have discussed was satisfactory when viewed from the perspective of relational theory.

The period's normative commitments took effect through a view of the legal subject focused on property rights and interests. Administrative law also placed considerable emphasis on the formal statuses of citizenship and domicile. I indicated a limited concern with protection of political and civil rights, which gestures at some sense of the subject as a political actor. Only a couple of commentators were explicitly alert to the effects that procedural safeguards played in constructing the relationship between the state and the individual as a democratic citizen.

Gordon's putatively apolitical 'pure' theory of jurisdiction aside, it seems that judicial intervention aimed to protect property rights. Narrow readings of privative clauses to permit judicial intervention – particularly in the labour union cases – had the effect of reinforcing the sense of the legal subject as locus of property rights.

The prevailing conception of administrative law regarded it as a body of rules. In other words, the writings of a majority of administrative law scholars and judges in the earlier period exemplified a positivist, rule-based conception. Michel Rambourg, for example, wrote that adminis-trative law is most often defined as 'un corps de règles spécifiques, exorbitantes du droit commun s'appliquant à l'administration et à ses activités' (1969, 2). Such a view reflected a positivist ethos widely held at the time. Admittedly, a tension surfaces between this view of adminis-trative law as rules and the conception of the common law that saw it as ready to fill in the gaps in statutes. Still, the earlier administrative law was far less open to, say, the interactional nature of law and the role of principles and values (Fuller 1969). The point should not, however, be overstated. Throughout the period, administrative law teachers increas-ingly considered the physiology of the administrative process, or put otherwise, 'the procedures, practices and substantive policies of ongoing public administration' (Christie 1971, 12). This phrase gets at what Fuller would have called administrative law as an enterprise. Ram-bourg himself acknowledged the sociologically richer view of adminis-trative law as a social system (1969, 34). At least one judge, Ivan Rand, presaged the contemporary focus on values, although the ethos was not widely accepted in their time (*Roncarelli* 1959, 141; Rand 1961, 190; 1951, 4; see also McWhinney 1959). Rand J.'s shared values bespoke a less rule-based, more values-based common law constitutionalism. Nonetheless, it was the notion of administrative law as an 'ensemble of rules' (Rambourg 1969, 10) that prevailed. Where, as in this historical period, a regime is so uncongenial to relational theory's concerns, it matters little how a relational inquiry is structured. But the succeeding period, which would show considerable impatience with many of the sterile classificatory rules presented in this chapter, and would turn, at critical junctures, to contextualism, will call for a separation of rela-tional theory's method from its normative commitments.

6 Contextualism Emerges

Scholars have not thoroughly explored the connections between the contextual methodology that has emerged within Canadian administrative law and the contextualism promoted by relational theorists and other strands of feminism. In what may be the only essay to examine Canadian administrative law from an explicitly feminist perspective, Alison Harvison Young suggests that the language of 'contextualisation' turns out not to indicate deep connections with feminism (1997, 333–4). I am less sure that this is the case. Her essay addresses mainly one level of contextualism, the propensity on the part of courts to regard administrative agencies contextually or, as Harvison Young prefers to say, functionally. She also discusses bias and what can be regarded as another level of contextualism, one applicable to individual bureaucrats. In this chapter I argue that contemporary administrative law has adopted a method of contextualism. It has come to produce contextual subjects. I will examine the development of a contextual methodology for both administrative agencies and individual bureaucrats, but I shall also identify the rise of a third level of contextualism, one applied to those individuals subject to administrative action. These second and third levels of contextualism produce legal subjects firmly embedded in their particular contexts. Viewed together, these three levels show considerable affinity for the contextualism advocated by relational theorists.

At the outset, possible divergences from relational theory call for mention. Some relational theorists speak of contextualism without saying much about formal rules or criteria. It is possible in philosophical discussions to argue for analytical approaches that depart radically from traditional methods. In legal settings, however, institutional practices and textual authorities such as statutory and doctrinal texts constrain the possibilities for change. The adoption of a methodology of contextualism recounted in this chapter turns out to be shot through with contradictory tendencies in which formalism resurges. At times, formalism's resurgence occurs simultaneously with a major advance in contextualism. The institutional practices of legal settings also prompt inquiry as to whether the organs that attempt to adopt a contextual methodology possess the capacity to do so successfully. Another possible divergence concerns the methodology of contextualism and its underlying normative commitments. Relational theorists sometimes imply that their relational inquiry and contextual methodology can be deployed neutrally, without explicit recourse to their normative commitments. They present the idea that focusing on relationships can help resolve political and legal quandaries. To the contrary, this chapter's study of contextualism in administrative law will highlight the imbrication of normative commitments and the contextual methodology through which they are realized. The upshot is recognition that the contextual methodology cannot be totally prior to the normative project and distinct from it. The story of contextualism's emergence begins with administrative procedure.

Agencies' Procedure

For a long time, the availability of certiorari to challenge a decision and the applicability of the rules of natural justice turned on the outcome of a classification of that decision as quasi-judicial or administrative. In the late 1970s the Supreme Court of Canada announced that in determining the applicability of procedural safeguards to administrative decision making, the classification was no longer necessary. *Nicholson v. Haldimand–Norfolk Regional Board of Commissioners of Police* (1978) concerned a police officer's dismissal during his probationary period. A regulation made under the police board's enabling legislation provided officers the right to a hearing and an appeal prior to any penalty. Yet it also carved out an exception that permitted the board to dispense with a constable's services within the first eighteen months. The police board contended that the officer, whose dismissal fell within that period, was dismissible at pleasure. It was, claimed the board, under no obligation to give notice, hear representations, or offer reasons before dispensing with the officer's services. Chief Justice Laskin, for a slim majority, rejected the view in the lower courts' judgments that there was 'no halfway house' between the full observance of natural justice and arbitrary removal (ibid., 321). He recognized the emergence of 'a notion of fairness involving something less than the procedural protection of traditional natural justice,' and favourably cited a judicial pronouncement that a general duty of fairness obtains in the administrative or executive field (ibid., 324). Behind the emergence of a duty of fairness, he wrote, stands the realization of the difficulty of the quasi-judicial/administrative classification of statutory functions. Most importantly, it is unjust to endow some decisions with procedural protection while denying others any at all. The source of this injustice is the fact that statutory decisions classified as administrative may raise the same serious consequences for those adversely affected as decisions classified as quasi-judicial (ibid., 325).[1] The proper approach is to undertake a contextual examination of the particular decision being made to determine what protections are warranted. As Michael Taggart puts it, the administrative/judicial dichotomy 'withered under the fairness sunlamp' (2003, 324).

One objection to this approach concerns the shift in judicial methodology it entails. Martin Loughlin argues that proponents of fairness fail 'to recognize the change in the method of legal discourse and function of the courts required' on adoption of the informal approach proposed to replace reliance on the quasi-judicial/administrative classification (1978, 236). In Loughlin's view, the more classical judicial role of interpreting and applying the rules of natural justice was consistent with the distinctiveness of the methods and functions of adjudication. (Loughlin may overestimate the conceptual clarity and thus the consistency with his own conception of the rule of law achieved by the smorgasbord of methods deployed in the classification exercise.) By contrast, the application of a flexible standard of procedural fairness demands an individualized consideration of substantive rationality, an examination that expands the set of factors the court must consider. Loughlin's charge could perhaps be reformulated. Yet the point of difference between him and proponents of procedural fairness is not that he recognizes the change in the method of judicial discourse and function while they do not. The disagreement, rather, is over the suitability – normatively and in terms of institutional capacity – of such a shift towards multifactored contextualism. Laskin C.J.C.'s adoption of contextual procedural fairness in *Nicholson* must be taken as premised on confidence in the ability of judges adequately to perform the contextual assessment.

Scholars have proposed a number of larger theories against which to situate the increase of procedural review by courts.[2] For the moment, the merits of the individual theories matters less than the link between the contextual method and a normative project of some description. Indeed, Eric Tucker makes a compelling argument that the uncertainty and arbitrariness of the classification exercise – one of its chief evils and thus a major factor in the argument for change – resulted from doubt on the part of judges as to the desirability of making such a distinction at all. In other words, the older cases were so unpredictable because judges, operating on an unarticulated normative basis, fudged the classification to include particular cases as quasi-judicial and thus procedurally reviewable (Tucker 1987, 584). Yet the story is perhaps more complicated still. Though normative commitments influence the use of contextualism, the converse is also the case. It is, in a sense, a contextualism not deterred by prior legal characterizations – despite those characterizations' claims to pre-empt further inquiry – that brings into view the similarity of the harms inflicted by acts falling on both sides of classification exercises.

The new approach announced in *Nicholson* leaves an ambiguity. The ambiguity is whether the new contextualism is meant to eliminate all classifications and sharp divisions slicing across the administrative state (Mullan 1987, 3–4). On one hand is the mention in the majority reasons of the difficulty in classifying decision-making processes as quasi-judicial or administrative. On the other hand, Laskin C.J.C. quoted a dictum 'that in the sphere of the so-called quasi-judicial the rules of natural justice run, and that in the administrative or executive field there is a general duty of fairness' (*Bates v. Lord Hailsham* 1972, 1378). Such a dictum preserves a distinction between the quasi-judicial and executive zones. What it adds is that the executive field is no longer a space devoid of procedural obligations. Indeed, in *Nicholson*'s wake, Canadian judges inscribed distinctions. One distinction is that administrative processes of a legislative character, such as the making of regulations, are exempt from procedural obligations and review (*Canada (A.G.) v. Inuit Tapirisat of Canada* 1980). A related distinction is that, to be reviewable for their procedure, decisions must affect individuals (*Cardinal v. Director of Kent Institution* 1985).

Procedural fairness now turns on two questions. The first, which may be called the threshold question, is whether there is a duty to act fairly. The application of the duty of fairness is triggered where an administrative decision affects 'the rights, privileges or interests of an individual' (ibid., 653). The impact on the individual must be 'important' and the decision 'a significant one' (*Knight v. Indian Head School Division No. 19*

1990, 677). If the threshold question is answered in the affirmative, the content question arises: what precisely satisfies fairness in the particular case? The emergence or re-emergence of these distinctions hints at some judicial discomfort with an unstructured contextual methodology. It is a reminder of the distance between political theory and institutionalized law that while judges attempted to replace formal classification procedures with a contextual methodology, existing statutes and ones subsequently enacted preserved those classifications (Leckey 2004, 333–5).

The extension of procedural fairness to administrative decision makers required courts to examine the decision maker's context. The 'eminently variable' demands of the duty of procedural fairness (*Knight* 1990, 682) were to be assessed 'in a particular legislative and administrative context' (*Cardinal* 1985, 654). L'Heureux-Dubé J. collected the case law's lessons about the content of procedural fairness. She held that the purpose of participatory rights within the duty of procedural fairness is 'to ensure that administrative decisions are made using a fair and open procedure, appropriate to the decision being made and its statutory, institutional, and social context' (*Baker v. Canada (Minister of Citizenship and Immigration)* 1999, para. 22). The content was to turn, among other things, on the process followed in making the decision (including its resemblance to adjudication), the statutory scheme (provision of statutory appeal procedures or not), and the choices of procedure made by the agency itself (ibid., paras. 23, 24, 27).

By this point, the reviewing courts have journeyed a long way from the statutory interpretation exercise – with its onerous consequences – of classifying a decision as quasi-judicial or administrative. Courts are now required to examine multiple dimensions of the administrative process. To limit the effect of this examination, *Nicholson* is predicated on a firm distinction between process and substance. The belief is that courts can supervise the procedures deployed by delegated decision makers without interfering, in a way impermissible under the prevailing conception of the separation of powers, with the substantive decisions through which legislatures and their delegates develop policy. Yet the effect is that courts have empowered themselves with a significant role in institutional design. The long-term impact of procedural review on the bureaucracy's internal management far exceeds that of substantive review for want of jurisdiction or error of law. After all, it is procedural review that requires bureaucracies to change how they function rather than simply to decide differently in a single file (Macdonald 1980b, 5–7). Indeed, procedural review may entail not only internal bureaucratic overhaul, but also legislative reform of the administrative scheme. The extreme example is perhaps the judicial holding that refugee claimants are entitled to a hearing (*Singh* 1985) and the legislative overhaul it prompted (Hurley 1996, 320).

Practically, one may inquire whether the form of typical judicial review proceedings provides courts with adequate information on which to base an assessment as to the institutional and social context of a particular decision maker. Lon Fuller writes in a discussion of institutional design that 'the architectural design of legal institutions and procedures obviously cannot be drawn by adjudicative decision' (1969, 178). One may question the legitimacy of courts' assuming this function. Loughlin argues that determining the procedures suitable in individual cases requires a substantive weighing of competing social interests, interests that cannot be quantified in terms of legal criteria so as to yield determinate outcomes (1978). My more modest point is simply that the way in which courts conceive themselves to be looking at administrative decision makers has fundamentally altered. They purport to take a contextual approach. A significant shift has occurred in the style of reasoning that reviewing courts use in procedural review, style in Loughlin's sense of 'a spirit, culture or set of values' (1992, 58; cf. Hacking 1982; Davidson 2001). When everything (relatively speaking) turned on the classification exercise of a decision-making process as quasi-judicial or administrative, a statement such as 'in practice Agency A operates with procedures P,' or 'A has itself explicitly chosen procedures P,' would have been irrelevant to the legal determination.

Questions arise about the appropriate roles of tribunals in developing procedures and of courts in policing such development. The concern here is the relative institutional capacities in light of contextualism. In determining the degree to which courts will defer to administrative agencies' procedural determinations, they oscillate between two positions. One shows glimmers of deference to agencies. It holds that, even where there is a duty of fairness, the board is master of its procedure and can choose how to carry out its duty. The object of procedural review is not to impose all the requirements of natural justice on administrative proceedings; tribunals need not assume judicial trappings (*Nicholson* 1978; *Knight* 1990, 685).[3] The other position calls for review of procedural decisions on a correctness standard. The notion is that the agency must rightly understand and satisfy its procedural obligations on pain of its decision's invalidity (*Cardinal* 1985, 661; see Evans et al. 2003, 276–80). A seeming contradiction is apparent between these stances.[4]

Another puzzling point concerns the judges' epistemic confidence that they will know a fair administrative hearing when they see one. Judges who envisage zero deference to agencies regarding the fairness of hearings presume that 'fair hearing' has a real referent against which particular administrative practices can be measured. But this is precisely what cannot be the case, at least if one takes seriously the many references to the contextually 'eminent variability' of the content of procedural fairness. It is not easy to reconcile the lip service to the variability of procedural fairness with its strict enforcement. The judicial stance that there is no margin of error as to the appropriate degree of fairness – that procedural fairness's dictates are satisfied or unsatisfied, and if the latter, the decision vitiated – indicates little scepticism about the possibility of a right answer in each scenario. Restricting deference to the precise means chosen of operationalizing a judicially determined degree of fairness makes little sense if the concept of fairness itself has no independent fixed content, varying instead from one institutional instantiation to the next. The approach that a court should adopt in deciding if the duty to act fairly was satisfied is 'thus close to empiric' (*Knight* 1990, 682). The contextual view of the diversity of administrative processes leans away from strict enforcement. This strong judicial enforcement in procedural matters raises the question of the judicial capacity for this task. The judicial capacity to see diverse contexts has, I suggest, outstripped judges' flexibility and creativity in devising procedure appropriately responsive to that diversity. In other words, the contextual recognition of administrative diversity that necessitated *Nicholson* ensures, in subsequent cases, the inadequacy of the judicial models of procedure to which judges remain bound (Loughlin 1978, 235).

The difficulty of finding language that does not distort or restrict a contextual approach to a diverse field becomes evident here. The governing metaphor, according to which varieties of procedural fairness occupy a spectrum stretching from a full criminal trial to nothingness, appears suspect. The metaphor of a spectrum implies that the difference between various procedures is quantitative – the degree of fairness – rather than qualitative (Lakoff and Johnson 2003). Inscribing a criminal trial at the top ensures that each other instantiation of procedural fairness is conceived of as trial procedures modified by a bigger or smaller minus sign. Certain procedural requirements can, admittedly, be figured without distortion on such a spectrum. The minus sign for a paper hearing is uncontroversially bigger than the minus sign for an oral hearing. Yet the utility of labouring to locate other forms of procedural fairness on the so-called spectrum is dubious. Consider the sort of procedure that might facilitate consultation when an agency exercises a power of delegated legislation. Such efforts to consult should not be invisible if later a court is concerned with globally assessing the agency's responsibility and accountability in exercising its delegated power. Yet there seems little use in situating a 'notice and comment' procedure concerning a draft rule, or an online discussion forum, on a spectrum between a trial and nothingness. The risk is that the spectrum metaphor might render invisible those means of participation that do not figure easily along it. Indeed, the notion that all administrative consultative and participatory practices are trial procedures with a minus sign is itself, contrary to the avowals of intent, acontextual.

Different administrative contexts are best served, not by imposing procedures through judicial means, but by letting the administration or Parliament devise their own. Complaints about the adversarial character of procedural fairness (Macdonald 1980a; Lacey 1992) serve as a call for creativity and proactivity on the part of legislatures and bureaucrats when they design and implement procedural structures. Much can also be asked of administrative decision makers. An onus lies on them to be reflective and self-critical about appropriate procedures within their respective settings. As Roy Sainsbury writes: 'Administrative justice is not limited to the external scrutiny of administrative practices. It also presents a series of challenges for administrative agencies themselves – a challenge to articulate what the concept (in its elements of accuracy and fairness) means in their particular setting, and a challenge to demonstrate how their internal operations meet these demands' (1992, 329). Here arguments can be made for improving administration by inculcating a greater sense of internal accountability and of the rule of law as a value internal to administration, rather than one imposed from above by judicial review (Macdonald 2004; Sossin 2004a; Halliday 2004).

Judges' cultural attachment to judicial procedures combines with administrators' superior knowledge of their individual contexts to militate in favour of judicial deference to procedural choices by agencies. Courts have gradually come to defer to agency decisions on substantive matters, in recognition of the legitimacy of the administrative state. This argument from legitimacy also extends to procedural matters (Brown and Evans 1998, vol. 2, 7–78 to 7–79; Mullan 1987). This larger study of contextualism highlights the peculiarity of promulgating a contextual approach that harnesses strict correctness review to contextually variable determinations. Another site for the rise of contextualism is courts' approach for determining the suitable stance in reviewing administrative decision makers' substantive determinations and exercises of discretion.

Agencies' Substantive Determinations

The Supreme Court of Canada has developed what it calls a 'pragmatic and functional approach' for determining the appropriate standard of review for a court reviewing a decision maker's substantive determinations. In *C.U.P.E., Local 963 v. New Brunswick Liquor Corp.* (1979), the Supreme Court of Canada declared that the legal determinations of expert administrative agencies within their jurisdiction (concerning their constitutive or enabling statute) warranted deference. Where boards were protected by a privative clause, their decisions were to be overturned only if patently unreasonable, that is, if the statute could not reasonably support the interpretation given by the board. This decision signals a recognition that specialized tribunals have developed expertise that they can and should be permitted to bring to bear on the legal questions before them. It simultaneously requires reviewing courts to look at the legal determinations by agencies within their jurisdiction to determine whether they are patently unreasonable or not. By contrast, questions concerning the limits of that jurisdiction remained subject to correctness review. The limits of jurisdiction were regarded as preliminary questions to be resolved prior to the real decision. Correctness here means the decision the reviewing court holds to be the single right one, the decision it would have made at first instance. In each case, the key question remained whether or not a particular question was preliminary and thus 'went to jurisdiction' (reviewable on correctness) or instead fell within jurisdiction (reviewable on patent unreasonableness). Dickson J.'s judgment sent conflicting signals. He called for deference by hinting that the class of jurisdictional questions should be defined with restraint. Courts should not, in his view, 'be alert to brand as jurisdictional, and therefore subject to broader curial review, that which may be doubtfully so' (ibid., 233). Yet the application of the patent unreasonableness standard to decisions made within jurisdiction ensures that the agency's decision becomes a legal artifact worth looking at, at least to some extent. Decisions within jurisdiction no longer subsist in a lawless void.

A decade later, in *U.E.S., Local 298 v. Bibeault* (1988), the Court distanced itself from what it called the formalistic analysis of the prelimi-

nary or collateral question. Beetz J. wrote that the sole question to pose
henceforth would be, 'Did the legislator intend such a matter to be
within the jurisdiction conferred on the tribunal?' (ibid., 1087). This
question was to be answered by what he called a pragmatic and functional analysis. This analysis would require the reviewing court to
examine the wording of the enactment conferring jurisdiction on the
administrative tribunal, the purpose of the statute creating the tribunal,
the reason for its existence, the area of expertise of its members, and
the nature of the particular problem. In *Bibeault*, the object of the
pragmatic and functional analysis was to determine whether the question the tribunal addressed was jurisdictional (subject to review on a
correctness standard) or non-jurisdictional (shielded by the privative
clause and subject to review only on the stringent patent unreasonableness standard). The irony of this judgment is that, while its methodology was one that appeared conducive to a contextual and deferential
stance towards tribunal decision making, its actual outcome was formal
and interventionist. The Court held that, in fact, the question was jurisdictional, and thus subject to correctness review, on the basis that it concerned a general term in the civil law. The complex relationship
between the rise of contextualism and formalism thus continues.

Several years later, the Court held that the expertise of a specialized
tribunal warranted deference to its legal decisions even when they were
not legislatively shielded by a privative clause (*Pezim* 1994). Furthermore, where there was a privative clause, it was not determinative but
was simply pertinent to the degree of deference (Dyzenhaus 2006c).
The effect of this can be that operational contextual factors outweigh
the explicit legislative text. This development testifies that the method
of contextualism is focused not only on the legislative text, but also on
how administrative agencies operate. It represents an effort not to interpret a statute, but to respond judicially to an institution. Soon after-
wards, the Court recognized an intermediate standard of review
between correctness and patent unreasonableness: the so-called reasonableness *simpliciter* standard. This standard is suitable, for example,
for decisions subject to a statutory appeal but where the tribunal has relevant expertise superior to that of the reviewing court (*Canada (Director
of Investigation and Research) v. Southam Inc.* 1996; see Comtois 2003,
62–3). The chief question animating the reasonableness standard is
whether the decision maker has provided reasons that, taken as a whole,
provide tenable support for the decision (*Law Society of New Brunswick v.
Ryan* 2003). The pragmatic and functional approach is no longer being

used to determine whether a question is jurisdictional or not. Instead, it helps the court conclude which of the three standards of review (correctness, reasonableness simpliciter, patent unreasonableness) is appropriate. Another resurgence of formalism calls for mention. This occurred in the Court's statement in *Southam* that questions which have precedential value are to be reviewed more stringently than fact-specific questions (1996, paras. 36–7). Such a suggestion stands at odds with *C.U.P.E.* (1979), in which the question held to be within jurisdiction, and thus reviewable on patent unreasonableness, was a precedent-setting matter of statutory construction.

The last major development in the pragmatic and functional approach was the Court's extension of the approach to discretionary decisions. Discretionary decisions had been traditionally regarded as essentially unreviewable, subject to a list of nominate grounds for abuse of discretion. In 1999, however, the Court pronounced in *Baker* that legal determinations and discretionary decisions are not different species; rather, each contains elements of the other.[5]

The pragmatic and functional approach inspires a number of critical observations. One may query the extent of its functionalism in the sense of concern with letting specialized government agencies carry out their assigned tasks. Such doubts arise in light of the tendency to find that where the question is a pure one of law, the correctness standard applies. Reviewing courts attempt to justify this move on the basis that, when it comes to statutory interpretation, they enjoy a residual general expertise (Leckey 2004, 346–50). It appears that courts have difficulty letting go in domains they associate with their purview, even where the specialized tribunals have developed significant and contextually relevant expertise. Some critics also charge that the approach fails the standard of pragmatism on the basis that it is too complicated. Like instances of contextualism in the family setting, it consists of an inclusive set of overlapping factors that may or may not apply in each case. Just as a tribunal's decision as to the appropriate content of procedural fairness is reviewable on a correctness basis, so a reviewing court's conclusion as to the outcome of the pragmatic and functional approach is subject to review on appeal on the same stringent standard. In other words, in each case the reviewing court must apply the pragmatic and functional approach correctly to arrive at the single 'right' standard of review (*Dr. Q* 2003, para. 43). This judicial obligation stands at odds with the view that the pragmatic and functional approach's dependence on context instates a large element of adjudicative latitude (Lahey and Ginn 2002, 263). The charge that the

approach is too complicated is a serious one if the approach's chief justification in the first place is that it eliminated the complicated and indeterminate classification of questions as jurisdictional or non-jurisdictional. A couple of points about the former method of classifying
questions as jurisdictional or non-jurisdictional must be kept in mind,
specifically regarding the old, acontextual style of reasoning.

The former method of classifying a question as jurisdictional necessitated examination of the question and of the statute. It required identifying the turf that the legislature had intended to carve away from the
residual jurisdiction of the superior courts and to confer on the administrative agency. The idea was that the question could be decisively
answered by examining the statute. There were alternative senses in
which an administrative agency's operations within its jurisdiction were
understood. One was that the agency was a law to itself, usually meant
pejoratively (cf. Macdonald 1987). Another was that within its jurisdiction, the agency was more or less lawless: within jurisdiction, the agency
applied government 'policy,' a matter of no concern to judges. Both
senses indicated a perception on the part of judges that the administrative state lacked legitimacy. The exercise of classifying questions as jurisdictional or non-jurisdictional was mandated by a Diceyan conception
of the separation of powers. The Diceyan justification for judicial review
was the rule of law's imperative to confine inferior courts within their
statutorily conferred jurisdiction for the purpose of vindicating legislative intent (the ultra vires doctrine) (Forsyth 2000b; cf. Craig 2000). So
long as courts did not touch decisions made within jurisdictions –
letting stand, for example, legal errors that did not implicate jurisdiction – those same courts could avoid looking inside the operations of
tribunals. The courts did not legitimate administrative decision making
by engaging with it and thus treating it as worthy of judicial attention.
The Diceyan model does not associate any sense of pragmatism or functionalism with the mission of reviewing courts.

Scholars have already argued ably that the three standards of review
towards which the pragmatic and functional approach points signal an
acceptance of the administrative state's legitimacy. As David Dyzenhaus
and Evan Fox-Decent argue, the standard of patent unreasonableness
requires the entry of judicial hands into what Diceyan judges would
have preferred to consider the 'legal void within the limits set by jurisdiction' (2001, 208). They show how the deferential standards of review
require that judges look at administrative decisions and in doing so
implicitly ratify the administrative state.

My addition to this conversation concerns the manner of operationalizing and securing that ratification. The pragmatic and functional approach demands of reviewing judges a novel way of seeing not only statutes and administrative decisions, but also, institutionally, the administrative state's organs. Recall how the bestowal of deference on the basis of a specialized tribunal's expertise absent a privative clause stemmed from an assessment that, in practice, the tribunal is best placed to decide, an exercise distinct from scanning the statute for a legislative command to which to defer. The pragmatic and functional approach requires judges to take into account a much broader set of concerns than occupied them when applying a test of jurisdiction. It calls for attention to context.

When an ostensibly flexible contextual methodology is introduced, key questions are how to make it workable and how long will it sustain its flexibility before it reifies.[6] The Supreme Court has enunciated four factors for its pragmatic and functional approach. They are not intended to be exhaustive, nor are they mutually exclusive. The Court has modelled its contextual methodology with varying degrees of success. One instance of success is the Court's recognition of what can helpfully be called non-technocratic expertise. A word about expertise more generally is in order (Socqué 2006). Dyzenhaus argues convincingly that the leading case in which the Supreme Court of Canada held that administrative tribunals were entitled to deference, *C.U.P.E.*, has a contradiction or tension embedded in it. The contradiction arises between a formal rationale for deference to a tribunal (a privative or preclusive clause) and a substantive rationale for deference (specialized expertise). The formal rationale reflects a Diceyan obeisance to the command of the supreme legislator. It is top-down in orientation. The substantive rationale is the more interesting and radical one because it reflects a bottom-up appreciation that a specialized administrative tribunal merits deference on the basis of its expertise (Dyzenhaus 1997). This expertise is technocratic. Where the tribunal members possess non-legal expertise and engage in an activity apparently removed from traditional processes of legal reasoning, the case for deference is made fairly readily on a technocratic basis. It is easily arguable that in deferring, say, to the Competition Tribunal's determination that a substantial lessening of competition has not occurred, or to a securities commission's determination that market actions do not warrant its intervention in the public interest, a reviewing court concedes little of its traditional terrain. This is not to say that judges have not in the past interfered with the work of specialized bureaucrats. Rather, in the past decades, the case for deference to technical expertise has largely been won.[7] When the Supreme Court structured the contextual approach by identifying the factor of tribunal expertise, it seemed to mean this species of technocratic expertise. What I intend to show now is that the Court has recognized that its initial incarnation of expertise needed to be broadened. The expansion took the form of the recognition of non-technocratic or democratic expertise.

In *Law Society of New Brunswick v. Ryan* (2003), the tribunal under review – a law society's disciplinary committee – consisted of lawyers and lay appointees. The lawyers had no prima facie claim to expertise of a kind foreign to the reviewing judge. As the Court remarked, judges will have been members themselves of a provincial law society, and will be familiar with the ethical and other standards of practice to which lawyers are held (ibid., para. 30). Despite this knowledge common to reviewing judges and the committee members, Iacobucci J. discerned three bases for attributing expertise to the tribunal relative to the reviewing court. One was the expertise generated in disciplinary hearings by repeated application of the relevant norms (conventional technocratic expertise). Another was that the lawyer members of the committee were current members of the law society and might, Iacobucci J. speculated, be more intimately acquainted with the everyday practice of law than judges who were no longer participating in solicitor–client relationships. This point was perhaps tenuous: the distinction between the expertise of a practitioner and that of a judge falls far short of the distinction between the expertise of an economist sitting on the Competition Tribunal and the economic acumen of a typical Federal Court judge. The basis for expertise most interesting for this discussion stemmed from the statutorily mandated presence of a lay person. In the Court's view, though lay persons have less knowledge of legal practice than lawyers or judges, they may be better placed to understand how particular forms of conduct and choices of sanctions would affect the general public's perception of the profession and their confidence in the administration of justice. These are, after all, concerns central to the legislation (ibid., para. 32). One may accept the proposition that a member of the general public may be better placed than a professional to speak for the attitudes of the general public, but it is peculiar to label that superior placement 'expertise.' The lay person is not one who, to draw on expertise's dictionary definition, is trained by practice or experience. Expertise in this regard might, by contrast, come from a professional public opinion pollster. The idea that the lay person speaks for the general public hints less at a concern for expertise in the technocratic sense in which functionalists typically call for deference to bureaucrats than at a concern for representation or democracy.

Attention to an administrative decision maker's democratic qualities also appears in *Chamberlain v. Surrey School District No. 36* (2002). That case concerned a school board's decision in which it declined to approve for optional classroom use three books depicting same-sex parented families. In reaching the standard of reasonableness simpliciter, the Chief Justice, speaking for the majority, incorporated under the rubric of expertise the school board's capacity to balance the interests of different groups, such as parents with widely differing moral outlooks, and children from many types of families. McLachlin C.J.C. wrote that it was the job of board members, as elected representatives, to bring community views into the educational decision-making process (ibid., para. 10). Taken into account here was a democratic consideration that was clearly part of the context. It was, however, remote from the technocratic concern that non-political bureaucrats benefit from specialized training and experience distinct from the skills of a reviewing judge.

In these two judgments, the Court demonstrated itself able to define the context in a way beyond that suggested by the previously set guideposts of its pragmatic and functional factors. The Court undertook in *Ryan* and *Chamberlain* a substantial analysis of each tribunal's operations in its context. Decisions delegated to government ministers show a further concoction of technocratic and non-technocratic expertise and democratic accountability. In such instances, the Court will say, variously, that the minister is likely to have the best information, and thus to acquire technical expertise (*Suresh* 2002), or to be politically accountable (*C.U.P.E. v. Ontario (Minister of Labour)* 2003, para. 18, Bastarache J., dissenting). In ministerial cases, both justifications typically have currency. The defining lines of contextualism thus shift.

Despite this possibility of redefining its terms, a contextual methodology may exclude information that seems relevant. To be clear, it is not the exclusion of factors per se that may be objectionable, but rather the exclusion of factors that reasons indicate ought to be included (Schauer 1988, 543). The four contextual factors set out for the pragmatic and functional approach do not refer explicitly to the board's appointment process. A New Brunswick case brings out this exclusion in the definition of the context. *Keddy* (2002) concerned the standard of review for a statutory appeal from an appeals tribunal's determination that the employee appellant, when injured, was acting in the course of her employment. An affirmative finding would have eliminated any tort claim, restricting the appellant's remedy to indemnification under the workers' compensation scheme. The majority of the court concluded that it was a question of law, reviewable on correctness. In his dissent, however, Robertson J.A. queried how the legislative draftsperson could indicate intent to displace the deference doctrine other than by including a statutory right of appeal (ibid., para. 25). He highlighted factors that, while arguably relevant, had not yet found comfortable accommodation in the pragmatic and functional approach, namely, the possibility that a right of appeal reflected a political compromise to satisfy competing interest groups and that the legislature was conscious that political factors not tied to the legislative objectives had historically influenced the appointment of tribunal members (ibid., para. 27). In the British context, Murray Hunt has proposed that the posture of deference adopted by a reviewing court should take into account the primary decision maker's democratic accountability (2003, 351). Such a consideration might tackle some of Robertson J.A.'s concerns, as might consciousness of a tribunal's reputation (Hawkins 1998). One can conjecture practical reasons why courts may not be well positioned to assess the appointment processes of tribunals, not least that such processes may change with the succession from one government to the next or more frequently. But the political considerations sketched in the dissent do not strike me as irrelevant. The majority's failure to find a place for them in applying the pragmatic and functional approach demonstrates the difficulty in maintaining a thoroughly contextual approach. Even if the Supreme Court insists that its set of four factors is not exhaustive, the reviewability of standard of review determinations on a correctness basis on appeal is likely to motivate lower court judges to stick closely to those factors already adumbrated.

Tension between the inclination to privilege judicial expertise in interpreting a statutory text and a more thoroughly contextual way of seeing underlies a further development. At issue in *Barrie Public Utilities v. Canadian Cable Television Assn.* (2003) was the Canadian Radio-television and Telecommunications Commission's (CRTC) determination that the applicable legislation empowered it to order utility companies to grant access to their power poles to cable television companies. Applying the pragmatic and functional approach, six justices settled on correctness. They did so largely on the basis that the question did not engage the CRTC's special expertise in the regulation and supervision of Canadian broadcasting and telecommunications. In Gonthier J.'s view, the meaning of 'the supporting structure of a transmission line' was a purely legal question, within the province of the judiciary. It followed that the exercise was one of 'pure statutory interpretation' for which the Court was better equipped. The majority, I suggest, got distracted by what I have elsewhere called methodological expertise. By this I mean the expertise required to make the particular decision. This way of assessing relative expertise is novel, and it will always drive towards intervention because, appropriately or not, a court will always consider itself more expert than a board at statutory interpretation (Leckey 2004, 347). Consequently, the majority neglected to examine as fully as precedents would have suggested the composition, institutional context, and practical ability of the tribunal at issue. The irony is that in this case, the CRTC had issued a set of lengthy and very judicial reasons justifying its statutory interpretation and the ensuing order. The functionalism driving the pragmatic and functional approach is stymied if, when it comes to interpreting even a board's enabling or home statute, that functionalism is held hostage to the reviewing court's a priori superior expertise at statutory interpretation. The introduction of methodological expertise regarding statutory interpretation is a Trojan horse for a return to Diceyan formalism and the priority of the ordinary courts. In such cases, the reviewing court downplays the importance of the context – the institutional capacity of the administrative tribunal and the contextual specificity of the setting in which the statutory scheme operates – in favour of an insistence on its own acontextual and ahistorical superiority in the form of its a priori expertise at statutory interpretation.

Another instance of a return to formalism is, arguably, the tendency for reviewing courts to presume the similarity of the set of tribunals to which the same subject matter has been assigned. In an understandable effort to sink some guideposts for themselves in the unmarked terrain of contextualism, courts develop rules of thumb. One is that human rights tribunals merit little deference; another is that labour boards and workers' compensation tribunals merit high deference. Such a practice is consistent with what Hunt calls the spatial metaphor: the idea that, within certain areas of judgment, the judiciary will automatically defer (2003, 345; see also Leckey 2004, 357–8). The result can be that courts do not consider contextual factors such as the manner in which a particular legislature has structured its tribunal in a given area, such as workers' compensation. Put another way, given the multiplicity of contextual factors, the subject matter cannot be presumed to be the salient and governing one (Leckey 2004, 350). This tendency to seek out consistent rules cutting through the morass of contextualism hints at constraints, derived from the imperatives of judicial practice, on the potential of a contextually open and particularistic method.

It is arguable that many judges fail to meet the standard set by the pragmatic and functional approach. Wade MacLauchlan finds it rare to see a sophisticated assessment of a decision maker's reasoning process and expertise (2001, 292). The authors of an empirical study are more sanguine, suggesting that lower court judges do, all in all, a decent job at applying the approach and adopting the new way of seeing the organs of the administrative state. Though judges often do not engage with decisions in their total factual and legal context as thoroughly as does the Supreme Court, the outcomes are globally in accord with the policy behind pragmatic functionalism (Lahey and Ginn 2002, 326). What is undisputable, however, is the degree of contextual dependency introduced by the approach: the current law 'recognizes, tolerates and indeed celebrates contextualism' (ibid., 264).

Part of my mission here has been to set the contextualism in the area of substantive review alongside the contextualism of review for procedural fairness. Administrative law doctrine regards the two areas as analytically distinct. There are, however, significant similarities regarding the methodology of contextualism and the periodic resurgence of formalism.[8] In both procedural and substantive review, the courts departed from a binary classification process (quasi-judicial/administrative in the one case; jurisdictional/non-jurisdictional in the other) in favour of a contextual, case-by-case approach. And in both cases, it took little time for some formal divisions and considerations to appear. A further dimension of contextualism concerns the view of the administrative decision maker as engaged and embedded.

Embedded Decision Makers

Alison Harvison Young (1997) argues that the feminist critique of impartiality raises important issues for the relationship between feminism and administrative law. In her view, the concept of bias – predicated on the judge as neutral and impartial – shows signs of strain. She observes that traditional conceptions of impartiality as objective and neutral have always been troublesome in administrative law contexts, such as labour relations, where expertise is valued. The basis for according deference to specialized decision makers is that they do not hear each matter before them as blank slates. Harvison Young discusses a case in which a board of inquiry was appointed to adjudicate a group of complaints by employees of systemic discrimination (*Great Atlantic & Pacific Co. of Canada* 1993). The respondent challenged the appointment of Professor Constance Backhouse as the Board of Inquiry on the basis that it gave rise to a reasonable apprehension of bias, Backhouse being a well-known feminist who had participated in a claim of systemic discrimination against Osgoode Hall Law School. Did Backhouse's experiences amount to expertise or to bias? Harvison Young identifies here a false dichotomy between what she calls the 'myth of tabula rasa impartiality' and the arbitrariness of whatever baggage a particular decision maker carries. She argues that approaches combining pluralism and feminism can diffuse the tension: the focus should shift from the 'baggage' that everyone has to the enterprise of making judgments within a context and a community (1997; also Nedelsky 1997).

Harvison Young is not alone among administrative law scholars in highlighting difficulties with the traditional law of bias. Trish Oberweis and Michael Musheno argue that 'identity, moral view and organizational culture interrupt the abstraction of law and influence the ways that laws are enacted, policies enforced, situations defined and outcomes evaluated' (2001, 96). In a discussion of administration and power differentials, Joel Handler makes the point about the embeddedness of administrative decision makers. He remarks that the powerful and powerless alike carry into their relationship 'their respective characters and self-conceptions, their root values, nurtured through immediate as well as past social relationships' (Handler 1992, 343). Their identities and origins (class, race, childhood, education, employment, relations with others, the everyday structures of their lives, their very different social locations) vitally affect their languages, social myths, beliefs, and symbols. Views of themselves and of others produce vastly different meanings and patterns in their encounters. Lorne Sossin pushes further still towards a contextually embedded conception of the administrative decision maker. He characterizes the case law on bias as evincing ambivalence towards personal relationships. The law recognizes that decision makers are products of social networks, professional communities, and personal experiences, and that the decision maker is consequently better; but evidence of personal opinions or connections to particular cases tends to trigger the impartiality principle. Sossin contends that bias's very nature is specifically contextual: it is not a general predisposition, but a specific injustice directed at particular individuals. It follows that impartiality can only be evaluated 'within the context of the relationship between the decision-maker and the party affected by the decision' (Sossin 2002, 821). That scholars reject the traditional definition of bias as inappropriately and unsustainably acontextual is perhaps unsurprising. Yet they have been joined in this enterprise by reviewing judges.

Our first instance is the crucial judgment *Baker* (1999). Mavis Baker was a Jamaican non-status migrant ('overstayer') with a handful of Canadian-born children. She sought exemption from the rule that non-citizens shall not be admitted or permitted to remain in Canada without legal authorization. She applied for permanent resident status on the basis of the general 'humanitarian and compassionate discretion' in the immigration legislation. The case is significant in so many ways (Dyzenhaus 2004a) that it is easy to overlook that the chief basis for disposing of the appeal was a finding of reasonable apprehension of bias on the part of the case officer. L'Heureux-Dubé J. identified the factors that led her to conclude that a well-informed member of the community would perceive bias (the standard test): Officer Lorenz's notes did not disclose the existence of an open mind or a weighing of the case's circumstances free from stereotypes. These notes connected Ms Baker's mental illness, her training as a domestic worker, and her several children with the conclusion that she would be a lifelong strain on Canada's social welfare system. What preoccupies me here is the way that L'Heureux-Dubé J. inflected the notion of impartiality as she examined those factors. Within the span of two paragraphs, three different formulations occur (I have taken the liberty of reversing their order). One refers simply to the officer's 'duty to consider impartially' the appellant's request for admission (*Baker* 1999, para. 48). This formulation suggests total consistency with a classical notion of impartiality as neutrality and objectivity. A second refers to 'the impartiality appropriate to a decision made by an immigration officer' (ibid., para. 48). This formulation hints at a more context-specific content to impartiality. It tacitly nods to the previous cases that have held that the degree of impartiality required of members of administrative tribunals depends on the circumstances, and that they should not be held, as a general rule, to the highest judicial standard (*Newfoundland Telephone Co.* 1992). It also suggests, without delineating the point, the specificity of the immigration setting. It is the third, most extended formulation that is the most remarkable.

L'Heureux-Dubé J. wrote: 'The context here is one where immigration officers must regularly make decisions that have great importance to the individuals affected by them, but are also often critical to the interests of Canada as a country. They are individualized, rather than decisions of a general nature.' L'Heureux-Dubé J. observed that immigration decisions demand special sensitivity: 'Canada is a nation made up largely of people whose families migrated here in recent centuries. Our history is one that shows the importance of immigration, and our society shows the benefits of having a diversity of people whose origins are in a multitude of places around the world' (*Baker* 1999, para. 47). But L'Heureux-Dubé J. was not merely reiterating the myth of Canada as a welcoming, multicultural, immigrant society (cf. Mawani 2004). She was setting up for the big punch: 'Because they necessarily relate to people of diverse backgrounds, from different cultures, races, and continents, immigration decisions demand sensitivity and understanding by those making them. They require a recognition of diversity, an understanding of others, and an openness to difference' (*Baker* 1999, para. 47).

Rather than concern with negative attributes – such as freedom from preconceived ideas – L'Heureux-Dubé J. was calling for *positive* attributes (recognition of diversity, understanding of others, openness to difference). These attributes collide with the traditional conception of impartiality. Within these paragraphs, the administrative decision maker is seen not as detached, but as connected to the applicant's context. Indeed, the decision maker is enjoined actively to reach towards the applicant with sensitivity, understanding, and openness. The earlier cases that recognized the suitability of flexible standards of impartiality, calibrated to particular administrative contexts, had tended to fasten on the decision maker's appointment or election process. It has been observed that in the case of boards composed of elected members, strict application of a reasonable apprehension of bias standard might undermine the very role entrusted by the legislature to the board. That is, elected board members have likely been elected on precisely the basis of holding preconceived, publicly declared views. In such circumstances, it may be sufficient if board members hear their cases with an open mind (*Newfoundland Telephone* 1992; *Old St. Boniface Residents Assn. Inc. v. Winnipeg (City)* 1990). But in L'Heureux-Dubé J.'s performance in *Baker*, it is not the administrative structure that is relevant, but instead the substantive content of the decisions to be made. Moreover, her signification does not attenuate the demands made of decision makers under the doctrine of impartiality, but intensifies them.

Baker enunciates a duty to give reasons for administrative decisions, and scholars have argued that this requirement blurs the line between procedure and substance (Dyzenhaus and Fox-Decent 2001, 217). The line is blurred further by L'Heureux-Dubé J.'s importation of what appear to be relevant factors for the substantive decision into the frame of mind required of the immigration officer, as a matter of procedural fairness. Admittedly, a clear hook for these requirements exists in the fact that the statutory provision at issue concerned a derogation from the general regime on a humanitarian and compassionate basis. An obligation on a decision maker to be, say, open to difference looks much more like a mandatory factor to be considered in exercising a statutory discretion – omission of which would render a decision unreasonable or patently unreasonable – than a condition of impartiality as it is conventionally understood. Yet L'Heureux-Dubé J.'s discussion of bias appears squarely within the section on procedural fairness. What is significant is the manner in which a conception of impartiality positively attuned to the context partially dissolves the line between process and substance. Contrary to the occasional claims of relational theorists, the context is not something to be examined in isolation from distinctly normative claims. Rather, L'Heureux-Dubé J.'s definition of the context and what attention to it demands is predicated on her normative conception of the place of immigration in Canadian history and the Canadian identity.

A couple of ways of reading the presentation of impartiality in *Baker* are possible. One sees it as evincing a normative stance of general sympathy towards vulnerable individuals who interact with the administrative state. This reading of the judgment would regard the traditional idea of impartiality as comporting a minimum of negative content (freedom from influence or from prior conclusions) as attenuated in favour of positive considerations that favour the vulnerable individual. Call this the vulnerability principle. A contrasting reading sees L'Heureux-Dubé J.'s configuration of impartiality as driven by the statutory scheme, specifically the textual inclusion of humanitarian and compassionate considerations. This reading views the judges as moving from the statutory text to a working out of the statutory directions in the context of the decision making. This reading attenuates the impartiality demanded of the decision maker on the basis that it is the decision maker's duty and institutional predisposition to be already inclining towards the legislature's objectives. Call this the legislative purpose principle. It is with this second reading in mind that it is fitting to canvass a couple of post-*Baker* cases.

In two cases decided in 2003, the Supreme Court of Canada rejected allegations of bias against administrative decision makers. The complainant in each case was a large corporation, the sort of party unlikely to attract sympathy on the basis of its vulnerability. Bell Canada, ensnared for years in sex discrimination litigation concerning the wages it paid to female employees, impugned the impartiality of the Canadian Human Rights Tribunal (*Bell Canada* 2003). Bell contended that, first, the Canadian Human Rights Commission's power to issue interpretive guidelines binding on the tribunal and, second, the tribunal chair's power to extend members' terms in ongoing inquiries undermined the tribunal's impartiality. Imperial Oil Ltd., for its part, attacked an order issued by the provincial minister of the environment that it decontaminate and restore a polluted site it no longer owned (2003). Imperial Oil argued that, since the minister had an interest in recovering the cost of the decontamination, he was insufficiently impartial in deciding whether to issue the order. (The record reveals a comedy of errors of prior botched decontamination efforts and civil suits against the government.) In both cases, the Supreme Court of Canada held that the decision makers under their respective statutory schemes satisfied all applicable duties of procedural fairness.[9] In *Bell Canada*, the Court held that the tribunal was not a free-standing court, but rather an instrument created by Parliament for the purpose of identifying and remedying discrimination. Accordingly, measures that channelled the tribunal's interpretation towards the eradication of discrimination, while perhaps unfavourable to respondents such as Bell Canada, did not detract from the contextually warranted degree of impartiality. In *Imperial Oil*, the Court held that the appellant corporation's argument treated the minister as a member of the judiciary, whose personal interest in a case would make him biased according to the usual test. By contrast, the contextual nature of the content of the duty of impartiality reflects that some administrative decision makers are ministers or officials performing policy-making discretionary functions. LeBel J. admitted that the environmental legislation's 'polluters pay' principle had created a conflict between the minister and the interests of those subject to the law. In other words, the minister was not expected to be neutral as to the outcome.[10] He was, however, required to follow precise procedural steps stipulated in the statute. The minister's role as manager of an environmental protection scheme in the service of the public interest in the environment did not render him insufficiently impartial. Indeed, it is peculiar to think that a ministerial decision maker would ever be other than embedded in an institutional and policy context (Luhmann 2001, 202). The oddness of applying a judicial test of impartiality to administrative decision makers highlights how much the conception of impartiality presumes a judge alone in his chambers. The idea of individual bias developed in respect of judges applies awkwardly, say, to entire departments of bureaucratic decision makers.

These cases are arguably compatible with both readings provided above of the requirement of impartiality in *Baker*. They are compatible with the vulnerability principle, provided that in each case one identifies the vulnerable parties as Bell's underpaid female employees and as those members of the public harmed by Imperial Oil's industrial degradation of the environment. Indeed, the judicial appreciation of the content of impartiality in these two cases appears to give greater weight to the collective interest, in a democratically defensible way, than did *Baker*, in which there was little consideration of the impact on the public of quashing Mavis Baker's deportation order. These judgments are also compatible with what I called the legislative purpose principle, acceptance of an administrative decision maker's inclining towards the implementation of a statutory objective (remedy of discrimination, environmental restoration) (Sossin 2005a, 439). When, as here, the legislative purpose is to aid vulnerable parties, it is unnecessary to decide between the two readings I have provided of impartiality in *Baker*.

To what extent is there a freestanding vulnerability principle where the legislative purpose does not privilege vulnerable parties? In *Baker*, L'Heureux-Dubé J. could hang the robust positive attributes of impartiality she required of the immigration officer on the peg of the statutory reference to humanitarian and compassionate grounds. What if, as becomes increasingly conceivable, Parliament amends the immigration scheme to take much greater account of national security concerns, drastically cutting down or eliminating textual reference to the humanitarian and compassionate values to which L'Heureux-Dubé J. refers? Or what if Parliament severely truncates the available procedures on the explicit basis of cutting costs? Is L'Heureux-Dubé J.'s robust configuration of impartiality specific to a case involving a vulnerable individual, or is the same approach conceivable as requiring, in the hypothetical example just sketched, an immigration officer to adopt a positive openness to the imperative of protecting the Canadian public and sparing the Canadian purse? Someone with a freestanding normative commitment to protecting vulnerable individuals – perhaps someone like L'Heureux-Dubé J. – would still need to engage with the new legislative priority of national security. But in doing so she would sense a tension, an obligation to reconcile what Sossin calls 'a variety of competing obligations' (2005a, 428). A proponent of solely the legislative purpose principle would feel no tension if the legislature deleted all reference to humanitarian and compassionate values. My suspicion is that the impartiality analysis in *Baker* evinces a vulnerability principle. What the discussion of impartiality in that judgment shows, then, is not simply a contextualization of decision making, or acknowledgment of decision makers as embedded, but rather the conjugation of context and normative commitments. It is time to turn to the way in which the procedural rights granted to subjects construct them as embedded in particular contexts.

Embedded Subjects

In *Baker*, L'Heureux-Dubé J. wrote that the heart of the analysis regarding participatory rights 'is whether, considering all the circumstances, those whose interests were affected had a meaningful opportunity to present their case fully and fairly' (*Baker* 1999, para. 30). For example, in *Knight* (1990), where a school board wished to dismiss an employee hired under contract, the duty of fairness was held to require the board to inform the employee of the reasons for his dismissal and to give him the opportunity to make representations. (Although there was never a formal hearing, the majority held that a series of meetings and negotiations had satisfied these procedural obligations.) A decade later, in *Baker*, L'Heureux-Dubé J. held that the 'meaningful opportunity' was satisfied in the circumstances by the opportunity to produce full and complete written documentation (1999, para. 34). The high-water mark of the right to an oral hearing in Canadian administrative law seems to have been *Singh*, the case of the refugee claimants who were granted a hearing in 1985.

The sceptic may object that in administrative law the right to participate, including the right to notice and an oral hearing, is nothing new. In the nineteenth century the 'justice of the common law' would stitch across the putative gaps in a statute so as to provide for participatory rights where administrative action threatened property rights. So, the objection would run, it is peculiar to argue that the administrative law of the past twenty-five or thirty years reveals a more contextual approach in contrast to prior practice on the basis of the granting of participatory rights. What is distinctly contextual, however, is the basis for the right to participate.

In the earlier period, participation rights accrued where a threat arose to a right but not to a mere interest or privilege. The assumption of such a rule was that the distinction between rights and privileges tracked a normative distinction between interests important and unimportant to subjects. It presumed that the deprivation of a privilege would not severely harm an individual. By contrast, today the right to participate depends on a variety of contextual factors, the impact of the decision on the individual significant among them. This impact is assessed in a more contextual manner, beginning with the individual, rather than with a classification of what is at stake. This factor calls the decision maker, and later the reviewing judge, to examine the legal subject before her in a careful, contextually sensitive way. Consequently, the legal subject emerges as less abstract than as, under the prior law, a holder of a property right or not. In *Nicholson*, for example, Laskin C.J.C. cited a passage by Lord Denning in which he viewed the duty of fairness as attracted by the subjection of a person to 'pains or penalties' (*Nicholson* 1978, 327–8, citing *Selvarajan v. Race Relations Board* 1976, 19). In *Baker*, the fact that the decision 'in practice ha[d] exceptional importance to the lives of those with an interest in its result – the claimant and his or her close family members' intensified the content of the duty of fairness (1999, para. 31). Finally, in *Suresh*, the procedural protections required when deportation to possible torture was at issue were affected by the outcome's 'serious personal, financial and emotional consequences' (2002, para. 118).[11] This attention to the impact of the decision produced a legal subject that suffered detriment in a number of ways (physical, emotional, financial), and who was also seen as suffering that detriment in relationship with family members.[12] The effect of assessing the content of procedural fairness on the basis of the multidimensional impact of the decision on the individual and her family is to produce a subject embedded in a particular web of relationships in a way consistent with relational theory's contextual methodology. Administrative law is now producing contextual subjects.

Examination of the accounts of the justification of participation rights shows the way that a contextual methodology intertwines with normative commitments. While the justifications can be organized in different fashions, there are essentially two kinds of justifications for procedure: instrumental and non-instrumental. Instrumental justifications hold that participation is an instrument to more optimal outcomes. Non-instrumental justifications hold that participation is an intrinsic good.

In debates on participation, the upper hand tends to go to instrumental justifications. In a substantial monograph on due process, D.J. Galligan concludes that the sole compelling and logically consistent basis for according a right of participation is that, instrumentally, it yields superior, more accurate outcomes. The idea is the empirical claim that participation will increase accuracy: the individual claimants are likely to be the principal source of relevant information and thus their involvement overcomes the evidentiary difficulties in decision making (Sainsbury 1992, 304). This information is crucial for the ability of the tribunal accurately to take the subject's context into account.[13] The conclusion is that there is no intrinsic value in participation for participation's sake (Galligan 1996, 143). Moreover, Galligan warns that excessive attention to participation can itself impede inquiry as to its efficacy: 'The danger then is that participatory procedures serve a function which is more ideological and symbolic than real' (ibid., 161). For Galligan, constant reaffirmation of the instrumental value of procedures is necessary to maintain rigour in testing their effectiveness.

Framing a non-instrumental account is problematic because such a view of participation seems to require the possibility of participation rights that make no difference to the outcome. Few find attractive the notion of a hearing with no possibility of changing the decision maker's mind just for the sake of letting the individual participate. Yet it is possible to read in L'Heureux-Dubé J.'s reference in *Baker* to a 'meaningful opportunity' to present one's case more than simply the instrumental ability accurately to convey information.[14] My suggestion is that the best way to make sense of this reference is a richer but still instrumental account of participation's effect on decision making. The assumption in the instrumental account I have just given is that optimal decision making is a matter of accurately collecting the proper pre-existing data. The alternative account I sketch now regards the opportunity to participate as constitutive of meaning. It is thus meaning-full in a strong sense. I mean a view of the world by which one is much less assured that the facts and the rules pre-exist the act of bringing them together in the act of decision making. Here one may assign much greater weight to the idea that the language and forms of communication unavoidably affect the content (White 1990, 23–5). One may consider that the 'facts' are not a static set of data. Rather, what might be discerned as 'the facts' may hinge, in part at least, on the questions that were asked and the manner of the asking. It is not a matter of indifference who supplies the decision maker with its inputs (Sainsbury 1992, 304, 328). Contrary to the implication of the mechanistic language of 'accuracy,' the facts provided by the individual affected will not be identical to those provided by alternative means. Finally, on this view, even the rules to be applied are not presumed as static and pre-existing. Indeed, one conception of discretion views the norm as being developed by the decision maker in dialogic relationship with the individual affected. The individual can be called on to express his particular situation and, most crucially, his conception of the values that should guide the decision maker (Cartier 2004, 83; 2002).[15] The applicable norm is not an input that yields the output of the individualized decision. Rather, the norm as applied is itself part of the output.[16] It is through collaboration between decision maker and affected individual in seeking out the inflection of the applicable norm in the particular circumstances that administrative discretion becomes consistent with autonomy, understood in the literal sense as 'one's own law' (Nedelsky 1989, 10–11). This view of participation, which progresses from the particularistic view of the subject to the claim that the subject should participate in constructing the norms that govern it, blends methodological and normative dimensions. It combines the contextual methodology which requires that the decision maker sensitively and attentively obtain as much information as practicable with the normative construction of relational autonomy. Yet it remains an instrumental account, since it is concerned with affecting the outcome.

The doctrinal exclusion of the duty of procedural fairness from exercises of legislative power calls for mention. This exclusion applies to primary legislation, secondary legislation, and policy statements affecting an indeterminate group. Geneviève Cartier criticizes this exclusion, arguing that its foundation is flawed and that cases on procedural fairness – notably *Knight* and *Baker* – pave the way for a judicial recognition of a duty to act fairly in the field of legislative decisions. Such a recognition would, she argues, be consistent with her conception of discretion as dialogue (Cartier 2003). The exclusion is consistent with a contextual methodology in the following sense. It could be supposed that it is impracticable for a decision maker to whom a legislative power has been delegated to consult the community at large in a substantially contextual and particularistic manner. Cartier suggests ways to make consultation meaningful (ibid., 257–62); my point is simply that a restriction of participation to particular cases is not inconsistent with an emphasis on the contextual view of legal subjects. The exclusion of legislative acts from review for procedural fairness arguably evinces judicial recognition of the practical constraints on successfully engaging with a large number of legal subjects using a methodology of contextualism.

Relational theory's contextualism is not only spatial but also temporal. It concerns developments across time. It attends to reliance and tacit or informal undertakings that arise while the formal status of the parties remains unchanged. The doctrine of legitimate expectations springs to mind here as one of the most obvious sites to investigate whether the contextualism in administrative law is temporal. Courts in Britain have recognized a doctrine of legitimate expectations with both procedural and, more controversially, substantive effect (Craig and Schønberg 2000; cf. Thomas 2000, ch. 3). In Canada, however, courts have been much more restrained. Canadian courts have declared the doctrine of legitimate expectations to have only a procedural effect and to exclude the legislative process from its reach (Wright 1997).

Despite this judicial restraint, the Supreme Court of Canada in a recent case granted the outcome that a substantive doctrine of legitimate expectations would warrant. *Mount Sinai Hospital Center* (2001) concerned the issuance by the Minister of Health and Social Services of a permit for the operation of the hospital. The hospital was a long-term treatment facility that was operating in a small town under a permit that no longer reflected the programs in operation. The hospital wished both to change the nature of its operating permit and to relocate to Montreal. The applicable legislation empowered the minister to issue permits when it was in the public interest to do so. Negotiations between the hospital and the ministry regarding the move had started in 1984. The minister promised the hospital that he would formally alter the permit to reflect the reality of its operations once the move to Montreal was accomplished. The government affirmed the promise several times. In 1991, once the hospital had moved to Montreal, it made a formal request to the minister for the permit to be regularized. Without giving the hospital an opportunity to make submissions, the minister informed the hospital that it would not receive the promised permit and that it would have to operate under the old, unaltered permit. The hospital brought an action in mandamus before the Superior Court, seeking an order that the minister issue the permit. Rather than granting the hospital's request, the Superior Court ordered that, as a procedural matter, the minister hear the hospital's submissions before deciding whether altering the permit was in the public interest. The court made this order on the basis that the minister's conduct had generated a legitimate expectation. The Court of Appeal allowed the hospital's appeal. On the basis of the doctrine of public law promissory estoppel, it ordered the minister, as a substantive matter, to issue the promised permit. The Supreme Court of Canada affirmed, issuing two sets of reasons, neither one of which relied on legitimate expectations. The majority reasons, written by Bastarache J., held that by promising the hospital that it would receive the modified permit, the minister had exhausted his statutory discretion. The minister's specific conduct indicated that his decision had been made, and the statute did not provide for the minister to change his mind. The minority reasons, written by Binnie J., quashed the decision on two further bases. Procedurally, the minister's failure to extend even minimal procedural fairness to the hospital warranted setting aside the decision to refuse the modified permit. Substantively, the minister's exercise of his discretion was patently unreasonable in virtue of the understanding of the public interest that he and his predecessors had defined over the years.

For present purposes, the differences between the majority and the minority approaches to the problem are less significant than their similarities. Each judge based his determination that an order of mandamus requiring the issuance of the permit was warranted on the pattern of interaction over time between the hospital and the ministry. For Bastarache J., the government's behaviour, though not implying actual issuance of the permit, resulted in an exercise of the ministerial discretion. His willingness to regard instances of conduct over time, cumulatively, appeared in the statement that the fact that the relevant course of dealings consisted of various elements over a long period constituted no bar to looking at 'the overall situation' and concluding that a decision had been made (*Mount Sinai* 2001, para. 100). He wrote, too, that what mattered was the course of conduct between the parties and the evidence documenting the relationship (ibid., para. 105). Binnie J. focused on 'an analysis of *the relationship* between the respondents and the Minister' (ibid., para. 4 [emphasis in original]) and the respondents' reliance on the minister, both obviously developed across time. He referred to a 'web of understandings and incremental agreements' and a 'web of relationships' (ibid., paras. 8, 10).

Cartier regards *Mount Sinai* as 'the Canadian answer' to English cases recognizing a doctrine of substantive legitimate expectations. She characterizes the Canadian solution as limiting the 'freedom of a public decision maker to backtrack on a particular, substantive promise to exercise discretion in a particular way' (unpublished, 246). She writes, too, that the view exemplified is that 'discretion requires that the decision made attests to its faithfulness and authenticity to a complex nexus of understandings and communications' (ibid., 260; see also 2006). She does not spell out fully what strikes me as most crucial here: that the exercise of discretionary power was constrained in light of the context of relationship between the institution and successive ministers that had developed across time. It is a temporally dynamic understanding of the stance of government towards the governed that is vindicated here. In the absence of the formal timely issuance of the permit, the web of conduct and communication shared by the parties over time led to a legally recognizable and enforceable obligation. At least for institutions, the context is arguably a temporal one.

It is important not, however, to overstate this point. In *Baker*, the Supreme Court held Ms Baker to have no legitimate expectation that altered the content of the duty of procedural fairness (1999, para. 29). It is significant that the Court in that judgment did not hold the Convention on the Rights of the Child to have given rise to any procedural legitimate expectations. Instead, it deferred consideration of the Convention's values until the moment of substantive review.[17] Admittedly, doctrinal reasons militated for reining in the doctrine of legitimate expectations in the Canadian context (but see Cartier 2006). Nonetheless, a claim that the courts' contextualism embraces a temporal dimension would be stronger were there a more robust doctrine of legitimate expectations, which is of course judicial recognition of relationships played out across time. The Court's choice in *Baker* to accomplish through *substantive* review what it might have done through legitimate expectations – a procedural doctrine – has implications for the relationship between subject and administrative decision maker. Substantive review of discretionary decisions emphasizes the setting in which the subject is figured as the relatively passive object on which the decision maker operates. Legitimate expectations, which Canadian courts have diluted, produce a juridical space in which legal subject and decision maker operate roughly as equals, able to send, receive, and interpret signals that alter their relationship and respective rights and obligations. Indeed, perhaps the appropriate observation is that the degree of equality between administrative decision maker and subject will significantly affect the way in which the context will be framed. It is a hospital, a relatively strong institutional player, that gets the benefit of the most temporally robust definition of the context that becomes relevant for administrative decision making and judicial review. Yet even here, neither camp of judges at the Supreme Court will explicitly attribute the result to legitimate expectations. Rather, the order to the minister is justified by reference to exhaustion of the ministerial discretion or the patent unreasonableness of any alternative course. Consider the contrast when, say, refugee claimants find themselves with a lengthy history of relationships with administrative officials. Such subjects are liable to find that a history of repeated applications and procedural moves constitutes a liability sowing suspicion on the part of immigration officials rather than an asset. Thus here, too, contextualism serves specific interests and conceptions and is not a neutral methodology.

This chapter has attempted to draw together strands of contextualism emerging through administrative law as it has developed over the past thirty years. Credence in contextualism's possibility and normative commitment to its appropriateness have had unifying effects. This chapter has also drawn together the separate streams of intervention in procedure and deference on substance. Courts now view administrative tribunals contextually. They do so in determining the content of procedural fairness and in picking the standard of review for agencies' substantive determinations. In their attenuation of the traditional notion of impartiality, courts have also adopted a view of administrative decision makers as contextually situated or embedded. Last, courts have, in determining the content of procedural fairness and articulating justifications for participation, added the impact of a decision on the individual. This addition has effectively instated a contextual view of the subject. Some approve of this contextualism; others, such as Loughlin, may reject it as inconsistent with courts' functions, their expertise, and the rule of law. Yet even critics should see what stands before them. And this contextualism is consistent with the contextual methodology of relational theory.

It seems at times that judges have manipulated contextualism to augment their interventions in administrative processes. Such an increase in judicial intervention makes it worth undertaking greater empirical inquiry into the effectiveness of judicial review (Richardson and Sunkin 1996). A recent empirical study completed in the United Kingdom demonstrated little impact of judicial review on the administration's workings. Simon Halliday's findings show that 'despite extensive and prolonged exposure to judicial scrutiny, unlawful decision-making was rife in each authority. In different (and sometimes subtle) ways the local authorities' administrative processes displayed considerable evidence of values and priorities which were in conflict with the norms of administrative law' (2000, 122; see also Richardson and Machin 2000; Sunkin and Pick 2001; cf. Thomas 2003). Halliday even suggests an inverse relationship between exposure to judicial review and the degree of internal self-scrutiny by agencies (2000, 122). If the effect of judicial review on behalf of an individual actually diminishes the probability that others will have justice done for them, it demands reflection. The empirical inefficacy of judicial review – critical scrutiny of agencies from the outside – militates in favour of greater scholarly and policy attention to internal accountability mechanisms.[18]

It is not easy to pinpoint the causes for this turn to contextualism, and doing so is not my present task. In accounting for the turn away from bright-line classifications, commentators often refer to the complexities and unpredictability of the exercises. It is perhaps preferable to focus on the increasing recognition, as an empirical matter, of the diversity of the administrative state's organs. The set of these organs does not divide neatly into two classes because it is so internally diverse (Sossin 2005a, 430). It is this internal diversity that presses administrative law to disaggregate, to split into discrete specializations. The sense of the unmanageableness of the abstract rules contributed to the turn to contextualism. Contextualism relinquishes the ambition to universal knowledge by contenting itself with shifting from one 'focus of particularity' to another (Geertz 2000, 134). Contemporary administrative law seems to be a field in which contextualism is congenially regarded, but often the contextualism discussed is a mode of statutory interpretation by reference to principles of good administration (Siegel 1998). The contextualism identified in this chapter, by contrast, is a larger approach than one limited to interpreting texts. This empirical recognition of institutional and practical diversity, in turn, has on two levels merged with normative concerns.

On one normative level, judges and lawyers came to doubt the extent to which dichotomies such as right/privilege effectively tracked what they perceived as the genuine interests of individuals. Their commitment to protecting individual subjects impelled them to revise their conception of the administrative state. Neither the judicial emphasis on acquired rights nor the functionalist allegiance to government proved ultimately persuasive. On another level, the turn to contextualism has provided expression for acceptance of the legitimacy of the administrative state. To see why, it is necessary to recall that two of the binary classifications that were eliminated in the adoption of contextualism had the effect of ruling swathes of administrative decision making largely unreviewable. I mean the effect, for purposes of procedural review, of labelling a decision administrative, and the effect, for substantive review, of finding a question to fall within jurisdiction. What animated these binary classifications was a sense that what lay on the unreviewable side of them was not law. Whatever the officials of the administrative state were doing when they made administrative or executive decisions, and when they trenched questions within jurisdiction, their enterprise was not a legal one. The move to dissolve the binary classifications necessarily eliminated the spatial conception of territories devoid of law, and in effect this recognition of signs of law within the purview of officials entails that the administrative state is legitimate (Sossin 2005a; Dyzenhaus 2005). Yet since administrative officials frequently exercise statutorily delegated discretion without the strict guidance of enacted rules, the conception of law has to change. The understanding of administrative law as chiefly an 'ensemble of rules' (Rambourg 1969, 10) has been replaced by a conception of administrative law as a set of values and practices.

In a number of instances, the move to contextualism galvanized a countermove in which formalism asserted itself. David Dyzenhaus suggests that this dance between contextual informality and formalism is deeply characteristic of the common law method more generally (2006b, 477; see generally Fuller 1976; Postema 2002).[19] The point for the present inquiry into the purchase of relational theory on administrative law is more modest. Some proponents of relational theory, departing from the descriptive premise that individuals are embedded, imply that adoption of a methodology of contextualism, one simply grounded in a better description of individuals, prompts desirable prescriptions and outcomes. In other words, methodology precedes and indeed effectuates normative change. This chapter's survey of developments in administrative law suggests, by contrast, that adoption of a methodology of contextualism has occurred in the service of specific normative views regarding the administrative state and the subjects whose cases it determines. Or, rather, that there is a complicated interrelation: at times a change in norms is implemented through a contextual method, at other times contextualism alters the sense of the relevant norms. The next chapter takes up the inquiry as to the suitability to administrative law of relational theory's normative commitments.

7 Administration and Relational Norms

This chapter investigates the appropriateness of relational theory's normative commitments in administrative law. The objective is to understand better both administrative law and relational theory. I engage here with several authors who argue for the appropriateness of relational theory's normative commitments to the broader canvas of administrative law. Joel Handler describes the effect of the administrative state on the relationships of individuals with one another and with the state, arguing that what characterizes the administrative state is relationships of interdependence. He offers an aspiration of dialogical and communitarian engagement between bureaucrats and citizens (1986; 1990; 1988; 1985; 1983). Jennifer Nedelsky adopts Handler's description of the interdependence engendered by the administrative state. She argues that the relationships that constitute the capacity for relational autonomy include not only those with family members, intimate associates, and teachers, but also potentially with bureaucrats and other agents of the state. Practices of participation devised in administrative law provide lessons for her project of reconceiving autonomy in relational terms on the basis that such practices have produced feelings of autonomy in their participants (Nedelsky 1989). Lorne Sossin argues for the desirability of augmenting the interdependence of the bureaucrat–citizen relationship. Somewhat polemically, he proposes an aspiration of intimacy in bureaucrat–citizen dealings (2002). These authors rest, explicitly or implicitly, on the tenets of relational theory.[1] I will test the merits of these strong arguments, and then test weaker instantiations of relational theory in the administrative setting. But before doing so, I want to examine another normative matter: the way in which human rights norms and attention to family relationships are rendered concrete in administrative law through a method of contextualism.

Rights Bearers Embedded in Relationships

This section uses relational theory to illuminate a narrow but critical district of administrative law. This is the set of discretionary decisions regarding immigration matters and the idea of the subject as rights bearer. Recent judicial and scholarly developments in relation to the conception of the bearer of rights bring administrative law, at least this cranny of it, closer to relational theory's normative project than anything discussed in the previous chapter. I begin by sketching the conception of the legal subject as bearer of human rights, connecting it with scholarship on the contextual application of human rights. I argue that discretionary decision making introduces another, finer-grained layer of contextualization. The inflection of human rights norms in particular cases gestures towards relational theory's normative commitment to relational autonomy.

Public law scholars have identified the emergence of the conception of the citizen as bearer of human rights. David Dyzenhaus observes the transformation of the idea of the individual from one subjected to the law, through the individual as citizen, to the individual as bearer of human rights (2006a). During the earlier period, administrative law protections in migration and mobility matters were afforded or denied on the basis of citizenship. The non-citizen had no rights in the area of immigration and was subject to the mercy of the state. Within administrative law, this conception of the legal subject as demarcated by citizenship has partially given way to a notion of the legal subject – irrespective of his or her inscription vis-à-vis the fixed conditions for civic membership – as a bearer of human rights.

This transformation has not been smooth or unanimous. Tension arises between this view and the classical liberal emphasis on citizenship as the marker of membership in the community. Courts have repeatedly reinscribed this emphasis when applying the Canadian Charter of Rights and Freedoms, affirming that non-citizens' holding no unqualified right to enter or remain in the country is immigration law's 'most fundamental principle' (*Canada (Minister of Employment and Immigration) v. Chiarelli* 1992, 733; see also Macklin 2004, 174, 192–3). The 'war on terror' further jeopardizes the idea of subject as rights bearer (Bell 2006; cf. Dyzenhaus 2006a). The view of the subject as rights bearer can also collide with projects on the left. From that perspective, 'new identities as individualistic bearers of rights' replace 'solidaristic mass movements with class-based identities' (Arthurs 2005, 826). It is, of course, arguable that non-citizens enjoyed few of the perquisites of class-based solidarity secured during the twentieth century.[2] On a philosophical level, Hannah Arendt contends that the fates of human rights and the nation-state are inextricable, a claim empirically grounded in the tragic lessons of statelessness learned in Europe between the wars (2000). For Arendt, statelessness or the loss of nationality status is 'tantamount to the loss of all rights' (Benhabib 2004, 50). Nonetheless, the view of the rights bearer – at least, confidence in the viability of such a view – is gaining ground (cf. Murphy and Whitty 2006).

One early instance of the shift is the *Singh* case (1985). In that judgment, the Supreme Court of Canada viewed refugee claimants – non-citizens, members of the class of individuals whose presence on Canadian soil had historically been regarded as a mere privilege, arbitrarily revocable – as included within the Charter's reference to 'everyone.' The judges held the claimants to be entitled to an oral hearing of their claims in virtue of the principles of fundamental justice in Section 7 of the Charter.[3] (Three of the six judges relied on the Canadian Bill of Rights 1960, but the inclusion of a refugee claimant as a 'person' in that instrument's s. 2(e) is equivalently momentous.) From the same perspective, it is significant that, in the Supreme Court of Canada's judgment in *Baker* (1999), the person who received the protection of the rule of law was a vulnerable overstayer whose continued residence on Canadian soil turned on an official's determination whether 'humanitarian and compassionate grounds' warranted an exception from the standard regime. As Dyzenhaus reads the judgment's import, the judges held themselves bound to consider Ms Baker, not as someone helpless in a virtually lawless void, but as an individual entitled to treatment in accordance with the values regarded by Canadians as constitutive of public order (2002a, 503).

A further indication of the subject as rights bearer is discernable in a recent change to the place of the Charter in domestic administrative proceedings. The administrative law question is the capacity of tribunals to adjudicate challenges to the constitutional validity – typically its compliance with the Charter – of their own enabling statute. Overruling its earlier case law (*Cooper v. Canada (Human Rights Commission)* 1996), the Supreme Court of Canada has now established a presumption that the statutory power on the part of an administrative decision maker to determine any legal question brings the capacity to hear allegations of constitutional invalidity (*Nova Scotia (Workers' Compensation Board) v. Martin* 2003). These judgments further constitute the subject as bearer of human rights in the sense that constitutional rights are no longer regarded as external to administrative proceedings and to the subject. It is implicit in the judgment that conducting administrative proceedings without reference to the subject's status as a bearer of human rights is problematic. The recent judgments diminish the juridical territory that is not suffused with constitutional rights. Constitutional rights, these judgments appropriately signal, should not be a matter restricted to the superior courts, although those institutions are conventionally viewed as juridically more reputable. Rather, constitutional rights are diffused throughout the space of government.

A number of scholars have addressed the way in which it is necessary to contextualize the construal and implementation of international human rights norms. It is trite to observe that norms cast at a high level of abstraction are not self-executing and that values such as dignity and equality necessarily acquire different meanings in different contexts. Once human rights are accepted as an abstract value, it becomes necessary to ground them in a community and in particular interests, to 'tailor' them to 'local values, social structures and institutional capacities' (Galligan and Sandler 2004, 32). Seyla Benhabib argues that universalist rights claims must be 'contested and contextualized, invoked and revoked, throughout legal and political institutions as well as in the public sphere of liberal democracies' (2004, 19). What is imperative, she contends, is 'reiterating the universal in concrete contexts' (ibid., 134; see also Forst 1999, 43; Merry 2006; Goodale and Merry 2007). Benhabib distinguishes the principle of rights from a schedule of rights, the latter being a specific legislative concretion of rights by a democratic sovereign (ibid., 93, 141). For example, she contemplates that individual states may prescribe the requirements with which immigrants must conform in order to obtain citizenship. The contextualization of human rights that Benhabib attends to operates at the state level by promulgation of general legislation. I intend now to contrast that form of contextualization with the way that, on an individual level, Canadian administrative law now requires the customized application of human rights norms in the making of individual discretionary decisions.

The Supreme Court of Canada's review of the exercise of discretion in *Baker* (1999) is notable on several levels. *Baker* extends the pragmatic and functional approach for determining the standard of review of administrative decisions to include discretionary decisions. L'Heureux-Dubé J. affirmed that though discretionary decisions will generally be granted considerable respect, discretion must be exercised in accordance with statutory boundaries, the rule of law, administrative law principles, the fundamental values of Canadian society, and Charter principles (ibid., para. 56). She also referred to the Convention on the Rights of the Child, ratified by the executive but never statutorily implemented. The values of international human rights law, she said, may help 'inform' the contextual approach to statutory interpretation and judicial review (ibid., para. 70).[4] On one level, the contextual approach to statutory interpretation refers simply to the widely accepted point that text only acquires meaning within a particular interpretive community or context. As such, contextualism in statutory interpretation is largely unremarkable. For international lawyers, it is significant that L'Heureux-Dubé J. regarded a ratified but unimplemented treaty as helpful (Moran 2004). What is relevant here, however, is the way that the Court modelled a contextual view of the *legal subject* in the service of specific normative commitments.

Dyzenhaus argues with others that the Court's reference to the factors constraining the exercise of discretion instantiates a conception of the principle of legality. This principle requires broadly expressed discretions to be read as always already subject to the common law's fundamental values, including values expressive of human rights. He locates this principle within a particular conception of democratic legal culture, the culture of justification, in which decision makers are required to justify their decisions by demonstrating how the decisions conform to the fundamental values or, where they depart from those values, that such departures are justifiable (Dyzenhaus, Hunt, and Taggart 2001, 34). These fundamental values have been judicially updated to include modern democratic values, among them fundamental human rights (ibid., 7). It is in light of these values that, within administrative law, the legal subject is increasingly regarded as a bearer of human rights irrespective of the inscriptions of nationality. Moreover, the fact that these values must be instantiated in particular cases, as the minister hears applications for the humanitarian and compassionate exemptions, means that the values are constantly being reiterated, to use Benhabib's word, not in state but in individual contexts.

Looking back at the issue of a requirement for administrative decision makers to provide reasons for their decisions underscores the significance of this development. One argument raised by opponents of such a requirement was the prediction that there would be nothing to say. Administrative decisions are essentially factual, on this view, and specifying reasons in each case would result in mere reiterations of the general policy. Many administrative cases are 'little else than a fact-finding inquiry followed by a political decision' (Wade 1949, 231). The move in *Baker* to require justification in individual cases signals the inadequacy of the reiteration of a political decision after a rehearsal of facts. What is demanded is that the decision maker particularize the political norm to the individual in his or her context. At issue is not the way that a statute contextualizes a human rights norm, but rather the way in which applying a human rights norm in an individual case – in an exercise of discretion mandated by statute – produces, by consequence, a contextual or embedded view of an individual affected by administrative action. This application of universal norms to individual subjects in their unique locations is consistent with the rejection of the universal subject in favour of unique agents in particular locations (Stychin 1995, 22–3).

Put differently, the rise of fundamental values, left at an abstract level, fails to tell the whole story. At least in this contested corner of administrative law, behind the screen of the vague set of values, a more particularized conception of the legal subject is emerging. Where one type of judge sees primarily a state prerogative, what one might call a human rights judge sees a person with a life and a family (Dyzenhaus 2004b, 3). To see this new view of the subject clearly, it is helpful to recall the older view, according to which once it was determined that the individual did not hold citizenship, no contextual inquiry was warranted or permissible. The old reliance on classifications of citizenship or alienage was static. An alien subject had the same entitlement or rights – that is, none to speak of – after twenty years as on the day he landed. The alien subject was viewed acontextually. By contrast, the conception emerging in *Baker* is contextual. It can be fruitfully elucidated in two respects by reference to relational theory.

The first concerns the legal subject's development over time. Relational theory's context is not only spatial but also temporal, referring to the notion of the historical self. There is a sense in *Baker* of the applicant herself and her children sinking roots in Canadian soil over time. The contextual examination of Ms Baker that L'Heureux-Dubé J. held to have been necessary would have entailed different considerations in the late 1990s than it would have in the 1980s when Ms Baker first arrived. Conceived of as a rights bearer, Mavis Baker should at all times have had the same rights – the right, say, to be treated according to Canada's constitutive values – but what those rights demand *in concreto* is in part a function of temporal and contextual considerations. The willingness to regard the subject as having interests that change –

deepen – over time is remarkable because, from perspectives much less sympathetic to people like Ms Baker, the duration of her illegal over-staying only aggravated the offence she committed against the Canadian state. That is not, however, L'Heureux-Dubé J.'s appreciation of matters. The approach that L'Heureux-Dubé J. performed shows affinity to relational theory's description of thick, embedded subjects and to its temporal contextualism.

The second, connected respect engages relational theory's normative commitment to autonomy-enhancing relationships. The majority of the Supreme Court held in *Baker* that the relevant context in which the statutory 'humanitarian and compassionate' values had to be worked out included a norm of international law protecting the best interests of any children. L'Heureux-Dubé J. held that for an exercise of discretion to have been reasonable in the case, it would have had to 'consider the children's best interests as an important factor, give them substantial weight, and be alert, alive and sensitive to them' (*Baker* 1999, para. 75). This respect connects to the first because sensitive assessment of children's best interests will, as in family law, necessarily evaluate the effects of time's passage (Philippe 2003), investigating the lives of the Canadian children over time. The assessment that L'Heureux-Dubé J. undertook is consistent with relational theory's normative commitments. The performance in *Baker* hints that the fundamental values are especially likely to find themselves engaged when intimate relationships are at stake. Here, then, the contextual methodology hooks up with relational theory's normative commitment to autonomy-enhancing thick relationships. *Baker* models an approach by which the diffuseness of international law's human rights norms is made manageable for the judge through a focus on a single very particular right that will always be realized in concrete ways for which evidence should be available: the best interests of the children. One may think of what Clifford Geertz calls 'a continuous dialectical tacking between the most local of local detail and the most global of global structure in such a way as to bring both into view simultaneously' (1979, 239).[5]

Obviously a great many international law norms and values jostle for judicial, administrative, and scholarly attention. Yet there was something particularly telling, for the Court, in the fact that Mavis Baker was a subject whose deepest relationships were imperilled. The Supreme Court of Canada seemed to see the value of the individual's dignity – a key attribute for the subject as bearer of human rights – as concretely realizable through an individual's intimate relationships in a particular context. The judicial performance is consistent with the normative commitment to preserving and enhancing those relationships that facilitate autonomy, relationships precisely like the filial bonds jeopardized in this case. Ms Baker and her children, the argument would go, will be best able to exercise a capacity for autonomy in relationship with one another and the community into which they have grown. The prior approach in administrative law based on citizenship required no foothold in context, but this approach does. *Baker* inaugurates a robust substantive emphasis on intimate relationships by the instrumentality of a contextual approach.

The potentially disruptive effects of such an emphasis have generated reaction. One judge insists that, contrary to some interpretations, the reasons in *Baker* do not call for children's interests to prevail. Thus the presence of children neither bars per se the deportation of a parent residing illegally in Canada nor calls for any particular result (*Legault* 2002, para. 12). It is perhaps in some measure such anxiety about the judicial commitments entailed by contextually grounded review that is discernible in the Supreme Court's retreat from the *Baker* approach. In *Suresh* (2002, paras. 26–41), the Court insisted, a bit stridently, that the standard of review for ministerial discretion is not reasonableness, as in *Baker*, but the most deferential standard of patent unreasonableness. This later judgment calls for acknowledgment that *Baker* probably represents the high-water mark of judicial intervention in the furtherance of family relationships via a contextual application of human rights norms. The judgment remains significant, however, both on its merits and for the chord it struck within the community of administrative law scholars, who swiftly nominated it to the pantheon of administrative law judgments (but see Birkinshaw 2004, 236, 243).

The normative commitments infusing the deployment of contextualism in *Baker* come more clearly into view when one considers the potential conflicts between this normative inflection of contextualism and the public interest. Might current configurations of contextualism require judges to take seriously the contextual interests of the individual without correspondingly providing a means for contextually taking the public interest into account? After all, the participation rights discussed in the previous chapter provide the subject with a way of making her case, but, arguably, the public is unrepresented. Lorne Sossin suggests that the public's primary concern regarding administrative decision making is that the values of impartiality, fairness, and reasonableness find expression. To situate these values vis-à-vis the somewhat unstable process/substance distinction, impartiality and fairness are procedural, reasonableness is substantive. Sossin proceeds to identify inherent tensions within the concept of public interest between the public's stake in ensuring that public officials do not exceed their statutory powers and its concern in seeing that those powers are exercised equitably (2002, 813). This characterization understates, however, the tensions between advancing the interests of the particular individual at issue and the broader public interest.

Sossin posits that what is reasonable in particular settings may change according to the nature and degree of the affected parties' vulnerability. The duty owed to vulnerable parties and the broader duty to uphold the public interest are complementary. The goal is not to accord vulnerable parties special benefits beyond their statutory entitlements, but simply to ensure that they receive the fullest possible benefit (ibid., 853). This argument is unproblematic if it means only that vulnerable parties should get the fullest benefit to which they are entitled. They should, and so should parties characterized as less vulnerable. If the legislature subsidizes the activities of large corporations, those corporations should receive their fullest statutory entitlement. The statement becomes problematic, however, if it leads to contextualized and sensitive attention being paid to vulnerable parties whose interests conflict with the public interest. The duty owed to vulnerable parties, to perceive their specific needs and circumstances, and the broader duty to uphold the public interest cannot, contrary to Sossin, be presumed complementary. In the case of a workers' compensation scheme based on a fixed pool for compensation, tensions can emerge between compensating individual workers and conserving the pool for future claimants.

A starker conflict arises within *Baker* itself. Dyzenhaus has suggested that no tension arises between individual and collective interests. Surely it is in the collective interest, he argues, that decisions such as Mavis Baker's be made in a humane and compassionate way. But taking the immigration legislation seriously as an expression of democratic will calls for acknowledgment that the issue in *Baker* was a discretionary derogation from the general regime. The values of the derogation are humanitarian and compassionate, but the immigration scheme presumes that a person in Mavis Baker's circumstances should be deported. Robert Thomas identifies a 'deep-seated conflict' between values of the liberal democratic state: to bolster their liberal credentials, governments recognize the right to seek asylum, but they must also satisfy the electorate's appetite for restrictive policies (2003, 510).[6] One can spar with different canons of statutory interpretation – the large interpretation of remedial legislation, say, versus the narrow construal of derogations. But an unhelpful blindness is evident in denying the occurrence of such conflicts.

Contextualism operationalized within a bilateral relationship between an administrative decision maker and the affected individual generates an asymmetry. It provides a great deal more information about the needs and circumstances of the latter, but may render still more difficult consideration of the public interest to the extent that it may be inconsistent with the most beneficial treatment of the individual. This is particularly the risk where, as in the immigration setting, courts appear to be infusing contextualism with the substantive norms of relational theory. One may insist, as does Geneviève Cartier, that the public interest structures the exercise of discretion as one of the 'fundamental elements' (unpublished, 273). Yet unless care is taken, the public interest is likely to be represented by rather abstract policy considerations, as opposed to contextually anchored evidence of immediate impact on the individual and on her family. The public interest constitutes a background, structuring element, whereas the affected individuals who get to participate actively are the parties (ibid., 272). The public interest may not stand on equal footing with the affected individual in terms of the quality and immediacy of evidence present for the decision maker. Contextualism, the *Baker* case at least suggests, may collaborate in redistributing resources from the collectivity to individuals.

After all this, a couple of deflationary observations about *Baker* are in order. The judgment remains the exemplar par excellence – or perhaps more accurately, as I conceded, the high-water mark – of attention within administrative law to relational theory's commitment to the intimate relationships that further relational autonomy. Yet even bracketing the retrenchment in *Suresh*, there is reason why *Baker*'s promise for relational theorists is equivocal. In chapter 6, I contrasted the decision to allow Ms Baker's appeal on the basis of the unreasonable exercise of discretion (an alternative basis to the procedural breach of impartiality) with the message that might have been sent by a recognition of legitimate expectations. In the exercise of discretion, the individual figures, to a degree, as the object on which the administration operates, an *administré*. The acknowledgment of the individual as a bearer of rights, one entitled to justification, palliates this arrangement, but the individual and the decision maker never relate as equals. What should be observed from relational theory's perspective is that the Court in *Baker* paid comparatively little attention to the relationship between Ms Baker and the bureaucrat. L'Heureux-Dubé J. held that the opportunity for Ms Baker to present her case on paper, rather than an oral hearing, satisfied the duty of procedural fairness. Where I detect attention to enhancing relationships in the interest of relational autonomy, the relationships scrutinized are those of the subject and her children. The fact of staying with her Canadian-born children presumably enhanced Ms Baker's relational autonomy. Furthermore, the obligations of reasonableness and of articulating those reasons, bearing on officials, ought to secure better treatment of applicants in Ms Baker's shoes, treatment better befitting rights bearers than *administrés* cowering in a lawless void. There are, however, disappointingly few signs of a 'focus on relationships,' along the lines of relational theory, that takes as its target the relationship *between the bureaucrat and the subject.* The relationships examined were not those between Mavis Baker and the immigration officials. Still less are there signs that in similar proceedings, future Mavis Bakers will likely experience a sense of exercising their capacity for relational autonomy. These potential sources of concern will inform the examination, in the next part, of relational theory's normative commitment to autonomy-enhancing relationships between citizens and the administration. Relational theory may fasten unhelpfully on one kind of relationship at the expense of another.

Framing Cautions for Relational Theory

To this point, I have not addressed at length the collective applicability of relational theory's elements in administrative law. I argued in the previous chapter that its contextual methodology is suitably applied. But I have left open the pertinence in this field of relational theory's normative commitment to relationships that enhance relational autonomy. Indeed, I have been non-committal in my assessment of the precise character of relational theory's normative commitments, and of their intensity or strength. I suggested in chapter 1 that the relational theoretic literature is ambiguous as to how much normative baggage, and what kind, the relational approach or inquiry entails. As there are two plausible constructions of the 'focus on relationships,' some ambiguity is detectable as to the breadth of the range of relationships that relational theorists will promote in the service of relational autonomy. Relational theorists might be open to the idea that any kind of relationship may promote relational autonomy (what I called the weak form). This weak normative commitment, which stands in a somewhat fuzzy stance towards relational autonomy, is simply to an inquiry into optimal relationships, whatever they turn out, after context-specific analysis, to be. The alternative, strong form of relational theory dictates a commitment to promoting a particular substantive kind of relationship, usually thick, intimate relationships of interdependence. This commitment derives directly from the description of relational autonomy.

In this book's chapters in the family setting, the constructive relationships that promote relational autonomy are thick, interdependent ones marked by continuity, love, respect, and other largely uncontroversial attributes of family ties. While there was some concern about the precise degree of thickness materialized through legally enforceable obligations in the family context – think of spousal support long after a divorce and the step-parent's child support obligation – the difficulties arise from the matter of drawing a line within a general approach to interdependent relations. Application of a 'relational approach' in such a setting does not invite inquiry into whether relational theorists bring to their project a prior commitment to the view that constructive, autonomy-enhancing relationships are going to be thick and interdependent. But the administrative law setting prompts precisely this investigation. In this setting, it is not a foregone conclusion that such relationships are desirable.

To anticipate, I argue that a strong, ex ante commitment to thick relationships, one inappropriate in this context, colours the relational studies of administrative law. Furthermore, in administrative law even the weak relational approach is problematic. I begin by examining scholarship on administrative law within relational theory, drawing out its authors' precommitment to thick, interdependent relationships in the administrative setting.

The Strong Version: Promoting Relational Autonomy through Thick Relationships

Jennifer Nedelsky's general discussion of relational autonomy hints that the sort of personal relationships she has in mind as enabling relational autonomy are thick relationships. As examples of relationships that enable people to be autonomous, she mentions relationships 'with parents, teachers, friends, loved ones.' It is not necessarily an exhaustive list, but she does not include species of relation that, intuitively, are unlikely ever to be thick, and that one is likely to think instinctively should operate by rather different norms of distance, dignity, and respect. She does not mention relations with prison guards or customs officers. Her suggestion that the most promising 'model, symbol, or metaphor for autonomy' is child rearing gestures further towards a particular, substantive view of relationships. Yet on the same page she writes that 'some of the relationships which either foster or undermine autonomy are not of an intimate variety,' referring to relationships that 'are part of the more formal structures of authority,' including employment relations and the public sphere (Nedelsky 1989, 12). In this last reference to relationships that are not intimate, a hint appears that she might be open to approaching administrative law without a commitment to thick relationships. But the child-rearing model for autonomy is prominent in her paper. Its force seems to imply, in turn, that it is improbable that, in particular settings, relational theory will accept that quite distant forms of interaction serve relational autonomy. In any event, this question is explored most fairly not at the level of general theoretical accounts of relational autonomy, but rather in fine-grained scrutiny of relational theoretic treatments of administrative law.

On my reading, the applications of relational theory in administrative law settings by Nedelsky and others indicate a prior substantive commitment. This commitment is not broadly to any kind of autonomy-enhancing relationships, but more narrowly to thick, equal, or interdependent relationships. In administrative law, relational theorists seem to model the strong version of a relational approach. Nedelsky's discussion of administrative law, for example, is framed as an inquiry into administrative law's lessons for relational autonomy. The idea is that some participatory structures within administrative law constitute settings in which citizens have experienced a feeling of autonomy. She considers at some length Joel Handler's example of special education, in particular the structure implemented in some schools in Madison, Wisconsin (Handler 1986, ch. 4). She lists the components of autonomy to which the legal developments discussed seem responsive: 'dignity, efficacy, competence, and comprehension, as well as defense against arbitrariness' (Nedelsky 1989, 28). These components appear fully consistent with an account of an appropriate administrative relation as rather distant. But there are crucial clues that what Nedelsky has in mind is a relationship between citizens and bureaucrats that is thicker and more substantive. She comments that Handler's 'language of negotiation and bargaining' fails to capture her own image of an 'optimal relationship' (ibid., 31). Yet negotiation and bargaining are not incompatible with the attributes of dignity, efficacy, competence, and comprehension. If what Handler describes falls short, it is only because Nedelsky's 'optimal relationship' exceeds the conditions for respecting the attributes she listed earlier.

Precisely what Nedelsky envisages soon emerges. She reproduces a quote from a family member that Handler includes in his book, and her gloss on it is revealing: 'One can see that the relationship has been helpful, supportive, and respectful, but to me it does not quite convey the sense of *fully equal partnership*' (ibid., 31n57 [emphasis added]). It is not enough, for Nedelsky, for a bureaucratic relation to be 'helpful, supportive, and respectful.' (Would that all bureaucratic relations equalled such a standard.) It should, rather, be a fully equal partnership. Importantly, the essay does not defend a caveat that there is something unique about the role of parents in their children's special education that makes a radically different kind of relation with bureaucrats appropriate in this case but not others. What is one to do with the idea of fully equal partnership?

The bureaucrat and the citizen, in their vertical relation, will never be equal in the sense that the former will risk consequences equivalent to those bearing on the latter. The bureaucrat's children will not have their special schooling changed, say, if the citizen prevails in her arguments, nor does the immigration official face deportation should a Mavis Baker make her case convincingly. The most that is possible is a conception of equality applicable horizontally within the class of citizens (Dyzenhaus 2000), as opposed to an idea of vertical equality as between citizens and officials. To give it the benefit of the doubt, perhaps 'fully equal partnership' stands as a shorthand for qualities such as respect and fairness. But if so, it is unclear in what measure the attributes 'helpful, supportive, and respectful' fall short. Nedelsky's references to her image of an 'optimal relationship' and the measuring stick of 'fully equal partnership' suggest that, as a relational theorist, she approaches administrative law with a solid idea of what appropriate relationships will be. They will resemble the ones appropriate in more intimate settings, such as the family.

Another commitment to thick, interdependent relationships is found in Sossin's work. Sossin proposes that interdependence and intimacy are aspirations for the bureaucrat–citizen relationship. He suggests that administrative law's key values – fairness, impartiality, and reasonableness – can be better instantiated through intimate relationships, ones characterized by interdependence, vulnerability, mutual respect, and trust. Intimacy does not undermine impartiality, fairness, and reasonableness in administrative decision making. Rather, on his view, it enhances interdependency and engagement (Sossin 2002, 843; see also 1994). His ideal of interdependency and intimacy favours transmission of the information critical for accurate decision making. Recognizing the interaction of bureaucrats and citizens 'as a personal relationship will enfranchise citizens, animate bureaucrats, and enhance the accountability of the administrative state' (Sossin 2002, 815). Sossin objects to the current legal regime governing administrative decision making. He does so on the basis that the package of legal rights, guarantees, and obligations that purport to protect individuals from arbitrary state action substantially impedes the formation of meaningful relationships between decision makers and affected parties (ibid., 815–16).

To be sure, these studies located within relational theory do not formulate an empirical claim that reciprocity and mutuality actually do structure all social relations. Many relational theorists, including ones discussed in this chapter, concede that strategic imperatives, domination, and violence characterize many social interactions (Goodin 1996, 513). But the most convincing reading of relational theoretic work in administrative law indicates that relational theorists bring with them an established idea of optimal relationship borrowed from other, more intimate settings. This is not surprising since, as one philosopher puts it, a central feature of relational feminist accounts is the normative 'possibility of mutuality, reciprocity, and communication as features of social interaction' (Allen 2004, 243). The consequence, though, is that relational theory can slip into an unattractive imperialism in claiming that all, or at least too many, relations should be thickly relational – indeed intimate – in relational theory's normative sense. Of course, the gesture is unattractive only if, as I believe, there are probative reasons why the claim is inapt.

The commitment to thick, interdependent relationships in administrative law is unhelpful. Even viewing the relation solely from the individual's perspective, the thickness of relationship hinted at by Nedelsky and explicitly called for by Sossin is unattractive. In situations in which the most intimate knowledge is at issue (medical records, financial and domestic details), it is precisely not a relation of intimacy but rather one of distance that many, at least in the dominant Anglo-American culture, are likely to prefer. I knew an old woman in a small town who, well into her eighties, drove to a neighbouring town to cash her Old Age Security cheques. She wished to withhold from the tellers and other clients in her local bank branch decisive proof that she was over sixty-five. This case is perhaps extreme, but it reveals a kernel of truth in the search that people may have for what I shall call, later in this chapter, respectful distance rather than intimacy. There should be space in which to acknowledge that treating people fairly – arguably one of administrative law's highest aims – is distinct from cultivating relationships of interdependence or intimacy with them. But this idiosyncratic matter of personal comfort is not, of course, the prime difficulty. The major problem with intimate administrative relationships concerns the public interest.

The commitment to thick, interdependent administrative relationships obscures the public interest. Nedelsky's vision of equal partnership does not make sense when one imagines a discretionary decision maker with fewer resources than are demanded by the set of citizens requesting a share. If the decision maker must allocate those resources in the service of the public interest, it is incoherent to think of her as standing in an equal partnership with the individual applicants. Consider the situations of schooling for children with special needs discussed by Handler and Nedelsky. In situations of limited resources – fewer spots in the program than there are eligible children, or a variable number of spots but the reality that the more children admitted, the less the individualized attention for those participating – the bureaucratic decision maker is confronted with a *polycentric* distributive problem. The polycentric task or question is a notion developed by Lon Fuller in his classic essay 'The Forms and Limits of Adjudication.' Fuller vividly visualizes a polycentric problem as a spider web. A tug on one strand distributes tensions after a complicated pattern throughout the web as a whole (Fuller 2001, 127). Polycentric controversies 'exhibit a blend of technical, factual, and political attributes that often seem nearly impossible to separate or accommodate within a single procedural framework' (Boyer 1972, 169). They are not well resolved by adjudicative or quasi-adjudicative proceedings, with their tendency to reduce matters to binary contests. In such instances, the decision maker should seek to make responsible, accountable decisions for all, but the idea of standing in a relation of equal partnership to each parent is unhelpful and ultimately obstructive.[7]

An aspiration of intimacy occludes considerations of the public interest by focusing myopically on the individual and her relationship with a decision maker. Discussion of reasons for administrative decisions bears out this risk. The background for this discussion is the enunciation in *Baker* of a duty, 'in certain circumstances,' to provide a written explanation for a decision (1999, para. 43). That judgment alters the default position at common law from one where reasons have to be provided only in exceptional circumstances to one where reasons are required when an administrative decision is critical to an individual's future. Sossin criticizes even this current practice of giving reasons as insufficiently intimate. He proposes reconceiving reasons as 'a measure of intimacy,' suggesting that reasons be assessed against not only the standard of legal sufficiency, as is current practice, but also 'the standard of meaningfulness, truth and honesty' (Sossin 2002, 838). Yet reasons are unlikely to nurture an intimate relationship since, unlike a right to participate, exercisable during the course of the interaction between the decision maker and the individual and partly constitutive of their relationship, reasons arrive at the end. But more importantly, the notions of equal partnership (Nedelsky) and intimacy (Sossin) inappropriately exclude the public interest. They do so by suggesting that when an administrative decision has been well made, it will be possible to persuade the individual affected to accept it. For them, the purpose of the relationship involves this process of persuasion and acceptance. This notion sets the standard too high; there are defensible decisions that the individual will never accept.

Admittedly, the variety of administrative scenarios is such that there are also settings in which the front-line decision maker is not allocating scarce resources as between competing candidates. In many cases it may be that the bureaucrat's task is to determine eligibility or ineligibility for a benefit on the sole basis of the applicant's file, without simultaneous reference to other competing candidates. This is perhaps the paradigmatic welfare case. Even here, I suspect, other factors likely distort the purity of this bilateral view of the decision maker and the applicant. Departments may be assessed quarterly or at year end on their aggregate acceptance or rejection rates. Subtle or not-so-subtle pressures may induce bureaucrats to treat candidates one way or another. But even assuming there are no public interest or third-party considerations in a bilateral decisional context, it is not plain why an optimal relationship should be thick and interdependent rather than modelled after the rather thinner aspiration I sketch presently.

Whence this thick aspiration for optimal administrative relationships? At a general level, it comes from relational theorists' having worked previously on thick, interdependent, autonomy-enhancing relationships in other settings and then regarding their forays into administrative law as a continuous part of that enterprise. At a more local level, part of its source may be the descriptive account of interdependence within the contemporary welfare state. A brief genealogical investigation will reveal that the strong normative commitment to thick relationships in administrative law is causally related to a problematic description of the position of subjects and of autonomy vis-à-vis the administrative state. The starting point is relational theorists' description of subjects and autonomy. I mean the understandings of subjects as socially embedded and of autonomy as constitutively relational. I have called this the descriptive premise. But by description here I mean, additionally, the basic account of how subjects stand towards the administrative state, something that proves foundational to relational theoretic administrative law scholarship. Errors in this description infect the later, normative stages of relational theory's engagement with the administrative state.

At several junctures, Handler sketches similar accounts of the contrast between what he calls classic liberalism and the contemporary era of the administrative state. Classical liberalism regards society as instrumental to the development of the individual. Government is rebuffed by the specification and enforcement of substantive rights through procedural due process remedies. This is liberal legalism. By contrast, in the contemporary welfare state, 'transactions between the citizen and the state call for continuing relationships, for cooperative efforts, rather than lawsuits ... They are not interested in keeping the government at bay. They want to work with the government to get what they want' (Handler 1985, 690–1). Here Handler is responding to Charles Reich's (1964) proposition that it is appropriate to characterize government benefits as property in the traditional, liberal legal way. So far this account is unproblematic.

The difficulty arises in the characterization of the relations between the state and its citizens. Handler writes: 'People, in their dealings with government, are in a social bond. They are not isolated individuals. They need cooperative relationships not zones of privacy. They are concerned not with the conditions of independence but with the conditions of *interdependence*' (Handler 1985, 691 [emphasis added]). 'Interdependence' is the problematic concept in Handler's and other relational theoretic accounts of administrative law. It is no slip of Handler's pen, occupying instead a central place in his work (see also 1983, 1276; 1990, 16). He presents this idea of interdependence not as the thrust of his normative argument, but rather as an accurate *descrip-*

tion of contemporary reality that furnishes the background necessary for his normative explorations in the service of community.

Nedelsky, for her part, adopts a similar account of the terrain. She writes that 'the characteristic problem of autonomy in the modern state is not, as our tradition has taught us, to shield individuals from the collective, to set up legal barriers around the individual which the state cannot cross … The task is to render autonomy compatible with the interdependence which collective power (properly used) expresses.' She continues: 'The problem of interdependence, individual autonomy, and collective power takes its characteristic modern form in the relation between citizens and administrative bodies' (Nedelsky 1989, 13 [footnote omitted]). Plain evidence that Nedelsky regards the idea of interdependence as forming part of her initial description appears later in the essay. She refers to 'the *reality* of interdependence shap[ing] the scope of collective action and control' and the importance of 'a *recognition* of interdependence' (ibid., 20, 21n32 [emphasis added]). In the legal setting, admittedly, recognition assumes variable degrees of constitutive or performative robustness. 'Recognition' of spouses as equals in family law legislation, for example, does not presuppose that they were already equal. It amounts instead to the legislature's acknowledgment that, at common law, they were not. But here it seems that Nedelsky assumes that the interdependence for which she urges recognition existed prior.[8]

The problem is that the language of interdependence mischaracterizes the rapport between citizens and bureaucrats. The dictionary stipulates that 'interdependence' requires dependence 'on each other' (Brown 1993, vol. 1, 1392). In this setting the term is misleading because the bureaucrats making discretionary decisions within ministries and departments do not depend on their citizen clients in a way remotely comparable to those citizens' dependence on them. Even if bureaucrats consult individuals before exercising discretion, and seek to foster a dialogue, along the lines proposed by Cartier, it will not follow that there is 'interdependence.' Cartier asserts that interdependence is inherent to her conception of discretion as dialogue (unpublished, 295), but it is unhelpful to transpose 'interaction' and 'interdependence.' Doing so implies a set of policy reactions that may be ill suited to the terrain.

The absence of interdependence marks even the special education setting that Handler describes. It is true that if subjects ceased requesting discretionary decisions in their favour – never again demanded workers' compensation, stopped applying for permits, never sought refugee protection – the bureaucrats' jobs would be jeopardized. But such a scenario is distant from any present reality. Once bureaucrats' dependence for their livelihood on a collective stream of applicants is eliminated, there is little sign of dependence on individual citizens sufficient to fuse citizens and bureaucrats in an interdependence of mutual need and mutual vulnerability. Admittedly, every bureaucrat herself relies on benefits administered by other bureaucrats elsewhere in the administrative state. Immigration officials have children in special education. Welfare case workers make their homes more energy efficient in response to government inducements and apply for subsidies. Tax clerks apply for veterans' pensions. It is not the case that there are discrete classes, those who apply for benefits from the welfare state and those who make discretionary decisions allocating those benefits. Viewing everyone collectively, there may be what Handler more appropriately characterizes as 'interconnectedness' (1985, 706). This is preferable to interdependence as it does not connote mutuality of dependence. Yet it remains the case that, within each individual transaction in which one citizen seeks something and another will decide the case, the rapport is not one of interdependence. It should not be theorized as if it were.

Some of the drive towards the strong form of a relational approach is perhaps also a consequence of terminology. Relational theorists employ the terms 'relationship' and 'relational' in significantly different ways. One is the personal sense of a bond between two individuals, what the dictionary calls the 'state or fact of being related; a connection, an association, *spec.* an emotional (esp. sexual) association between two people' (Brown 1993, vol. 2, 2534). Much of the time, relational theorists talk about relationships in this acceptation: the personal, especially emotional connection between individuals. Nedelsky does so when she notes that it is not isolation, but relationships 'with parents, teachers, friends, loved ones' that aid the development and experience of relational autonomy (1989, 12; 1990, 169; see also Ball 2005, 357–9).

Another usage of *relationship* is the more impersonal sense of a connection between one thing and another. The sense can be, to use the dictionary's language again, the impersonal 'particular way in which one thing stands in connection with another.' It is this meaning of relation that is in play when Christine Koggel speaks of the relation between individuals and abstractions such as a matrix of 'social practices and political contexts' (1998, 131). Nedelsky herself speaks of such relations, referring to 'social-structural relationships' and those less intimate relationships that are 'part of the more formal structures of authority,' including 'employment relations as well as the officially "public" sphere' (1989, 11–12). Given the reliance in the literature on Handler's work, it is worth observing that he defines 'social autonomy' as 'a relational concept' concerning 'the relationship between the agent's desires and some set of constraints' (1990, 16). Handler's relation between a *desire* and a complex of *constraints* is markedly different from a constructive personal relationship between, say, a child and a favourite teacher. He is not talking about the contributions of a subject's personal relationships to her capacity for autonomy.

Part of the troubles arising from a pre-commitment to thick, interdependent administrative relationships derives, I suspect, from inattention to differentiable senses of 'relationship.' Thus at junctures relational theorists use 'relationship' to include both personal and impersonal relations, but when it comes to theorizing how to enhance 'relationships,' it is as if they have in mind exclusively personal relationships.[9] If one is inattentive to the distinctions, it is easy enough, when examining public law, to slip from discussing the way in which citizens stand in connection with the state (relation) to discussing or theorizing that connection as if it were an association, even an emotional one, between two people (relationship). Use of the word 'relationship' can initiate an unhelpful anthropomorphism of the administrative state, one that generates unproductive policy prescriptions.[10] Talk of relationships, with its connotation of personal connection, is metaphorical. It is not of course the case that other ways of analysing administrative law do not themselves rely on metaphor. The unavoidable pervasiveness of metaphor in thought and language has been ably documented (Lakoff and Johnson 2003, 247). The point, rather, is that where, as in relational theory, relationship is the central idea, it is especially crucial to be critically alert to its anthropomorphic, metaphorical character.[11] My sense is that the extensive theorizing on relationships, most of it accomplished in settings where thick relations do matter, has coloured the term 'relationship' so much that it is difficult to apply it in an extended fashion, sensitive to relational theory, without importing the stronger normative commitments.

A glance back at administrative impartiality reinforces the inappropriateness of the idea that optimal administrative relationships are thick. In *Baker* (1999), L'Heureux-Dubé J. gestured towards a substantive and demanding conception of the decision maker's impartiality.

The judgment imposes obligations on the bureaucratic decision maker in respect of the vulnerable individual. The bureaucrat is enjoined to reach towards the vulnerable applicant for a humanitarian and compassionate exception with 'a recognition of diversity, an understanding of others, and an openness to difference' (ibid., para. 47). Even there, at what is arguably the zenith of judicial exhortations for bureaucratic mental and emotional involvement, the relationship is not a mutual one. The bureaucrat does not depend on the individual, nor is the individual bound to corollary obligations vis-à-vis the bureaucrat. The individual is not invited to be open to the conditions of the decision maker, and it would appear peculiar if she were. It is thus problematic that the factual account of interdependence and the ambiguous meanings of 'relationship' prove influential when relational theorists employ their relational approach and trace out the implications of their normative commitments.

A sense that intimacy and interdependence are not, after all, desirable qualities in administrative settings emerges from Sossin's own work. He addresses institutional responses to the problem of vulnerability. In settings where the most crucial interests are at stake, an advocate, guardian, or intermediary may facilitate an administrative process. As he observes, these intermediaries are often said to owe their vulnerable clients a fiduciary duty. One way of addressing vulnerability in the administrative relationship more broadly is to view that relationship as giving rise to fiduciary-like obligations (2002, 850–3; see also Sossin 2003, 179–80; also Criddle 2006). He hastens to clarify that he is not suggesting the imposition of a duty to act in the interests of the affected individual. Rather, he is attempting to make the point that some social, institutional, and legal contexts place decision makers in a greater position of public trust than others. This suggestion illuminates the fundamental contradiction between the reality of disproportionate distributions of power and the ideals of intimacy, interdependence, or equal partnership. Fiduciary or trust-like duties are conceptually and practically incompatible with mutuality and interdependence. The settings in which fiduciary duties are recognized towards vulnerable individuals – doctor–patient, priest–parishioner, trustee–beneficiary – are decidedly asymmetrical. A person in a position of strength bears responsibilities towards the other, and, if all goes well, the vulnerable person benefits from the fiduciary's exercise of his powers (see generally Fox-Decent 2005). These relationships are neither intimate, nor equal, nor interdependent. One has only to think of *Norberg v. Wynrib* (1992), in which some judges characterized a physician's exchange with his patient of drugs for sexual favours as a breach of the physician's fiduciary duty. Rent seeking aside, problems of the worst kind of abuse seem to arise in fiduciary relationships precisely when those relationships become intimate.

That Sossin sees utility in references to fiduciary duty and the public trust bearing on administrative decision makers indicates his awareness, on some level, of the major difficulties with the ideal of intimate relationship between affected individuals and administrative decision makers. Moreover, the public dimension of the state's relations ensures that it cannot engage in a bilateral relation without concern for the competing interests of the collectivity. The Crown cannot be an ordinary fiduciary, precisely because 'it wears many hats and represents many interests, some of which cannot help but be conflicting' (*Wewaykum Indian Band v. Canada* 2002, para. 96; see also Fox-Decent 2005, 264–5).

A further dimension of the unattractiveness of a strong relational approach in administrative law comes from examination of an area of administrative law that is already genuinely characterized by a high degree of interdependence. This area will underscore the difference between the relationships that individuals have with the administration and those of corporate entities. I am thinking of public–private partnerships, that grey zone penetrated at times by principles and rules of administrative law but regulated more by contract law. It is in the contractual relationships between organs of the state and various consortia and associations of the private sector that one is likeliest to find the highest degree of interdependence in terms of closeness, informality, exchange of information, and mutual reliance (Freeman 2000a; 2000b; Vincent-Jones 2000; 1999; Deakin and Michie 1997). Trust is increasingly acknowledged to be an important feature in successful long-term commercial relations, which also rely on implicit understandings and shared conventions (Campbell and Collins 2003, 25; Wightman 2003; Collins 1996). Yet trust in commercial or commercial–administrative relations does not likely characterize the kind of autonomy-enhancing relating envisaged by relational theory. The fact that these relations function best absent recourse to formal dispute resolution mechanisms is a telling point: 'business as usual' is a cooperative state in which mutual self-interest lubricates the relationship, punctuated occasionally by disputes. But the relations that individuals are likely to have with the administration are not analogous.

It may be revealing that the example in the previous chapter that modelled the greatest attention to temporally defined context concerned the relation between a government ministry and a hospital. In *Mount Sinai*, Binnie J. stated that if it were a private law case, he would agree that the elements of promissory estoppel were present (2001, para. 46). Promissory estoppel is a private law doctrine that operates where there is a promise that the promisor should reasonably expect to have induced substantial action on the part of the promisee and where injustice will arise if the promise is not enforced. There is a hint in Binnie J.'s speculation that closeness and mutuality through informal dealings, even of an institutional kind, are likelier appropriate in a private law rather than a public law setting. Equivalent private law doctrines are less likely to apply by analogy where what lies under scrutiny is a government decision affecting a single vulnerable individual. The difference in power and resources in such circumstances rules any idea of mutuality out of the question: the decision maker does not depend on the individual in any remotely equivalent way. Rather, the decision maker wields substantial power against the individual. If one does not attempt to 'enhance' the relationship between institutions and the bureaucracy by making them closer and more interdependent, what is the normative content by which one substantiates the 'focus on relationships'? It will be something other than the commitment provided by the strong form of relational theory.

Before turning to the weaker version of a relational approach, a caveat is in order. A prior commitment to a particular model of autonomy-enhancing relationship on the part of some relational theorists does not prove, as a matter of induction, that all possible relational theorists necessarily share that commitment. But it is revealing that these forays of relational theory into administrative law largely manifest this commitment. It suggests that the descriptive premise and enterprise of focusing on relationships are frequently linked to certain substantive views. But it is time to test that hypothesis by investigating the possibility of a less robust form of relational theory, a weaker 'focus on relationships' in the administrative law setting. Such a weak form of relational theory would examine relational contexts but would not show a prior commitment to a particular model of relationship as optimal.

The Weak Version: Promoting Optimal Relationships of Varying Kinds

I begin by identifying key features of the administrative setting for theorizing optimal relationships. Then I sketch my view of the appropriate model for the bureaucrat–citizen relation and examine whether a plausible incarnation of relational theory might conceivably accept it. My view seeks to be compatible with the more accurate description of affairs I have tried to reach by sweeping aside the notion of interdependence. A further influential factor, in theorizing optimal administrative relationships, is the rarity of continuity in the bureaucrat–citizen relation. The assumption that the relations between the bureaucrats of the modern administrative state and citizens are analogous to (personal) relationships is misleading. Often the citizen will not interact in a sustained way with the same bureaucrats. Cases get passed from one bureaucrat to another. Officials change positions. Cabinets, the members of which are nominally responsible for exercising significant statutory discretion, are regularly shuffled. Think of the succession of ministers of health and social services who fingered the hospital file in *Mount Sinai Hospital Center* (2001). If one speculates that it was not the ministers themselves but their subordinates who handled the dossier, the number of potential players increases further. For analytical clarity, it is important to bear in mind that 'the relationship' between ministry and hospital is not remotely a personal one. Frequently there is little chance of continuity in the citizen– or client–bureaucrat relation. Such sustained personal interactions may, admittedly, occur more often in some of the areas on which Joel Handler focuses his research, such as education for children with special needs (1986, ch. 3, 4). In such cases, a case worker may have sustained responsibility. But even there, turnover is likely to be a constant factor. The typical relation between a citizen and a bureaucrat is likely to differ significantly in duration from those in the family setting, a locus in which relational theory's analytic purchase is more self-evident.

Moreover, even where the same bureaucrat handles a case for a long time, the power imbalance precludes the possibility of any thick relation of interdependence or intimacy. Consider those individual–bureaucrat relations that may be regarded as radically asymmetrical and non-optimal. I refer to situations in which vulnerable individuals find themselves cast more as supplicants for government largesse than as citizens. At times, the asymmetry of power and resources may be such that the applicant who presents herself to the administrative decision maker is not the authentic subject who pre-existed the administrative process. Rather, she is a subject reconstituting herself in conformity with her best understanding of what the decision maker will want most to hear. A refugee hearing, for example, imposes significant explicit and, less obviously, implicit constraints and incentives in response to which individuals re-form their narratives and reinvent themselves. They feel pressure to recite the story they believe their adjudicators wish to hear (Macklin 1999, 137–8; see also Valverde 2007). In a refugee hearing, the scenario may be slightly peculiar: officially, the tribunal members and an individual encounter one another for the first time, but the individual may be operating on the basis of a rich oral history of compatriots' prior strategies, successes, and failures. The tribunal members, in turn, may be influenced by past dealings with that individual's fellow nationals. Admittedly, bureaucrats respond to role expectations and are themselves partly constituted by discourses of power. There is no authentic subject untainted by relations of power (Weberman 2000, 264). But bureaucrats are not impelled to reconstruct themselves in the hope of securing a favourable decision. The power dynamic here points away from a model of optimal relationship as thick and interdependent towards something quite different.

A slightly different point calls for mention. A 'focus on the relationship,' depending as it does in the literature on the description of interdependence, risks obscuring the power relation between bureaucrats and individuals in another way. The risk is that attention to the relationship will shift concern from the achievement of satisfactory substantive outcomes (instrumental) towards the development of administrative relationships as if they were an end in themselves (non-instrumental). Attention to the quality of the administrative relationship – whether, as in the strong version, its intimacy, or in the weak version, its character in some other sense – can suppress more important debate over appropriate substantive standards (Lacey 1992, 379). Where the most vulnerable individuals are involved, material needs are likely so pressing that little surplus energy permits them to relish participation in democratic life.[12] Those most vulnerable subjects who contend for a welfare benefit or status as a refugee are unlikely to have the mental and physical energy to engage in democratic participation for its own sake. It is ironic that Handler and Nedelsky's language of interdependence has the effect of masking dependence and vulnerability, since both scholars are explicitly concerned in their work with dependence and power (Handler 1988, 1093; 1995; 2004; Nedelsky 1989, 13, 27; 1990, 169).

In such settings, the relation is arguably pathological. In the refugee case, it is disputable, to use Foucault's terms, whether the relation is one of power – which is only exercisable over free subjects, only to the extent they are 'free' – or one of domination (Rabinow and Rose 2003, 126ff.). Given the dimension of domination, there are perhaps conceptual constraints on relational theory's capacity for constructive intervention. Fruitful as it is in some settings, relational theory's language of enhancing, fortifying, or promoting existing relationships precludes a radical reconstruction or transformation of a relation. It presumes, I think, the relation's redeemability. The transformation in the field of immigration and refugee law, from a view of non-citizens as supplicants begging for privileges the administration of which was utterly unreviewable, to one of non-citizens as rights bearers, surpasses what could plausibly be called an enhancement in a relationship. It amounts, rather, to a conceptual overhaul. The recognition of rights on the part of individuals attempts to even the scales substantively, and in doing so drastically reconfigures the relation and its discursive field. All the issues raised by this reconfiguration are not yet resolved. A tension persists between recognition of the rights bearer and the delegation of discretion to ministers and other officials. For example, Canadian courts have not satisfactorily resolved the conjunction of human rights and administrative discretion (Macklin 2004; Mullan 2004).

A further indicator away from thick relationship is the recent recognition of the importance of human rights. The person as rights bearer, at least in those areas of administrative law touching non-citizen subjects' mobility, is incompatible with the informal coziness of thick relationships. Rights on the part of the citizen have been recognized precisely because that citizen is not remotely equal to the bureaucrat and the state. If they were more equal, one would want to emphasize rights much less and instead emphasize informal forms of relating, as in the commercial institutional cases. But it is in the administrative setting where individuals are most vulnerable that formal protections can be most necessary. The conception of rights bearer instates an entitlement to treatment with dignity and fairness, qualities that are better understood as palliating a relation of dependence rather than characterizing one of interdependence. For those who occupy a wrongfully subordinated position, rights can be a 'marker of citizenship' and of the entitlement to participate (Williams 1987a, 431; 1987b; also Goodin 1996, 513). The idea of the rights bearer does not draw the parties closer, but instead interposes a formal barrier between them. But the legal right is not the chief source of the distance. Bureaucrats and individuals may be so different – so foreign to each other in terms of class, culture, and material resources – that it is better to attempt to manage the distance than to initiate a closeness that is not really possible (Macklin 1999). In contrast with the refugee example, in regulatory settings the regulators and the staff of the regulated industries are likelier to come from similar backgrounds and to have similar education and credentials. Indeed, in some regulated fields – financial services, say, or pharmaceuticals – there is considerable mobility from government to the private sector and back as individuals accumulate expertise in one setting and seek a purchaser for it in the other. Obviously no comparable back-and-forth movement characterizes areas such as refugee claims, and the optimal administrative relation should reflect that.

A paradox arises. It was a contextualism consistent with relational theory's methodological element that helped lay the groundwork for recognizing non-citizens as bearers of rights. Nevertheless, the transformation of the relation between the individual and the state entailed by such recognition surpasses the enhancement of existing relations within the purview of relational theory. Indeed, some sense of the limits of enhancing relationships and of the irredeemable quality of some relations marked by severe asymmetries of power and material resources emerges in Nedelsky's recent work. Discussing welfare, she suggests that only some form of guaranteed annual income can shift the deeply entrenched patterns. In other words, she now thinks that what is best is not fostering an existing relationship – within which the bureaucrat exercises discretion in assessing the applicant's fit to a set of prescribed criteria – but eliminating that relationship entirely, replacing it with an uncontroversial, non-discretionary entitlement on the part of the citizen (Nedelsky unpublished a; also Goodin 1996, 513). Where the relations are most oppressive, relational theory's project of promoting constructive relationships may find itself stretched beyond its conceptual capacity.

These factors and antinomies in mind, my conjecture is that the objective should be to secure respectful, fair, and dignified treatment for individuals, consistent with the public interest. Bureaucrats should demonstrate contextual sensitivity while maintaining a distance concomitant with the power differential. In other words, striving for a contextual sensitivity does not require the closeness connoted by intimacy or interdependence. The optimal bureaucrat–citizen relationship is one of respectful distance.

It is time now to give relational theory the benefit of the doubt by assuming that its normative commitment is variable enough to accept a wide spectrum of optimal relationships, including ones characterized by respectful distance. Perhaps relational theory's normative commitments can harbour the sort of relation between citizens and bureaucrats that I have argued should be characterized by dignity, fairness, and respect for rights.

My intuition is that by this point, relational theory has stripped itself to a degree that it becomes unrecognizable to itself. It is possible to argue that the model of relation I have sketched is consistent with relational theory on the basis that it promotes the subject's autonomy in the specificity of the bureaucratic setting. Its ultimate prescriptions, however, are identical to those of mainstream liberalism, and the objection swiftly arises that the relational theoretic literature operates on the assumption that the outcomes towards which it gestures differ from the offerings of mainstream liberalism. Nedelsky recounts a telling challenge in this regard in which a philosopher colleague queries why relational autonomy in the public law sphere does not end up in a restatement of the old liberal argument that rights must be balanced against the public good. She replies that what has changed is that the value of autonomy will be recognized as inextricable from the social context in which individuality arises (Nedelsky 1989, 35–6). But in administrative law, I suggest, the tension between the collectivity and the individual is such that even this social understanding of autonomy ought to cash out into a fairly conventional liberal conception of the appropriate relation between citizens and the administration, one that includes the notion of the individual as a bearer of human rights. The contextual methodology aside, the distinctiveness of a relational approach in this setting appears to be fading. It is perhaps worth recalling here suggestions that 'more sophisticated forms of liberalism and relational feminism may tend in the end to converge' (Goodin 1996, 513).

This question of diluting relational theory aside, there is a further dimension in which relational theory's inquiry seems a bad fit in administrative law. Relational theory's classic formulation speaks of 'fostering' existing relationships. In administrative law, it is strong institutional repeat players who are likeliest to develop such ongoing relations with bureaucrats. Think of a pharmaceutical company and a food and drug regulator, or a financial services institution and a securities regulator. 'Enhancing' the administrative relation here poses clear threats of conflicts with the public interest. If one attempts to enhance or promote the bureaucrat–individual relation, one may find the chair of a regulatory agency ensconced cozily in a private box at an arena with captains of the regulated industry. This image is not especially attractive and conjures concerns about industry capture. While it is chiefly the repeat players such as major industries and their regulators who have the time and resources to invest in deepening their administrative relationships, the public probably do not desire such relations to be too thick. One may think of the rich literature on 'repeat players' in civil litigation (Galanter 1974). Where the public interest and the interest of, say, a regulated industry are often in conflict, there is arguably a public interest in maintaining a somewhat adversarial relationship rather than fostering and enhancing that relationship. One might wish the relation to retain an adversarial strain, to keep – ideally – the regulator sharp and the industry honest. Is it helpful to say that what one is doing, in nourishing this healthy antagonism, is promoting, enhancing, or fostering the contextually mandated kind of constructive relationships? It is perhaps possible but seems a stretch. In arriving at such an articulation of the mandate, relational theory has come a long way from its other, stronger incarnations.[13]

Further challenges arise in operationalizing even the weak form of relational theory's 'focus on relationships.' Administrative law presents a challenge to such a theoretical enterprise in the dizzying variety of levels and kinds of relation. Even bracketing personal relationships, the class of relations is diverse. It should not be assumed that the relation between a citizen and a front-line case officer, a citizen and a review tribunal, a citizen and an appeals tribunal, a citizen and a reviewing court, a citizen and an appellate court, an institution and a regulator, an agency and a reviewing court, and a reviewing court and an appellate court are analogous. It is plain that the 'relationship between courts and tribunals' (Jacobs and Kuttner 2002, 618) should be understood as other than a personal relationship. '*The relationship* between the respondents and the Minister' in *Mount Sinai* (2001, para. 4 [emphasis in original]) is a distinctly different thing from, say, the relationship in family law between unmarried cohabitants.

The contextualism outlined in the previous chapter can plausibly operate as between the different levels of administrative relations. Indeed, judges insist that it should. Contextualism in such instances refers to the way that individuals with decision-making authority apprehend the case in front of them and the way that reviewing judges assess the work of delegated decision makers. Contextualism can function effectively in impersonal, institutional settings, drawing attention to an agency's practices to supplement a statutory text that may be silent on the question of procedure or of a decision maker's expertise. A reviewing court may examine a securities commission contextually for its procedural practices or for its technical expertise without treating relations as personal ones. Given the qualitative differences among relations within the administrative state, though, the purposive 'focus on relationships' calls for greater caution. Theorists posing the inquiry, 'What relationships do we wish to promote?' – and attempting to concretize the normative commitment to relationships that enhance relational autonomy – need to be conscious that many of the relations in administrative settings are impersonal, institutional rapports marked by a significant asymmetry of power and resources. Where closeness arises, it does so, undesirably, in pathological cases of agency capture.

More problematically, even kept normatively weak, open to any view of optimal relationship, a relational inquiry stacks the deck towards the bilateral bureaucrat–individual relationship. A focus on the relationship per se loses sight of other interests. The focus on reasons within Sossin's relational account, whether as conducive to intimacy between bureaucrat and individual or as ameliorative of some other kind of relationship between them, ignores the crucial precedential function of reasons as they relate to parties currently outside the set of administrative relations. Reasons guide the conduct of other individuals who will interact with the administration in the future (*Via Rail Canada* 2000, para. 20). Another element of administrative reasons is the public good of a culture of justification in which exercises of state power are legitimated by their public justification, even if the affected individual does not agree with that justification (Dyzenhaus and Fox-Decent 2001; Liston 2004; Craig 1994, 283). This legitimation function of reason giving depends on a culturally embedded intuition about the character of non-arbitrary decision making (Lindseth 2005).[14] These crucial public, communal dimensions of the provision of reasons seem to escape a relational focus on administrative relations.

Is there a cruel irony here? Relational theory rejects liberal atomism in favour of social relationships. In administrative law, it theorizes state–citizen relations as interdependent and then focuses on the individual bureaucrat–citizen relation as if it were a personal relationship. The effect is to emphasize the qualities of this bilateral relation rather than the consequences of individual administrative decisions for the larger community. A focus on relationship, which it seems will fasten inexorably on individuals dealing with bureaucrats, has difficulty taking into consideration other people who will occupy those roles in future cases and the other people outside those roles who are nonetheless affected by the transactions within them. The normative content one pours into it aside, the very form of a focus on relationship foregrounds and suppresses different interests in a problematic way. Administrative law presents significant challenges for applying relational theory, in strong or weak forms. A further problematic dimension of relational theory remains, one perhaps linked to relational theory more generally.

Institutional and Structural Relations

I have argued already that a relational approach, one that strives to theorize and promote optimal relationships between bureaucrats and individuals, can overlook the public interest. Indeed, the very notion of a 'focus' on relationship, itself a metaphor, implies concentrating on some things, bringing them into view clearly, and relegating other things to the fuzzy periphery. What it also grasps poorly is the dual character of administrative law as simultaneously articulating the relationship between the administration and individuals and the relationship *between the administration and the courts* as a matter of political theory and political economy.

In her exploration of administrative law's lessons for relational autonomy, Nedelsky examines *Goldberg v. Kelly* (1970), the case in which the U.S. Supreme Court adopted the view that welfare payments are the kind of benefit that cannot be taken away without 'due process.' Nedelsky reads this development as entailing that 'recipients will experience their relations to the agency in a different way'; 'a hearing designates recipients as part of the process of collective decision-making rather than as passive, external objects of judgment' (1989, 27). She draws from the judgment the idea that the 'relationship can be shaped by the nature of the decision-making and the citizen's role in it. The nature of the citizen's relation to the agency ... need not be dictated by the substance of the agency's power' (ibid., 28). This analysis is preceded by the definitional statement that administrative law 'mediates between governmental agencies and the citizens subject to their decisions' (ibid., 27). Now, it is possible to think about good relationships between individuals and the bureaucracy at a purely theoretical level, without attention to the means for implementing changes. It is also possible to attempt to initiate change to those relationships through internal mechanisms of accountability and good governance (Macdonald 2004). But it remains the case that administrative law, in lawyerly discourse and, it seems, for relational theorists, is conceived of as devised by reviewing courts. Administrative law is what judges impose on the administration.

Work of relational theory in administrative law shows a relational approach as focusing on individual relationships and as failing to take into account that administrative law also mediates between courts and government agencies. The predisposition to attend to personal relationships – even the weak focus, on the optimal bureaucrat–citizen relationship, whatever it turns out to be – has helped obscure a plane of institutional interaction. It is radically incomplete to analyse judicial impositions of procedure for the changes they effect to the bureaucrat–citizen relationship without observing that they also rewrite the relation between bureaucrats and their judicial overseers. Relational theory has acknowledged rather poorly that administrative law disputes 'serve as proxies for a two-hundred-year-old political controversy: should the invisible hand of the market or the visible hand of the state determine the course of our lives?' (Arthurs 1985, 196 [endnote omitted]).[15] Little sense is apparent of administrative law functioning 'within an interest-driven set of competing power relationships' (Leyland and Woods 1997, 393). Is this a contingent lapse on the part of a couple of relational theorists' forays into administrative law, or does it have deeper roots in the project?

I noted earlier that relational theorists use their crucial term 'relationship' to refer, alternately, to personal relationships and to more impersonal relations. There may be a sense that lumping together interpersonal dealings with structural market conditions and ideologies of racism and patriarchy as 'relationships' provides the fullest possible scope for assessing the constraints on autonomy and the possibilities for enhancing that capacity. The idea is perhaps that unless you call them all 'relationships,' a relational approach cannot take them all into account. What the administrative law example suggests, however, is that use of an explicitly relational focus on relationship introduces its own blind spots. The ambition to assess all connections as relationships may outpace the practical ability to realize it. The idea of a 'focus on relationships' sheds sharp light on personal relationships, but it can throw institutional dealings into obscurity. Casting the net of the focus on relationship too wide may ultimately disserve its project. The valuable work theorizing and examining constructive personal relationships may, I suggest, have made it difficult to examine institutional and structural configurations under the same rubric as part of the same inquiry. It is perhaps the case that the ambitions ascribed to relational theory's relational approach are too burdensome for an inquiry into relationships. My motivation in making this suggestion is not to downplay the importance of these impersonal factors in enabling or constraining autonomy. To the contrary, my claim is that these institutional and structural factors are too important to be treated as 'relationships,' too influential to be eclipsed by a focus on individual relationships, as seems to have happened in these administrative law studies. It is here, finally, that I can return to my suggestion in chapter 1 that it is worth distinguishing a subject's *context* from her *relationships* because more flexibility and openness remains in assessing contextual factors than relationships. Obviously, either inquiry will bring baggage, but context perhaps less than relationships. A contextual inquiry, though it requires normative guidelines, is less committed ex ante to particular norms of good relationship.

What is best taken from relational theory in this setting is the need for contextual sensitivity on the part of administrative decision makers. This contextualism aids in the application of human rights norms in discretionary decision making, as called for in *Baker* (1999).

I have argued that relational theory seems not to be open to fostering relations characterized by distance, respect, and rights in the service of autonomy. Instead, it favours ideals of equal partnership, interdependence, and intimacy in the administrative relationship. These aspirations are, as I have argued, problematic and should not be adopted. The developments discussed in chapter 6 are best characterized as giving rise to a contextual approach, but not as instantiating a substantive commitment to intimacy or to the advancement of relational autonomy through administrative relationships. Problematic theorizing about administrative relations has derived, in some measure, from inaccurate descriptions of the contemporary administration–citizen relations as interdependent and from unreflective anthropomorphism, treating relations with the administration like interpersonal relationships.

I identified problematic tendencies in the relational literature on administrative law: the failure to distinguish between different kinds of relations (referring to personal and impersonal relations without differentiation as 'relationships') and the reliance on an account of the contemporary administrative state as having established interdependence in citizen–state dealings. It is these tendencies, I argued, that are partly responsible for the inappropriate normative focus within relational theory on equal, interdependent, and intimate citizen–state relations (what I called the strong version of a relational focus).[16] The tendency to view the citizen–bureaucrat relation as a personal relationship leads to aspirations of intimacy, equality, and interdependence. This view can occlude the public interest by seeking to place the individual on equal footing with the administrative decision maker. Alternatively, it can disserve the individual's substantive interests by focusing exclusively on the quality of relation with the administration, not the outcome. Another tendency, which presumes the interdependence of bureaucrats and citizens, obscures the power differentials and discrepancy in resources between bureaucrats and vulnerable individuals. This last effect is a painful one for relational theorists, as their contextual method is expressly concerned with identifying such structural features. The description of interdependence in the administrative state can, however, foreclose contextual inquiry into the reality of relations.

I presented an account of desirable citizen–bureaucrat relations as marked by respect, dignity, distance, and contextual sensitivity on the part of the bureaucrat. After closely reading relational theoretic work in administrative law, I concluded that relational theory seems not to be open to the conclusion that such a relation is the one which, in the administrative law setting, best fosters relational autonomy. Instead, relational theorists appear committed – in what I tendentiously suggested was an imperialistic way – to the promotion of thick, interdependent, intimate relationships in administrative law, irrespective of the context. Yet such a normative commitment to enhancing the bureaucrat–citizen relation can, counterproductively, detract from efforts to transform that relation by altering the material conditions that render the citizen vulnerable. Indeed, I suggested that in the administrative field, relational theory's potential is constrained by its emphasis on 'enhancing' and 'promoting' existing relationships, a conceptual emphasis that can preclude radical transformation. Undue attention to the bilateral bureaucrat–citizen relation can detract from consideration of the polycentric character of distributive problems affecting many parties. It also detracts from consideration of the institutional, structural relationship between the judiciary and the administration.

A jurisdictional dilemma ensues. One horn entails saying that relational theory is applicable everywhere, but that in some settings – I submit administrative law to be one of them – it will be drastically diluted. Only the weak form will be appropriate. Moreover, since even the weak form of a content-neutral 'focus on relationship' tends to highlight bilateral interactions and occlude institutional ones, relational theorists would need to enlarge their research agenda in administrative law considerably and with great caution. Absent such caution, in administrative law, 'focus on relationship' can detract from constructive attention to power relations and substantive outcomes.

The other horn requires concluding that the writ of relational theory, in its full form, runs, with less dilution, in a narrower field, perhaps most suitably in private law. Relational theorists who are interested in maximizing their theory's impact should take notice that arguments for relational autonomy are much more persuasive in the family setting, say, than arguments for interdependence, equality, and intimacy in bureaucrat–citizen relations. Demarcating a reduced domain of application for relational theory is a task that can be made easier by thinking, not of a general 'focus on relationships,' but of the two elements that I have argued can be broken out: the contextual methodology and the normative commitment. The contextual method is more flexible and open to different normative configurations. It applies more widely than relational theory's normative commitments, articulated fully. Despite efforts to frame a neutral form of relational inquiry, the normative commitment seems always to be lurking somewhere, and it is best acknowledged.

Indeed, it is recognition that optimal relationships take different forms, not only the model of thick, interdependent ones, that underwrites this book's argument that the legal subject now produced is a *contextual* one, not a relational one. Amy Allen, canvassing the range of feminist perspectives on subjectivity, discerns 'a shared insight of these related feminist perspectives on the relational self: namely, that mutual, reciprocal, communicative social interactions are necessary for the formation, sustenance, and repair of the self' (2004, 240). Such interactions are doubtless valuable, but the emphasis they install on thick relationships is precisely the reason why this book, concerned as it is not only with family law settings but also with administrative law settings, prefers to speak of contextual subjects. A discourse of relational subjects in administrative law would likely succumb to the same problems I have identified in this chapter in connection with relational theory's relational approach in administrative law.

8 Conclusion

This book has argued for the emergence of a new view of legal subjects in family law and administrative law. In both fields, legislative, judicial, and scholarly practices now constitute *contextual subjects*. That is, these legal fields reflect the contextual subject that has emerged in what some call 'post-liberal theory' (Reece 2003, 13). In another sense, the book also claims that family law and administrative law are now themselves contextual subjects. Family law and administrative law have adopted a methodology of contextualism. I have made these arguments using relational theory. In turn, I have also used these substantive fields of law to make arguments about relational theory. The ways in which contextualism advances different normative commitments in the two fields demonstrate the separability of relational theory's key elements. Instead of regarding relational theory as a single enterprise of 'focusing on relationships,' it is better to split it into a *contextual method* and its *normative commitments*.

Contextualism departs from what I called relational theory's descriptive premise, the view of individuals as partially constituted by their context, including their various relationships. In law, contextualism resists exclusive reliance on formal statuses and categories. It holds that the application of legal rules and regimes should, where possible, be particularized. Contextualization fits, along with specificity and the 'accommodation of incoherence,' in what Desmond Manderson nicely calls 'legal geography.' It contrasts with legal geometry's abstraction, reification, and 'denial of incoherence' (Manderson 2000, 170). Context typically extends spatially and temporally. The temporal dimension reflects relational theory's description of the self as historically constituted, projected through time. It is, let me say provisionally, an enemy of formalism. In practice, it often erodes dichotomies. It does so by driving towards categories' underlying objectives and criticizing a dichotomy's crudeness by identifying similarities between cases assigned to both categories. In this respect, contextualism resembles functionalism.

Functionalism in administrative law means concern with law's consequences and government's improvement of social welfare through administrative agencies, not courts. Where administrative agencies are concerned, functionalism and contextualism are perhaps interchangeable (Harvison Young 1997, 333–5).[1] Functionalism fails, however, to capture the dimension I have tried to bring out by drawing on the discourses of subjectivity. It does not grasp the way that contextualism, in both family law and administrative law, produces a new conception of the *legal subject*. Mavis Baker is conceived as a subject rooted in her family and social context (*Baker* 1999). She occupies a subject position not entailed by the functionalist commitment to taking seriously an administrative decision maker's 'purpose and nature' (Harvison Young 1997, 334). Functionalism does not speak positively to the contextualized view of the subject as bearer of rights.

In family law, similarly, contextualism and functionalism overlap to some extent. Functionalism in that field implies concern for facilitating the functions of financial and affective support that families perform. Here again, once functionalism identifies the salient functions of the institution, it is likely to paint using broad, possibly *acontextual* strokes. A functionalist definition of the family concerned with securing financial and emotional support for household members will find few reasons for distinguishing between blended families that are superficially similar on the basis that one type has been constituted only recently. Functionalism may not grasp contextualism's temporal dimension. In family law, as in administrative law, functionalism bears on institutions – administrative tribunals, households – but is unlikely to concern itself with the manner in which legal practices produce subjects.

Family law and administrative law produce subjects embedded in context, especially thick relationships. The subjects in these fields are increasingly ones that change across time, such that reliance and patterns of interaction can tilt the analysis towards particular outcomes. The move towards contextualism repudiates overarching, universal characterizations in favour of more specific, contingent identities. In family law, recognition of a person as married to another once entailed a robust package of rights and obligations. Today a contextual approach may lead to different kinds of obligations towards different people and a much more fragmented sense of family identity. A cohabiting couple will be recognized as a conjugal unit for some purposes but not others. More than two parent figures may owe support for a child's upbringing. This contextual approach, with its emphasis on the particular, can be seen as consistent with theoretical explorations of the death of the universal subject. As Carl Stychin recounts, the postmodern rejection of all projects claiming to be universal deconstructed the unity of the subject, revealing subjects to be 'plural, fragmentary, and contingent' (1995, 20). Subjectivities are now 'fluid rather than solid, contextual rather than universal' (Flax 1993, 93 [reference omitted]; also Reece 2003).

Perhaps contextualism will help legal regimes become more sensitive to diverse individuals' important interests. A risk arises, however, of exaggerating and romanticizing the ability of legal regimes fully to recognize people as they are or perceive themselves to be. In a book on standing in public law litigation, Joseph Vining argues that in the law's eyes the individual remains always merely a personification of social values and interests (1978). His point is that legal processes are neither equipped nor inclined to take a comprehensive view of the subject that encompasses multiple dimensions. By adopting a contextual approach to particular human beings in their social and economic contexts, contemporary courts and legislatures focus explicitly on specific values and narrow bundles of rights. Yet these institutions may remain hobbled in their capacity to perceive individuals as complex, unitary beings (Baker 1981, 339). Contextualism volleys ever more information at judges, inviting increasingly close scrutiny. Yet there can be a darker side to a contextualism that entails such heightened scrutiny of subjects. In Canada, where recognition of same-sex couples has been achieved in courts, it has not arrived through arguments for privacy. Submitting claims under the equality guarantee, applicants essentially invited judges to examine their unions in detail so as to conclude that they are conjugal, committed, and functionally equivalent to heterosexual relationships and that it is thus appropriate to compare them to heterosexual marriages. It is not universally accepted, however, that it is appropriate for the state's gaze to intrude so much into intimate relationships.[2] Even if one believes in the value of the public recognition of such relationships that recourse to a methodology of contextualism has secured, such recognition is not without its ambivalence and costs. A pessimist may see contextualism as preparing what Giorgio

Agamben calls 'a tacit but increasing inscription of individuals' lives within the state order' (1998, 121).

This contextualism, I have argued, can be connected to a methodology called for as part of feminist political philosophers' relational approach. The other element of relational theory to be drawn from the 'relational approach,' I argued, is a normative commitment to promoting relational autonomy through thick, interdependent relationships. It draws attention to those conditions necessary for sustaining and nourishing relationships that enhance people's capacity for self-development. The normative commitment also extends to palliating the effects of harmful relationships. It translates into a preference for relational continuity. It is worthwhile distinguishing this normative commitment from relational theory's descriptive premise because relational theory's criticism of liberalism as atomistic misunderstands substantial elements of the liberal tradition. If, as I suggested in chapter 1, liberalism accepts that individuals are formed within relationships and communities, such acceptance indicates that the nub of relational theorists' disagreement with liberals is not the descriptive premise. Rather, disagreements will arise over the appropriate *normative* response to the particulars of humans' embedded existence. This sets the emphasis squarely on relational theorists' normative position.

The Substantive Chapters Reviewed

Family Law

I argued in chapter 2 that relational theory illuminates family law during the period 1950 to 1975. Family law, at that time, produced a thick legal subject, one embedded – to an extent asphyxiating for some – in social relations and religious traditions. In contrast to relational theory's exhortations, family law showed itself to be markedly acontextual in methodology. A couple of statuses structured the field dichotomously: married/unmarried and legitimate/illegitimate. For the most part, lacking the privileged status entailed an unpleasant packet of negative consequences without contextual examination as to whether particular circumstances warranted other treatment. Subjects were thick, but not contextual. Once a subject had been inscribed on the map produced by the governing statuses, details about that subject's life were unnecessary. Certain states of fact, such as unmarried cohabitation and same-sex relationships, were virtually invisible. Indeed, homosexual relations were unthinkable as potential conjugal relationships. The set of privileged family relationships was conceived of formally and abstractly. The law, particularly Quebec's civil law, focused more on a universal iconic ideal of Married Woman than on particular married women. Abstention from contextual examination characterized, similarly, the judicial production of a rule preferring the biological link joining birth parent and child over a functional relationship between the same child and a prospective adoptive parent. The resolution of property disputes between spouses was also acontextual, a stance exemplified in the majority reasons in *Murdoch v. Murdoch* (1973). Yet despite this acontextualism, the family law of the earlier period paid considerable attention to relationships.

The dichotomies furnished by marriage and legitimate filiation provided institutional responses to the inquiry as to what kinds of relationships were suitably fostered. Two critical differences separated this family law from one with which relational theorists could ally themselves. First, the autonomy to which subjects could aspire was differentiated sharply along gender lines. Second, family law regarded as constructive only those relationships legitimate in the eyes of church (usually) and state.[3] In several instances (actions for breach of promise to marry, immutability of marriage contracts, and withdrawal of the birth parent's consent to adoption), judges and legislatures used comparatively formal tools (contract doctrine, rigid rules) to protect subjects whose vulnerability stemmed from thick relationships. These examples intimate that relational theory's alignment of contract and formalism with atomist liberalism should be regarded not as conceptual, but as empirical and contingent.

Chapter 3 argued that in the contemporary period, family law has aligned itself much more closely with the elements of relational theory. Contemporary family law is characterized by a contextual methodology and by a normative commitment to deep relationships marked by a greater aspiration of gender equality and diminished attention to relationships' formal status. The developments in matrimonial property and alimony demonstrate substantial attention to context. They recognize that despite the absence of formal evidence, in practice both spouses contribute valuably to the marriage as a shared economic enterprise. Laskin J.'s dissent in *Murdoch* exemplified attention to the particular features of a marriage and a conception of family roles that focused more on performance than on formal status. In contrast with the preceding period, attention shifts from the promotion of legitimate relationships. Legislatures and courts eroded the distinctions between married and unmarried couples. They also granted children's status independence from the civil status of the parents. As in the earlier period, the subject of family law is a thick one, but one no longer defined vis-à-vis a grid of legitimacy. Courts normalized adoption, acknowledging with less reluctance the viability of a parental bond not dependent on biological ties. One striking example of contextualism was the ascription of child support obligations to step-parents on the basis of the lived interaction within the family. Another was the legislative recognition of unmarried couples in the form of a support obligation and judicial recognition in the form of equitable remedies. Last came the recognition of same-sex couples.

When viewing family law through the lens of relational theory, continuities become apparent. The contextual methodology and the normative commitment to thick relationships are discernible across the entire contemporary period. The effect is that, contrary to the arguments of some family law and constitutional law scholars, the litigation of family cases under the Canadian Charter of Rights and Freedoms did not effect a seismic change to the landscape. The changes to family law wrought by Charter litigation are themselves consistent with the prior turn to contextualism and the recognition and promotion of thick relationships without regard to their formal status. It is through a contextual method that the human rights in the Charter were rendered concrete in the family field. Family subjects are now not only thick, but also contextual.

Chapter 4's study of explicit and implicit private ordering within adult relationships clarified the critical importance of spelling out normative positions within relational theory. Adopting contextualism and a weak 'focus on relationships' are insufficient for addressing difficult disputes. The point of departure was a trilogy of recent judgments. *Miglin v. Miglin* (2003) addressed the judicial approach when weighing a separation agreement that reduces or waives the spousal support obligation otherwise owing. The question was essentially the degree to which parties would be held to bargains departing from statutory entitlements in the face of changing circumstances subsequent to contract formation and separation. *Hartshorne v. Hartshorne* (2004) examined a similar question, except that the spouses had derogated contractually from the general regime on entering marriage. It was thus a period of married life that intervened between the agreement and the wife's claim. *Nova Scotia (A.G.) v. Walsh* (2002) considered, in light of the Charter's guarantee against discrimination, the legislature's restriction of a matrimonial property regime to married couples. At issue were the patrimonial consequences constitutionally attributable to cohabitants who had never crossed 'la formalité du seuil' (Cornu 1998, 154). The judges of the Supreme Court of Canada divided in all three cases. In each, a majority enforced the legal consequences of action (the contracts in *Miglin* and *Hartshorne*) and of inaction (failure to marry in *Walsh*).

The cruder reading of this division regards the majority and minority judges as sharply polarized. It views the majority as adopting an acontextual methodology and accepting the parties' private ordering uncritically. On this reading, the majority is seen as holding that 'a contract is a contract,' irrespective of the context. Admittedly, underdeveloped references to autonomy and choice in the majority judgments provide fodder for this construction. The same reading regards the minority in the three cases as adopting a contextual method and demonstrating a normative commitment to palliating the detrimental effects of thick relationships, undeterred by prior formal ordering. But the superior reading, I argued, is that the majority and minority shared crucial points of agreement, ones consistent with relational theory. All judges took a contextual approach to the statutes and legal subjects before them. All were alert to obligations arising independently of the mechanisms of formal ordering. All accepted that subjects form deep relationships, the consequences of which are unpredictable ex ante. Where the judges diverged is their fine-grained normative response to instances of private ordering. The challenge consisted in striking an appropriate balance between deference to the context of thick relationships, which drives towards determinism, and respect for individual choice, a value which the minority judges – and relational theorists – were unwilling to jettison.

These disputes highlight the value and limits of relational theory. That all the judges accepted the key elements of relational theory testifies to its attractions and achievement in having thoroughly articulated widely shared moral and political intuitions. The divergences in these judgments illustrate, however, that unanimity as to these elements fails to dictate specific outcomes in difficult cases. Put another way, individuals who concur in adopting relational theory's elements may still disagree over the precise balance to strike between recognition of a subject's embeddedness in thick relationships and the imperative of protecting that subject's autonomy by staking out a position short of determinism. This tension inheres in the most sophisticated accounts of relational autonomy. It is necessary to move beyond advocacy for a 'focus on relationship' and begin attempting to work through concrete trade-offs. Relational theory's contextualism and normative commitment fit well with contemporary family law, but the work is just beginning.

Administrative Law

Turning to another field where relational theory has been applied, chapter 5 examined administrative law from 1950 until 1975. Administrative law at the time was a new field. Lawyers, judges, and scholars were adapting to the development of the welfare state and the implementation of distributive programs by government agencies. Relational theory's elements aided, negatively, in telling the story of earlier administrative law. Relatively little concern fastened on the relation between individuals and the bureaucracy. Judicial and scholarly attention focused instead on the contentious relation between courts and agencies. This institutional rivalry is perhaps understandable given the administrative state's novelty. Judges during this era appear to have been reacting to the rise of the administrative state and their perceived loss of institutional prestige rather than purposively designing productive relations either between courts and the administration or between the administration and individuals. As in family law during the earlier period, the method used by judges and administrative law scholars was largely acontextual. Administrative and legal processes constituted subjects affected by government action as an amalgam of the results of classification exercises. Processes classified as quasi-judicial could be challenged by application for certiorari and were subject to review for a government actor's failure to satisfy the demands of natural justice. By contrast, processes classified as administrative were largely immune from review. Judges and doctrinal writers developed various tests for use in the classification exercise, which for the most part were applied acontextually. In classifying a particular administrative act, judges typically did not examine contextual factors such as the impact of the government action on the affected individual.

Several conceptions of citizenship marked administrative law. One was the view of the subject as member of the national community in opposition to aliens. In the field of immigration, aliens could claim no rights, only privileges. Aliens' naturalization or deportation processes were thus unreviewable. Another conception of citizenship focused on the property owner, who stood in opposition to beneficiaries of mere privileges, such as professional licences. The former was much likelier to enjoy procedural guarantees. The last conception contrasted democratic participants with passive objects of administration, what French writers call *les administrés*. Individuals on the wrong side of these distinctions were largely invisible. During the historical period, administrative law revealed little interest in the interdependent relationships of interest to relational theorists. A strong sense of an adversarial relationship between the administration and individuals obtained. Procedural constraints arose chiefly in cases where the administration threatened the property interests of individuals, a circumstance that reinforced the ideals of negative liberty, bounded individuals, and government non-interference. Moreover, the conception of natural justice applicable in quasi-judicial proceedings showed its pedigree in the protections of a criminal trial. Administrative law was conceived of chiefly as a body of rules rather than a set of embedded institutional practices or values. The effect was to produce thin, abstract legal subjects. In subsequent decades, however, administrative law did not maintain this remoteness from relational theory's elements.

Chapter 6 traced the emergence in administrative law of a contextual methodology during the contemporary period. It identified the rise of a contextual view taken by judges towards various organs of the administrative state. Contextualism rose to replace reliance on two dichotomies. One, which determined the necessity for an agency of satisfying the procedural requirements of natural justice, distinguished quasi-judicial from administrative acts. The other, which determined whether a tribunal's decision was reviewable for error, distinguished questions that were 'jurisdictional' from those that were not. In both cases, judges have adopted contextualism, rejecting those dichotomies in favour of locating individual cases along a spectrum. The contextual approach instated in these two enterprises requires courts to examine not only the pertinent enabling statute, but also empirical features of the agency's practice.

In what may indicate broader tendencies within contextualism, a formal instinct to reinstate clear divisions resurged from time to time. It appears that there may be limits on how much contextualism can reasonably be borne. Furthermore, when assessing claims of bias, courts have tended to regard individual bureaucrats as contextually embedded. The chapter also identified the rise of contextualism in the relation between administrative agencies and individual subjects. Inclusion of the impact of the decision on the individual as a factor in

determining the procedural entitlements, and the increase in procedural requirements generally, collaborated in producing contextualized subjects. Chapter 6 indicated, then, the presence within contemporary administrative law of the contextual methodology associated
with relational theory and some purposive attention to structuring relations. Contextualism is an attractive methodology for use in this
domain, populated as it is with a diverse variety of institutions and practices uneasily subjected to formal rules and marked, instead, by vast
swathes of discretion.

Chapter 7 turned to relational theory's normative element in the
administrative setting. I traced the particularly contextual way in which
international human rights norms have been applied in administrative
law judgments. In connection with *Baker v. Canada* (1999), I identified
an attention in the area of discretionary decision making regarding
immigration to the thick relationships of individuals consistent with
relational theory's normative commitment. Fundamental values and the
conception of the individual as bearer of human rights at times play out
in terms of supporting the individual's family relationships. There are,
of course, other ways in which human rights can be pertinent to administrative processes. But given the prevalence of human rights claims in
the immigration and asylum settings, such rights appear to be invoked
in the interests of family unity and stability. I suggested the possibility
that contextual advancement of this normative commitment might set
itself in conflict with the public interest. The interests of the individual
affected by administrative action are taken into detailed account, but a
contextual approach does not necessarily provide effective means for
considering the more general collective interest.

Then I turned to the broader question of the suitability of relational
theory's normative commitment in administrative law as it would apply,
not to an individual and her family members, but to the relation
between an individual and the organs and bureaucrats of the administrative state. I identified problems in the account of the administrative
state that some relational theorists use as their point of departure,
notably the description of interdependence, and in insufficiently differentiated uses of 'relationship' and 'relational.' The metaphor of
'relationship' calls for caution. Relational theorists' emphasis on the
need for constructive relationships can shift with scant discussion to the
idea that all or at least most relationships should be constructive relationships in the same sense of fostering relational autonomy. I contended that intimacy and interdependence are unsuitable aspirations

for the relationship between the administration and individuals. The power differential between bureaucrats and vulnerable individuals impedes the development of such qualities. Moreover, in the circumstances where bureaucrat–citizen intimacy is likely to arise, such intimacy is unattractive and has the potential of undermining the bureaucrat's duty to advance the public interest. I thus rejected the application of a strong version of a relational approach in administrative law. But I also identified difficulties with the weak version, the relational inquiry that ostensibly has no pre-commitment to thick relationships. Even the weak 'focus on relationship' may inhibit relational theory from aiding in a radical transformation of drastically asymmetrical relations. Furthermore, attending as it seems to do to bilateral relationships between individuals and bureaucrats, the weak focus on relationship has blind spots. It detracts from consideration of the public interest, the role that procedural requirements such as reasons have for subjects other than the parties to a decisional process. And it makes it hard to attend to another crucial element of administrative law. This is the axis of institutional rivalry between courts and the administration. Both a commitment to developing thick relationships between bureaucrats and individuals (the strong version) and a commitment to seeking to pursue optimal relationships (the weak version) show little space to attend to administrative law's structural and institutional questions.

My argument was not that administrative law should adopt a thin, atomistic, acontextual view of subjects. Rather, it was that, even accepting the embeddedness of subjects, it is still appropriate to aspire to attributes for the administrative relationships such as respectful distance rather than intimacy and interdependence. This argument against the adoption of relational theory's normative element, while accepting the methodology of contextualism, reinforces the separability of these elements. Contextualism's utility is not confined to the narrower ambit of the theory's normative commitments.

Contextual Subjects and Relational Theory

It is the administrative law case study that brings out best why I refer to *contextual* legal subjects rather than *relational* legal subjects. Relational theorists have bestowed on the idea of the relational subject an emphasis on 'the possibility of mutuality, reciprocity, and communication as features of social interaction' (Allen 2004, 243) that makes it difficult to theorize other kinds of social interaction through its lens. The contextual subject, by contrast, captures the sense of contingency, particular-ity, and context-specific needs and provides a better starting point for theory (e.g., Reece 2003, 13–14). I do not deny that subjects interacting with the bureaucracy are, in other areas of their life, caught up in thick relationships. But to speak of them as relational subjects for the pur-poses of administrative law analysis unhelpfully tips the scales in advance. Feminist talk of the relational subject tends to assume 'the pos-sibility of nonstrategic, mutual, reciprocal, cooperative, communicative interactions with others and to stress the importance of such relations for developing and maintaining a sense of self' (Allen 2004, 249). This assumption detracts from good theorizing in administrative law. Recall that where signs of relational theory's normative commitment appeared the most in an authoritative text of administrative law, the concern was not the relationship between a subject and the administration, but rather that between a subject and her own family members.

It is appropriate here to return once more to the idea that two con-ceptions of a relational approach are intelligible, one strong, one weak. The strong one is concerned with enhancing the autonomy of individ-uals – often with special attention to women, presumably for remedial reasons – understood relationally. It wants to promote the thick, inter-dependent relationships that facilitate the capacity for autonomy. The strong conception understands the set of interdependent relationships as inscribing a jurisdictional boundary. This is at least an inference to draw from Martha Minow and Mary Shanley's statement that an approach based on relational rights and responsibilities 'should draw attention to the claims that arise out of relationships of human interde-pendence' (1996, 23). The strong conception's mandate is promoting *a particular kind of relationship*. Its writ is accordingly constrained by the requirement for there to be interdependent relationships on site.

The weak conception, as it presents itself, is less a political project than a 'framework.' The weak version's 'focus on relationship provides a useful framework for exploring ... issues and arguments more fully' (Nedelsky 1993a, 355). It helps 'to identify the issues at stake' (ibid., 344). It is a tool to be used preliminarily for serious normative thought and debate. As proof of its neutrality worthy of the Swiss, the relational 'framework seeks to offer a better way of understanding the claims even of the positions to which it is clearly unsympathetic' (ibid., 346). The weak conception seeks to assess situations through its lens of the descriptive premise of subjects as embedded and to identify and analyse the way that existing rights structure existing relationships. It is not concerned with particular kinds of relationships, but with relationships tout court. Its intended audience are people who do not think about relationships at all. The ambition is that this weak exercise helps solve problems.[4]

The weak conception prompts the objection that it underestimates the extent to which other theoretical approaches are already and always relational in the weak sense of fostering *some* conception of appropriate relationships. All selves and all rights, in public and private law, are thoroughly relational. Hegel's account of subjectivity involving the master and the slave is 'inevitably relational' (Frazer and Lacey 1993, 175). In Evan Fox-Decent's apt phrase, a 'relational aspect does not confer any normative laurels' (2005, 272). What differs from one institutional setting to another is the kind of relationship that a right promotes. Within private law, it is perhaps property law that provides the most promising toehold for the view that classical liberal conceptions of rights are not self-consciously relational or fail to attend to relationships. Property rights are often figured as boundaries or barriers, and the idea persists that an owner can enjoy his property rights in isolation (Nedelsky 1990). The civil law, for example, conceives of a real right as an unmediated relationship between the right holder and the thing (Cornu 2003, para. 982). One can imagine a sole individual on an island making use of objects, but surely it is sterile to suppose that in doing so she exercises a right. Rights necessitate a social context and a complex of relationships (cf. Kasirer 2002b). The civilian idea of abuse of right is more self-evidently relational (art. 7 C.C.Q.). Wesley Hohfeld's scheme of four types of rights is relational (2001). Contract and tort, however conceived, are relational in the weak sense. Formal theories of private law predicated on corrective justice have the effect of advancing a particular conception of appropriate relationships (Weinrib 1995).

The weak version – relational theory's call merely to 'focus on relationships' – is not per se novel or productive. Admittedly, some scholars working with relational theory occasionally concede the novelty point. Martha Minow and Mary Shanley observe that contractarian liberals acknowledge human relationships, but treat them all as chosen and susceptible to bargaining in the market (1996, 20). Brenda Cossman acknowledges that the so-called autonomous self is profoundly relational, 'as much a product of its social relationships as the sense of self as connected and dependent' (1990, 357). Where relational theorists disagree with a juridical approach or regime, then, it is not that they are sensitive to relationships and their opponents are oblivious to them. Relational theory's most valuable contributions do not lie in drawing attention to the fact that rights structure relationships and always have (Nedelsky 1993b, 13). They lie elsewhere.

Furthermore, I showed in chapter 1 with reference to work by relational theorists that efforts to apply the weak conception or neutral relational framework seem to morph, unsignalled, into more normative enterprises. Thus Minow and Shanley propose that a focus on relational rights and responsibilities might examine the same-sex marriage question 'by considering the place of such proposed relationships in the lives of those immediately involved and those in the surrounding community' (1996, 23). Their explicit support for 'sexual equality and diversity of family forms' (ibid., 4) intimates that they believe the upshot of their relational focus would be to open marriage to same-sex couples (see also Ball 2005). But what propels the analysis to such an outcome is the *normative* commitment to family diversity, not the relational or contextual focus. Reference to opponents of same-sex marriage, who could follow relational theory by adopting the contextual method and some of its normative commitments, clarifies the point. Such opponents would share with relational theorists the objective of fostering constructive relationships, but they would contend that homosexual relationships are suitably regarded as destructive (Finnis 1994). Moreover, a contextual assessment might well weight significantly the views of those in the surrounding community who feel that recognizing same-sex marriage would debase existing marriages.[5] It is recognition that treatment of same-sex relations ultimately turns on a normative or moral commitment that motivates recent efforts within political theory to articulate the case for such unions' substantive worth (Ball 2003).

This specific example aside, the slippage from the weak conception to the normative considerations of the strong conception happens because the idea of a focus on relationships *is derived from* a normative account of relational autonomy and a belief that relational autonomy is a desideratum. The focus on relationship, cut off from the normative commitments associated with the strong form, pushes out tendrils reaching for those commitments or rapidly withers. Its independent life seems brief. That this is so is a problem only for those who wish to defend space for a weak, content-neutral relational approach. It is troubling only for those who think that a relational approach is a helpful way to broach conflicts in fields where intimate, thick relationships are plainly impossible: relations between bureaucrats and individuals, between industries and regulators, perhaps between one trading bloc and another, between an international organization and a national economy. The weak conception is necessary if one is going to assess structural and institutional interactions as relationships, because it is crazy to personify them and attempt to make their relationship thick and interdependent. But for those content to adopt the strong relational approach, in which the focus on relationships is nourished by its normative commitments, there is no difficulty. It then becomes possible to respond to the jurisdictional dilemma I depicted at the end of the previous chapter by saying that relational theory works well only in some settings.

My own sense is that relational theory is best restricted to the strong form and to settings where thick relationships are appropriate and the question is what inducements and material and legal supports they require to flourish. It is most apt at theorizing relations in which the personal element has significant intrinsic value. The relationships with parents, teachers, friends, and loved ones, to which Nedelsky refers in elucidating the relational character of autonomy (1989, 12; 1990, 169), cannot be eliminated without a loss. They are relationships that the individual wishes to keep. It is in these circumstances that relational theory's discourse of enhancing and supporting constructive relations is most apt. Part of the difficulty with introducing relational theory in administrative law is that in that setting, the individual citizen is likely to be less concerned with enhancing the relation linking her with the administration than with obtaining her desired outcome. Reducing citizens' interactions with bureaucrats to the purely instrumental level goes too far. Some democratic value marks citizens' participating in their political community by engaging in processes with their executive government (Dyzenhaus 2000; Cartier 2002). But it is prudent not to exaggerate this value. It is arguably the proportion of instrumental to non-instrumental elements in the relation that calibrates the plausibility of relational theory, which by virtue of its core commitments focuses on the relationship rather than the substantive ends. Relational theory, one may conjecture, works best where the relation has a robust element of intrinsic worth.[6] Where the relation is a personal one with substantial value for the participants, reference to 'relationship,' with its connotations of personal, emotional affiliation, can be less metaphorical and more literal.

Admittedly, relational theorists may have wide-ranging interests. They may be interested in physics as well as family, in botany as well as pedagogy. They may wish, in some of their scholarly work, to theorize appropriate modes of interaction between impersonal institutions of one kind or another. Or they may attempt to discern the impact of structural, macroeconomic forces on the distribution of labour within the economy of the household. They may undertake, from a position of neutrality, to defuse disputes by seeking to identify the ultimate ends or highest values of the different people involved and to clarify the issues truly in dispute. These are worthy activities. But I think they are not helpfully regarded as part of the relational approach. They are fundamentally different enterprises from most of what goes on under the rubric of a relational approach and relational theory. And it muddies the core projects of a relational approach to combine them with these other activities. It is my hope that the extended surveys of legal developments in family law and administrative law help clarify relational theory's rich resources – and its limits. Its contributions lie in a normative, robust project of identifying and promoting good relationships. Those contributions are much less useful at shedding light, neutrally, on areas where the relational critics assess there to be currently no attention, or at least insufficient attention, to relationships.

Once this strong, substantive version is accepted, relational theory's value is most easily seen. In family law, for example, its exploration of the potential conflicts between enhancing the individual's interest in autonomy and that individual's relationships, between according space to individual agency and recognizing the influences of social forces, provides a starting point for solving problems.

Perhaps torn between the strong and weak versions of their approach, relational theorists are often reticent in expressing their normative commitments. They label as descriptive or methodological concerns that are better acknowledged as fully normative. Failing to bring out their normative commitments can deprive relational theorists of the tools for criticizing relationships they know instinctively to be bad ones. Without candid acknowledgment of the normative part of their program, relational theorists can find themselves conceding that a number of substantive regimes they disapprove of are 'relational' because they promote some kind of relationship. Laws or contracts drastically restricting access to divorce, for example, arguably 'promote relationships.' But I suspect that most relational theorists would evaluate the costs of such measures to women's autonomy as unacceptably high. Compare the views of conservative communitarians, who favour reducing the possibilities for exit from marriage (Spaht 1998; see Reece 2003, ch. 3). As Amy Allen argues: 'Feminists should be careful to distinguish different modes of relationality and the differential impact that they have' (2004, 251).

It is the strong conception that provides the resources for criticizing family law's past. Recall the emphasis on legitimacy in the earlier period, one that had the effect of marginalizing unmarried couples and penalizing illegitimate children. In their writings on the family, relational theorists adopt what they call a relational approach to family relationships. Most relational theorists view family law as concerned chiefly with supporting thick relationships of care and interdependence, irrespective of their formal or informal character. (Recall that the account of relational theory in chapter 1, by its emphasis on individual choice in attachments and on diversity of relational forms, excludes those conservative communitarians who seek primarily to shore up marriage.) Relational theorists detect, in their theory, the resources necessary to criticize the bad old days of the earlier period and to justify subsequent developments. Indeed, proponents of relational theory are likely to advocate that contemporary family law evolve further still in recognizing alternative family forms. What a glance backward to mid-century illuminates is the conjunction, in a regime that is substantively unattractive, of a description of subjects as embedded and a commitment to fostering constructive relationships. The difference between relational theorists and defenders of the early period is not, crucially, a 'focus on relationships.' The architects of the earlier regimes – successive legislatures and generations of judges, the redactors of Quebec's nineteenth-century civil code – focused on desirable relationships. The points of disagreement lie in the appropriate methodology and the substantive definition of desirable relationships. The historical period of family law hints that relational theory's analytical traction does not derive from anything so content-neutral as the weak version of its 'focus on relationships.' What the second and third chapters reveal as distinctive about relational theory's perspective on the family is its contextual methodology, informed by a normative commitment to deep relationships irrespective of their formal status.

Within administrative law, the denial of procedural review to non-citizens presumably sought to intensify the bonds of solidarity among Canadian nationals; membership must, in some views, have its privileges. Here again the task for a relational theorist confronting such a regime is likely to be not an undifferentiated 'focus on relationships,' but rather a hard-headed determination that it is illegitimate or unjust to promote one set of relationships at another's expense. The differences between the legal regimes I have examined show relational theory's contributions to be its methodology of contextualism and, in settings such as family law, its normative commitment to thick, interdependent relationships.

It calls for clarification that the connection between relational theory and these legal fields is not causal. What relational theory provides is a theoretical account within which the legal developments can be examined and better understood. Relational theory's explanatory value will come further into view by distinguishing the different kinds of contributions it may make to law.

Relational Theory, Liberalism, and Contributions to Law

This book's sustained surveys of family law and administrative law suggest that the rich critical and constructive contributions that relational theory – the strong, normative conception – has to make in legal settings will be one of three kinds. The first is methodological. The second is normative. The third is a hybrid – concerning how norms influence context – that has not yet received adequate attention. Relational theory's contributions will, I suggest, have greater influence and clarity if they are framed self-consciously in relation to these three kinds.

Relational theorists make their first, methodological kind of contribution by promoting contextualism where legal analysis excludes consideration of the context. The restriction of child support obligations by virtue of the law of filiation in the Civil Code of Québec contrasts, as acontextual, with the contextual and functional approach called for by the Supreme Court of Canada in evaluating whether a step-parent has stood 'in the place of a parent' (*Chartier* 1998). Relational theorists would likely favour the latter. The virtual invisibility of unmarried couples in the civil law, an object of scholarly criticism, is another instance of acontextualism. Yet another legal site in which relational theorists might have made a methodological contribution was the characterization of a process as administrative on the basis of a formal test. The turn to the imposition of procedural requirements on the basis that the decision, examined contextually, will have a significant impact on the individual is consistent with relational theorists' convictions. It was, likewise, acontextual to regard parole as a mere privilege on the basis of its legal origin in total abstraction from the impact it has on the subject affected and the ways that, in other circumstances, the liberty interest attracts legal protections.

It is at this methodological level that the limited Canadian legal literature on contextualism situates itself. In the leading study, Shalin Sugunasiri thoughtfully traces the development of contextualism as a method of Charter construction and statutory interpretation more broadly (1999). He analyses the methodological disagreement among judges of the Supreme Court of Canada in a family law case, *Willick v. Willick* (1994), noting that the majority and concurring judges avowed themselves to be following a contextual method. The difference between the two camps, he argues, is that the contextualism of one camp was more 'thoroughgoing' than that of the other; the disagreement turned on the 'extent of contextualization' (Sugunasiri 1999, 140, 142). He views this disagreement as one of degree, not kind. Another scholar focuses more narrowly on contextualism in Charter interpretation. Danielle Pinard worries about contextualism's analytical location (at assessment of the substantive right or Section 1) and its relationship with traditional rules of evidence (2002; 1996; 2001). Contextualism remains, in these studies, a method for construing enacted text (Siegel 1998; cf. Aman 2006). It is not, as I have argued it to have become in family law and administrative law, a way more generally of conceiving of legal subjects. Neither Sugunasiri's account nor those of Pinard contemplate the turn to contextualism in developing common law doctrines of administrative law. If contextualism is merely a means of textual interpretation, why should the 'justice of the common law' take a contextual view of administrative agents and subjects, or why should the common law of bias adopt contextualism? Administrative law, like family law, stands as evidence that the contextualism followed in Canadian courts is much more than a way of interpreting enactments. It is a way of viewing, interpellating, and thus producing subjects and the organs of the administrative state. Attention to the constitution of legal subjects deepens the appreciation of contextualism's breadth.

Relational theorists make their second, explicitly normative kind of contribution by criticizing legal rules and practices that do not promote autonomy-enhancing relationships. Having set aside the weak conception of a relational approach, I want now to focus on the imperatives of articulating the normative commitments. Relational theorists are critical of preferences for the sort of interaction understood as typical between self-interested strangers. (As an empirical matter, of course, individuals may show more regard for strangers than narrow conceptions of self-interest dictate.) They oppose to it their preference for a high degree of interdependence and intimacy in the interest of relational autonomy. The disagreement between the majority and minority judges in the domestic private ordering cases in chapter 4 turned, I argued, on fine-grained normative decisions as to how to balance acknowledgment of subjects' embeddedness in thick relationships against their autonomy. It is a normative judgment call, one on which relational theorists have much to say, whether a subject's interests are ultimately best served by enforcement of the state's default regime or recognition of the subject's freedom to contract around that regime.

Legal fields such as family law suggest that relational theorists would do well to articulate their normative positions more fully. It is inadequate in family law to begin with a description of the individual as constituted within relationships and a social context and to attempt to deduce policies from that. Even when a contextual methodology is adopted, one aimed at seeing subjects as embedded, a stage arrives where normative decisions must be taken. This point may disconcert those liberals who wish the state to be neutral as between conceptions of the good life. I refer here to the liberal view that so long as different ways of life respect justice, the state should not assess their merits. On this neutral or antiperfectionist liberal view (Kymlicka 2002, 17–18), the state tells people what is rightfully theirs and what rightfully belongs to others. It insists that people adjust their conceptions of the good life to respect others' rightful claims.

Yet the ongoing performance of family law penetrates to the core of decisions as to what constitutes a good life. A bundle of state benefits awarded on the basis of family membership provides incentives towards one kind of relationship over others. It is intended to do so. The state's furnishment of inducements through a family law regime, income taxation, and government programs instantiates a particular conception of what constitutes a good life for that state's citizens (notably monogamous conjugality). Such state actions depart from liberal neutrality and inaugurate a game of state perfectionism. By perfectionism, I mean the idea that there can be an account of the good human life or the intrinsically desirable life, one characterized by certain properties constitutive of human nature. State perfectionism is the notion that the state has a role to play in promoting its citizens' achievement of such desirable lives (Hurka 1993; Sher 1997; Wall 1998; Galston 1991). Contemporary family law poses difficulties for the neutralist here because deep-seated disagreement exists over the type of family structures that should be recognized. Indeed, it is difficult to explain, let alone justify, the place given to marriage and its performance as a juridical and social institution without reference to a contingent particular vision of the good. This marriage example is worth exploring further.

Daniel Weinstock has sketched a neutralist justification of state marriage. He argues that the state may provide civil marriage, compliant with the strictures of state antiperfectionism, as a means of increasing social capital (Weinstock 2005, 52). In his view, this objective justifies civil marriage's major features, though he acknowledges that the reasons why individuals marry likely differ from this state objective. Yet the social capital objective does not necessarily justify the exclusion of relations involving more than two persons or of non-conjugal relations.[7] More decisive, I think, is the insurmountable gap between the theoretical justification of state marriage as an instrument for augmenting social capital and the reality of the state's discursive and material performance of civil marriage. It may be that the state's current practices are not justifiable by a model of strict state neutrality. But it remains for the legal theorist to make sense of them. The social capital justification, like the view of legally acknowledged same-sex relationships as an instrument for the downloading of social costs, neglects important symbolic elements. No neutralist objective related to social capital could justify the legislative and judicial performance of marriage, which Jean Carbonnier has aptly described as 'a civil sacrament' (2001, 310). In interpreting and applying the legal rules of marriage, judges perform and reproduce a discourse of marriage that far exceeds its instrumental function. Even the legislative texts constituting Quebec's civil union send clear approbative messages, ones irreducible to ambitions for social capital (Kasirer 2002a, 51). From the field of family law in practice, the thin understanding of marriage on which neutralist arguments are predicated is unrecognizable. It is perhaps the proposal for replacing civil marriage with a registry of mutual obligations – occasionally mooted during the same-sex marriage debate – that most vividly flushes out the rich, normative symbolism in which civil marriage is inextricably implicated. Such proposals help people swiftly discover their sense that the state's civil marriage is an approval of the goodness of one kind of life. My own view is that the Canadian recognition of same-sex marriage is likely to be best justified by reference to a robust perfectionist account of the good of recognizing chosen intimate relationships (Ball 2003, 100ff.).[8] In any event, these matters are not, as I have argued above, ones captured by a mere 'focus on relationships,' but are instead thoroughly normative.

As this discussion shows, the relationship between relational theory and liberalism is an ambiguous one. It is unclear at times whether relational theory is meant to criticize liberalism from the inside, or to attack it from an external point.[9] Some scholars see it as part of what they call postliberalism (Reece 2003). Given the diversity within liberalism, it is reasonable to think that relational theory can find a berth within it. Indeed, my objection that relational theory overstates its criticism of liberalism as atomistic suggests that relational theory is valuable for its rich expression of understandings already within liberalism. This reflection on state perfectionism and family law, arising from observation of the considerable currency of relational theory's normative commitment in contemporary family law, suggests that relational theory may find resonances worth pursuing with liberal perfectionism. Work by Kimberly Yuracko solidifies the need for such pursuit (2003). She argues that feminists should make their substantive commitments more explicit, and that those commitments are perfectionist ones (ibid., 87). 'Feminist values,' writes Yuracko, 'should more openly enter the political fray and join the social debate about ... public policy' (ibid., 134). It may well be the case, too, that given relational theory's political project, substantive rather than procedural or content-neutral conceptions of relational autonomy are preferable. This book testifies to the importance of relational theory's normative commitment, for, while I have not attempted an exhaustive assessment of what has caused the legal turn to contextualism, it seems to be something undertaken at least much of the time in the service of prior normative commitments, rather than the inverse.

A further point regarding relational theory's stance towards liberalism calls for mention. Relational theorists often perceive themselves to be speaking, as do many feminists, from the margins. Theirs is a minority view, opposed to a dominant, oppressive status quo. The self-understanding is, as I suggested in chapter 1, one of speaking relational truth to liberal power. So if relational theory can find a berth within liberalism, that militates in favour of revising the self-understanding. It is worth noticing the extent to which the legal establishment – think of the Supreme Court of Canada judgments discussed in previous chapters – operates on the basis of core elements of relational theory and relational accounts. What follows is that the potential for future work is not advocacy for attention to relationships at a big level, but detailed work on how best to hammer out attention to constructive relationships in the rules and interstices of governance.

A more interesting kind of contribution that relational theorists can make to law remains. Relational theorists' third, hybrid kind of contribution concerns the norms that inform contextualism. The norms that define the context in which legal subjects are constituted are controversial. Relational theory has not yet attended adequately to this kind of conflict. Yet my account of family and administrative law shows it to occur frequently and to produce significant consequences for individuals ensnared in litigation and the public interest. Recourse to a contextual approach depends on norms that demarcate the boundaries of what will be regarded as part of the context. Kim Scheppele observes that it is surprising 'how much of social life proceeds with standards for description being implicit, but well-understood, highly complex, but used in practice by a great many social actors' (1987, 1108). José Medina points out, similarly, that 'contexts are structured by tacit norms' (2003, 662). Applying legal categories such as identities or, indeed, virtually any adjudication or decision making requires a process of seeing some features as salient and being blind to others (ibid., 663; see also Medina 2006, ch. 2). Martha Minow and Elizabeth Spelman argue that 'the call for context itself tacitly signals both that the selection of some context is unavoidable, if only by default, and that the selection of one context over another implies a preference for one set of analytic categories rather than another' (1990, 1605; see also 1626). The call 'to look at context typically represents a call to focus on some previously neglected features. It does not, however, mean focusing on all possible features' (ibid., 1629). Relational theory has, to date, focused much more on advocating contextualism than on closely examining the ways that contingent, contestable, and powerful norms always underwrite and structure such contextualism, prescribing how to frame appropriate contexts in different settings. The important question, as Minow and Spelman have identified, is this: 'Which context should matter, what traits or aspects of the particular should be addressed, how wide should the net be cast in collecting the details, and what scale should be used to weigh them?' (ibid., 1629).

Nor have legal scholars plumbed the matter satisfactorily. Danielle Pinard discusses cases in which the Supreme Court's definition of the context is held to include values. Indeed, it is a matter of concern for her that the Court's contextualism in Charter cases embraces (unsystematically, in her estimation) law, facts, and values (Pinard 2002, 337).[10] But she does not carry the argument through to the point of examining norms not just as included in or excluded from a context, but rather as actively constituting or governing one. Nancy Hirschmann calls for the interrogation of various contexts 'to understand how barriers are created, understood, and defined by and within specific contexts, and hence how options and choices are created, understood, and defined' (2003, 95).[11] Emphasizing the constraining role of negative social constructions, she argues that freedom requires the 'creation of new contexts' (ibid., 205). Hirschmann is speaking of actual contexts in the form of social conditions and attitudes, materialized and institutionalized in ways that impede the exercise of freedom. Yet her call for the 'creation of new contexts' is also applicable, one step removed, when one thinks of the judicial construction of contexts that influence adjudication. A number of the important legal disagreements examined in this book concern the normative construction of juridically salient contexts. In many instances, the key debate turns not on whether contextualism is appropriate or not, but rather on whether something is appropriately included within the relevant context or excluded from it. Some exclusions will be good ones (Schauer 1988, 543). Relational theory underscores the roles played by rights, context, and institutional structures in constructing relationships. The point can also be turned on its head: relationships play a role in constructing rights, context, and structures. A context will come into view shaped by the already existing relationships.

As the summary of the substantive chapters showed, it is in the family law of the contemporary period that the elements of relational theory are simultaneously most present. General agreement obtains on the appropriateness of contextualism and the normative commitment to autonomy-enhancing thick relationships. Disagreements within Canadian contemporary family law seem to be internal debates on the terrain of relational theory. It is unhelpful, however, to obscure the role of normative matters in delineating contexts, which can be sites of vivid dispute. In delineating context, is there a preference for conjugal over non-conjugal thick relationships, and if so, why? What if both kinds enlarge the capacity for relational autonomy? The question matters because some answers to it will eliminate certain relationships from sustained examination of the role they play in individuals' lives. Is there a limit on the number of persons who can together form these thick relationships, and if so, what should that limit be and on what justification? Long before one encounters the explosive issue of polygamy, this question arises in connection with the number of 'parents' a child may have. Should the law distinguish between the number of parental figures that may accrue to a child through the formation and dissolution of sequential family units and the number that may intentionally form and register a family ex ante?[12] Does one exclude all non-biological parent figures from the relevant context as legal strangers? (Richman 2002). When assessing an application to vary a custody order, should the total context be assessed afresh, or can the status quo rightfully claim some priority? (*Gordon v. Goertz* 1996). When contextually evaluating the best interests of a child in a custody dispute, do the child's mixed race and the respective races of the parents enter the context? (*Van de Perre v. Edwards* 2001). These issues are best discussed in terms of the norms that structure contextualism: they are controversial points among people self-avowedly applying a contextual approach. They are not matters resolvable by underscoring the need for thinking about relationships or for adopting contextualism. People on different sides are already aware of the critical importance of relationships for enhancing subjects' capacity for autonomy. Their difficulty is working out how best to do so.[13] These matters are decidedly not – to use the language from Shalin Sugunasiri's study of contextualism – merely quantitative ones about contextualism's 'extent.'

To return for a moment to the same-sex marriage debate, framing the question as a discrimination claim under the Charter – a strategic imperative – drastically narrowed the admissible context. In doing so, it impeded debate on the broader substance of marriage in the contemporary era. In *Halpern v. Canada (A.G.)* (2003), the Ontario Court of Appeal maintains its focus strictly on the claimants, not on (heterosexual) others already married: 'The purpose and effects of the impugned law must at all times be viewed from the perspective of the claimant. The question to be asked is ... not whether the law takes into account the needs, capacities and circumstances of opposite-sex couples' (ibid., para. 91). The court's application of the equality jurisprudence was impeccable; my concern is that single-minded application of the equality jurisprudence fails to do justice to the range of concerns that family law implicates. A contextual or relational approach sensitive to the place of same-sex relationships in the lives of members of a community, such as that of Minow and Shanley, noted earlier, would reasonably include the reactions of those whose heterosexual marriages stand to lose the exclusivity of their club. Indeed, assessing the same-sex marriage issue solely as a matter of the constitutional right of gay men and lesbians excludes the public character of family law and of state marriage. If governments had initiated the recognition of same-sex relationships, instead of awaiting judicial orders, they might have undertaken a broader contextual examination of the collective interest. It would have been preferable to have framed the matter outside the terms of a constitutional right claim in a way that could have considered the interests of other members of society. The social significance of marriage that justified the inclusion of same-sex couples is such that the rest of society has an interest in discussing that institution's boundaries.[14]

In administrative law, defining the relevant context implicates similar normative issues. In American administrative law, scholars and judges debate at length whether the context in which agencies' organic statutes are to be understood includes legislative history (Siegel 1998, 1029). Contextual methods in the Canadian setting such as the pragmatic and functional approach for determining the standard of review necessarily emphasize some factors and exclude others. This contextual approach, in its current incarnation, does not easily accommodate certain factors, such as the political character of agency appointments.[15] It is also unclear whether the reviewing judge should rely more on the agency's features specified in the statute or on the characteristics of the agency in practice. For example, it may be that, though the organic statute does not demand it, a majority of a board's members will have legal training. Is such de facto expertise relevant in assessing the deference owed to the agency? I argued in chapter 7, in connection with *Baker*, that one effect of the contextualized subject arising from the particularistic application of human rights norms is that administrative decision makers are required to take into account the interests of any children of affected individuals. To what extent does the context so defined still include the public interest that motivated passage of the immigration legislation? A substantially larger set of questions about context centre on the definition of administrative law itself. Harry Arthurs insists that the definition of administrative law should capture 'the experiences not just of jurists but of the citizens, communities, corporations, civil servants, commentators, and politicians who consume and produce it.' He would regard as relevant to the context of assessing administrative decisions 'politics, economics, culture, social change, and discursive strategies' (Arthurs 2005, 803; see also Macdonald 2005, 453).

Norms and Context

To this point, my account of the relation between norms and context has been too crude, or rather, incomplete. The relation is not, as the previous paragraphs imply, a unilateral one. The verbs that come to mind for what norms do to context – govern, define, structure – connote an exaggerated sense of precision and decisiveness, of instrumental vigour and efficacy. They occlude the way that attention to context sometimes prompts changes in the legal norms and the jurisdictional boundaries. Polygamy is an incendiary example in family law, provoking visceral opposition. It becomes too easily a red herring in debates over same-sex marriage (Corvino 2005). In its own right, however, it remains an open question. It is impossible to rule out a priori the possibility that persons in polygamous (or, presumably, polyandrous) domestic configurations will one day amass the contextual evidence that will lead others to rethink their views. It was, as I argued above, contextual examination that led judges to see the functional similarities between same-sex and opposite-sex couples. In administrative law, it is arguably a contextualism that imposes pressure on the most foundational boundaries of controls on power. The distinction between public and private exercises of power and the idea that state power beyond national borders is immune to the rule of law, to give two examples, are perhaps best contested and undermined by contextual examinations of how power is actually exercised on the distant side of the line that orthodoxy consecrates as public law's frontier. The relation between norms and context is thus one of mutual amendment and reenforcement in ways not fully predictable.[16] It is by attention to this complicated relation between norms and contexts that relational theory will best be able to advance its substantive commitment to promoting relational autonomy.

Relational theory situates itself, for the most part, within political philosophy. One might object that this book unjustly draws direct comparisons between the theory's elements and developments within the legal system. My own view is that relational theorists discuss legal examples frequently enough that they can be regarded as having invited lawyers to take their theory seriously and see what connections can be found between theoretical discussions and the practice of law.

It appears that relational theory can reject too categorically what it regards as a paradigmatically liberal emphasis on contract. I observed in chapter 2 that close attention to judicial treatment of one kind of contract – the promise to marry – shows the judges to have been serving normative commitments akin to relational theory's. The judges' formal, contractual approach turned out, on scrutiny, to function in the service of precisely the sort of relational interests dear to relational theorists. Relational theory thus overlooks potential instances of attention to its normative concerns if it regards its normative commitment as indissolubly glued to contextualism. And it is blind to discrete possibilities within the legal system for protecting relational interests by recourse to contract if it rejects as irredeemably tainted what it regards as the chilly brew of liberalism–formalism–atomism–contractualism. The values that contract serves cannot be presumed to be constant. There can be a paradoxical acontextualism in presuming that contract always advances a vision of bargaining atoms. In chapter 4, I noted instances where relatively strict enforcement of contracts – say of a sperm donor's waiver of his paternal rights – might be appropriate. The relational literature is occasionally vague as to whether by contract within liberal legalism it is referring to the ideal of contract within political theory or the actual practice of contract within legal systems. If the latter, relational theory might benefit from greater engagement with the rich sociolegal research on implicit and informal dimensions of contract (Campbell, Collins, and Wightman 2003). In the adoption cases in the 1950s, formal rules favouring the blood ties may have been used to favour vulnerable unmarried mothers in a setting where a less formal analysis would have had difficulty taking their interests into account once they had granted their consent for their children's adoption. To my suggestion that relational theory's contextualism can be adopted in administrative law without the normative commitments, these examples add the suggestion that sometimes methods other than informal particularism can serve relational theory's ends. Thus, while relational theory's method of contextualism makes a valuable contribution in many settings, it is perhaps too categorical to presume that contextualism is always the suitable method in law's empire. For its part, formalism, as Frederick Schauer argues, may be a useful tool in some parts of the legal system and not others (1988, 547).

As a subset of political philosophy, relational theory can enjoy the luxury of advocating contextualism without regard for the rules of evidence or practice's demands of precedent and predictability. Danielle Pinard's lawyerly concern with contextualism and the rules of evidence is not one that relational theorists tend to address (1996, 176–7). As a methodology, contextualism can be difficult to apply. As has been noted in the constitutional setting, there are institutional difficulties in managing 'the doctrinal consequences of a more complex view of human subjectivity' (Abrams 2001, 72) and, in the criminal setting, adopting a contextual and relational view of autonomy (Nedelsky unpublished b). Unsurprisingly, the limited Canadian literature presents competing views of contextualism's transparency and ease. Sugunasiri characterizes the Supreme Court of Canada's contextualism as 'exceedingly rigorous in terms of analysis and accountability' (1999, 172). Pinard, disagreeing sharply, argues that it is as if entry into the world of context 'liberates judges from all constraints' (2002, 356). It is of course possible to over-state the practical simplicity of the former acontextual approaches I noted for family law and administrative law in chapters 2 and 5. Applying the binary classification exercises of administrative law proved highly complicated, and in family law, conflict of laws prescribed Byzantine rules for determining whether couples were married or divorced in the eyes of Canadian law. A further point for political theorists to consider in the legal context is the normative weight of legislation. Judges are not able simply to ask themselves what kinds of relationships are best promoted and set about achieving their vision. The majority judges in the domestic contracting cases, for example, plainly felt that the legislation signalled the will of the legislatures that the spouses' agreements have weight. And in the administrative law setting, too, legislation imposes important constraints.

I have recounted the demise of several major organizing categories in administrative law and family law. In administrative law, a contextual approach did away with the classification of acts as quasi-judicial or administrative. Moreover, the need to classify processes cannot be fully replaced by a contextual exercise of locating processes on a spectrum of required procedure. At the very least, Section 7 of the Charter, triggered only when the right to life, liberty, and security of the person is threatened, stubbornly requires a classification exercise. I also noted the tendency for formalism to resurge in administrative law from time to time. Even in the process of elaborating an ostensibly contextual approach, formalism reinserts itself.

As for family law, the contextual expansion of categories such as couple and parent has not, obviously, done away with the field's fundamental structure. The fact that more relationships fall within a parent–child regime in the Divorce Act does not alter the basic structure by which parental relationships are privileged. It can be argued that the emergence of contextualism in family law has better included some non-traditional relationships, assimilating them to the traditional ones.

But others remain outside. Where a child has no other father, judges may tend to find that a stepfather has stood 'in the place of a parent.' What is unclear is whether this tendency indicates more the abiding cultural force of patriarchal conceptions or a more general discomfort with unstructured contextualism and a need for signposts as judges navigate the morass of contextualism. After all, contextualism cannot mean that judges take up their task 'from scratch' each time (Nedelsky unpublished b, 20). It is probably a case of both sympathy for patriarchy and acknowledgment of the need for guidance: this preference for there to be a 'father' on the scene evinces some discomfort with the openness of a contextual approach unmoored from traditional views of parenthood. There have also been moves towards formal rules in the form of guidelines for child support and, more recently, spousal support. These parliamentary initiatives show a preference for greater certainty and less reliance on the case-by-case contextual application of norms by judges.

The relationship between contextualism and formalism may be less adversarial than I have hinted so far. Perhaps the two are necessarily linked and what happens is ebb from one to the other. David Dyzenhaus suggests the possibility 'that the common law way requires a constant to-and-fro between attempts to loosen the grip of rules and formal categories by articulating principles and attempts to stabilize and make principles predictable by formalizing them' (2006b, 477). The imperatives of governance and adjudication may impose implicit constraints in how far contextualism can dissolve categories. If this is so, it may be less important to criticize all exclusionary divisions for their effects than to develop more sophisticated means for normatively evaluating exclusions as better or worse than others (cf. Cossman 2007).

The relation of norms and context has special bearing in the human rights setting. In both family law and administrative law, this book has recounted processes through which human rights norms have been rendered concrete through a contextual approach. Recall the equality cases concerning families in chapter 3 and the indirect application of international human rights norms in the review of discretionary decision making in chapter 7. Such a process is not purely parochial and has relevance for other national settings. In the United Kingdom, for example, judges interpreting the Human Rights Act 1998 in administrative law cases will do well to adopt a contextual view of the administrative decision makers and of the subject matter, as Murray Hunt advocates (2003). The promise of that instrument's incorporation of the

European Convention on Human Rights into municipal law will be better realized through a contextual approach to judicial review, rather than one which, formally, regards certain domains as the unreviewable bailiwick of the executive branch.

In family law, the Canadian experience has parallels worth exploring further with European experiences. One feature is the highly contextual, fact-specific way in which the constitutional equality right was concretized in family law cases. Another, not tied to human rights, is a feature flowing from the structure of Canadian federalism that generates a rough analogy with member states of the European Union. I am thinking of the tension or dialectic between a formal and abstract approach to the definition of family at one level of regulation and a more contextual approach at another level. In the Canadian family setting, this is evident when comparing the Civil Code of Québec's strict reliance on juridical filiation for the delineation of all parent-like obligations with the federal Divorce Act's contextual approach to identifying persons who have stood in the place of a parent. The comparison arises when the national law of a European country, say France, defines family in a formal, abstract way, without reference to any context aside from the traditional categories of civil status, and then must interact with European human rights law. Article 8 of the European Convention on Human Rights has been interpreted as the right 'de mener une vie familiale normale' (Millard 1995, para. 184). This reference to 'normality' requires consideration of the social milieu in which it inserts itself – it must be understood contextually (ibid., para. 204; see Diduck 2003, 202–4). Courts have held that the possibilities of normal families exceed the strict set of relations founded on marriage and the model of the legitimate family (*Marckx* 1979; *Keegan* 1994), although the approach 'maintains an emphasis on the traditional married heterosexual couple as the core of the notion of family' (Reid 2004, 359). For the European Court of Human Rights, 'la vie familiale normale est une vie familiale de fait, qui s'incarne dans le lien familial: elle ne s'arrête pas aux formes reconnues par le droit, et englobe au moins les relations entre proches parents, reconnues ou non' (Millard 1995, para. 206). If the criterion of normalcy is thoroughgoingly normative, it is nonetheless one that can only be rendered concrete case by case (ibid., paras. 211, 195) through a contextual approach that takes into account signs of family life beyond juridical ones. This process has been one of the 'difficult imbrication' of French and European jurisprudence (ibid., para. 174). The difficulties are attributable to a number of factors,

including substantive attachment to traditional family law and national-
istic resistance to European norms.[17] But another factor is surely resistance to the methodological shift entailed by the adoption of a contextual approach to family that threatens the *droit commun*'s promulgation
of abstract, unchanging categories.[18] This book's studies speak to the
complications of different legal orders, following different normatively
inflected methodologies, operating in the same institutional space and
on the same territory.

Before closing, it is critical to address an objection pertinent to this
question of defining context and of adopting contextualism as opposed
to an abstract method. Some argue that it is unhelpful and even misleading to speak of a choice between abstraction and context. Minow
and Spelman identify 'a defect in the usual rhetoric of contextualism:
the usual rhetoric mistakenly implies a binary distinction between
abstraction and context, when at best there are constant interactions
between them' (1990, 1625). The choice lies 'between which particulars
within a situation to attend to' (ibid., 1608n41). Furthermore, as an
empirical matter, 'abstract theories are in some sense rooted in particular contexts and operate within contexts with real and particular effects
that often benefit some people more than others ... Moreover, the contextualist uses categories to select which particular details matter. Those
categories can be generalized. The binary distinction between abstraction and contextualism is not only mistaken, but also obscures these
important points of interdependence between them' (ibid., 1628).

A couple of elements in this objection merit response. One is consistent with my account of the interrelation of norms and context. This is
the point that contextualism will use or construct categories to select
which details matter. Another is the notion that abstract theories are
rooted in contexts and operate to serve some interests more than
others. I would not deny that abstract rules of, say, family law distributed
their benefits unequally across all subjects bound by them. But the presence of inducements and self-interest in legal production does not eliminate the conceptual possibility of an abstract approach. Something is
lost if one historicizes instances of abstract methodology so as to equate
them to contextualism. Analytical purchase of past practices is diminished if one treats the legal regimes detailed in chapters 2 and 5 as contextual, distinguishable from the regimes of the later chapters in virtue
only of *which* particulars they attended to. What the legal realist observation that abstract theories 'benefit some people more than others'
elides is the phenomenon experienced by judges and other legal par-

ticipants: their sense of being bound by a method of abstraction. Law and its methods are not only *rapports de force*. Rules and techniques developed under the rubric of abstraction may have reflected the situation and advantages of the privileged classes who devised them. But it remains the case that judges and legislatures experienced themselves to be practising an abstract methodology. Moreover, once abstract legal rules and regimes that pick out certain features are developed, other features drop away. The ones picked out by the rules are coded as juridical and the rest are coded as irrelevant. In the historical period, the features that tended to be coded as relevant were formal features that could be found in the statute book and the register of civil status. Though the political philosopher, the political scientist, or the social historian may emphasize the common elements of shifting force and self-interest, a lawyer will not be indifferent to the textual source of the elements coded as legally relevant or their normative import. Judges in the historical periods discussed in this book sensed themselves to be bound by abstract analytical tools. Indeed, at junctures they expressed regret that they could not hold otherwise, as they in fact wished to do. By contrast, there is a sense in recent decades that it has become permissible and indeed mandatory to identify and discuss contextual factors. The difference is more than a shift of emphasis within contextualism. It has material consequences for legal practice, including the pressure it may impose on traditional rules of evidence (Pinard 2002; 1996; 2001).

Contextualism continues to have significant potential in family law and administrative law. As its sway increases, its institutional effects call for further examination. Its complex relation with norms – those it changes, and the norms that influence it – invites systematic exploration. The normative commitments that it serves in the family setting, notably the promotion of autonomy-enhancing relationships irrespective of their formal status, stand to be articulated more explicitly, rather than buried in thick descriptions of the subject or a contextual method. In administrative law, by contrast, relational theory should be cautious not to anthropomorphize the administrative state in a way that occludes the realities of dependence and asymmetries of power. Relational theory has been so successful, in a sense, that its next stage challenges it to come to terms with that success. It is no longer productive simply to exhort people to focus on relationships or the fact of subjects' social embeddedness. For relational theory, these victories have been won. What calls for relational theorists' energies now is fine-grained study of the dynamic interrelation of norms and context. In numerous settings, despite unanimous adoption of a thick description of the subject and a method of contextualism, normative disagreements subsist. It is in such settings that relational theory's task remains. It is the labourious, disputatious working out of how best, given the limits on law's instrumental capabilities and the attendant costs, to promote relational autonomy. And the lawmaker's, judge's, and legal scholar's task remains thinking through how best to respond to the new contextual subjects.

Notes

1. Introduction

1 Legal culture is a controversial notion in comparative law, though the controversies do not matter greatly for this book's purposes. For recent interventions in the debates, see, for example, Legrand 2006; Glenn 2004; Nelken 2004; Nelken and Feest 2001; Cotterrell 2006; 1997; and Friedman 1997.

2 Acknowledgment within relational theory that the attack on liberal atomism has been overstated is made in Koggel 1996, 128; and Friedman 2003, 16.

3 This rejection of readings of Kant as atomistic includes, ironically, the charge that such readings of Kant by communitarians and relational theorists are acontextual in overlooking that Kant, himself 'embedded in history,' is responding to a particular set of arguments and ethical imperatives (Brender and Krasnoff 2004, 2).

4 It may be helpful to parallel the distinction between the descriptive premise and the normative response to it with a distinction drawn by Charles Taylor in an effort to clarify the issues in the so-called liberal–communitarian debate of the 1980s. He distinguishes ontological claims about human nature from advocacy claims about what policies to espouse. For Taylor, ontological questions concern 'what you recognize as the factors you will invoke to account for social life.' Advocacy issues 'concern the moral stand or policy one adopts' (1997, 181–2).

5 Compare the rich literature on relational contracts, which approaches contract from sociology rather than political theory. The *locus classicus* is Macneil 1980. For an important Canadian study, see Belley 1998.

6 At the same time, concern for the subject's relational autonomy entails attention to the consequences of relationships, including measures to palliate the collapse of an economically interdependent relationship and the material and psychological means for exit from one that is destructive. The thoroughly normative character of relational continuity is clarified by the point that autonomy sometimes requires the severing of destructive relational ties (Friedman 1997, 55–6).

7 I need to acknowledge that Nedelsky herself recognizes that the relational framework is 'itself normative' and that it is not neutral with respect to 'conventional liberal conceptions of autonomy,' which she regards as mistaken (1993a, 345, 346). Nevertheless, her claim is that a relational approach has analytic purchase prior to and distinct from the question of what kind of relationships are appropriate in a given context.

8 It does not matter for present purposes whether relational theorists regard relational autonomy as the ultimate value, or whether they see it as contributing to a still higher value. Nedelsky now sees relational autonomy as a component of what she calls the capacity for creative interaction (unpublished b). Compare Nancy Hirschmann's carefully reasoned focus on freedom, instead of on autonomy (2003, 39).

9 Similarly, it is a normative, not a descriptive, concern that it is necessary to take account of the 'interpersonal dependency, reciprocity and responsibility involved in family relationships' (Shanley 1995, 103).

10 It is not only within feminist political theory that scholars advocate contextualism. A non-exhaustive sampling of disciplines that have examined contextualism (philosophy, sociology, political science, linguistics, science, and education) appears in Sugunasiri 1999, 127–8n1.

2. Thick Subjects in the Past

1 The conservatism is perhaps unsurprising, given civilian jurists' sense that the civil law of the family in Quebec partakes in a historical continuity extending from the Roman republic (Deleury, Rivet, and Neault 1974; Pineau 1965–6, 201–3).

2 I trace the complex historical relationship between civil and religious marriage more fully in Leckey 2006.

3 'Matrimonial regime characterized by the formation of a common mass composed of all or part of the property of the spouses ... It is generally agreed that the mass of property created by the regime is held in indivision by the spouses despite a possible inequality of the powers of adminis-

tration accorded to husband and wife' (*Private Law Dictionary of the Family* 1999, 25–6, *s.v.* 'community (of) property regime').

4   The detail about the jaw appears only in the subsequent hearing *Murdoch v. Murdoch* (1976, para. 11).

5   The provision was s. 17 of the Married Women's Property Act, 1882. This approach permitted courts 'to do justice for the parties' by avoiding the rigid requirement of property law that beneficial title depends on proof of a direct financial contribution (Jacobson 1975, 562).

6   The trial judge's account is puzzling. MacDonald J. found that Mrs Murdoch banked the insurance moneys in her own name and that Mrs Nash considered the money 'to be her daughter's money to use as her daughter saw fit.' But the judge found that this relationship between mother and daughter was a relationship between them, 'not a relationship which involved the defendant.' He accordingly accepted Mr Murdoch's evidence that the moneys he received periodically were a loan from Mrs Nash (*Murdoch* 1971, para. 15).

7   The trial judge rested the grant of custody on the child's satisfaction in his present school. Contemporary readers will find it peculiar that, given evidence of Mr Murdoch's physical assault of Mrs Murdoch, the trial judge's chief concern was to avoid awkwardness: 'I did not question him [the child] in any way that I felt would embarrass him, or suggest the existence of any conflict, or misunderstanding between his father and mother, and he expressed no feeling in that respect to me' (*Murdoch* 1971, para. 10).

8   There is arguably a punitive flavour to the Appellate Division's disposition of Mrs Murdoch's appeal in sole reliance on *Pigott v. Pigott* (1969). In that case, a husband was ordered, in proceedings relating to partition of the matrimonial home, to pay his wife a monthly amount for rental accommodation. In later proceedings, he argued successfully that his maintenance obligation to the wife should be reduced on account of the order relating to the rent money. Then, having reduced his alimony obligation, the husband appealed the first order respecting the payments for accommodation. The Court of Appeal held that, having relied to his benefit on the first order, he could not later appeal from it. A husband reducing his obligations to his wife by reference to an order and then attempting to overturn that order is distinguishable from a woman, such as Mrs Murdoch, who accepts a partial victory in order to subsist but appeals from the partial defeat. It is mysterious how the majority judges expected that women in Mrs Murdoch's situation who abstained from endorsing the maintenance portion of such an order would feed themselves pending

appeal. Support for my suggestion that the *Murdoch* situation is readily distinguishable from *Pigott* is found in the fact that Laskin J., who dissented at the Supreme Court in *Murdoch*, signed on to *Pigott* while at the Ontario Court of Appeal.

9 Contemporary opposition to the legalization of same-sex marriages often characterizes homosexual relations as 'unnatural' in opposition to 'natural' heterosexual marriages. The historical discourse of legitimacy hints that such opponents have reversed the point: it is the relation arising without the law's benediction that is natural.

10 Art. 165 C.C.L.C. obligates husband and wife 'to maintain and bring up their children' ('nourrir, entretenir et élever leurs enfants'), while art. 240 C.C.L.C. confers on the illegitimate child 'the right to demand maintenance' ('le droit de réclamer des aliments').

11 The dictionary defines 'coupling' as both 'joining in couples' and 'sexual intercourse' (Brown 1993, vol. 1, 531). The term thus perches between joining in couples, which in family law implies conduct capable of attracting social recognition, and mere sexual contact. *Coupling* thus captures the unmarried heterosexual relations discussed above and the homosexual contact addressed here. The lexical choice to say 'homosexual' rather than 'same-sex' is deliberate; reference to same-sex relations connotes a non-judgmental stance absent at the time, while 'homosexual' better captures the ethos of the period's legal and medical apparatuses.

12 To this extent, the dichotomy legitimate/illegitimate functions similarly to heterosexuality and homosexuality in some legal regimes. Like heterosexist rules, too, the regime of legitimacy rewarded members of the default class on the 'right' side of the line by assigning advantages to a characteristic for which those members were in no way personally responsible (Halley 1993, 85).

13 The judges exemplify the tendency lamented by John Willis in the administrative law context of construing statutes narrowly on the basis that they, unlike judicial decisions, merely interfere with the law and legal philosophy, rather than participating constructively in its development (1935, 60). For a subtler account of judges and legislatures as sharing sovereignty, which contrasts with the formal view of legislatures as issuing commands and judges as interpreting and applying them, see Allan 2004.

14 See also *Hepton* 1957, 607 (child's welfare primarily 'within the warmth and security of the home provided by his parents'); *Re Baby Duffell* 1950, 744 ('well settled that the mother of an illegitimate child has a right to its custody').

3. Contextual Subjects in the Present

1 This dissent is significant doctrinally for inaugurating the constructive, as opposed to resulting, trust as a remedy available in matrimonial disputes (Rogerson 1985, 538). A resulting trust is implied on the basis of the parties' intentions; a constructive trust is created by operation of law where unjust enrichment or fraud would make it unconscionable for the holder of legal title to profit from the beneficial title.

2 On this point, Martland J. relied on the trial judge's finding. Laskin J. noted that the basis of the trial judge's conclusion appeared to be Mr Murdoch's evidence in chief, in which he said that his wife's activities around the ranch were 'just about what the ordinary rancher's wife does. Most of them can do most anything' (*Murdoch* 1973, 444).

3 The fullest account of the physical conflict appeared in a subsequent judgment, where the judge wrote that 'as a result of a fracas in their home, the wife's jaw was broken, necessitating her hospitalization ... The wife alleges that it was her husband who broke her jaw. The husband alleges that both the wife and her mother, during an argument ... were pulling his hair while he was at the dinner table and in an effort to extricate himself from their clutches, his wife was thrown about and broke her jaw against the refrigerator.' The judge added instructively that there was 'no doubt from the evidence that harmony did not prevail in the Murdoch household' (*Murdoch* 1976, paras. 11, 12).

4 I think it was, similarly, an abstract ideal of Wife that rendered impossible or unthinkable violence by men against women, causing Martland J. to smooth physical violence into 'marital difficulties.'

5 Indeed, late in his reasons Laskin J. distinguished Mrs Murdoch's 'strenuous labours' from 'mere housekeeping chores,' which would not per se support a constructive trust (*Murdoch* 1973, 457). The effect was that women's traditional tasks remained unvalued and invisible.

6 In distinguishing the rhetorical construct from the actual person involved in the litigation, I am following Janet Halley (2006, 295, 348).

7 An action for unjust enrichment arises when three elements are satisfied: (1) the defendant is enriched; (2) the plaintiff suffers a corresponding deprivation; and (3) there is no juristic reason for the enrichment.

8 Excluding misconduct is perhaps easier said than done; it can be difficult to extract the conduct of one spouse, ruled out as irrelevant, from the conditions of the other spouse that the legislation stipulates are relevant. A spouse's conduct may have such an impact on the other spouse that, in

the judge's assessment, it reduces the latter's economic capacities and prospects (*Leskun v. Leskun* 2006).

9 There is a clear contrast with the determination that child support should be regularized by guidelines (Federal Child Support Guidelines, SOR/97-1775), although there is a movement towards the adoption of guidelines for spousal support as well; see Carol Rogerson and Rollie Thompson, 'Spousal Support Advisory Guidelines: A Draft Proposal' (January 2005), online: Department of Justice Canada http://www.justice.gc.ca/en/dept/pub/spousal/project. Cynics might suspect that the child support guidelines, while attempting to minimize litigation, have probably redirected the energy of obstreperous parents from legal argument about the children's reasonable needs to underemploying themselves or otherwise minimizing their declared income (*Moffatt* 2003; *Riel* 2003).

10 McLachlin J., concurring, was reluctant to authorize judicial notice in the service of a contextual approach. She advocated a 'common-sense, non-technical view of causation' (*Moge* 1992, 882). The deeper point of L'Heureux-Dubé J.'s performance was common sense's complicity in the detrimental consequences for women of prevailing social and economic arrangements. This is precisely the point Susan Drummond gets at when arguing that judicial notice of the feminization of poverty 'exposes the arbitrariness of the taken-for-granted, in this case that women's labour in the home is appropriate behaviour – appropriate to womanhood' (2000, 29).

11 Even today, adoption arguably remains discursively inferior, still a mimetic filiation. See, for example, art. 578, para. 1 C.C.Q., which states that adoption 'creates the same rights and obligations as filiation by blood.' For recent scholarship from Quebec on adoption, see Roy 2006; Lavallée 2005.

12 But see Family Law Act 2003, ss. 12 (Surrogacy), 13 (Assisted conception); arts. 538ff. C.C.Q. (Filiation of Children Born of Assisted Procreation). See particularly art. 539.1 C.C.Q., which stipulates that 'if both parents are women, the rights and obligations assigned by law to the father, insofar as they differ from the mother's, are assigned to the mother who did not give birth to the child.' The amendments have generated substantial criticism from Quebec legal scholars (e.g., Ouellette, Joyal, and Hurtubise 2005; Joyal 2003; Philips-Nootens and Lavallée 2003; Pratte 2003; but see Bureau 2003). For the argument that filiation as a legal fiction in the latest reforms has antecedents in Roman law, see Savard 2006.

13 Reconciling this judicial statement with the posited federal regulation of child support, which contemplates differential treatment for a potential

debtor who is a person standing in the place of a parent (Federal Child Support Guidelines, s. 5), is admittedly a challenge.

14 Objection to this variety is the gravamen of Huband J.A.'s dissent in *Monkman v. Beaulieu* (2003), where he argues that the diversity of in loco parentis relationships recognized by the provincial legislation renders inappropriate the importation of *Chartier* from the federal legislation to the provincial statute.

15 'Same-sex' is a more appropriate qualifier than 'gay' or 'homosexual,' since the traditional requirements for marriage bear on sex, not sexual orientation.

16 The slight inconsistency between La Forest J.'s justifications for the two classes of couples included in the pension regime calls to mind the analysis of homophobic discourses that they 'are composed of a potentially infinite number of different but functionally interchangeable assertions, such that whenever any one assertion is falsified or disqualified another one – even one with a content exactly contrary to the original one – can be neatly and effectively substituted for it' (Halperin 1995, 33). In La Forest J.'s case, if marriage is so crucial to society, how can one condone the injury done to it by the unmarried couples' failure to wed?

17 Quebec's willingness to create a new consensual civil status, combined with its reluctance to ascribe obligations to unmarried couples, indicates a conception of the legal subject more fixed on freedom of choice than that prevailing in other provinces.

18 A further dimension in which the privatization literature is unduly reductive is its inattention to the psychic and symbolic benefits attained through public recognition of relationships newly characterized as family. Expansion of the legal 'family' must be more than – to use Cossman's characterization – a 'regulatory instrument for the enforcement of private support obligations for economically dependent family members' (2002a, 169). Such analyses occlude the celebratory dimensions of Quebec's civil union and of same-sex marriage (Kasirer 2002a; MacDougall 2001).

19 For fuller development of the argument that a focus on the Charter dimensions of family law should be corrected by a return to the understanding of family law as private law, see Leckey 2007b.

20 Compare discussion of the gesture of the majority of the U.S. Supreme Court, which, to establish a basis for application of the constitutional right to privacy, transformed an instance of casual gay sex into a 'more enduring' relationship (Rollins 2005, 176). It appears difficult to provide constitutional space for same-sex relationships without regarding them as good

and deeply meaningful. By contrast, outside the American setting one would be less inclined to assume that a right to privacy depends on the value of what one does under its cover.

4. Contracting and Disputes within Relational Theory

1 There were contentions that the decisions inappropriately deviated from precedents in constitutional law and family law. The constitutional claim is that the focus in *Walsh* on personal choice conflicts with *Miron v . Trudel* (1995), in which the majority had required an insurer to treat unmarried cohabitants the same as married couples on the basis that unmarried couples had not made a meaningful choice. A typical family law claim is that the majority reasons are inconsistent with cases from the 1990s in which the Supreme Court had expanded the spousal support obligation. Criticisms of this kind overstate the departures from constitutional and family law precedents.

2 Carol Rogerson's account of *Miglin* departs temporarily from the view of the majority and minority reasons as exemplifying radically opposed positions, suggesting that the majority reasons speak in two voices, one contextual, the other ideologically liberal, and that the judgment 'is open to multiple interpretations' (2003, 321). She also notes the possibility that the division between the dissent and the majority is 'driven as much by different views of Mrs. Miglin's spousal support entitlement ... as by different views of the appropriate weight to be given to spousal agreements' (ibid., 325). But she concludes nonetheless that the ideologically liberal voice dominates, even adopting the familiar lexicon of atomistic liberalism to characterize the majority reasons (ibid., 310, 323). Its contextual voice overwhelmed by its liberal voice, *Miglin* stands in an 'idealized world' in which 'spouses are formal equals making rational choices to protect their own self interest' (ibid., 323).

3 In neither *Miglin* nor *Hartshorne* did the dissenting judges hold explicitly that the claimant's vulnerability during the bargaining process was sufficient to vitiate the contract. LeBel J. in *Miglin* abstained from drawing any conclusions about the negotiating environment on the basis that the trial judge had made no findings of fact on the issue, but he noted that Ms Miglin said she felt pressure (2003, para. 244). In *Hartshorne*, Deschamps J. wrote that indications of Ms Hartshorne's vulnerability during negotiation failed to demonstrate unconscionability, but ought to have alerted the judge to the possibility of unfairness (2004, para. 90).

4 The Petri dish for testing certain critics' commitment to a gendered view of emotion may be the first major case in which two lesbians dispute a domestic agreement. Would the mere ascription of emotion to the applicant carry the same weight? The experience with obscenity – where the imperative of preventing men's exploitation of women has been held (awkwardly) applicable to same-sex materials – indicates that gay men and lesbians cannot assume that they bypass heavy-handed judicial application of MacKinnon-style feminism (Cossman 2002c, 492–3).

5 It may be worth noting the character of Ms Hartshorne's domestic labours. The dissenting judges wrote of Mr Hartshorne's 'benefit from his wife's work in the private sphere' (*Hartshorne* 2004, para. 91). The politically charged 'private sphere,' rather than the milder term 'home,' evokes a substantial literature detailing men's systemic failure to value women's reproductive and domestic labours while profiting from them. See also the argument that upholding the Hartshornes' contract has negative implications for law reforms sought by feminists to compensate women for their unpaid work in the home (Shaffer 2004a, 435). Yet throughout the marriage, the Hartshornes had a nanny and a housekeeper (*Hartshorne v. Hartshorne* 2002, para. 19), making it erroneous to imply that Mr Hartshorne believed it possible to exact from women for nothing the caring work traditionally consigned to them.

6 Janet Halley illuminates the way in which an interpretive stance predicated on these dichotomies renders invisible certain features of a relationship and structures an observer's apprehension of the context (2006, 319–63). Reading against the grain along Halley's lines highlights dimensions of *Hartshorne* obscured by the presumption that contracting subordinates women. Ms Hartshorne's lawyer advised that the proposed contract was so unfair as to be unenforceable. For opponents of enforcement, this fact favoured Ms Hartshorne: the deal's flagrant unfairness aggravated Mr Hartshorne's pressuring her to sign it on threat of cancelling the wedding and humiliating Ms Hartshorne in front of the guests. But recall Mr Hartshorne's stipulation that he would marry Ms Hartshorne only if shielded from potential property division by a marriage agreement. To the extent that Ms Hartshorne trusted her legal advice, she believed she was marrying Mr Hartshorne in violation of his minimum conditions for consent.

7 A methodological caveat is appropriate: in this chapter I do not undertake a systematic study of the post-*Miglin* jurisprudence. It is possible that the early cases decided under *Miglin* found too easily that substantial compli-

ance with the legislative objectives had been attained. For concern that even bad contracts can survive scrutiny under the *Miglin* test, see Tétrault 2005, 869. Frankly, it is too soon to know what the judgments will come to mean over time (Leckey 2007a, 40–1).

8 It does not matter for my purposes that the majority judges arguably understated the importance of emotion and trust in even commercial settings, a point substantiated by recent empirical work in the field of contract (Belley 1998).

9 For cases where the husband took advantage of the wife's vulnerability, see *Freake v. Freake* (2003); *Rogerson v. Rogerson* (2004); *Reinhardt v. Reinhardt* (2004); *Goudie v. Stapleford* (2004); *Fazal v. Fazal* (2004); *Slipak v. Slipak* (2004); *J.D. v. R.S.* (2004); and *B.R. v. B.I.* (2004). Compare the scarcer stripe of case where it is the wife pressuring the husband: *M.E.O. v. S.R.M.* (2003, para. 72); and *R.P. v. E.M.Z.* (2004, para. 157). See also the refusal to let the wife allege subsequently that she was vulnerable when she had legal counsel and, more importantly, was the one who had insisted on having the prenuptial contract: *Culen v. Culen* (2003).

10 For post-*Miglin* cases where agreements have been set aside where the parties lacked a sense of having a choice, and thus did not exercise a capacity of autonomy, see *Gauthier v. Gauthier* (2004); and *Slipak v. Slipak* (2004).

11 For the view of *Hartshorne* as a warning to women lawyers that 'their legal training places them at risk of never receiving a sympathetic ear from a judge,' see Boyd and Young 2004, 567. Treating the majority's approach to Ms Hartshorne's professional qualification as a lack of sympathy fails to canvass adequately the possibility that legal training may constitute a valid reason for upholding a person's contracts. In *Walsh*, that most contextually feminist of judges, L'Heureux-Dubé J., discounted cohabitants' 'choice' to remain unmarried by observing that 'most people are not lawyers' (2002, para. 143). In so doing, was she tacitly conceding that the minority of the population who *are* lawyers may more justly be held to their choices?

12 Note that in Quebec, the granting of an opt-out to unmarried couples would give them a more flexible property regime than applies to married couples, who cannot opt out of the family patrimony. Could married couples in that province raise a Charter challenge on the basis that the law denied them, on the basis of their marital status, the benefit of a flexible matrimonial regime?

13 It is Gonthier J. in his reasons concurring with the majority who made the most valiant stab at defending the line drawn exactly here. Observing that

the division of matrimonial assets and spousal support have different objectives, he wrote that the former is a contractual matter, while the latter, as it applies to unmarried couples, responds to social concerns about dependency as a result of common law relationships (*Walsh* 2002, para. 204). There is a truth in this, at least with respect to Ontario. In that province the support obligation was extended to unmarried couples in reaction to statistics about reliance on public assistance by former common law wives. But see Conway and Girard 2005, 728–9. For readings of *Walsh* from within Quebec, where Gonthier J.'s distinction resonates with civil law doctrine and family law tradition, see D.-Castelli and Goubau 2005, 177; Pineau and Pratte 2006, para. 379.

14 Some of the post-*Walsh* private law cases, in which unmarried cohabitants formulated claims in unjust enrichment for proprietary rights, suggest that judges, at least in this private law setting, have not taken the Supreme Court's holding on the Charter challenge in *Walsh* as prescribing a view of unmarried cohabitants as self-interested atoms able to protect themselves fully by formal contracts. It is in Quebec that recent changes are most significant. The Civil Code of Québec specifies no mutual support obligation applicable as between de facto spouses (Tétrault 2005, 549–51). Throughout the 1990s, Quebec courts were relatively sluggish in accepting claims in unjust enrichment from separated cohabitants. The Quebec Court of Appeal has recently eased the path for cohabitants to make such claims. The court enunciates two presumptions: first, a correlation between impoverishment and enrichment after a de facto union of long duration; second, the absence of justification for the enrichment (*B. (M.) v. L. (L.)* 2003; see Baudouin 2005, para. 585). There is little sense that courts' equitable jurisdiction is being petrified by the reinstallation of abstract bargaining atomistic subjects in family law. For the implications of these cases for theories on the importance of the Charter in family law, see Leckey 2007b.

15 I have suggested elsewhere that scholars seeking to advance debate and policy making might productively situate themselves in relation to four hypotheses: first, the majority judges boldly applied an abstract, conceptual, or ideological approach to domestic contracting. Second, the majority judges applied an abstract approach but, unnerved by the political optics, insisted on labelling what they did as contextual. Third, the majority judges signalled a sincere intention to apply contextualism but botched the job. Fourth, the majority judges actually applied contextualism, although it yielded results unappetizing to the antienforcement camp (Leckey 2007a, 37–8).

5. Thin Subjects in the Past

1 These five areas accounted for 153 of the 210 administrative law cases at Osgoode Hall in 1972. Other subjects were securities regulation, expropriation and compensation, immigration, and miscellaneous municipal government activities. For a detailed presentation of statistics, see Angus 1974, 188.

2 I am not unaware of the perils of attempting even these definitions. Harry Arthurs argues persuasively that the term 'administrative law' 'acquires real meaning only when it is located within specific contexts of time and place, of institutional function and social reality. The mid-nineteenth century is not the late twentieth; England is not Canada or the United States; adjudication is not rule-making or enforcement; business markets are not labour markets, and welfare benefits are not television licences' (1985, 195–6).

3 For the argument that it was the error of the functionalists to overlook their rich philosophical heritage, see Loughlin 2005, 402–3.

4 Gordon points out dourly that problems as to locus standi arise only when certiorari is sought for an illegitimate use, that is, for the quashing of an administrative order; where the order is judicial, there is a *lis*, which necessarily implies parties (1955, 484).

5 One might conjecture, after Judith Butler, that the materiality of the citizen's body is a discursive effect of the administration's practices (1993).

6 A variation is Gordon's view, namely, that judicial processes recognize existing rights while administrative ones create new rights, interests, and liabilities. The issue for Gordon was recognition versus creation, not right versus interest (1933, 113).

7 According to some accounts, an act's nature is a function of its procedural elements, so once judicial procedures befit that process, its nature is no longer quasi-judicial. Beetz suggests that 'it is not inconceivable' that it would be advantageous to subject certain non-judicial functions such as quasi-legislative ones to procedures, such as a duty to give notice, hold public hearings, and hear from interested parties (1965, 255).

8 A distinction between administrative and judicial reasons, on the basis of officials' practical expertise, is sketched in Dyzenhaus 2002a, 469n46.

9 A rare whiff of the idea of reasons as justification emerges from a criticism of the quasi-judicial/administrative distinction. The objection that the reasons for characterizing a particular type of decision are not made apparent and that labels substitute unsatisfactorily for reasons presupposes

that reasons could provide satisfaction of the kind associated with justification (Jobson 1972, 288).

10 Indeed, it is a strategy to cast notions of citizenship as pre-political (Butler 1995a). For a relational theorist's exploration of citizenship, see Nedelsky 2001.

11 Willis refers disdainfully to review of decisions under the Immigration Act, speaking of a court 'with the sweating immigrant before it' (1961, 258). The thinness of Willis's concern with what could be called the 'vulnerability principle' is assessed in Dyzenhaus 2005, 691–4.

12 I cannot unpack this fragment here, but it reveals a tension: the discretion is not unfettered, but governed by policy considerations. The obvious question arises as to what, if any, recourse Gordon would have envisaged when a discretion was exercised in a way inconsistent with any rational conception of policy or expediency.

6. Contextualism Emerges

1 If extended, this line of reasoning can also raise the matter of the exercise of power by non-governmental entities, so-called 'private governments' (Macaulay 1986; also Leckey 2003). State action doctrines operate to prevent this extension of judicial scrutiny.

2 Left functionalist critics such as Harry Arthurs see judicial intervention as a jealous effort on the part of conservative judges to thwart implementation of the administrative state's redistributive agenda (1979). A less parochial view – one, that is, less attuned to the specifically Western, twentieth-century rise of the welfare state – understands procedural review as a 'rejudicialisation' expressive of a political and cultural desire to subject official action to traditional norms of justice, a pattern that has occurred in other contexts (Lindseth 2005). Others may argue, through a Marxist lens, that the trend of proceduralization is a systemic response to a crisis stemming from the conditions of modern capitalism (Tucker 1987). Rule-of-law liberals argue that judicially imposed requirements of procedural fairness operate in the service of a culture of justification (Dyzenhaus and Fox-Decent 2001).

3 *Baker v. Canada (Minister of Citizenship and Immigration)* included an agency's own procedural choices among the factors that affect the content of procedural fairness (1999, para. 27). The other factors are the nature of the decision being made and the process followed in making it; the nature of the statutory scheme; the importance of the decision to those affected; and legitimate expectations (ibid., paras. 23–6).

4 The set of these factors developed since *Nicholson*, and authoritatively collected in *Baker*, bears a tension between form and substance. The nature of the statutory scheme and the terms of the decision maker's enabling statute are formal factors. The importance of the decision to the individual is a substantive factor. The procedural choice made by the agency itself is arguably a hybrid factor. Its characterization depends on whether what justifies its inclusion is the pedigree of the procedural choice (that it was made by the agency) or its presumed basis in administrative technical expertise. The mix of formal and substantive factors parallels the paradox of formal and substantive rationales for deference to agency substantive determinations (privative clause versus expertise) (Dyzenhaus 1997, 290), a paradox that persistently generates tension and contradictory outcomes.

5 I should acknowledge that three years after *Baker*, the Supreme Court appeared to beat a retreat by declaring that patent unreasonableness review of discretionary decisions is identical to review for the old nominate grounds for abuse of discretion (*Suresh v. Canada (Minister of Citizenship and Immigration)* 2002; see Mullan 2004, 41–7).

6 For a classic presentation of the cyclical moves from standards to rules and back again, see Kennedy 1976.

7 That does not mean, of course, that the meaning of expertise is plain or uncontroversial. One commentator urges the Supreme Court of Canada 'à saisir l'occasion offerte par un litige pour établir une grille d'analyse qui permettrait aux tribunaux supérieurs de départager de façon cohérente et systématique le décideur administratif de celui qui ne l'est pas' (Socqué 2006, 375). He writes that the Court 'laisse entendre en certaines occasions que la spécialisation des fonctions constitue le produit de la conjugaison des facteurs de l'expertise du décideur, de l'objet de la loi à l'examen ainsi que de la présence ou de l'absence d'une clause privative et de l'existence d'un droit d'appel. En d'autres occasions, la Cour suprême établit plutôt une adéquation entre les notions de spécialisation des fonctions et d'expertise relative, adéquation qui résulte de la confusion au sein d'un seul et unique ensemble conceptuel de la notion de spécialisation des fonctions et de celle de l'expertise' (ibid., 372–3).

8 The failure to hold contextualism in substantive review beside contextualism in procedural review regrettably narrowed the scope of Harvison Young's study (1997). Perhaps because she quickly labels the approach regarding substantive review as 'functionalist,' she does not address the developments in procedural review, which are repeatedly labelled 'contextual.'

9 At issue in these two cases was essentially the statutory arrangement that conferred decision-making power on a tribunal or person. An objection may arise in the form of the rule that common law requirements of procedural fairness bend before a statute inconsistent with them. This rule, the objection would run, precludes such attacks on statutory arrangements. But in these cases, quasi-constitutional guarantees of tribunal impartiality applied (in *Bell Canada*, s. 2(e) of the Canadian Bill of Rights 1960, and in *Imperial Oil*, s. 23 of Quebec's Charter of Human Rights and Freedoms).

10 Lorne Sossin argues that the judgment raises what he calls the thornier problem of how to distinguish the duties of the minister acting as an administrative decision maker from those of a minister as a member of the political executive (Cabinet) (2005b, 52n178). Elsewhere, Sossin also argues that LeBel J.'s resolution of the matter was insufficiently contextual (though he does not put it quite like this) in failing to recognize a grey zone between acting for personal gain and acting in the public interest. The intermediate grey zone, according to Sossin, includes acting for partisan gain, a type of conduct that may trigger partiality concerns (2004b, 69).

11 At issue in *Suresh* was s. 7 of the Charter, but the Court underscored the connection between the principles of fundamental justice in s. 7 and the common law of administrative law.

12 See recognition of the 'monumental' importance, in financial and emotional costs, of a governmental funding decision for children and their families in *N. (R.) (Litigation Guardian of) v. Ontario (Minister of Community, Family and Children's Services)* (2004, para. 28).

13 An intriguing suggestion that tribunals may in certain respects be technically superior to courts at apprehending the relevant context appears in *Paul v. British Columbia (Forest Appeals Commission)* (2003, para. 36). The suggestion is made that the more relaxed evidentiary rules of administrative tribunals 'may in fact be more conducive than a superior court to the airing of an aboriginal rights claim.'

14 Similarly, hints of a dignity-based view of the duty to provide reasons are discernable in L'Heureux-Dubé J.'s statement that where a decision is critical to a person's future, 'it would be unfair ... not to be told why the result was reached' (*Baker* 1999, para. 43).

15 This thicker but still instrumental view of participation is probably consistent with Lon Fuller's articulation of the need for participation to permit decision makers a 'clear and full understanding' of the subject's situation (1955, 1315), particularly when viewed against the backdrop of Fuller's many writings on reciprocity.

16 One may think here of Charles Taylor's discussion of following a rule, where he writes that 'practice not only fulfills the rule, but also gives it concrete shape in particular situations. Practice is, as it were, a continual interpretation and reinterpretation of what the rule really means' (1997, 178).

17 By contrast, the Australian approach has been to recognize ratified but unincorporated treaties under the doctrine of legitimate expectations (Dyzenhaus, Hunt, and Taggart 2001, 10–12).

18 Some think that the efficacy of judicial review is not susceptible of empirical measurement. Harry Arthurs writes: 'Nor, as it turns out, do judicial review or appeal always operate effectively *in terrorem* to ensure administrative compliance with legislative policy or fair procedures. The doctrine is too incoherent, the outcomes too random, the very object of review too elusive and ill-defined to support any credible assessment of the net results of judicial intervention' (1985, 200 [endnote omitted]).

19 See similarly the discussion of the necessary relationship between structured decision making and contextual or situated decision making in Wells 1990.

7. Administration and Relational Norms

1 Geneviève Cartier submits that the exercise of administrative discretion is appropriately conceptualized as a dialogue between decision makers and affected individuals, and refers directly to Nedelsky's relational theory (unpublished, 292–7). Relational theory is not, however, central to her argument, and the dialogue she envisions does not entail a relation as intimate as those contemplated by other scholars.

2 Nor, for that matter, did women. Many of the achievements of organized labour reinforced a gendered division of labour, consigning women to unpaid work and focusing on securing a living wage for men fortunate enough to work for unionized employers (Fudge and Tucker 2001).

3 It has been argued that the *Singh* ruling may have aggravated the situation of refugee claimants: the application of the Charter to refugee claimants on Canadian soil prompted a government response by which measures were designed to force claimants to obtain entrance visas abroad, beyond the Charter's reach (Arthurs and Arnold 2005, 99–101).

4 But Jutta Brunnée and Stephen Toope worry that the weak verb 'inform' diminishes international law's status in Canadian law rather than augmenting it (2004, 370–5).

5 For another judicial performance of this contextual examination, see Evans J.A.'s concurrence in *Hawthorne v. Canada (Minister of Citizenship and Immigration)* (2002), another case concerning potential deportation to Jamaica. He models the contextual character of the enterprise explicitly, taking as the relevant point of departure the child's present existence in Canada, not her previous life in Jamaica and what could be conjectured about a return to that life. What concerns him is the crucial part that the child's mother played in her life in Canada, and the effect on her best interests of continuing life in a new country without her mother or other relatives (ibid., para. 43).

6 By linking liberal credentials with asylum seekers, Thomas underemphasizes mainstream liberalism's historical commitment to defending a closed community (Dauvergne 1999).

7 The Supreme Court of Canada has recognized the idea of polycentricity, holding that judges should review more deferentially when the administrative decision in issue is polycentric. Bastarache J. wrote: 'While judicial procedure is premised on a bipolar opposition of parties, interests, and factual discovery, some problems require the consideration of numerous interests simultaneously, and the promulgation of solutions which concurrently balance benefits and costs for many different parties' (*Pushpanathan v. Canada* 1998, para. 36).

8 Sossin, too, refers to interdependence, but not as a description of present circumstances. He describes actual citizen–bureaucratic relations as remote, alienating, and objectifying. For him, interdependence is a form in which it would be desirable to 'recast' the administrative relationship (Sossin 2002, 811). It is part of the content of his normative argument, not a putatively factual precondition.

9 Compare the suggestion that part of the trouble results from a 'simple fallacy' within relational feminism in failing adequately to distinguish 'rights' from 'right relations' (Goodin 1996, 511).

10 A similar concern that people unjustifiably predicate governmental discourse on informal conversation among friends, with its attractive features of equality, openness, and mutual respect, is framed in Waldron 1999, 70. See also Hiebert 2002 and a reviewer's concerns with the relational approach developed there (Kahana 2005, 133–41).

11 'Dialogue' is another term current in political and legal theory with less than optimal clarity as to the relative weights of its metaphoric and literal meanings. When scholars refer to the relation of Parliament and the Supreme Court of Canada as a dialogue, it seems at moments that they

actually envisage a conversation analogous to one between two humans. The term 'dialogue' has been used often enough in this setting that it is becoming a dead metaphor. By contrast, characterization of the pattern of interactions between the Supreme Court of Canada and various social groups and institutions as a dance (Van Praagh 2001, 618) is obviously an anthropomorphic metaphor and a challenge to the reader to reflect on it.

12 One may think here of Dyzenhaus's 'ideal of free and equal citizenship,' an ideal of the active citizen 'who is not a mere subject of the law,' but a citizen 'equipped with resources to participate in the making of the law and to hold officials to account' (2000, 172). I suspect Dyzenhaus is speaking of procedural resources, but equipping the citizen with more material resources is surely another crucial prerequisite for free and equal citizenship.

13 It is perhaps worth briefly locating this book's argument on relational theory and administrative law vis-à-vis sociolegal research on relational contracts. Despite the shared adjective, the two literatures are quite distinct, and the relational contract literature does not typically address the concerns of bureaucratic fairness targeted by relational theorists. Relational contract theory concerns itself with long-term commercial relations, as opposed to the transactional contracts associated with neoclassical contract law. It assumes that both sides have an interest in maintaining the relationship, and indeed, that the relationship's continuity is a freestanding good for both. Relational contract theorists are concerned with the way in which power shifts over long relationships, as where one party has invested more deeply than the other in idiosyncratic expenditures (Macneil 1980; Feinman 2000). Nominally free marketplace relationships thus present risks of coercion and dependence (Gordon 1985). By contrast, the administrative relations in which vulnerable individuals interact with the state are not ones in which the bureaucrat has an interest in maintaining the relationship, nor in which the parties begin as nominal equals but change as a result of their relationship-specific investments and other sunk costs over time. Relational contract theories insights are most relevant to public–private partnerships: 'Recognizing privatization as a relational phenomenon shifts the locus of efficiency and accountability from contractual specificity and enforcement to encouraging flexibility and fostering mutual responsibility for program goals' (Davidson 2006, 264). This is, of course, the setting where, I have argued, relational theory is problematic.

14 The link between non-arbitrary action and the articulation of reasons is glimpsed in the French terminology by which a decision for which

reasons is provided is *motivée* and one without reasons is *non motivée*, as if motivation for action and articulation of reasons for doing so are inseparable.

15 It is of course the case that some rights-based liberal accounts of administrative law also fail to attend adequately to the way in which administrative law configures the relation between courts and the administration. But this failing has been repeatedly remarked on by left functionalist critics and others. Moreover, liberal theorists see administrative law as connecting to a political theory of the separation of powers, or rather their necessary interconnectedness (Dyzenhaus 2000; 2006a). Relational theory has not yet done so.

16 Some of the criticisms raised here of relational work on administrative law resonate with theorizing on citizenship and the political order more generally (cf. Nedelsky 2001; Dietz 1989; and Goodin 1996).

8. Conclusion

1 My caveat about this point derives from functionalism's tendency to slide from careful attention to the administrative body to a blunt confidence in the capability of every agency. Think of John Willis's ideological faith that, without evidence in a given case, the administration was necessarily expert and should, accordingly, be left alone to do its job (1935). There has also been a judicial tendency, in applying the pragmatic and functional approach, of concluding that all boards assigned roughly the same task merit the same degree of deference, irrespective of differences in their statutory constitutions.

2 It is perilous to essay in an endnote a comment on the relative merits of privacy versus substantive due process as a road for same-sex relationship recognition in the United States. It bears noting, however, that even the constitutional right to privacy does not apply without a measure of scrutiny of the conduct at issue, or at least that its protections apply to relationships already validated (e.g., as conjugal) by the state. For recent interventions, see Cohen 2002; Citron and Shanley 2005; Rollins 2005; Marcus 2006; Greene 2006.

3 A qualification: Where, as in the earlier period, family law's purpose is a formal one – to promote legitimate relationships – it is arguable that the charge of acontextualism is a category mistake. If the objective is to promote legitimate relationships and penalize illegitimate ones, it is consistent to abstain from contextual examination of the functional similarities of legitimate and illegitimate unions.

4 Compare the argument that 'rights debated in terms of relationship seem to me to overcome most of the problems of individualism without destroying what is valuable in that tradition' (Nedelsky 1993b, 15). Nedelsky makes a still stronger claim as to relational theory's problem-solving utility: 'when we understand rights as relationships ... we can not only *move beyond long standing problems*, but we can create a conceptual and institutional structure that will facilitate inquiry into the new problems that will inevitably emerge' (ibid., 26 [emphasis added]).

5 I acknowledge that a contextual assessment of the kind prescribed by Minow and Shanley can alter some people's normative commitments. Some people who once opposed same-sex marriage have changed their mind on witnessing how same-sex relationships function in context. But if the conviction is firm enough that a species of relationship is pathological or destructive, social approbation of that relation as normal will only intensify the revulsion. Indeed, a major argument against same-sex marriage is precisely that it normalizes such relationships.

6 Relational contract theory, too, presupposes that both parties have an investment in the relationship's continuance (Macneil 1980). For this reason, it does not apply well in the administrative setting.

7 Weinstock's justification for excluding polygamy is the difficulty in assigning and enforcing support obligations with more than two parties. As I have discussed in chapter 3, however, Canadian law currently accepts the possibility of child support obligations and corollary access or custody rights respecting more than two parents. I am unconvinced that the spousal support obligation is radically different. As for enduring non-conjugal relations, such as those between cohabiting siblings, they may be rarer than conjugal unions, but a number of them seem far more stable than a sizable proportion of marriages.

8 Recent perfectionist accounts admittedly fall short of such a theory. Galston concedes that 'families without children may well approximate arrangements that touch the vital interests of their immediate members only, and principles of individual freedom and choice may be most appropriate' (1991, 286). Sher acknowledges that homosexuality frustrates a natural goal in not yielding the sexual organs' reproductive outcome, but he rejects the claim that homosexuality is indecent and consequently disvaluable (1997, 216–17).

9 Compare Nedelsky (the imperative of 'rejecting its [autonomy's] liberal incarnation') (1989, 14) and her later suggestion that the liberal tradition has been 'not so much wrong as seriously and dangerously one-sided in its emphasis' (1993b, 13). For further acknowledgment that relational theory

seeks to alter an emphasis from inside liberalism, see the clarification that 'it is really a matter of bringing to the foreground of our attention what has always been the background reality' (ibid., 14; see also 18). See also the discussion of the location of accounts of rights as relational vis-à-vis liberalism in Brennan 2004, 94–5. Others note that 'liberalism faces a new challenge of doing justice to the profoundly intersubjective nature of autonomy,' but that 'there are, to be sure, resources within liberalism for accommodating this expanded scope [*recognitional* autonomy]' (Anderson and Honneth 2005, 145; cf. Goodin 1996).

10   In a similar way, the suggestion that 'each moment of legal consciousness unites a vision of law with a method of analysis' (Leyland and Woods 1997, 375) does not specify that it is the vision of law that defines the contours of the method of analysis. See the notion that context consists of '*principles* underlying administrative law' (Siegel 1998, 1043).

11   Acknowledgment of the interactive character of context is also made in Dietz 1989, 1, where Dietz recognizes as 'imperative the task of seeking out, *defining, and criticizing* the complex reality that governs the ways we think, the values we hold, and the relationships we share' (emphasis added).

12   Compare in this regard *Chartier* 1998 and the successful application for a declaration under provincial legislation that three persons were a child's parents in *A.A. v. B.B.* (2007).

13   Concluding a study in the course of which it becomes apparent that 'social-context analysis fails to achieve feminist and anti-discrimination goals in these cases,' two authors state that their study serves 'as a warning against assumptions that a contextualized analysis necessarily serves the interests of all women and as a call for further feminist research on the operation and limitations of social-context analysis in judicial settings' (Lawrence and Williams 2006, 332).

14   Individuals genuinely concerned about the formation of individual identity and the attainment of intimacy 'can't afford to be neutral about the terms on which family life is lived' (Regan 1993, 4). A liberal perfectionist argues, I think persuasively, that it is imperative to 'reject the thesis that questions of family structure are purely private matters not appropriate for public discussion and response' (Galston 1991, 285).

15   See similarly the discussion of the potential clash between contextualism's 'preference for sensible and efficient administrative procedures' where Congress 'has deliberately saddled an agency with procedures that impede its ability to carry out its mission' to secure the votes of legislators opposed to the agency's creation in Siegel 1998, 1111.

16 A further complication for the lawyer attempting to understand the relationship between context and norms is raised by James Boyd White. In the constitutional setting, he objects that a view of texts as taking their meaning from their context 'denies the possibility that a people might wish to use a text to change their context, to constitute an idealized version of themselves in their laws that would alter who they were' (1990, 137).

17 For discussion of the attitudes of private law commentators towards fundamental rights in connection with reforms of family law, including their serving as 'a sensitive barometer of nationalist sentiment,' see Leckey 2007d, 187.

18 If France, for example, has resisted recognition of homosexual families and homosexual filiation, it may find itself unable to do so for much longer (Bach-Ignasse 1998; Borrillo and Pitois 1998; Wintemute 2004, 57–60; 2005, 195).

Works Cited

Abel, Albert S. 1972. 'The Dramatis Personae of Administrative Law.' *Osgoode Hall Law Journal* 10: 61.
– 1962. 'Appeals against Administrative Decisions: In Search of a Basic Policy.' *Canadian Public Administration* 5: 65.
– 1961. Book Review of *Judicial Review of Administrative Action* by S.A. de Smith. *University of Toronto Law Journal* 14: 135.
Abrams, Kathryn. 2005. 'Legal Feminism and the Emotions: Three Moments in an Evolving Relationship.' *Harvard Journal of Law and Gender* 28: 325.
– 2001. 'The Legal Subject in Exile.' *Duke Law Journal* 51: 27.
– 1999. 'From Autonomy to Agency: Feminist Perspectives on Self-Direction.' *William and Mary Law Review* 40: 805.
Agamben, Giorgio. 1998. *Homo Sacer: Sovereign Power and Bare Life*, trans. Daniel Heller-Roazen. Stanford: Stanford University Press.
Allan, T.R.S. 2004. 'Legislative Supremacy and Legislative Intention: Interpretation, Meaning, and Authority.' *Cambridge Law Journal* 63: 685.
Allen, Amy. 2004. 'Foucault, Feminism, and the Self: The Politics of Personal Transformation' in Taylor and Vintges 2004a: 235.
– 2000. 'The Anti-Subjective Hypothesis: Michel Foucault and the Death of the Subject.' *Philosophical Forum* 31: 113.
Aman, Alfred C., Jr. 2006. 'The Importance of Being Contextual: Deference South of the Border.' In Huscroft and Taggart 2006: 351.
Anderson, Joel, and Honneth, Axel. 2005. 'Autonomy, Vulnerability, Recognition, and Justice.' In Christman and Anderson 2005: 127.
Angus, W.H. 1974. 'The Individual and the Bureaucracy: Judicial Review – Do We Need It?' *McGill Law Journal* 20: 177.
Appiah, Kwame Anthony. 2005. *The Ethics of Identity*. Princeton: Princeton University Press.

Arendt, Hannah. 2000. 'The Perplexities of the Rights of Man.' In Peter Baehr, ed., *The Portable Hannah Arendt*. New York: Penguin: 31.

Arnup, Katherine, and Boyd, Susan. 1995. 'Familial Disputes? Sperm Donors, Lesbian Mothers, and Legal Parenthood.' In Didi Herman and Carl Stychin, eds., *Legal Inversions: Lesbians, Gay Men, and the Politics of Law*. Philadelphia: Temple University Press: 77.

Aronson, Mark. 1997. 'A Public Lawyer's Responses to Privatisation and Outsourcing.' In Taggart 1997: 40.

Arthurs, Harry W. 2005. 'The Administrative State Goes to Market (and Cries "Wee, Wee, Wee" All the Way Home).' *University of Toronto Law Journal* 55, no. 3: 797.

– 1985. *'Without the Law': Administrative Justice and Legal Pluralism in Nineteenth-Century England*. Toronto: University of Toronto Press.

– 1983. 'Protection against Judicial Review.' *La Revue du Barreau* 43: 277.

– 1980. 'Jonah and the Whale: The Appearance, Disappearance, and Reappearance of Administrative Law.' *University of Toronto Law Journal* 30: 225.

– 1979. 'Rethinking Administrative Law: A Slightly Dicey Business.' *Osgoode Hall Law Journal* 17: 1.

Arthurs, Harry W., and Arnold, Brent. 2005. 'Does the *Charter* Matter?' *Review of Constitutional Studies* 11: 37.

Bachelard, Gaston. 1983. *La formation de l'esprit scientifique. Contribution à une psychanalyse de la connaissance objective*. 12th ed. Paris: Vrin.

Bach-Ignasse, Gérard. 1998. 'Familles et homosexualités.' In Borrillo 1998: 122.

Bailey, Martha J. 2004. 'Marriage *à la carte*: A Comment on *Hartshorne* v. *Hartshorne*.' *Canadian Journal of Family Law* 20: 249.

– 1989–90. '*Pelech, Caron*, and *Richardson*.' *Canadian Journal of Women and the Law* 3: 615.

Baker, G. Blaine. 1981. 'Legal Identity: From Maine and Durkheim to Graveson, Tribe, and Vining: An Essay on "Legal Identity: The Coming of Age of Public Law," by Joseph Vining.' *University of Western Ontario Law Review* 19: 307.

Bala, Nicholas. 2001. 'The Charter of Rights and Family Law in Canada: A New Era.' *Canadian Family Law Quarterly* 18: 373.

– 1994. 'The Evolving Canadian Definition of the Family: Towards a Pluralistic and Functional Approach.' *International Journal of Law, Policy and the Family* 8: 293.

Balkin, J.M. 1993. 'Understanding Legal Understanding: The Legal Subject and the Problems of Legal Coherence.' *Yale Law Journal* 103: 105.

Ball, Carlos A. 2005. 'This Is Not Your Father's Autonomy: Lesbian and Gay

Rights from a Feminist and Relational Perspective.' *Harvard Journal of Law and Gender* 28: 345.

– 2003. *The Morality of Gay Rights: An Exploration in Political Philosophy*. New York: Routledge.

Bamforth, Nicholas, and Leyland, Peter, eds. 2003. *Public Law in a Multi-layered Constitution*. Oxford: Hart Publishing.

Barbe, Raoul P., ed. 1969. *Droit administratif canadien et québécois*. Ottawa: Éditions de l'Université d'Ottawa.

Barclay, Linda. 2000. 'Autonomy and the Social Self.' In Mackenzie and Stoljar 2000a: 52.

Barlow, Anne, and James, Grace. 2004. 'Regulating Marriage and Cohabitation in 21st Century Britain.' *Modern Law Review* 67: 143.

Baudouin, Jean-Louis. 2005. *Les obligations*. 6th ed. by Pierre-Gabriel Jobin with Nathalie Vézina. Cowansville: Yvon Blais.

– 1966. 'Examen critique de la situation juridique de l'enfant naturel.' *McGill Law Journal* 12: 157.

Baudouin, Louis. 1967. 'La famille face à un code moderne.' *La Revue du Barreau* 27: 221.

– 1962. 'Le marchandage juridique de l'adultère de la femme au cours de la liquidation des intérêts pécuniaires des époux en cas de séparation de corps.' *La Revue du Notariat* 64: 229.

– 1954–5. 'Immutabilité ou mutabilité des conventions matrimoniales?' *McGill Law Journal* 1: 259.

– 1951. 'Validity of Marriage between Two Roman Catholics Solemnized by Protestant Minister – Nature of Marriage in Quebec.' *Canadian Bar Review* 29: 437.

Baxter, Ian F.G. 1963. 'The Contract to Marry.' *La Revue du Barreau* 23: 44.

– 1961. 'Recognition of Status in Family Law: A Proposal for Simplification.' *Canadian Bar Review* 39: 301.

Beaman, Lori G. 1999. 'Sexual Orientation and Legal Discourse: Legal Constructions of the "Normal" Family.' *Canadian Journal of Law and Society* 14, no. 2: 173.

Beetz, J. 1965. 'Uniformité de la procédure administrative.' *La Revue du Barreau* 25: 244.

Bell, Colleen. 2006. 'Subject to Exception: Security Certificates, National Security, and Canada's Role in the "War on Terror."' *Canadian Journal of Law and Society* 21, no. 1: 63.

Belley, Jean-Guy. 2001. 'Une justice de la seconde modernité: proposition de principes généraux pour le prochain *Code de procédure civile*.' *McGill Law Journal* 46: 317.

– 1998. *Le contrat entre droit, économie et société: étude sociojuridique des achats d'Alcan au Saguenay-Lac-Saint-Jean.* Cowansville: Yvon Blais.

Bender, Leslie. 1993. 'An Overview of Feminist Torts Scholarship.' *Cornell Law Review* 78: 575.

Benhabib, Seyla. 2004. *The Rights of Others: Aliens, Residents and Citizens.* Cambridge: Cambridge University Press.

Benhabib, Seyla, et al. 1995. *Feminist Contentions: A Philosophical Exchange.* New York: Routledge.

Bergeron, Viateur. 1961. 'La légitimation et l'adoption de l'enfant né hors du mariage (II).' *Les Cahiers de Droit* 4, no. 3: 16.

– 1960. 'La légitimation et l'adoption de l'enfant né hors du mariage (I).' *Les Cahiers de Droit* 4, no. 2: 14.

Bird, Colin. 1999. *The Myth of Liberal Individualism.* Cambridge: Cambridge University Press.

Birkinshaw, Patrick. 2004. Book Review of D. Dyzenhaus, ed., *The Unity of Public Law. Oxford University Commonwealth Law Journal* 4: 235.

Bordeleau, Jean-Marc. 1968. 'Homosexualité et nullité de mariage.' *Studia Canonica* 2: 223.

Bordo, Susan. 2005. 'Adoption.' *Hypatia* 20, no. 1: 230.

Borgeat, Louis. 1994. 'Les enjeux méconnus de l'autre droit administratif.' *Canadian Bar Review* 73: 299.

Borrillo, Daniel, ed. 1998. *Homosexualités et droit.* Paris: Presses Universitaires de France.

Borrillo, Daniel, and Pitois, Thierry. 1998. 'Adoption et homosexualité: analyse critique de l'arrêt du Conseil d'État du 9 octobre 1996.' In Borrillo 1998: 139.

Bosniak, Linda. 2000. 'Citizenship Denationalized.' *Indiana Journal of Global Legal Studies* 7: 447.

Bottomley, Anne, and Wong, Simone. 2006. 'Shared Households: A New Paradigm for Thinking about the Reform of Domestic Property Relations.' In Diduck and O'Donovan 2006: 39.

Boyd, Susan B. 2000. 'The Impact of the Charter of Rights and Freedoms on Canadian Family Law.' *Canadian Journal of Family Law* 17: 293.

– 1996. 'Best Friends or Spouses? Privatization and the Recognition of Lesbian Relationships in *M.* v. *H.*' *Canadian Journal of Women and the Law* 13: 321.

– 1994. '(Re)placing the State: Family, Law and Oppression.' *Canadian Journal of Law and Society* 9: 39.

– 1989. 'Child Custody, Ideologies, and Employment.' *Canadian Journal of Women and the Law* 3: 111.

Boyd, Susan B., and Young, Claire F.L. 2004. 'Feminism, Law, and Public Policy: Family Feuds and Taxing Times.' *Osgoode Hall Law Journal* 42: 545.

Boyer, Barry B. 1972. 'Alternatives to Administrative Trial-Type Hearings for Resolving Complex Scientific, Economic, and Social Issues.' *Michigan Law Review* 71: 111.

Boyle, James. 1991. 'Is Subjectivity Possible? The Postmodern Subject in Legal Theory.' *University of Colorado Law Review* 62: 489.

Brender, Natalie, and Krasnoff, Larry. 2004. 'Introduction.' In Natalie Brender and Larry Krasnoff, eds., *New Essays on the History of Autonomy: A Collection Honoring J.B. Schneewind.* Cambridge: Cambridge University Press: 1.

Brennan, Samantha. 2004. 'The Liberal Rights of Feminist Liberalism.' In Amy R. Baehr, ed., *Varieties of Feminist Liberalism.* Lanham: Rowman and Littlefield: 85.

Brierley, John E.C., and Macdonald, Roderick A., eds. 1993. *Quebec Civil Law: An Introduction to Quebec Private Law.* Toronto: Emond Montgomery.

Brighenti, Andrea. 2007. 'Visibility: A Category for the Social Sciences.' *Current Sociology* 55: 323.

Brison, Susan J. 2000. 'Relational Autonomy and Freedom of Expression.' In Mackenzie and Stoljar 2000a: 280.

– 1997. 'Outliving Oneself: Trauma, Memory, and Personal Identity.' In Meyers 1997b: 12.

Brisson, J.-M., and Kasirer, N. 1996. 'The Married Woman in Ascendance, the Mother Country in Retreat: From Legal Colonialism to Legal Nationalism in Quebec Matrimonial Law Reform, 1866–1991.' *Manitoba Law Journal* 23: 406.

Bromley, P.M. 1957. *Family Law.* London: Butterworths.

Brown, Donald J.M., and Evans, John M. 1998. *Judicial Review of Administrative Action in Canada.* Looseleaf, 2 vols. Toronto: Canvasback.

Brown, Lesley, ed. 1993. *The New Shorter Oxford English Dictionary*, 2 vols. Oxford: Clarendon Press.

Brown, Wendy, and Halley, Janet. 2002. 'Introduction.' In Wendy Brown and Janet Halley, eds. *Left Legalism/Left Critique.* Durham: Duke University Press: 1.

Brun, H. 1974. 'La mort de la "discrétion administrative."' *Canadian Bar Review* 52: 426.

Brunnée, Jutta, and Toope, Stephen J. 2004. 'A Hesitant Embrace: *Baker* and the Application of International Law by Canadian Courts.' In Dyzenhaus 2004a: 357.

Bryan, Penelope Eileen. 1999. 'Women's Freedom to Contract at Divorce: A Mask for Contextual Coercion.' *Buffalo Law Review* 47: 1153.

Bureau, Marie-France. 2003. 'L'union civile et les nouvelles règles de filiation: tout le monde à bord pour redéfinir la parentalité.' In Lafond and Lefebvre 2003: 385.

Butler, Judith. 2004. *Undoing Gender*. New York: Routledge.

– 2000. *Antigone's Claim: Kinship Between Life and Death*. New York: Columbia University Press.

– 1999. *Gender Trouble: Feminism and the Subversion of Identity*. New York: Routledge [1990].

– 1997a. *Excitable Speech: A Politics of the Performative*. New York: Routledge.

– 1997b. *The Psychic Life of Power: Theories of Subjection*. Stanford: Stanford University Press.

– 1995a. 'Contingent Foundations: Feminism and the Question of "Postmodernism"' in Benhabib et al. 1995: 35.

– 1995b. 'For a Careful Reading' in Benhabib et al. 1995: 127.

– 1993. *Bodies That Matter: On the Discursive Limits of 'Sex.'* New York: Routledge.

Cadava, Eduardo, Connor, Peter, and Nancy, Jean-Luc, eds. 1991. *Who Comes after the Subject?* New York: Routledge.

Campbell, Angela. 2007. 'Conceiving Parents through Law.' *International Journal of Law, Policy and the Family* 21: 242.

Campbell, David, and Collins, Hugh. 2003. 'Discovering the Implicit Dimensions of Contracts.' In Campbell, Collins, and Wightman 2003: 25.

Campbell, David, Collins, Hugh and Wightman, John, eds. 2003. *Implicit Dimensions of Contract: Discrete, Relational, and Network Contracts*. Portland: Hart Publishing.

Canadian Bar Association. 1948. 'Administrative Law and the Canadian Bar Association.' *Canadian Bar Review* 26: 1333.

Caparros, Ernest. 1994. 'Le patrimoine familial: une qualification difficile.' *Revue générale de droit* 25: 251.

Carbonnier, Jean. 2001. *Flexible droit: pour une sociologie du droit sans rigueur*. 10th ed. Paris: L.G.D.J.

– 1955. *Droit civil*, t. 1. Paris: Presses Universitaires de France.

Cartier, Geneviève. unpublished. 'Reconceiving Discretion: From Discretion as Power to Discretion as Dialogue.' SJD diss., Faculty of Law, University of Toronto, 2004.

– 2006. 'A "Mullanian" Approach to the Doctrine of Legitimate Expectations: Real Questions and Promising Answers.' In Huscroft and Taggart 2006: 185.

– 2004. 'The *Baker* Effect: A New Interface between the Canadian Charter of Rights and Freedoms and Administrative Law – The Case of Discretion.' In Dyzenhaus 2004a: 61.

- 2003. 'Procedural Fairness in Legislative Functions: The End of Judicial Abstinence?' *University of Toronto Law Journal* 53, no. 3: 217.
- 2002. 'La discrétion administrative: une occasion de dialogue entre citoyens et tribunaux?' In Stephen G. Coughlan and Dawn Russell, eds., *Citizenship and Citizen Participation in the Administration of Justice.* Montreal: Thémis: 233.
Castel, J.G. 1958. 'Canadian Private International Law Rules Relating to Domestic Relations.' *McGill Law Journal* 5: 1.
Cavarero, Adriana. 2000. *Relating Narratives: Storytelling and Selfhood,* trans. Paul A. Kottman. New York: Routledge.
Chaikoff, Patricia Madely. 1964. 'Adoption in Ontario: An Agnostic's Position.' *Osgoode Hall Law Journal* 3: 23.
Chambers, Lori. 2007. *Misconceptions: Unmarried Motherhood and the Ontario Children of Unmarried Parents Act, 1921–1969.* Toronto: University of Toronto Press for the Osgoode Society.
Cherniak, Lawrie, and Fien, Cy. 1974. 'Common Law Marriages in Manitoba.' *Manitoba Law Journal* 6: 85.
Chitty, R.M.W. 1964. 'The Justice of the Common Law.' *Chitty's Law Journal* 12: 127.
Chodorow, Nancy Julia. 1986. 'Toward a Relational Individualism: The Mediation of Self through Psychoanalysis.' In Heller, Sosna, and Wellbery 1986: 197.
Christie, Innis M. 1971. 'The Nature of the Lawyer's Role in the Administrative Process.' In Law Society of Upper Canada 1971: 1.
Christman, John. 1991. 'Autonomy and Personal History.' *Canadian Journal of Philosophy* 21, no. 1: 1.
Christman, John, and Anderson, Joel, eds. 2005. *Autonomy and the Challenges to Liberalism: New Essays.* Cambridge: Cambridge University Press.
Citron, Jo Ann, and Shanley, Mary Lyndon. 2005. 'Sexuality, Marriage, and Relationships: The Radical Potential of *Lawrence.*' In Hirsch 2005: 209.
Code, Lorraine. 2000. 'The Perversion of Autonomy and the Subjection of Women: Discourses of Social Advocacy at Century's End.' In Mackenzie and Stoljar 2000a: 181.
Coderre, J. 1965. 'Adoption, a Critical View of the Law.' *Meredith Lectures* 1965: 36.
Cohen, Jean L. 2002. *Regulating Intimacy: A New Legal Paradigm.* Princeton: Princeton University Press.
Collier, Richard. 2006. 'Feminist Legal Studies and the Subject(s) of Men: Questions of Text, Terrain and Context in the Politics of Family Law and Gender.' In Diduck and O'Donovan 2006: 235.
- 2001. 'Straight Families, Queer Lives? Heterosexual(izing) Family Law.' In Stychin and Herman 2001: 164.

Collins, Hugh. 1996. 'Competing Norms of Contractual Behavior.' In David Campbell and Peter Vincent-Jones, eds., *Contract and Economic Organisation: Socio-Legal Initiatives.* Aldershot: Dartmouth: 67.

Comtois, Suzanne. 2003. *Vers la primauté de l'approche pragmatique et fonctionnelle: Précis du contrôle judiciaire des décisions de fond rendues par les organismes administratifs.* Cowansville: Yvon Blais.

Conway, Heather, and Girard, Philip. 2005. '"No Place Like Home": The Search for a Legal Framework for Cohabitants and the Family Home in Canada and Britain.' *Queen's Law Journal* 30: 715.

Coontz, Stephanie. 2005. *Marriage, a History: From Obedience to Intimacy or How Love Conquered Marriage.* New York: Viking.

Copjec, Joan, ed. 1994. *Supposing the Subject.* New York: Verso.

Corbett, D.C. 1960. 'Administrative Powers under the Immigration Act' in Hodgetts and Corbett 1960: 483.

Cormie, D.M. 1961. 'The Nature and Necessity of Administrative Law.' *Canadian Bar Papers* 1.

Cornu, Gérard. 2003. *Droit civil: Introduction: Les personnes, les biens.* Paris: Montchrestien.

– 1998. *L'art du droit en quête de sagesse.* Paris: Presses Universitaires de France.

Corry, J.A. 1960. 'The Prospects for the Rule of Law.' In Hodgetts and Corbett 1960: 544.

Corvino, John. 2005. 'Homosexuality and the PIB Argument.' *Ethics* 115: 501.

Cossman, Brenda. 2007. *Sexual Citizens: The Legal and Cultural Regulation of Sex and Belonging.* Stanford: Stanford University Press.

– 2002a. 'Family Feuds: Neo-Liberal and Neo-Conservative Visions of the Reprivatization Project.' In Brenda Cossman and Judy Fudge, eds., *Privatization, Law, and the Challenge of Feminism.* Toronto: University of Toronto Press: 169.

– 2002b. 'Lesbians, Gay Men, and the *Canadian Charter of Rights and Freedoms.' Osgoode Hall Law Journal* 40: 223.

– 2002c. 'Sexing Citizenship, Privatizing Sex.' *Citizenship Studies* 6: 483.

– 2000. 'Developments in Family Law: The 1998–99 Term.' *Supreme Court Law Review* (2d) 11: 433.

– 1994. 'Family Inside/Out.' *University of Toronto Law Journal* 44, no. 1: 1.

– 1990. 'A Matter of Difference: Domestic Contracts and Gender Equality.' *Osgoode Hall Law Journal* 28: 303.

Cossman, Brenda, and Ryder, Bruce. 2001. 'What Is Marriage-Like Like? The Irrelevance of Conjugality.' *Canadian Journal of Family Law* 18: 269.

Cotterrell, Roger. 2006. 'Comparative Law and Legal Culture.' In Mathias

Reimann and Reinhard Zimmermann, eds., *The Oxford Handbook of Comparative Law*. Oxford: Oxford University Press: 709.

– 1997. 'The Concept of Legal Culture.' In Nelken 1997: 13.

Craig, Paul P. 2000. 'Ultra Vires and the Foundations of Judicial Review.' In Forsyth 2000a: 47.

– 1997. 'Public Law and Control over Private Power.' In Taggart 1997: 196.

– 1994. 'The Common Law, Reasons, and Administrative Justice.' *Cambridge Law Journal* 53: 282.

Craig, Paul P., and Schønberg, Søren. 2000. 'Substantive Legitimate Expectations after *Coughlan*.' *Public Law* 2000: 684.

Cretney, Stephen. 2003. *Family Law in the Twentieth Century: A History*. Oxford: Oxford University Press.

Criddle, Evan J. 2006. 'Fiduciary Foundations of Administrative Law.' *UCLA Law Review* 54, no. 1: 117.

Cullity, M.C. 1972. 'Property Rights during the Subsistence of Marriage.' In Mendes da Costa 1972, vol. 1: 179.

Damasio, Antonio R. 1994. *Descartes' Error: Emotion, Reason, and the Human Brain*. New York: Putnam.

Dauvergne, Catherine. 1999. 'Amorality and Humanitarianism in Immigration Law.' *Osgoode Hall Law Journal* 37: 597.

Davidson, Arnold I. 2001. *The Emergence of Sexuality: Historical Epistemology and the Formation of Concepts*. Cambridge, MA: Harvard University Press.

Davidson, Nestor M. 2006. 'Relational Contracts in the Privatization of Social Welfare: The Case of Housing.' *Yale Law and Policy Review* 24: 263.

D.-Castelli, Mireille, and Goubau, Dominique. 2005. *Le droit de la famille au Québec*. 5th ed. Saint-Nicolas: Presses de l'Université Laval.

Deakin, Simon, and Michie, Jonathan, eds. 1997. *Contracts, Co-operation, and Competition: Studies in Economics, Management, and Law*. Oxford: Oxford University Press.

Dehler, David. 1962. 'Inter-Faith Adoption.' *Canadian Bar Journal* 5: 367.

Deleury, Édith, Rivet, Michèle, and Neault, Jean-Marc. 1974. 'De la puissance paternelle à l'autorité parentale: une institution en voie de trouver sa vraie finalité.' *Les Cahiers de Droit* 15: 779.

De Smith, S.A. 1968. *Judicial Review of Administrative Action*. 2nd ed. London: Stevens and Sons.

Dewar, John. 1998. 'The Normal Chaos of Family Law.' *Modern Law Review* 61: 467.

Dicey, A.V. 1959. *Introduction to the Study of the Law of the Constitution*. 10th ed. London: Macmillan.

Diduck, Alison. 2003. *Law's Families.* London: LexisNexis.

– 1995. 'The Unmodified Family: The Child Support Act and the Construction of Legal Subjects.' *Journal of Law and Society* 22: 527.

Diduck, Alison, and O'Donovan, Katherine, eds. 2006. *Feminist Perspectives on Family Law.* New York: Routledge.

Diduck, Alison, and Orton, Helena. 1994. 'Equality and Support for Spouses.' *Modern Law Review* 57, no. 5: 681.

Dietz, Mary G. 1989. 'Context Is All: Feminism and Theories of Citizenship.' In Jill K. Conway, Susan C. Bourque, and Joan W. Scott, eds., *Learning about Women: Gender, Politics, and Power.* Ann Arbor: University of Michigan Press: 1.

Dodds, Susan. 2000. 'Choice and Control in Feminist Bioethics.' In Mackenzie and Stoljar 2000a: 213.

Donchin, Anne. 2000. 'Autonomy and Interdependence.' In Mackenzie and Stoljar 2000a: 236.

Donner, Wendy. 1991. *The Liberal Self: John Stuart Mill's Moral and Political Philosophy.* Ithaca: Cornell University Press.

Douglas, Mary. 1986. *How Institutions Think.* Syracuse: Syracuse University Press.

Douglas, Mary, and Ney, Steven. 1998. *Missing Persons: A Critique of the Social Sciences.* Berkeley and Los Angeles: University of California Press.

Drummond, Susan G. 2000. 'Judicial Notice: The Very Texture of Legal Reasoning.' *Canadian Journal of Law and Society* 15, no. 1: 1.

Dubler, Ariela R. 2003. 'In the Shadow of Marriage: Single Women and the Legal Construction of the Family and the State.' *Yale Law Journal* 112: 1641.

Dummett, Ann, and Nicol, Andrew. 1990. *Subjects, Citizens, Aliens and Others: Nationality and Immigration Law.* London: Weidenfeld and Nicolson.

Dussault, René. 1969. 'Les contrôles sur l'administration au Québec.' In Barbe 1969: 511.

Dyzenhaus, David. 2006a. *The Constitution of Law: Legality in a Time of Emergency.* Cambridge: Cambridge University Press.

– 2006b. 'David Mullan's Theory of the Rule of (Common) Law.' In Huscroft and Taggart 2006: 448.

– 2006c. 'Disobeying Parliament? Privative Clauses and the Rule of Law.' In Richard W. Bauman and Tsvi Kahana, eds., *The Least Examined Branch: The Role of Legislatures in the Constitutional State.* Cambridge: Cambridge University Press: 499.

– 2005. 'The Logic of the Rule of Law: Lessons from Willis.' *University of Toronto Law Journal* 55: 691.

– ed. 2004a. *The Unity of Public Law.* Portland: Hart Publishing.

– 2004b. '*Baker*: The Unity of Public Law?' In Dyzenhaus 2004a: 1.

– 2002a. 'Constituting the Rule of Law: Fundamental Values in Administrative Law.' *Queen's Law Journal* 27, no. 2: 445.

– 2002b. 'Formalism's Hollow Victory.' *New Zealand Law Review* 2002: 525.

– 2000. 'Form and Substance in the Rule of Law: A Democratic Justification for Judicial Review?' In Forsyth 2000a: 141 .

– 1997. 'The Politics of Deference: Judicial Review and Democracy.' In Taggart 1997: 279.

– 1996. 'The Legitimacy of Legality.' *University of Toronto Law Journal* 46: 129.

Dyzenhaus, David, and Fox-Decent, Evan. 2001. 'Rethinking the Process/ Substance Distinction: *Baker* v. *Canada*.' *University of Toronto Law Journal* 51, no. 3: 193.

Dyzenhaus, David, Hunt, Murray, and Taggart, Michael. 2001. 'The Principle of Legality in Administrative Law: Internationalisation as Constitutionalisation.' *Oxford University Commonwealth Law Journal* 1, no. 1: 5.

Eisenberg, Melvin Aaron. 1995. 'The Limits of Cognition and the Limits of Contract.' *Stanford Law Review* 47: 211.

Elshtain, Jean Bethke, and Buell, John. 1991. 'Families in Trouble.' *Dissent* 38: 262.

Eribon, Didier. 2004. *Insult and the Making of the Gay Self.* Trans. Michael Lucey. Durham: Duke University Press.

Estey, W.Z. 1971. 'Usefulness of the Administrative Process.' In Law Society of Upper Canada 1971: 307.

Evans, Dylan, and Cruse, Pierre, eds. 2004. *Emotion, Evolution, and Rationality.* Oxford: Oxford University Press.

Evans, J.M., Janisch, H.N., Mullan, David J., and Risk, R.C.B. 2003. *Administrative Law: Cases, Text, and Materials.* 5th ed. by David J. Mullan. Toronto: Emond Montgomery Publications.

Feinman, Jay M. 2000. 'Relational Contract Theory in Context.' *Northwestern University Law Review* 94, no. 3: 737.

Fineman, Martha Albertson. 1995. *The Neutered Mother, the Sexual Family, and Other Twentieth Century Tragedies.* New York: Routledge.

– 1983. 'Implementing Equality: Ideology, Contradiction, and Social Change: A Study of Rhetoric and Results in the Regulation of the Consequences of Divorce.' *Wisconsin Law Review* 1983: 789.

Finnis, John. 1994. 'Law, Morality, and "Sexual Orientation."' *Notre Dame Law Review* 69: 1049.

Flax, Jane. 1993. *Disputed Subjects: Essays on Psychoanalysis, Politics, and Philosophy.* New York: Routledge.

Fletcher, George P. 1993. *Loyalty: An Essay on the Morality of Relationships.* New York: Oxford University Press.

Fontaine, Paul. 1927. 'Conventions matrimoniales.' *La Revue du Notariat* 30: 73.

Forst, Rainer. 1999. 'The Basic Right to Justification: Toward a Constructivist Conception of Human Rights.' *Constellations* 6: 35.

Forsyth, Christopher, ed. 2000a. *Judicial Review and the Constitution*. Portland: Hart Publishing.

– 2000b. 'Of Fig Leaves and Fairy Tales: The Ultra Vires Doctrine, the Sovereignty of Parliament, and Judicial Review.' In Forsyth 2000a: 29.

Foster, Henry H., Jr. 1968. 'Divorce: The Public Concern and the Private Interest.' *Western Ontario Law Review* 7: 18.

Foucault, Michel. 1990a. *The History of Sexuality. Volume 1: An Introduction.* Trans. Robert Hurley. New York: Vintage.

– 1990b. *The History of Sexuality. Volume 2: The Use of Pleasure.* Trans. Robert Hurley. New York: Vintage.

– 1988. *The History of Sexuality. Volume 3: The Care of the Self.* Trans. Robert Hurley. New York: Vintage.

Fox-Decent, Evan. 2005. 'The Fiduciary Nature of State Legal Authority.' *Queen's Law Journal* 31: 259.

Fraser, F. Murray, and Kirk, H. David. 1984. '*Cui Bono?* Some Questions Concerning the "Best Interests of the Child" Principle in Canadian Adoption Laws and Practices.' In Katherine Connell-Thouez and Bartha Maria Knoppers, eds., *Contemporary Trends in Family Law*. Toronto: Carswell: 105.

Fraser, Nancy. 1995. 'False Antitheses.' In Benhabib et al. 1995: 59.

Frazer, Elizabeth, and Lacey, Nicola. 1993. *The Politics of Community: A Feminist Critique of the Liberal–Communitarian Debate.* Toronto: University of Toronto Press.

Freeman, Jody. 2003. 'Extending Public Law Norms through Privatization.' *Harvard Law Review* 116: 1285.

– 2000a. 'Private Parties, Public Functions, and the New Administrative Law.' *Administrative Law Review* 52: 813.

– 2000b. 'The Private Role in Public Governance.' *New York University Law Review* 75: 543.

– 1994. 'Defining Family in *Mossop v. DSS*: The Challenge of Anti-Essentialism and Interactive Discrimination for Human Rights Legislation.' *University of Toronto Law Journal* 44, no. 1: 41.

Friedman, Lawrence M. 1997. 'The Concept of Legal Culture: A Reply.' In Nelken 1997: 33.

Friedman, Marilyn. 2005. 'Autonomy and Male Dominance.' In Christman and Anderson 2005: 150.

– 2003. *Autonomy, Gender, Politics.* New York: Oxford University Press.
– 1997. 'Autonomy and Social Relationships: Rethinking the Feminist Critique.' In Meyers 1997b: 40.
– 1989. 'Feminism and Modern Friendship: Dislocating the Community.' *Ethics* 99: 275.
Fudge, Judy. 1989. 'The Privatization of the Costs of Social Reproduction: Some Recent Charter Cases.' *Canadian Journal of Women and the Law* 3: 246.
Fudge, Judy, and Tucker, Eric. 2001. *Labour before the Law: The Regulation of Workers' Collective Action in Canada, 1900–1948.* Don Mills: Oxford University Press.
Fuller, Lon L. 2001. 'The Forms and Limits of Adjudication.' In Kenneth I. Winston, ed., *The Principles of Social Order: Selected Essays of Lon L. Fuller.* Rev. ed. Portland: Hart Publishing: 101.
– 1976. *Anatomy of the Law.* Westport: Greenwood Press.
– 1969. *The Morality of Law.* Rev. ed. New Haven: Yale University Press.
– 1955. 'Freedom – A Suggested Analysis.' *Harvard Law Review* 68: 1305.
Galanter, Marc. 1974. 'Why the "Haves" Come Out Ahead: Speculations on the Limits of Legal Change.' *Law and Society Review* 9: 95.
Galligan, D.J. 1996. *Due Process and Fair Procedures: A Study of Administrative Procedures.* Oxford: Clarendon Press.
– 1982. 'Judicial Review and the Textbook Writers.' *Oxford Journal of Legal Studies* 2: 257.
Galligan, Denis, and Sandler, Deborah. 2004. 'Implementing Human Rights.' In Simon Halliday and Patrick Schmidt, eds., *Human Rights Brought Home: Socio-Legal Perspectives on Human Rights in the National Context.* Portland: Hart Publishing: 23.
Galston, William A. 1991. *Liberal Purposes: Goods, Virtues, and Diversity in the Liberal State.* Cambridge: Cambridge University Press.
Gavigan, Shelley A.M. 2000. 'Mothers, Other Mothers, and Others: The Legal Challenges and Contradictions of Lesbian Parents.' In Dorothy E. Chunn and Dany Lacombe, eds., *Law as a Gendering Practice.* Don Mills: Oxford University Press: 100.
Geertz, Clifford. 2000. *Available Light: Anthropological Reflections on Philosophical Topics.* Princeton: Princeton University Press.
– 1979. 'From the Native's Point of View: On the Nature of Anthropological Understanding.' In Paul Rabinow and William M. Sullivan, eds., *Interpretive Social Science: A Reader.* Berkeley and Los Angeles: University of California Press: 225.

Gilligan, Carol. 1982. *In a Different Voice: Psychological Theory and Women's Development.* Cambridge, MA: Harvard University Press.

Girard, Philip. 2005. *Bora Laskin: Bringing Law to Life.* Toronto: University of Toronto Press for the Osgoode Society.

– 1987. 'From Subversion to Liberation: Homosexuals and the Immigration Act 1952–1977.' *Canadian Journal of Law and Society* 2: 1.

Glenn, H. Patrick. 2004. 'Legal Cultures and Legal Traditions.' In Mark Van Hoecke, ed., *Epistemology and Methodology of Comparative Law.* Oxford: Hart Publishing: 7.

Goodale, Mark, and Merry, Sally Engle, eds. 2007. *The Practice of Human Rights: Tracking Law between the Global and the Local.* Cambridge: Cambridge University Press.

Goodin, Robert E. 1996. 'Structures of Political Order: The Relational Feminist Alternative.' In Ian Shapiro and Russell Hardin, eds., *Political Order.* Nomos 38. New York: New York University Press: 498.

Gordon, D.M. 1966. 'Jurisdictional Fact: An Answer.' *Law Quarterly Review* 82: 515.

– 1955. 'Certiorari and the Problem of Locus Standi.' *Law Quarterly Review* 71: 483.

– 1954. Case Comment on *Smith and Rhuland Ltd. v. The Queen ex rel. B. Andrews. Canadian Bar Review* 32: 85.

– 1933. '"Administrative" Tribunals and the Courts.' *Law Quarterly Review* 49: 94.

– 1932. Case Comment on *R. v. London County Council. Canadian Bar Review* 10: 198.

Gordon, Robert W. 2005. 'Willis's American Counterparts: The Legal Realists' Defence of Administration.' *University of Toronto Law Journal* 55: 405.

– 1985. 'Macaulay, Macneil, and the Discovery of Solidarity and Power in Contract Law.' *Wisconsin Law Review* 1985: 565.

Goulet, Jean. 1965–6. 'La protection juridique de l'amour.' *Les Cahiers de Droit* 7: 243.

Green, Bernard, and Winter, R.I. 1965. 'The Ontario Legitimacy Act, 1961–62.' *University of Toronto Law Journal* 16: 181.

Greene, Jamal. 2006. 'Beyond *Lawrence:* Metaprivacy and Punishment.' *Yale Law Journal* 115: 1862.

Hacking, Ian. 1986. 'Making Up People.' In Heller, Sosna, and Wellbery 1986: 222.

– 1982. 'Language, Truth, and Reason.' In Martin Hollis and Steven Lukes, eds., *Rationality and Relativism.* Cambridge, MA: MIT Press: 48.

Hahlo, H.R. 1972. 'Nullity of Marriage.' In Mendes da Costa 1972, vol. 2: 651.

Halley, Janet E. 2006. *Split Decisions: How and Why to Take a Break from Feminism.* Princeton: Princeton University Press.

– 1993. 'The Construction of Heterosexuality.' In Michael Warner, ed., *Fear of a Queer Planet: Queer Politics and Social Theory.* Minneapolis: University of Minnesota Press: 82.

Halliday, Simon. 2004. *Judicial Review and Compliance with Administrative Law.* Portland: Hart Publishing.

– 2000. 'The Influence of Judicial Review on Bureaucratic Decision-Making.' *Public Law* 2000: 110.

Halperin, David M. 2002. *How to Do the History of Homosexuality.* Chicago: University of Chicago Press.

– 1995. *Saint Foucault: Towards a Gay Hagiography.* New York: Oxford University Press.

Handler, Joel F. 2004. *Social Citizenship and Workfare in the United States and Western Europe.* Cambridge: Cambridge University Press.

– 1995. *The Poverty of Welfare Reform.* New Haven: Yale University Press.

– 1992. 'Discretion: Power, Quiescence, and Trust.' In Hawkins 1992: 331.

– 1990. *Law and the Search for Community.* Philadelphia: University of Pennsylvania Press.

– 1988. 'Dependent People, the State, and the Modern/Postmodern Search for the Dialogic Community.' *UCLA Law Review* 35: 999.

– 1986. *The Conditions of Discretion: Autonomy, Community, Bureaucracy.* New York: Russell Sage Foundation.

– 1985. 'Continuing Relationships and the Administrative Process: Social Welfare.' *Wisconsin Law Review* 1985: 687.

– 1983. 'Discretion in Social Welfare: The Uneasy Position in the Rule of Law.' *Yale Law Journal* 92: 1270.

Hartog, Hendrik. 2000. *Man and Wife in America: A History.* Cambridge, MA: Harvard University Press.

Harvison Young, Alison. 2001. 'The Changing Family, Rights Discourse and the Supreme Court of Canada.' *Canadian Bar Review* 80: 749.

– 2000. 'This Child Does Have 2 (Or More) Fathers ... : Step-parents and Support Obligations.' *McGill Law Journal* 45, no. 1: 107.

– 1998. 'Reconceiving the Family: Challenging the Paradigm of the Exclusive Family.' *American University Journal of Gender, Social Policy, and the Law* 6: 505.

– 1997. 'Feminism, Pluralism and Administrative Law.' In Taggart 1997: 331.

Hawkins, Keith, ed. 1992. *The Uses of Discretion.* Oxford: Clarendon Press.

Hawkins, R.E. 1998. 'Reputational Review I: Expertise, Bias and Delay.' *Dalhousie Law Journal* 21, no. 1: 5.

Haywood, Chris, and Mac an Ghaill, Máirtín. 2003. *Men and Masculinities: Theory, Research and Social Practice.* Philadelphia: Open University Press.

Heller, Thomas C., Sosna, Morton, and Wellbery, David E., eds. 1986. *Reconstructing Individualism: Autonomy, Individuality, and the Self in Western Thought.* Stanford: Stanford University Press.

Herman, Didi. 1990. 'Are We Family? Lesbian Rights and Women's Liberation.' *Osgoode Hall Law Journal* 28: 789.

Herring, Jonathan. 2005. 'Why Financial Orders on Divorce Should Be Unfair.' *International Journal of Law, Policy, and the Family* 19: 218.

Hewart of Bury, Lord. 1929. *The New Despotism.* London: Ernest Benn.

Hiebert, Janet L. 2002. *Charter Conflicts: What Is Parliament's Role?* Montreal: McGill-Queen's University Press.

Hirsch, H.N., ed. 2005. *The Future of Gay Rights in America.* New York: Routledge.

Hirschmann, Nancy J. 2003. *The Subject of Liberty: Toward a Feminist Theory of Freedom.* Princeton: Princeton University Press.

Hodgetts, J.E., and Corbett, D.C., eds. 1960. *Canadian Public Administration.* Toronto: Macmillan of Canada.

Hogg, P.W. 1974. 'Judicial Review: How Much Do We Need?' *McGill Law Journal* 20: 157.

– 1973. 'The Supreme Court of Canada and Administrative Law, 1949–1971.' *Osgoode Hall Law Journal* 11: 187.

Hohfeld, Wesley Newcomb. 2001. *Fundamental Legal Conceptions as Applied in Judicial Reasoning,* ed. David Campbell and Philip Thomas. Aldershot: Ashgate.

Horwitz, Morton J. 1992. *The Transformation of American Law, 1780–1860.* New York: Oxford University Press.

Howe, Adrian. 2001. 'Homosexual Advances in Law: Murderous Excuse, Pluralized Ignorance, and the Privilege of Unknowing.' In Stychin and Herman 2001: 84.

Hucker, John. 1975. 'Immigration, Natural Justice, and the Bill of Rights.' *Osgoode Hall Law Journal* 13: 649.

Hunt, Murray. 2003. 'Sovereignty's Blight: Why Contemporary Public Law Needs the Concept of "Due Deference."' In Bamforth and Leyland 2003: 337.

Hurka, Thomas. 1993. *Perfectionism.* New York: Oxford University Press.

Hurley, Mary C. 1996. 'Principles, Practices, Fragile Promises: Judicial Review of Refugee Determination Decisions before the Federal Court of Canada.' *McGill Law Journal* 41: 317.

Huscroft, Grant, and Taggart, Michael, eds. 2006. *Inside and Outside Canadian*

Administrative Law: Essays in Honour of David Mullan. Toronto: University of Toronto Press.

Jackson, Emily. 2006. 'What Is a Parent?' In Diduck and O'Donovan 2006: 59.

Jacobs, Laverne, and Kuttner, Thomas S. 2002. 'Discovering What Tribunals Do: Tribunal Standing before the Courts.' *Canadian Bar Review* 81: 616.

Jacobs, Melanie B. 2004. 'When Daddy Doesn't Want to Be Daddy Anymore: An Argument against Paternity Fraud Claims.' *Yale Journal of Law and Feminism* 16: 193.

Jacobson, Peter M. 1975. 'Recent Proposals for Reform of Family Property Law.' *McGill Law Journal* 21: 556.

– 1974. '*Murdoch v. Murdoch*: Just about What the Ordinary Rancher's Wife Does.' *McGill Law Journal* 20: 308.

Jobson, Keith. 1972. 'Fair Procedure in Parole.' *University of Toronto Law Journal* 22: 267.

Jones, Caroline. 2006. 'Parents in Law: Subjective Impacts and Status Implications around the Use of Licensed Donor Insemination.' In Diduck and O'Donovan 2006: 75.

Joyal, Renée. 2003. 'La filiation homoparentale, rupture symbolique et saut dans l'inconnu. Quelques réflexions à la lumière de l'évolution récente.' In Lafond and Lefebvre 2003: 307.

Kahana, Tsvi. 2005. 'Constitutional Cosiness and Legislative Activism.' *University of Toronto Law Journal* 55: 129.

Kasirer, Nicholas, ed. 2003. *Le droit civil, avant tout un style?* Montreal: Thémis.

– 2002a. 'Convoler en justes noces.' In Lafond and Lefebvre 2003: 29.

– 2002b. 'Le droit robinsonien.' In Kasirer 2002c: 1.

– ed. 2002c. *La solitude en droit privé.* Montreal: Thémis.

– 1995. 'Testing the Origins of the Family Patrimony in Everyday Law.' *Les Cahiers de Droit* 36: 795.

– 1994. '*Couvrez cette communauté que je ne saurais voir.* Equity and Fault in the Division of Quebec's Family Patrimony.' *Revue générale de droit* 25: 569.

Kennedy, Duncan. 1976. 'Form and Substance in Private Law Adjudication.' *Harvard Law Review* 89: 1685.

Kittay, Eva Feder. 1999. *Love's Labor: Essays on Women, Equality and Dependency.* New York: Routledge.

Klein, Suzanne Silk. 1985. 'Individualism, Liberalism, and the New Family Law.' *University of Toronto Faculty of Law Review* 43, no. 1: 116.

Kline, Marlee. 1993. 'Complicating the Ideology of Motherhood: Child Welfare Law and First Nation Women.' *Queen's Law Journal* 18: 306.

– 1992. 'Child Welfare Law, "Best Interests of the Child" Ideology, and First Nations.' *Osgoode Hall Law Journal* 30: 375.

Knetsch, Jack L. 1984. 'Some Economic Implications of Matrimonial Property Rules.' *University of Toronto Law Journal* 34: 263.

Koggel, Christine M. 1998. *Perspectives on Equality: Constructing a Relational Theory.* Lanham: Rowman and Littlefield.

Kronby, Malcolm. 1959. 'Administration of the Immigration Act.' *Osgoode Hall Law Journal* 1, no. 2: 1.

Kymlicka, Will. 2002. *Contemporary Political Philosophy: An Introduction.* 2nd ed. Oxford: Oxford University Press.

– 1989. 'Liberal Individualism and Liberal Neutrality.' *Ethics* 99: 883.

Lacey, Nicola. 1992. 'The Jurisprudence of Discretion: Escaping the Legal Paradigm.' In Hawkins 1992: 361.

Lafond, Pierre-Claude and Lefebvre, Brigitte, eds. 2003. *L'union civile: Nouveaux modèles de conjugalité et de parentalité au 21ᵉ siècle.* Cowansville: Yvon Blais.

Lahey, William, and Ginn, Diana. 2002. 'After the Revolution: Being Pragmatic and Functional in Canada's Trial Courts and Courts of Appeal.' *Dalhousie Law Journal* 25: 259.

Lakoff, George, and Johnson, Mark. 2003. *Metaphors We Live By.* Chicago: University of Chicago Press.

Lane, Joel. 1994. 'Michel Foucault.' In Peter Daniels and Steve Anthony, eds., *Jugular Defences: An AIDS Anthology.* East Haven: Oscars Press.

Laskin, Bora. 1952. '*Certiorari* to Labour Boards: The Apparent Futility of Privative Clauses.' *Canadian Bar Review* 30: 986.

Lavallée, Carmen. 2005. *L'enfant, ses familles et les institutions d'adoption: regards sur le droit français et le droit québécois.* Montreal: Wilson and Lafleur.

Law Commission of Canada. 2001. *Beyond Conjugality: Recognizing and Supporting Close Personal Adult Relationships.* Ottawa: Minister of Public Works and Government Services.

Law Society of Upper Canada. 1971. *Administrative Practice and Procedure.* Toronto: Richard De Boo.

Lawrence, Sonia N., and Williams, Toni. 2006. 'Swallowed Up: Drug Couriers at the Borders of Canadian Sentencing.' *University of Toronto Law Journal* 56, no. 4: 285.

Leckey, Robert. 2007a. 'Contracting Claims and Family Law Feuds.' *University of Toronto Law Journal* 57, no. 1: 1.

– 2007b. 'Family Law as Fundamental Private Law.' *Canadian Bar Review* 86, no. 1: 69.

– 2007c. 'Prescribed by Law/Une règle de droit.' *Osgoode Hall Law Journal* 45, no. 3: 571.

– 2007d. 'Private Law as Constitutional Context for Same-Sex Marriage.' *Journal of Comparative Law* 2, no. 1: 172.

– 2006. 'Profane Matrimony.' *Canadian Journal of Law and Society* 21, no. 2: 1.
– 2004. 'Territoriality in Canadian Administrative Law.' *University of Toronto Law Journal* 54, no. 3: 327.
– 2003. 'Employing Fairness.' *Canadian Journal of Law and Society* 18, no. 2: 45.
– 2002a. 'Chosen Discrimination.' *Supreme Court Law Review* (2d) 18: 445.
– 2002b. 'Harmonizing Family Law's Identities.' *Queen's Law Journal* 28, no. 1: 221.
– 2002c. 'Relational Contract and Other Models of Marriage.' *Osgoode Hall Law Journal* 40, no. 1: 1.
Legrand, Pierre. 2006. 'Comparative Legal Studies and the Matter of Authenticity.' *Journal of Comparative Law* 1, no. 2: 365.
Lemieux, Denis. 2006. 'The Codification of Administrative Law in Quebec.' In Huscroft and Taggart 2006: 240.
Lessard, Hester. 2006. 'Charter Gridlock: Equality Formalism and Marriage Fundamentalism.' *Supreme Court Law Review* (2d) 33: 291.
Leyland, Peter, and Woods, Terry. 1997. 'Public Law History and Theory: Some Notes Towards a New Foundationalism: Part 1.' In Peter Leyland and Terry Woods, eds., *Administrative Law Facing the Future: Old Constraints and New Horizons*. London: Blackstone Press: 374.
L'Heureux-Dubé, Claire. 2001. 'What a Difference a Decade Makes: The Canadian Constitution and the Family Since 1991.' *Queen's Law Journal* 27, no. 1: 361.
Lindseth, Peter. 2005. '"Always Embedded" Administration: The Historical Evolution of Administrative Justice as an Aspect of Modern Governance.' In Christian Joerges, Bo Stråth, and Peter Wagner, eds., *The Economy as a Polity: The Political Construction of Modern Capitalism*. London: UCL Press: 117.
Liston, Mary. 2004. '"Alert, Alive and Sensitive": *Baker*, the Duty to Give Reasons, and the Ethos of Justification in Canadian Public Law.' In Dyzenhaus 2004a: 113.
Lloyd, Genevieve. 2000. 'Individuals, Responsibility, and the Philosophical Imagination.' In Mackenzie and Stoljar 2000a: 112.
Loughlin, Martin. 2005. 'The Functionalist Style in Public Law.' *University of Toronto Law Journal* 55, no. 3: 361.
– 1992. *Public Law and Political Theory*. New York: Oxford University Press.
– 1978. 'Procedural Fairness: A Study of the Crisis in Administrative Law Theory.' *University of Toronto Law Journal* 28: 215.
Luhmann, Niklas. 2001. *La légitimation par la procédure*, trans. Lukas K. Sosoe and Stéphane Bouchard. St-Nicolas: Presses de l'Université Laval.
Macaulay, Stewart. 1986. 'Private Government.' In Leon Lipson and Stanton

Wheeler, eds., *Law and the Social Sciences.* New York: Russell Sage Foundation: 445.

Macdonald, Roderick A. 2005. 'Call-Centre Government: For the Rule of Law, Press #.' *University of Toronto Law Journal* 55, no. 3: 449.

– 2004. 'The Acoustics of Accountability – Towards Well-Tempered Tribunals.' In András Sajó, ed., *Judicial Integrity.* Boston: Martinus Nijhoff: 141.

– 1987. 'On the Administration of Statutes.' *Queen's Law Journal* 12: 488.

– 1980a. 'Judicial Review and Procedural Fairness in Administrative Law: I.' *McGill Law Journal* 25: 520.

– 1980b. 'Judicial Review and Procedural Fairness in Administrative Law: II.' *McGill Law Journal* 26: 1.

Macdonald, Roderick A., and Sandomierski, David. 2006. 'Against Nomopolies.' *Northern Ireland Legal Quarterly* 57: 610.

MacDougall, Bruce. 2001. 'The Celebration of Same-Sex Marriage.' *Ottawa Law Review* 32: 235.

– 2000. *Queer Judgments: Homosexuality, Expression, and the Courts in Canada.* Toronto: University of Toronto Press.

MacIntyre, Alasdair. 1984. *After Virtue: A Study in Moral Theory.* 2nd ed. Notre Dame: University of Notre Dame Press.

Mackenzie, Catriona, and Stoljar, Natalie, eds. 2000a. *Relational Autonomy: Feminist Perspectives on Autonomy, Agency, and the Social Self.* New York: Oxford University Press.

– 2000b. 'Introduction: Autonomy Refigured.' In Mackenzie and Stoljar 2000a: 4.

Macklin, Audrey. 2004. 'The State of Law's Borders and the Law of States' Borders.' In Dyzenhaus 2004a: 173.

– 1999. 'Truth and Consequences: Credibility in Refugee Determination.' In International Association of Refugee Law Judges, *Realities of Refugee Determination on the Eve of a New Millennium.* Haarlem: IARLJ: 134.

MacLauchlan, H. Wade. 2001. 'Transforming Administrative Law: The Didactic Role of the Supreme Court of Canada.' *Canadian Bar Review* 80: 281.

Macneil, Ian R. 1980. *The New Social Contract: An Inquiry into Modern Contractual Relations.* New Haven: Yale University Press.

Magnus, Kathy Dow. 2006. 'The Unaccountable Subject: Judith Butler and the Social Conditions of Intersubjective Agency.' *Hypatia* 21, no. 2: 81.

Manderson, Desmond. 2000. *Songs without Music: Aesthetic Dimensions of Law and Justice.* Berkeley and Los Angeles: University of California Press.

Marcus, Nancy C. 2006. 'Beyond *Romer* and *Lawrence:* The Right to Privacy Comes Out of the Closet.' *Columbia Journal of Gender and Law* 15: 355.

Markle, W. Ward. 1964. 'Catholic Adoptions in Ontario.' *Osgoode Hall Law Journal* 3: 27.

Marshall, T.H. 1950. *Citizenship and Social Class and Other Essays.* Cambridge: Cambridge University Press.

Marty, Gabriel, and Raynaud, Pierre. 1956. *Droit civil,* t. 1. Paris: Sirey.

Mashaw, Jerry L. 2005. 'Between Facts and Norms: Agency Statutory Interpretation as an Autonomous Enterprise.' *University of Toronto Law Journal* 55, no. 3: 497.

Mawani, Renisa. 2004. '"Cleansing the Conscience of the People": Reading Head Tax Redress in Multicultural Canada.' *Canadian Journal of Law and Society* 19, no. 2: 127.

Mayrand, Albert. 1963. 'Problèmes juridiques nés de la rupture des promesses de mariage.' *La Revue du Barreau* 23: 1.

McCamus, John D. 1993. 'Family Law Reform in Ontario.' *Special Lectures of the Law Society of Upper Canada* 1993: 451.

McLeod, Carolyn, and Sherwin, Susan. 2000. 'Relational Autonomy, Self-Trust, and Health Care for Patients Who Are Oppressed.' In Mackenzie and Stoljar 2000a: 259.

McLeod, James G. 2004. Annotation to *Hartshorne v. Hartshorne. Reports of Family Law* (5th) 47: 10.

McWhinney, Edward. 1959. Case Comment on *Roncarelli v. Duplessis. Canadian Bar Review* 37: 503.

Medina, José. 2006. *Speaking from Elsewhere: A New Contextualist Perspective on Meaning, Identity, and Discursive Agency.* Albany: SUNY Press.

– 2003. 'Identity Trouble: Disidentification and the Problem of Difference.' *Philosophy and Social Criticism* 29: 655.

Mendes da Costa, D., ed. 1972. *Studies in Canadian Family Law.* 2 vols. Toronto: Butterworths.

Merry, Sally Engle. 2006. *Human Rights and Gender Violence: Translating International Law into Local Justice.* Chicago: University of Chicago Press.

Meyer, David D. 2006. 'Parenthood in a Time of Transition: Tensions between Legal, Biological, and Social Conceptions of Parenthood.' *American Journal of Comparative Law* 54: 125.

Meyers, Diana Tietjens. 2004. *Being Yourself: Essays on Identity, Action, and Social Life.* Lanham: Rowman and Littlefield.

– 1997a. 'Emotion and Heterodox Moral Perception: An Essay in Moral Social Psychology.' In Meyers 1997b: 197.

– ed. 1997b. *Feminists Rethink the Self.* Boulder: Westview.

Millard, Eric. 1995. *Famille et droit public: Recherches sur la construction d'un objet juridique.* Paris: L.G.D.J.

Minow, Martha. 1990. *Making All the Difference.* Ithaca: Cornell University Press.

– 1985. 'Forming Underneath Everything That Grows: Toward a History of Family Law.' *Wisconsin Law Review* 1985: 819.

Minow, Martha, and Shanley, Mary Lyndon. 1996. 'Relational Rights and Responsibilities: Revisioning the Family in Liberal Political Theory and Law.' *Hypatia* 11, no. 1: 4.

Minow, Martha, and Spelman, Elizabeth V. 1990. 'In Context.' *Southern California Law Review* 63: 1597.

Mitchell, Graeme G. 2003. 'Developments in Constitutional Law: The 2002–2003 Term – A Tale of Two Courts.' *Supreme Court Law Review* (2nd) 22: 83.

Moran, Mayo. 2004. 'Authority, Influence, and Persuasion: *Baker*, Charter Values, and the Puzzle of Method.' In Dyzenhaus 2004a: 389.

Mossman, Mary Jane. 1994. 'Gender Equality, Family Law, and Access to Justice.' *International Journal of Law, Policy, and the Family* 8: 357.

– 1992. '*Les Belles Soeurs*: Unquiet Questions about Gender and Family Justice.' *Queen's Law Journal* 17: 465.

– 1989. 'Individualism and Community: Family as a Mediating Concept.' In Allan C. Hutchinson and Leslie J.M. Green, eds., *Law and the Community: The End of Individualism?* Toronto: Carswell: 205.

– 1985. 'Toward "New Property" and "New Scholarship": An Assessment of Canadian Property Scholarship.' *Osgoode Hall Law Journal* 23: 633.

Mossman, Mary Jane, and MacLean, Morag. 1986. 'Family Law and Social Welfare: Toward a New Equality.' *Canadian Journal of Family Law* 5: 79.

Mullan, David J. 2004. 'Deference from *Baker* to *Suresh* and Beyond – Interpreting the Conflicting Signals.' In Dyzenhaus 2004a: 21.

– 2001. *Administrative Law.* Toronto: Irwin Law.

– 1987. 'Natural Justice – The Challenges of *Nicholson*, Deference Theory, and the *Charter*.' In Neil R. Finkelstein and Brian MacLeod Rogers, eds., *Recent Developments in Administrative Law.* Toronto: Carswell: 1.

– 1980. 'Mr. Justice Rand: Defining the Limits of Court Control of the Administrative and Executive Process.' *University of Western Ontario Law Review* 17, no. 2: 65.

– 1975. 'Fairness: The New Natural Justice?' *University of Toronto Law Journal* 25: 281.

Murphy, Jason. 2001. 'Dialogic Responses to *M. v. H.*: From Compliance to Defiance.' *University of Toronto Faculty of Law Review* 59: 299.

Murphy, Thérèse, and Whitty, Noel. 2006. 'A Question of Definition: Feminist Legal Scholarship, Socio-Legal Studies and Debate about Law and Politics.' *Northern Ireland Legal Quarterly* 57, no. 3: 539.

Mykitiuk, Roxanne. 2001. 'Beyond Conception: Legal Determinations of Filiation in the Context of Assisted Reproductive Technologies.' *Osgoode Hall Law Journal* 39: 771.

Nedelsky, Jennifer. unpublished a. 'Reconceiving Autonomy: Sources, Thoughts and Possibilities.' [unpublished revision, 20 August 2004, on file with author].

– unpublished b. 'Rights and the Fully Human Self.' [on file with author].

– 2001. 'Citizenship and Relational Feminism.' In Ronald Beiner and Wayne Norman, eds., *Canadian Political Philosophy: Contemporary Reflections.* Oxford: Oxford University Press: 131.

– 1997. 'Embodied Diversity and the Challenges to Law.' *McGill Law Journal* 42, no. 1: 91.

– 1996. 'Should Property Law Be Constitutionalized? A Relational and Comparative Approach.' In G.E. van Maanen and A.J. van der Walt, eds., *Property Law on the Threshold of the 21st Century.* Apeldoorn: Maklu: 417.

– 1993a. 'Property in Potential Life? A Relational Approach to Choosing Legal Categories.' *Canadian Journal of Law and Jurisprudence* 6: 343.

– 1993b. 'Reconceiving Rights as Relationship.' *Review of Constitutional Studies* 1, no. 1: 1.

– 1990. 'Law, Boundaries, and the Bounded Self.' *Representations* 30: 162.

– 1989. 'Reconceiving Autonomy: Sources, Thoughts and Possibilities.' *Yale Journal of Law and Feminism* 1, no. 1: 7.

Nelken, David. 2004. 'Comparing Legal Cultures.' In Austin Sarat, ed., *The Blackwell Companion to Law and Society.* Oxford: Blackwell Publishing: 113.

– ed. 1997. *Comparing Legal Cultures.* Aldershot: Dartmouth.

Nelken, David, and Feest, Johannes, eds. 2001. *Adapting Legal Cultures.* Oxford: Hart Publishing.

Noddings, Nel. 1984. *Caring: A Feminine Approach to Ethics and Moral Education.* Berkeley and Los Angeles: University of California Press.

Noreau, Pierre. 2002. 'Construction et déconstruction du lien social en droit privé: Le cas de la monoparentalité.' In Kasirer 2002c: 133.

Nussbaum, Martha C. 2001. *Upheavals of Thought: The Intelligence of Emotions.* New York: Cambridge University Press.

– 1999. *Sex and Social Justice.* New York: Oxford University Press.

– 1986. *The Fragility of Goodness: Luck and Ethics in Greek Tragedy and Philosophy.* New York: Cambridge University Press.

Oberweis, Trish, and Musheno, Michael. 2001. *Knowing Rights: State Actors' Stories of Power, Identity, and Morality.* Burlington: Ashgate.

O'Connor, Peg. 2005. 'Identity Trouble and the Politics of Privilege.' *Symposia on Gender, Race, and Philosophy* 1 (online: http://web.mit.edu/sgrp).

O'Donovan, Katherine, and Marshall, Jill. 2006. 'After Birth: Decisions about Becoming a Mother.' In Diduck and O'Donovan 2006: 101.

Olsen, Frances E. 1983. 'The Family and the Market: A Study of Ideology and Legal Reform.' *Harvard Law Review* 96: 1497.

Ontario. 1968. *First Report of the Royal Commission Inquiry into Civil Rights*, vol. 1. Toronto: Queen's Printer (Chair: J.C. McRuer).

Ouellette, Françoise-Romaine, Joyal, Reneé, and Hurtubise, Roch, eds. 2005. *Familles en mouvance: Quels enjeux éthiques?* Quebec: Presses de l'Université Laval.

Ouellette, Monique. 1980. *Droit des personnes et de la famille*. 3rd ed. Montreal: Thémis.

Pépin, Gilles. 1997. 'La loi québécoise sur la justice administrative.' *La Revue du Barreau* 57: 633.

– 1969. 'Les tribunaux administratifs.' In Barbe 1969: 551.

Philippe, Catherine. 2003. 'Le temps et le droit de la famille.' In Anne Guineret-Brobbel Dorsman, ed., *Le Temps et le Droit*. Paris: Presses Universitaires Franc-Comtoises: 125.

Philips-Nootens, Suzanne, and Lavallée, Carmen. 2003. 'De l'état inaliénable à l'instrumentalisation: La filiation en question.' In Lafond and Lefebvre 2003: 337.

Pinard, Danielle. 2002. 'La "méthode contextuelle."' *Canadian Bar Review* 81: 323.

– 2001. 'Charter and Context: The Facts for Which We Need Evidence, and the Mysterious Other Ones.' *Supreme Court Law Review* (2nd) 14: 163.

– 1996. 'Le contexte factuel d'élaboration et d'application comme facteur d'interprétation de la norme juridique.' In Pierre-André Côté and Jacques Frémont, eds., *Le temps et le droit*. Cowansville: Yvon Blais: 171.

Pineau, Jean. 1972. *La famille*. Montreal: Presses de l'Université de Montréal.

– 1965–6. 'L'autorité dans la famille.' *Les Cahiers de Droit* 7: 201.

Pineau, Jean, and Pratte, Marie. 2006. *La famille*. Montreal: Thémis.

Popovici, Adrian, and Parizeau-Popovici, Micheline. 1971. *L'amour et la loi: Mariage, union libre, enfants adultères, séparation, divorce*. Montreal: Éditions du Jour.

Postema, Gerald J. 2002. 'Philosophy of the Common Law.' In Jules Coleman and Scott Shapiro, eds., *The Oxford Handbook of Jurisprudence and Philosophy of Law*. Oxford: Oxford University Press: 588.

Pratte, Marie. 2003. 'La filiation réinventée: L'enfant menacé?' *Revue générale de droit* 33: 541.

– 1982. 'Les nouvelles règles relatives à la filiation.' *Revue générale de droit* 13: 159.

Prémont, J. 1962. 'Recours contre les décisions administratives: Contrôle et appel en matières administratives.' *Canadian Public Administration* 5: 55.

Private Law Dictionary of the Family and Bilingual Lexicons. 1999. Cowansville: Yvon Blais.

Rabinow, Paul, and Rose, Nikolas, eds. 2003. *The Essential Foucault: Selections from Essential Works of Foucault, 1954–1984.* New York: New Press.

Rambourg, Michel. 1969. 'Notions générales sur le droit administratif canadien et québécois.' In Barbe 1969: 1.

Rand, Ivan C. 1961. 'Except by Due Process of Law.' *Osgoode Hall Law Journal* 2: 171.

– 1960. 'Some Aspects of Canadian Constitutionalism.' *Canadian Bar Review* 38: 135.

– 1954. 'Man's Right to Knowledge and Its Free Use.' *University of Toronto Law Journal* 10: 167.

– 1951. 'The Role of an Independent Judiciary in Preserving Freedom.' *University of Toronto Law Journal* 9: 1.

Réaume, Denise. 2006. 'The Relevance of Relevance to Equality Rights.' *Queen's Law Journal* 31, no. 2: 696.

Reece, Helen. 2003. *Divorcing Responsibly.* Oxford: Hart Publishing.

Regan, Milton C., Jr. 1999. *Alone Together: Law and the Meanings of Marriage.* New York: Oxford University Press.

– 1993. *Family Law and the Pursuit of Intimacy.* New York: New York University Press.

Reich, Charles. 1964. 'The New Property.' *Yale Law Journal* 73: 733.

Reid, Karen. 2004. *A Practitioner's Guide to the European Convention on Human Rights.* 2nd ed. London: Thomson.

Reid, Robert F. 1971. *Administrative Law and Practice.* Toronto: Butterworths.

Richardson, Genevra, and Machin, David. 2000. 'Judicial Review and Tribunal Decision Making: A Study of the Mental Health Review Tribunal.' *Public Law* 2000: 494.

Richardson, Genevra, and Sunkin, Maurice. 1996. 'Judicial Review: Questions of Impact.' *Public Law* 1996: 79.

Richman, Kimberly. 2002. 'Lovers, Legal Strangers, and Parents: Negotiating Parental and Sexual Identity in Family Law.' *Law and Society Review* 36: 285.

Risk, R.C.B. 1983. '"This Nuisance of Litigation": The Origins of Workers' Compensation in Ontario.' In David H. Flaherty, ed., *Essays in the History of Canadian Law,* vol. 2. Toronto: The Osgoode Society: 418.

Rivero, Jean. 1965. 'A propos des métamorphoses de l'administration d'aujourd'hui: Démocratie et administration.' In *Mélanges offerts à René Savatier.* Paris: Dalloz: 821.

Roach, Kent. 1989. 'The Administrative Law Scholarship of D.M. Gordon.' *McGill Law Journal* 34, no. 1: 1.

Rogers, I. MacF. 1953. Case Comment on *Re Ross and Bd. of Commrs. of Police for Toronto. Canadian Bar Review* 31: 807.

Rogerson, Carol J. 2003. 'Developments in Family Law: The 2002–2003 Term.' *Supreme Court Law Review* (2nd) 22: 273.

– 2001. 'The Child Support Obligation of Step-Parents.' *Canadian Journal of Family Law* 18, no. 1: 9.

– 1985. 'From *Murdoch* to *Leatherdale*: The Uneven Course of Bora Laskin's Family Law Decisions.' *University of Toronto Law Journal* 35: 481.

Rollins, Joe. 2005. 'Lawrence, Privacy, and the Marital Bedroom: A Few Telltale Signs of Ironic Worry.' In Hirsch 2005: 169.

Roy, Alain. 2006. *Le droit de l'adoption au Québec: adoption interne et internationale.* Montreal: Wilson and Lafleur.

– 2002. *Le contrat de mariage réinventé: perspectives socio-juridiques pour une réforme.* Montreal: Thémis.

Sainsbury, Roy. 1992. 'Administrative Justice: Discretion and Procedure in Social Security Decision-Making.' In Hawkins 1992: 295.

Sandel, Michael. 1982. *Liberalism and the Limits of Justice.* Cambridge: Cambridge University Press.

Savard, Anne-Marie. 2006. 'La nature des fictions juridiques au sein du nouveau mode de filiation unisexuée au Québec; un retour aux sources?' *Les Cahiers de Droit* 47, no. 2: 377.

Schauer, Frederick. 1988. 'Formalism.' *Yale Law Journal* 97: 509.

Scheppele, Kim Lane. 1987. 'The Re-vision of Rape Law.' *University of Chicago Law Review* 54: 1095.

Schlag, Pierre. 1990. 'The Problem of the Subject.' *Texas Law Review* 69: 1627.

Schneewind, J.B. 1998. *The Invention of Autonomy: A History of Modern Moral Philosophy.* Cambridge: Cambridge University Press.

Scott, F.R. 1948. 'Administrative Law, 1923–1947.' *Canadian Bar Review* 26: 268.

Shachar, Ayelet. 2005. 'Religion, State, and the Problem of Gender: New Modes of Citizenship and Governance in Diverse Societies.' *McGill Law Journal* 50, no. 1: 49.

Shaffer, Martha. 2004a. 'Developments in Family Law: The 2003–2004 Term.' *Supreme Court Law Review* (2nd) 26: 407.

– 2004b. 'Domestic Contracts, Part II: The Supreme Court's Decision in *Hartshorne v. Hartshorne.' Canadian Journal of Family Law* 20: 261.

Shanley, Mary L. 1995. 'Unwed Fathers' Rights, Adoption, and Sex Equality: Gender-Neutrality and the Perpetuation of Patriarchy.' *Columbia Law Review* 95: 60.

Sheppard, Colleen. 1995. 'Uncomfortable Victories and Unanswered Questions: Lessons from *Moge.' Canadian Journal of Family Law* 12: 283.

Sher, George. 1997. *Beyond Neutrality: Perfectionism and Politics.* New York: Cambridge University Press.

Siegel, Jonathan R. 1998. 'Textualism and Contextualism in Administrative Law.' *Boston University Law Review* 78: 1023.

Singer, Jana B. 1992. 'The Privatization of Family Law.' *Wisconsin Law Review* 1992: 1443.

Socqué, Mathieu. 2006. 'La notion d'expertise du décideur administratif aux fins de l'application de la méthode pragmatique et fonctionnelle.' *Les Cahiers de Droit* 47, no. 2: 319.

Sommers, Christina Hoff. 1994. 'Philosophers Against the Family.' In Markate Daly, ed., *Communitarianism: A New Public Ethics.* Belmont: Wadsworth: 321.

Sossin, Lorne. 2005a. 'From Neutrality to Compassion: The Place of Civil Service Values and Legal Norms in the Exercise of Administrative Discretion.' *University of Toronto Law Journal* 55, no. 3: 427.

– 2005b. 'Speaking Truth to Power? The Search for Bureaucratic Independence in Canada.' *University of Toronto Law Journal* 55, no. 1: 1.

– 2004a. 'Boldly Going Where No Law Has Gone Before: Call Centres, Intake Scripts, Database Fields, and Discretionary Justice in Social Assistance.' *Osgoode Hall Law Journal* 42: 363.

– 2004b. 'Developments in Administrative Law: The 2003–2004 Term.' *Supreme Court Law Review* (2nd) 26: 31.

– 2003. 'Public Fiduciary Obligations, Political Trusts, and the Equitable Duty of Reasonableness in Administrative Law.' *Saskatchewan Law Review* 66: 129.

– 2002. 'An Intimate Approach to Fairness, Impartiality, and Reasonableness in Administrative Law.' *Queen's Law Journal* 27, no. 2: 809.

– 1994. 'Redistributing Democracy: An Inquiry into Authority, Discretion and the Possibility of Engagement in the Welfare State.' *Ottawa Law Review* 26, no. 1: 1.

Spaht, Katherine Shaw. 1998. 'Louisiana's Covenant Marriage: Social Analysis and Legal Implications.' *Louisiana Law Review* 59: 63.

Stoljar, Natalie. 2000. 'Autonomy and the Feminist Intuition.' In Mackenzie and Stoljar 2000a: 94.

Stranger-Jones, L.I. 1951. *Eversley's Law of Domestic Relations.* 6th ed. London: Sweet and Maxwell.

Stychin, Carl F. 1995. *Law's Desire: Sexuality and the Limits of Justice.* New York: Routledge.

Stychin, Carl, and Herman, Didi, eds. 2001. *Law and Sexuality: The Global Arena.* Minneapolis: University of Minnesota Press.

Sugunasiri, Shalin M. 1999. 'Contextualism: The Supreme Court's New Stan-

dard of Judicial Analysis and Accountability.' *Dalhousie Law Journal* 22, no. 1:
126.

Sunkin, Maurice, and Pick, Kathryn. 2001. 'The Changing Impact of Judicial
Review: The Independent Review Service of the Social Fund.' *Public Law*
2001: 736.

Taggart, Michael. 2003. 'Reinventing Administrative Law.' In Bamforth and
Leyland 2003: 311.

– ed. 1997. *The Province of Administrative Law*. Oxford: Hart Publishing.

Tallin, G.P.R. 1956. 'Artificial Insemination.' *Canadian Bar Review* 34: 1.

Taylor, Charles. 1997. *Philosophical Arguments*. Cambridge, MA: Harvard University Press.

– 1989. *Sources of the Self: The Making of the Modern Identity*. Cambridge, MA:
Harvard University Press.

– 1985. *Human Agency and Language*. Cambridge: Cambridge University Press.

Taylor, Dianna, and Vintges, Karen, eds. 2004a. *Feminism and the Final Foucault*.
Urbana and Chicago: University of Illinois Press.

– 2004b. 'Introduction: Engaging the Present.' In Taylor and Vintges 2004a:
1.

Tétrault, Michel. 2005. *Droit de la famille*. 3rd ed. Cowansville: Yvon Blais.

Thomas, Robert. 2003. 'The Impact of Judicial Review on Asylum.' *Public Law*
2003: 479.

– 2000. *Legitimate Expectations and Proportionality in Administrative Law*. Portland: Hart Publishing.

Thompson, D.A. Rollie. 2003. Annotation to *Walsh v. Bona*. *Reports of Family
Law* (5th) 32: 87.

Trebilcock, Michael J., and Keshvani, Rosemin. 1991. 'The Role of Private
Ordering in Family Law: A Law and Economics Perspective.' *University of
Toronto Law Journal* 41: 533.

Tucker, Eric. 1987. 'The Political Economy of Administrative Fairness: A Preliminary Inquiry.' *Osgoode Hall Law Journal* 25: 555.

Valverde, Mariana. 2007. 'Toronto: A "Multicultural" "Urban Order."' In
Andreas Philippopoulos-Mihalopoulos, ed., *Law and the City*. London: Rout-
ledge-Cavendish: 191.

Van Praagh, Shauna. 2001. 'Identity's Importance: Reflections of – and on –
Diversity.' *Canadian Bar Review* 80: 605.

Vasterling, Veronica. 1999. 'Butler's Sophisticated Constructivism: A Critical
Assessment.' *Hypatia* 14, no. 3: 17.

Vincent-Jones, Peter. 2000. 'Contractual Governance: Institutional and Organi-
sational Analysis.' *Oxford Journal of Legal Studies* 20: 317.

– 1999. 'The Regulation of Contractualisation in Quasi-Markets for Public Services.' *Public Law* 1999: 304.

Vining, Joseph. 1978. *Legal Identity: The Coming of Age of Public Law.* New Haven: Yale University Press.

Wade, H.W.R. 1949. '"Quasi-judicial" and Its Background.' *Cambridge Law Journal* 10: 216.

Wade, Sir William, and Forsyth, Christopher. 2004. *Administrative Law.* 4th ed. Oxford: Oxford University Press.

Waldron, Jeremy. 1999. *Law and Disagreement.* New York: Oxford University Press.

Walker, R.H.E. 1965. 'The Disintegrating Marriage.' *Meredith Lectures* 1965: 8.

Wall, Steven. 1998. *Liberalism, Perfectionism and Restraint.* Cambridge: Cambridge University Press.

Walters, Mark D. 2003. 'Incorporating Common Law into the Constitution of Canada: *EGALE v. Canada* and the Status of Marriage.' *Osgoode Hall Law Journal* 41: 75.

Warner, Michael. 1999. *The Trouble with Normal: Sex, Politics, and the Ethics of Queer Life.* New York: Free Press.

Watson, Alan. 1993. *Legal Transplants: An Approach to Comparative Law.* 2nd ed. Athens: University of Georgia Press.

Weberman, David. 2000. 'Are Freedom and Anti-Humanism Compatible? The Case of Foucault and Butler.' *Constellations* 7: 255.

Weinrib, Ernest Joseph. 1995. *The Idea of Private Law.* Cambridge, MA: Harvard University Press.

Weinstock, Daniel M. 2005. 'Une philosophie politique du mariage.' *Comprendre* 6: 41.

Weitzman, Lenore J. 1985. *The Divorce Revolution: The Unexpected Social and Economic Consequences for Women and Children in America.* New York: Free Press.

Wells, Catharine. 1990. 'Situated Decisionmaking.' *Southern California Law Review* 63: 1727.

West, Robin. 1997. *Caring for Justice.* New York: New York University Press.

– 1988. 'Jurisprudence and Gender.' *University of Chicago Law Review* 55, no. 1: 1.

White, D.G. 1969. 'The Demise of Palm Tree Justice.' *Saskatchewan Law Review* 34: 291.

White, James Boyd. 1990. *Justice as Translation: An Essay in Cultural and Legal Criticism.* Chicago: University of Chicago Press.

Whitehead, Barbara Dafoe. 1992. 'A New Familism?' *Family Affairs* 5: 1.

Wightman, John. 2003. 'Beyond Custom: Contract, Contexts, and the Recognition of Implicit Understandings.' In Campbell, Collins, and Wightman 2003: 143.

Williams, Patricia. 1987a. 'Alchemical Notes: Reconstructing Ideals from Deconstructed Rights.' *Harvard Civil Rights–Civil Liberties Law Review* 22: 401.

– 1987b. 'Taking Rights Aggressively: The Perils and Promise of Critical Legal Theory for Peoples of Color.' *Law and Inequality* 5: 103.

Williams, Rowan. 2000. *Lost Icons: Reflections on Cultural Bereavement.* Edinburgh: T & T Clark.

Willis, John. 1974. 'Canadian Administrative Law in Retrospect.' *University of Toronto Law Journal* 24: 225.

– 1968. 'The McRuer Report: Lawyers' Values and Civil Servants' Values.' *University of Toronto Law Journal* 18: 351.

– 1961. 'Administrative Law in Canada.' *Canadian Bar Review* 39: 251.

– 1959. 'Administrative Decision and the Law: The Canadian Implications of the Franks Report.' *University of Toronto Law Journal* 13: 45.

– 1938. 'Statute Interpretation in a Nutshell.' *Canadian Bar Review* 16: 1.

– 1935. 'Three Approaches to Administrative Law: The Judicial, the Conceptual, and the Functional.' *University of Toronto Law Journal* 1: 53.

Wintemute, Robert. 2005. 'From "Sex Rights" to "Love Rights": Partnership Rights as Human Rights.' In Nicholas Bamforth, ed., *Sex Rights.* Oxford: Oxford University Press.

– 2004. 'L'adoption, les futurs parents gays et lesbiens et la convention européenne.' In Vladimir Martens, ed., *Citoyenneté, discrimination et préférence sexuelle.* Brussels: Publications des Facultés universitaires Saint-Louis: 41.

Wright, David. 1997. 'Rethinking the Doctrine of Legitimate Expectations in Canadian Administrative Law.' *Osgoode Hall Law Journal* 35: 139.

Yuracko, Kimberley A. 2003. *Perfectionism and Contemporary Feminist Values.* Bloomington: Indiana University Press.

Cases

A.A. v. B.B. 2007. 83 O.R. (3d) 561 (C.A.).

Alspector v. Alspector. [1957] O.R. 14 (H.C.), aff'd, [1957] O.R. 454 (C.A.).

Anderson v. Luoma. 1986. 50 R.F.L. (2d) 127 (B.C.S.C.).

B. (M.) v. L. (L.). 2003. 231 D.L.R. (4th) 665 (C.A.).

B.R. v. B.I. [2004] J.Q. No. 8278 (Sup. Ct.).

Baker v. Canada (Minister of Citizenship and Immigration). [1999] 2 S.C.R. 817.

Barrie Public Utilities v. Canadian Cable Television Assn. [2003] 1 S.C.R. 476, 2003 SCC 28.

Bates v. Lord Hailsham. [1972] 1 W.L.R. 1373.

Bell Canada v. Canadian Telephone Employees Association. [2003] 1 S.C.R. 884, 2003 SCC 36.

Board of Health for Saltfleet Township v. Knapman. [1954] O.R. 360 (H.C.), aff'd, [1955] 3 D.L.R. 248 (Ont. C.A.), aff'd, [1956] S.C.R. 877.

Bracklow v. Bracklow. 1999. [1999] 1 S.C.R. 420.

Brebric v. Niksic. 2002. 60 O.R. (3d) 630 (C.A.), leave to appeal refused, [2003] 1 S.C.R. vi.

C.U.P.E. v. Ontario (Minister of Labour). [2003] 1 S.C.R. 539, 2003 SCC 29.

C.U.P.E., Local 963 v. New Brunswick Liquor Corp. [1979] 2 S.C.R. 227.

Calgary Power Ltd. v. Copithorne. [1959] S.C.R. 24.

Canada (A.G.) v. Inuit Tapirisat of Canada. [1980] 2 S.C.R. 735.

Canada (A.G.) v. Mossop. [1993] 1 S.C.R. 554.

Canada (Director of Investigation and Research) v. Southam Inc. 1996. [1997] 1 S.C.R. 748.

Canada (Minister of Employment and Immigration) v. Chiarelli. [1992] 1 S.C.R. 711.

Cardinal v. Director of Kent Institution. [1985] 2 S.C.R. 643.

Caron v. Caron. [1987] 1 S.C.R. 892.

Chamberlain v. Surrey School District No. 36. [2002] 4 S.C.R. 710, 2002 SCC 86.

Chartier v. Chartier. 1998. [1999] 1 S.C.R. 242.

Cooper v. Canada (Human Rights Commission). [1996] 3 S.C.R. 854.

Cooper v. Wandsworth Board of Works. 1863. 14 C.B. (N.S.) 180.

Corbiere v. Canada (Minister of Indian and Northern Affairs). [1999] 2 S.C.R. 203.

Culen v. Culen. 2003. 338 A.R. 308, 2003 ABQB 480.

Dr. Q v. College of Physicians and Surgeons of British Columbia. [2003] 1 S.C.R. 226, 2003 SCC 19.

Egan v. Canada. [1995] 2 S.C.R. 513.

Eldridge v. British Columbia (Attorney General). [1997] 3 S.C.R. 624.

Ex parte Worlds. 1967. 65 D.L.R. (2d) 252 (Alta. S.C.).

Falkiner v. Ontario (Ministry of Community and Social Services). 2002. 59 O.R. (3d) 481 (C.A.), leave to appeal granted, [2003] 1 S.C.R. ix, appeal discontinued.

Fazal v. Fazal. [2004] O.T.C. 31 (S.C.J.).

Forrest v. Price. 1992. 48 E.T.R. 72 (B.C.S.C.).

Freake v. Freake. 2003. 230 Nfld. & P.E.I.R. 346, 2003 NLSCUFC 23, aff'd (2004), 238 Nfld. & P.E.I.R. 203, 2004 NLCA 39.

Gauthier v. Gauthier. 2004. 9 R.F.L. (6th) 312 (Ont. S.C.J.).

Goldberg v. Kelly. 1970. 397 U.S. 254.

Gordon v. Goertz. [1996] 2 S.C.R. 27.

Goudie v. Stapleford. 2004. 5 R.F.L. (6th) 55 (Ont. S.C.J.).

Great Atlantic & Pacific Co. of Canada v. Ontario (Human Rights Commission). 1993. 13 O.R. (3d) 824 (Div. Ct.).

Guy v. Guy. 1982. 35 O.R. (2d) 584 (S.C.).

Halpern v. Canada (A.G.). 2003. 65 O.R. (3d) 161 (C.A.).

Hartshorne v. Hartshorne. [2004] 1 S.C.R. 550, 2004 SCC 22.

Hartshorne v. Hartshorne. 2002. 220 D.L.R. (4th) 655, 2002 BCCA 587.

Hawthorne v. Canada (Minister of Citizenship and Immigration). 2002. [2003] 2 F.C. 555, 2002 FCA 475.

Hearn v. Hearn. 2004. 352 A.R. 260, 2004 ABQB 75.

Hepton v. Maat. [1957] S.C.R. 606.

Imperial Oil Ltd. v. Quebec (Minister of the Environment). [2003] 2 S.C.R. 624, 2003 SCC 58.

In re Gage; Ketterer v. Griffith. [1962] S.C.R. 241.

J.D. v. R.S. [2004] J.Q. No. 13490, J.E. 2005–208 (Sup. Ct.), aff'd, 2005 QCCA 269.

J.E.D. v. E.P.D. 2003. 42 R.F.L. (5th) 334, 2003 BCSC 1250.

Keddy v. New Brunswick (Workplace Health, Safety and Compensation Commission). 2002. 247 N.B.R. (2d) 284 (C.A.), leave to appeal refused, [2002] 4 S.C.R. vi.

Keegan v. Ireland. 1994. 291 Eur. Ct. H.R. (Ser. A).

Kelly v. Kelly. 2004. 72 O.R. (3d) 108 (C.A.).

King v. Low. [1985] 1 S.C.R. 87.

Knight v. Indian Head School Division No. 19. [1990] 1 S.C.R. 653.

Knodel v. British Columbia (Medical Services Commission). [1991] 6 W.W.R. 728 (B.C.S.C.).

L'Alliance des Professeurs Catholiques de Montréal v. Labour Relations Board of Quebec. [1953] 2 S.C.R. 140.

Law Society of New Brunswick v. Ryan. [2003] 1 S.C.R. 247, 2003 SCC 20.

Layland v. Ontario (Minister of Consumer & Commercial Relations). 1993. 14 O.R. (3d) 658 (Div. Ct.).

Legault v. Canada (Minister of Citizenship and Immigration). [2002] 4 F.C. 358, 2002 FCA 125, leave to appeal refused, [2002] 4 S.C.R. vi.

Leskun v. Leskun. [2006] 1 S.C.R. 920, 2006 SCC 25.

M. v. H. [1999] 2 S.C.R. 3.

M. v. M. 1972. 24 D.L.R. (3d) 114 (P.E.I. S.C.).

M.C. v. P.B. [2003] R.J.Q. 2719 (C.A.).

M.E.O. v. S.R.M. 2003. 39 R.F.L. (5th) 361, 2003 ABQB 362, aff'd (2004), 346 A.R. 351, 2004 ABCA 90.

Marckx v. Belgium. 1979. 31 Eur. Ct. H.R. (Ser. A).

Miglin v. Miglin. [2003] 1 S.C.R. 303, 2003 SCC 24.

Miron v. Trudel. [1995] 2 S.C.R. 418.

Moffatt v. Moffatt. 2003. 67 O.R. (3d) 239 (S.C.J.).

Moge v. Moge. [1992] 3 S.C.R. 813.

Monkman v. Beaulieu. 2003. 170 Man. R. (2d) 182, 2003 MBCA 17.

Moss v. Moss. [1897] P. 263.

Mount Sinai Hospital Center v. Quebec (Minister of Health and Social Services). [2001] 2 S.C.R. 281, 2001 SCC 41.

Murdoch v. Murdoch. 1976. 1 A.R. 378 (S.C. (T.D.)).

Murdoch v. Murdoch. 1973. [1975] 1 S.C.R. 423.

Murdoch v. Murdoch. 1972. 95 A.R. 118 (S.C. (A.D.)).

Murdoch v. Murdoch. 1971. 95 A.R. 119 (S.C. (T.D.)).

N. (R.) (Litigation Guardian of) v. Ontario (Minister of Community, Family and Children's Services). 2004. 70 O.R. (3d) 420 (Div. Ct.).

Nakkuda Ali v. Jayaratne. [1951] A.C. 66 (P.C.).

Newfoundland Telephone Co. v. Newfoundland (Board of Commissioners of Public Utilities). [1992] 1 S.C.R. 623.

Nicholson v. Haldimand-Norfolk Regional Board of Commissioners of Police. 1978. [1979] 1 S.C.R. 311.

Norberg v. Wynrib. [1992] 2 S.C.R. 224.

Nova Scotia (A.G.) v. Walsh. [2002] 4 S.C.R. 325, 2002 SCC 83.

Nova Scotia (Workers' Compensation Board) v. Martin; Nova Scotia (Workers' Compensation Board) v. Laseur. [2003] 2 S.C.R. 504, 2003 SCC 54.

Old St. Boniface Residents Assn. Inc. v. Winnipeg (City). [1990] 3 S.C.R. 1170.

Ontario Securities Commission v. Dobson. 1957. 8 D.L.R. (2d) 604 (Ont. H.C.).

Paul v. British Columbia (Forest Appeals Commission). [2003] 2 S.C.R. 585, 2003 SCC 55.

Pelech v. Pelech. [1987] 1 S.C.R. 801.

Pettkus v. Becker. [1980] 2 S.C.R. 834.

Pezim v. British Columbia (Superintendent of Brokers). [1994] 2 S.C.R. 557.

Pigott v. Pigott. [1969] 2 O.R. 427 (C.A.).

Pushpanathan v. Canada (Minister of Citizenship and Immigration). [1998] 1 S.C.R. 982.

R. v. Leong Ba Chai. [1954] S.C.R. 10.

R.L. v. D.L. [2004] J.Q. No. 11664 (Sup. Ct.).

R.P. v. E.M.Z. [2004] J.Q. No. 6439, J.E. 2004–1946 (Sup. Ct.).

Racine v. Woods. [1983] 2 S.C.R. 173.

Rathwell v. Rathwell. [1978] 2 S.C.R. 436.

Re Agar; McNeilly v. Agar. 1957. [1958] S.C.R. 52.

Re Baby Duffell; Martin v. Duffell. [1950] S.C.R. 737.

Re Goldstein and Brownstone. 1970. 15 D.L.R. (3d) 102 (Man. C.A.).

Re Mugford. 1969. [1970] 1 O.R. 601 (C.A.), aff'd, [1970] S.C.R. 261.

Re Ross and Board of Commissioners of Police for Toronto. [1953] O.R. 556 (H.C.).

Re Wells. 1962. 33 D.L.R. (2d) 243 (B.C.C.A.).

Reinhardt v. Reinhardt. 2004. 8 R.F.L. (6th) 340 (Ont. S.C.J.).

Richardson v. Richardson. [1987] 1 S.C.R. 857.

Riel v. Holland. 2003. 67 O.R. (3d) 417 (C.A.).

Rogerson v. Rogerson. 2004. 222 N.S.R. (2d) 324, 2004 NSSF 37.

Roncarelli v. Duplessis. [1959] S.C.R. 121.

Selvarajan v. Race Relations Board. [1976] 1 All E.R. 13 (C.A.).

Singh v. Minister of Employment and Immigration. [1985] 1 S.C.R. 177.

Slipak v. Slipak. [2004] O.J. No. 25 (S.C.J.).

Smith and Rhuland Ltd. v. The Queen. [1953] 2 S.C.R. 95.

Sorochan v. Sorochan. [1986] 2 S.C.R. 38.

Suresh v. Canada (Minister of Citizenship and Immigration). [2002] 1
  S.C.R. 3, 2002 SCC 1.

T. v. T. 1975. 24 R.F.L. 57 (Man. Q.B.).

Thompson v. Thompson. [1961] S.C.R. 3.

U.E.S., Local 298 v. Bibeault. [1988] 2 S.C.R. 1048.

Van de Perre v. Edwards. [2001] 2 S.C.R. 1014, 2001 SCC 60.

Via Rail Canada v. Canada (National Transportation Agency). 2000.
  [2001] 2 F.C. 25 (C.A.).

Wewaykum Indian Band v. Canada. [2002] 4 S.C.R. 245, 2002 SCC 79.

Willick v. Willick. [1994] 3 S.C.R. 670.

Legislation

An Act Instituting Civil Unions and Establishing New Rules of Filiation. S.Q. 2002, c. 6.

An Act Respecting adoption. S.Q. 1923–24, c. 75.

An Act Respecting the Legal Capacity of Married Women. S.Q. 1964, c. 66.

An Act Respecting Civil Marriage. S.Q. 1968, c. 82.

An Act to Amend The Child Welfare Act, 1954. S.O. 1958, c. 11.

An Act to Amend the Child Welfare Act, 1954. S.O. 1956, c. 8.

Adoption Act. S.Q. 1969, c. 64.

The Adoption Act. R.S.O. 1950, c. 7.

Adoption Act. S.O. 1921, c. 55.

Adult Interdependent Relationships Act. S.A. 2002, c. A–4.5.

Amendments Because of the Supreme Court of Canada Decision in M. v. H. S.O. 1999, c. 6.

Canadian Bill of Rights. S.C. 1960, c. 44.

Charter of Human Rights and Freedoms. R.S.Q. c. C–12.

The Child Welfare Act, 1965. S.O. 1965, c. 14.

Child Welfare Act. S.O. 1958, c. 11.

The Child Welfare Amendment Act. 1969. S.O. 1968–69, c. 9.

The Children of Unmarried Parents Act. R.S.O. 1950, c. 51.

Civil Marriage Act. S.C. 2005, c. 33.

Divorce Act. R.S.C. 1985, c. 3 (2d Supp.).

Divorce Act. S.C. 1967–68, c. 24.

Family Law Act. S.A. 2003, c. F–4.5.

Family Law Act. R.S.O. 1990, c. F.3.

Family Relations Act. R.S.B.C. 1996, c. 128.

Immigration Act. R.S.C. 1952, c. 145.

Law Reform (2000) Act. S.N.S. 2000, c. 29.
The Legitimacy Act, 1961–62. S.O. 1961–62, c. 71.
Marriage Act. R.S.N.S. 1954, c. 269.
Marriage Act. R.S.O. 1950, c. 222.
Married Women's Property Act, 1882. 45–46 Vict., c. 75 (U.K.).
Modernization of Benefits and Obligations Act. S.C. 2000, c. 12.

Index

A.A. v. B.B., 100, 299n12

Abel, Albert S., 143, 152–3, 154, 155

Abrams, Kathryn, 4, 5, 6, 8–9, 109, 110, 272–3

An Act Instituting Civil Unions and Establishing New Rules of Filiation, S.Q. 2002, c. 6, 101

An Act Respecting Adoption, S.Q. 1923–24, c. 75, 55

An Act Respecting Civil Marriage, S.Q. 1968, c. 82, 37

An Act Respecting the Legal Capacity of Married Women, S.Q. 1964, c. 66, 41

An Act to Amend the Child Welfare Act 1954, S.O. 1956, c. 8, 61

An Act to Amend the Child Welfare Act 1954, S.O. 1958, c. 11, 61

administrative agency. *See* administrative tribunal

administrative function, 141, 153–5. *See also* quasi-judicial function

administrative law: definition of, 142–3, 240, 270, 290n2; functionalist critics of, 145–6, 173, 207, 246, 297n1. *See also* judicial review, critics of

administrative state, 26, 143, 170, 196, 277; legitimacy of, 144–5, 147, 166, 182, 186, 208; opposition to, 144–5, 149–50; relationships of interdependence in, 209, 223; —, critique of, 223, 226–9, 233, 239, 242–3, 254–5; stories of rise of, 141–2; support for, 145, 147, 149, 291n2

administrative tribunal, deference for, 147; procedural determinations, 180–2; substantive determinations, 183–91, 206, 292n4, 297n1

administrative tribunal, expertise of, 147, 183–5, 192–3, 292nn4, 7; democratic, 188–9; methodological, 190–1; practical, 270, 290n8; technocratic, 187–8, 238

administrative tribunal, jurisdiction of, 151, 183–7, 192, 207–8, 253; Charter challenge to, 211–12; pure theory of, 148–50, 174. *See also* privative clause

adoption, 55–61, 86, 99, 249; acceptance of, 80–1, 249–50, 284n11; character as subversive and con-